THE LIFE AND LETTERS

of

WASHINGTON ALLSTON

Library of American Art

THE LIFE AND LETTERS

of

WASHINGTON ALLSTON

By Jared B. Flagg

Kennedy Galleries, Inc. · Da Capo Press
New York · 1969

This edition of *The Life and Letters of Washington Allston*
is an unabridged republication of the first edition published
in New York in 1892.

Library of Congress Catalog Card Number 68-27719

Copyright, 1892, by Charles Scribner's Sons

Published by
Kennedy Galleries, Inc.
20 East 56th Street, New York, N.Y. 10022
and
Da Capo Press
A Division of Plenum Publishing Corporation
227 West 17th Street, New York, N.Y. 10011

LIFE AND LETTERS

OF

WASHINGTON ALLSTON

Portrait of Allston.

From the original by George W. Flagg, N. A.

THE LIFE AND LETTERS

OF

WASHINGTON ALLSTON

BY

JARED B. FLAGG N.A. S.T.D.

WITH REPRODUCTIONS FROM ALLSTON'S PICTURES

NEW YORK

CHARLES SCRIBNER'S SONS

MDCCCXCII

TROW DIRECTORY
PRINTING AND BOOKBINDING COMPANY
NEW YORK

*T*O the memory of Richard H. Dana, Sr., without whose intelligent and careful labor in gathering material for his proposed life of Allston, I should not have begun my work; and to his daughter, Miss R. Charlotte Dana, without whose encouraging co-operation and sympathy, I should neither have begun nor finished it, this Biography is gratefully dedicated.

PREFACE

THE author of this Biography, impelled by repeated requests of relatives and friends of Allston, has with diffidence attempted the work, too long delayed, of gathering together such memories, written and verbal, as were still to be found, for the purpose of constructing a suitable memorial of America's great painter.

Others have preceded me in the work, but for want of material at hand have been obliged to content themselves with slight and insufficient records of a life known to be rich in all the elements requisite to interest, instruct, and elevate.

Dunlap, Washington Irving, Mrs. Jameson, Tuckerman, Sweetser, Miss Peabody, and R. H. Dana, Jr., have contributed valuable outlines, but in no instance has the work been carried to that measure of fulness which justice to the subject demands. This conviction of inadequacy in the various sketches of Allston's life has given urgency to the request that I should undertake the task which would have been done by abler hands had the elder Dana lived to fulfil his loving purpose. From his notes and unfinished manuscripts, together with the many and valuable letters which he had gathered, it is evident that he intended to leave, as the crowning labor of his life, a book worthy of himself and of Allston.

The present is a day of specialties, of classification and directness. Philosophy is eliminated from narrative, and reflections, speculative or critical, are out of place in the story of a life. How far the canon of criticism enforcing this elimination may be carried without overreaching and missing its purpose, I will not presume to decide; doubtless it may be carried to an objectionable extreme. I have obeyed the edict of the critical public in this matter so far as to feel almost like apologizing for the measure of my obedience.

My first plan included the treatment of various questions of art, as they would arise naturally in contemplating the life of an artist. This I believed would be to carry out the design of my predecessor in the work.

I cannot say that in my forbearance the public has lost anything of special value; but I can say, that in the case of the elder Dana such forbearance would have involved great loss; had he lived to finish his Life of Allston, biographical narration would have been embellished by the philosophical reflections of a mind whose every expression is the embodiment of intelligence and the evidence of poetic sensibility. In familiarizing myself with his work, cut short by death, I have been continually impressed with the thought that he was, above all others, qualified as Allston's biographer. To no other theme could he have brought the fulness of his intellect, his power of discrimination and analysis, with such loving homage. His admiration for Allston was boundless. He regarded him as one in whom were centred all high qualities with the least possible admixture of the earthy. So imbued with a sentiment of exalted esteem, he could devote the tribute of his rare scholarship and brilliant imagination as a free-will offering to the memory of his distinguished relative.

In studying his notes and plan for the book, I have been not only certified of a great loss, but have felt embarrassed in the attempt to enter into his labors. I have been oppressed with a sense of inability to carry the work to that degree of fulness and finish which he had in view. His copious memoranda and notes have afforded me the greatest assistance.

From all sources open to me I have gathered and appropriated whatever would add to the completeness and interest of my work. For assistance obtained from living witnesses I am chiefly indebted to Allston's niece, Miss R. Charlotte Dana, and his nephew, George W. Flagg.

LIST OF REPRODUCTIONS FROM ALLSTON'S PAINTINGS

PAGE

CONTENTS

CHAPTER V.

CHAPTER VI.

CHAPTER VII.

CHAPTER VIII.

CHAPTER IX.

CHAPTER X.

CHAPTER XI.

CHAPTER XII.

CHAPTER XIII.

CHAPTER XIV.

CHAPTER XXXI.

CHAPTER XXXII.

WASHINGTON ALLSTON

CHAPTER I.

ALLSTON'S PARENTAGE.—HIS CHILDHOOD.—SCHOOL-DAYS IN CHARLES-
TON AND NEWPORT.—ACQUAINTANCE WITH KING AND MALBONE.
—ENTRANCE AT HARVARD COLLEGE.

The South Carolina Allstons trace their descent from a baro-
nial family in the Norse settlement in Northumberland. Their
immediate ancestor, John, who adhered to the fortunes of the
Duke of Monmouth in his unsuccessful rebellion, to escape
his leader's sad fate, probably, came over about the year 1685,
and settled in the rich rice country bordering the Waccamaw
River, where he and his descendants became a wealthy and influential family. About the same time there emigrated to Carolina,
and settled in St. James' Parish, Berkley, James Moore, a grandson, as tradition tells, of the brilliant and famous Roger Moore
(or More), leader of the Irish rebellion of 1641. He was made
Governor of the colony in 1700. He married the only child of a
former Governor, Sir Joseph Yeamans, Bart., by whom he had a
son, James, who was also made Governor in 1719, having before
then, as commander of the forces of the colony, gained great distinction in wars against the Indians. Ramsey, in his "History
of South Carolina," says of Colonel Moore: "He was a man
excellently qualified for being a popular leader in perilous adventures ; in every new enterprise he had been a volunteer, and in
all his undertakings was resolute, steady, and inflexible."

His son John married Rachel Villeponteux, a Huguenot lady. Their son John married Elizabeth Vanderhorst, also a Huguenot, and their daughter, Rachel Moore, was the mother of Washington Allston. This last-named John Moore became very rich, which was proven, as well as his patriotism, by his lending the government, for carrying on the War of Independence, the very considerable sum, in those times, of fourteen thousand pounds, in gold. His three daughters are mentioned in a historical scrap as among the most beautiful women of the colony, and the excellent portrait of Rachel (habitually called by the *petit nom* of "Cettie," as others of her family were), now owned by her descendant, Miss Helen Allston, of Charleston, shows that she certainly merited the compliment. She was married January 19, 1775, to William Allston, son of John and Deborah, a captain in the war, and a widower at the time, having two sons by a former wife. He is mentioned in James's "Life of Marion" in these terms:

"During the struggle of the year 1781, Captain William Allston, of True Blue, on Little River, All Saints Parish, served under Marion. He was a firm patriot and good soldier; indeed he may well be enumerated among the martyrs to the cause of his country."

The children of this marriage were—Mary, born in 1778; Washington, whose birth is registered in the family Bible thus: "My son Washington was born Friday night, half after eleven o'clock, the fifth of November, 1779," and William Moore, born 1781.

Mrs. Allston, having had a French grandmother on the father's side and a French mother, was, as to blood, three-fourths French. Charleston was largely peopled with Huguenot refugees in those times; her aunt, Elizabeth Moore, was married to one of them, a gentleman named Neufville (corrupted since to Neville), and of the loves of a son of theirs and his cousin

Rachel, a story has come down which may properly be related here, since such readers as may become interested in the life of her son may want to know something of the mother. Early in their lives the two cousins, much thrown together during childhood, as we may presume, became lovers, and when young Neufville, as was usual with scions of the Carolina aristocracy, was sent to England to be educated, they were affianced lovers, expecting to be united when he should have completed his studies and made the tour of Europe. It would not have been strange if so long a separation and the many attractions and allurements besetting a youth abroad in the world had weakened the ties of first love, so far as the man was concerned, though, as will be seen, the woman was true. Certain it is that his letters became less and less frequent, and finally ceased altogether; there was a report of his death when the eligible and attractive widower Allston began to pay her attentions. She repelled them, of course; but her parents, and especially her mother, strongly desired the match, and so strongly seconded the cause of the suitor that Rachel finally yielded, though not until after she had been made to believe that Neufville was dead.

As was usual with planters on the Waccamaw River, Captain Allston had both a "plantation house" near his rice-fields and a "sea-shore house" not far distant, where was found in summer-time a refuge from heat as well as malaria. Opposite this last, in the spring of 1778, and after his family had been removed to it, a ship was wrecked. The crew took to the boats and pulled for the shore, where storm-driven waves rolling up a level beach made breakers of such height as to render their chances of safely "beaching" desperate. All but one perished in the attempt. He, not a sailor, but a passenger, when he had clambered out of the surf, made his way to the nearest habitation. In answer to his inquiries, the servants who admitted him informed him it was the house of Captain Allston, who was not then at home, but said that they would inform their mistress. Soon the door of the room in which he was waiting opened and the mistress entered. He gazed at her in speechless astonishment. She started back, and uttering the name of him who she thought was sleeping with the dead in a distant land, fell to the floor in a swoon. When she recovered, Neufville had left the house, and shortly after tidings were received of his death from yellow fever in Charleston.

This narrative reads so like a conventional romance that it is difficult to credit it as a record of facts; yet such it is. An experience so impressive could not fail to exert a lasting influence. We may assume that it did much to chasten, much to establish that poise of character, and to develop those high qualities of womanhood for which the mother of Washington Allston was conspicuous. Self-reliance, tender-heartedness, frankness, generosity, and firmness were characteristics she bequeathed to her progeny.

In 1781 Captain Allston, on his return from the famous battle of Cowpens, was seized with a mysterious illness, from which he died. It was believed he was poisoned by a trusted servant. Just before his death, at his request, the infant Washington was brought to his bedside; he then uttered these prophetic words: "He who lives to see this child grow up will see a great man." The young mother cherished the prediction of the dying father as a sacred legacy. Every incident of Washington's childhood indicating genius would recall the words of the sick-room in corroboration of her ambition and expectations regarding him. It was a voice from the borders of the spirit world, a solemnly impressive and true prophecy of his future greatness. She never doubted it, and she reared him as in the light of that prophecy. How far the reflex influence of her mind thus biassed was an element in the development of his character, we cannot tell, and yet we may not reasonably ignore or deny it.

The spring after Captain Allston's death, Lord Cornwallis selected as his head-quarters the plantation of the Widow Allston, and, with his staff, took up his abode in her house. His Lordship and officers were extremely gallant and courteous, conducting themselves rather as gentlemen on a visit to a friend than as representatives of a hostile army in the house of one of the enemy. The utmost consideration and deference were shown in the endeavor to conform to the customs of the house; nothing on the premises was injured, and the widow was pleased by their gentle and considerate deportment. One day at dinner, having learned through the servants that there was an infant in the house named Washington, his Lordship politely requested the young mother to present them to the little general; she assented, and the child was carried around the table, receiving the admiration and playful caresses of all present.

Born on a Southern plantation Allston was surrounded by influences favorable to the development of that ideality which was so richly manifested in his life. The pet of the negroes on a large plantation undergoes a novitiate, in barbaric magic and superstition, potential in the highest degree in developing imagination and fancy. The boy Washington was sensible and sturdy enough to be able to listen without injury to stories of ghosts and goblins in which the African delights. The Southern negro is never so happy as when relating to infantile gentry legends and myths to startle and alarm. No training could be more effective in peopling the shades of night with spectral forms to terrify, than that to which this child of genius was subjected. The love of the dramatic and tragic which was ever a conspicuous element in his character; that ideality that was continually reaching for and presenting visions of the invisible; that love of imagery in the realms of the spectral and supernatural; in short, the tendency toward the marvellous, not only of his brush but of his pen and conversation, it is not too much

to say was in great part a legitimate result of the influence of
the negroes acting upon his highly imaginative nature.   In later
years, while repeating the ghost stories learned in his childhood,
he would say that the excitement he experienced in being frightened by those stories was delightful to him.   He craved excitement, and to such a degree that, even though mingled with fear,
it did not lose its relish.   There was in him an affinity for the
purely ideal which belongs not to ordinary minds, but is the
property of the true poet.

The current of the talent of which he partook so largely can
be traced back many generations to a distinguished Dutch ancestor, Vanderhorst, a contemporary of Rubens, who was famous
as an illustrator of books, and associated with the great artist in
that work.

Dr. Henry C. Flagg was chief of the medical staff of Greene's
army; he was the son of a wealthy shipping merchant of Newport, R. I., in her days of commercial prominence.   He remained
in the South after the war, and the widow of Captain Allston
became engaged to him, much against the wishes and Southern
prejudices of her family.   Her mother considered the officers of
Greene's army a set of Northern adventurers, socially, and in
every way beneath the gentry of the South.   The landholders—
the Southern planters—were regarded by themselves as the
aristocracy, the nobility of the country.   They sent their sons to
the North to be educated, it is true; but learning alone could
not give that social elevation which is based on ownership of
land.   Mrs. Moore was so imbued with this arrogant spirit that
she bitterly opposed her daughter's marriage to a Northern
officer.   It was not the personality of the suitor, but his birth
and origin to which she objected.   To her earnest remon-
strances Mrs. Allston replied that she had married once to please
her family, and she was now determined to please herself.   This
persistence was at the cost of her patrimony.   After marrying

thus against the will of her family, her father said she had married a Yankee adventurer, and poverty should be her portion.

Dr. Flagg, the step-father of Washington Allston, manifested the deepest interest in his early training. He placed him at Mrs. Colcott's school, in Charleston, where he was thoroughly grounded in rudimentary studies. As a punishment for some offence the school-mistress once placed him in solitary confinement. After two hours, hearing no demonstrations of penitence, she opened the door of the room where he was confined, and found him drawing a ship on the bottom of a wooden chair with a piece of chalk. She was so pleased with this drawing that she kept the chair locked up during her life, occasionally showing it as a memento of the early days of the great artist.

In relation to the first evidence of his artistic talent, Allston writes : " To go back as far as I can, I remember that I used to draw before I left Carolina, at six years of age (by the way no uncommon thing) ; and still earlier, that my favorite amusement, much akin to it, was making little landscapes about the roots of an old tree in the country, meagre enough, no doubt; the only particulars of which I can call to mind were a cottage built of sticks, shaded by little trees, which were composed of the small suckers (I think so called), resembling miniature trees, which I gathered in the woods. Another employment was the converting the forked stalks of the wild ferns into little men and women, by winding about them different-colored yarn. These were sometimes presented with pitchers made of the pomegranate flower. These childish fancies were straws by which, perhaps, an observer might have guessed which way the current was setting for after-life. And yet, after all, this love of imitation may be common to childhood. General imitation certainly is ; but whether adherence to particular kinds may not indicate a permanent propensity, I leave to those who have studied the subject more than I have to decide."

"But even these delights would sometimes give way to a stronger love for the wild and marvellous. I delighted in being terrified by the tales of witches and hags, which the negroes used to tell me, and I well remember with how much pleasure I recalled these feelings on my return to Carolina; especially on revisiting a gigantic wild grape-vine in the woods, which had been the favorite swing for one of these witches."

While at school in Charlestown he learned to prepare oil colors, and in his vacations locked himself in his room, where he commenced a picture of the eruption of Vesuvius. When this, his first effort in oil was shown, his family were so surprised by its excellence that they feared lest he might disgrace them by becoming a painter. His step-father, thinking to overcome this dangerous tendency, sent him to Newport to prepare for college, under the tuition of a Mr. Rogers. This course, however, instead of turning him from the pursuit of art, only confirmed him in his determination to be an artist.

Of his youth, Allston writes: "I concluded my last letter with the amusement of my childhood, my next step will be to my boyhood. My chief pleasure now was in drawing from prints, of all kinds of figures, landscape and animals. But I soon began to make pictures of my own; at what age, however, I cannot say. The earliest compositions that I can remember were the storming of Count Roderick's castle, from a poor (though to me delightful) romance of that day, and the 'Siege of Toulon.' The first in India ink, the other in water-colors. I cannot recall the year in which they were done. To these succeeded many others, which have likewise passed into oblivion. Though I never had any regular instructor in the art (a circumstance, I would here observe, both idle and absurd to boast of), I had much incidental instruction, which I have always through life been glad to receive from anyone in advance of myself. And, I may add, there is no such thing as a self-taught artist, in the ignorant acceptation of the word; for the greatest genius that ever lived must be indebted to others, if not by direct teaching, yet indirectly through their works.

"I had, in my school-days, some of this latter kind of instruction from a very worthy and amiable man, a Mr. King, of Newport, who made quadrants and compasses, and occasionally painted portraits. I believe he was originally bred a painter, but obliged, from the rare calls upon his pencil, to call in the aid of another craft. I used at first to make frequent excuses for visiting his shop to look at his pictures; but finding that he always received me kindly, I went at last without any, or rather with the avowed purpose of making him a visit. Sometimes I would take with me a drawing, and was sure to get a kind word of encouragement. It was a pleasant thing to me, some twenty years after this, to remind the old man of these little kindnesses."

In Newport Allston made the acquaintance of Malbone, the foremost miniature painter of his day, of whom he writes: "I became acquainted with Malbone but a short time before he quitted Newport, a circumstance which I then remember regretting exceedingly, for I looked up to him with great admiration; our not meeting earlier was owing, I suppose, to his going to another school, and being some years older than myself. I recollect borrowing some of his pictures on oiled paper to copy."

The new influence exerted over young Allston by these men tended to confirm him more and more, and to aid him in his inextinguishable purpose. Moreover, the scenery about Newport, so grandly different from that of the low country of South Carolina, in which his childhood was passed, stimulated his imagination and developed still further his taste for painting.

While in Newport, engaged in his preparatory studies, he was a favorite in the best society; there he met the sister of the celebrated Unitarian clergyman, Dr. William Ellery Channing.

This lady, to whom he became engaged, exerted a very strong influence upon his after-course. Channing entered college a year before Allston, and in " Dana's Memoranda" we find the following interesting extracts of letters written him by Allston at that time :

" The first letter," says Mr. Dana, " is without date, and relates a dream which Allston had, of walking slowly on the hill in Newport, and seeing a spacious mansion, overshadowed by a lofty elm—nature and art in rivalry set all off with bowers and woodbine—a fair lady in a bower, who blushes at seeing him, then comes forward, and he falls upon his knees before her, while she confesses to having perceived an attachment.

" At the close, he says : ' Give my love to Ned, and tell him that I have at last finished "Mount Vesuvius." ' On the back of the letter is written 'Sophomore,' which doubtless refers to C.'s year at college. This letter shows somewhat of the after-man, extremely youthful in character as it is ; however, boys were truly boys in those days ; but then what men they made !

" In a letter dated March 22, 1795, from Newport, he says : ' My temper is naturally quick and resentful for a few minutes, but, believe me, in the cooler time of reflection I repine in secret if I have offended. I wish to make reparation, but a foolish pride, which too many think honorable, stops me and obliges me to do a thing which I inwardly abhor.'

" In June, 1795, he writes : ' I am sorry to tell you that I am disappointed of my expectation of seeing you at Cambridge as a fellow-student, as my father-in-law has fixed on Providence College. Mr. Taylor, contrary to our expectation at his entrance, as usher, is generally esteemed, and resembles Mr. Hawes more than any tutor we have had since the departure of that grave-comic-foolish-wise man. Apropos, I think it my duty to warn you to guard your heart against the fatal shaft of Cupid, which has so often left dreadful monuments of its triumph by the temptation of minds which,—" O, horribile dictu, mihi frigidus horror membra quatit, gelidusque coit formidine sanguis." Shall I proceed, or shall I forbear? Well, now my emotion has subsided, I will proceed, and without keeping you in further suspense; you must know that Eben Richardson, that wonderful luminary of Newport City, has fought a terrible battle with that little devil Cupid, who has vanquished him (though not past recovery) with a dose of ratsbane. But poor Eben, repenting after the battle, declared his defeat, and begged assistance of the doctor.'

" To the same, December 19, 1795, he says: 'I would not willingly hurt any human being, much less one whom I had called my friend.' (I remember his once telling me that when at Newport he was fond of shooting, but that having once wounded a bird, and being obliged to wring its neck to put it out of pain, he never fired at another.)

" In the same letter he says, 'I thank you for the satisfaction you express at my intention of entering Cambridge.' He then asks for a particular account of the examination, 'and what parts of the Greek Testament and Cicero' he had better study."

Upon the completion of his preparation he entered Harvard. His course under Mr. Rogers had been so thorough that the college curriculum made but small demands upon his time, so that he was enabled to devote several leisure hours daily to painting.

CHAPTER II.

At Cambridge Allston renewed his acquaintance with Malbone, of whom he says : " When I entered college I found him
established in Boston.   He had reached the maturity of his
powers, and was deservedly ranked the first miniature painter of
the country.   Malbone's merits as an artist are too well known
to need setting forth by me ; I shall therefore say but few words
on that head.   He had the happy talent among his many excellencies of elevating the character without impairing the likeness ;
this was remarkable in his male heads ; and no woman ever lost
any beauty from his hand ; nay, the fair would often become still
fairer under his pencil.   To this he added a grace of execution
all his own.   My admiration of Malbone induced me at this
time to try my hand at miniature, but it was without success,
I could make no hand of it; all my attempts in this line being
so far inferior to what I could then do in oil that I became dis-
gusted with my abortive efforts and I gave it up.   One of these
miniatures, or rather attempts at miniatures, was shown me several years later, and I pronounced it ' without promise,' not
knowing it to be my own work.   I may add, I would have said
the same had I known it.   I may observe, however (for I know
not why I should not be as just to myself as to another person),
that I should not have expressed a similar opinion respecting

its contemporaries in oil, for a landscape with figures on horseback, painted about this time, was afterward exhibited at the Somerset House."

"My leisure hours at college were chiefly devoted to the pencil, to the composition equally of figures and landscapes; I do not remember that I preferred one to the other; my only guide in the choice was the inclination of the moment. There was an old landscape at the house of a friend in Cambridge (whether Italian or Spanish I know not) that gave me my first hints in color in that branch: it was of a rich, deep tone, though not by the hand of a master—the work, perhaps, of a moderate artist, but one who lived in a good age, when he could not help catching something of the good that was abroad. In the coloring of figures the pictures of Pine, in the Columbian Museum in Boston, were my first masters. Pine had certainly, as far as I recollect, considerable merit in color. But I had a higher master in the head of Cardinal Bentivoglio, from Vandyke, in the college library, which I obtained permission to copy one winter vacation. This copy of Vandyke was by Smybert, an English painter, who came to this country with Dean, afterward Bishop, Berkeley. At that time it seemed to me perfection, but when I saw the original, some years afterward, I found I had to alter my notions of perfection. However, I am grateful to Smybert for the instruction he gave me—his work rather. Deliver me from kicking down even the weakest step of an early ladder."

There is an incident of interest connected with this copy of Vandyke which we may in passing venture to give. When Copley sent out to be exhibited in the Royal Academy his picture of a boy wearing a turban, Sir Joshua Reynolds said to Mr. West, "The man who painted that picture has studied Vandyke." West replied that he could assure him the man had never seen a Vandyke. Both statements were true, for while Copley had never seen an original Vandyke, he had diligently studied this copy by Smybert, which had so captivated Allston.

Allston showed early in life that his powers were not confined to landscape or graver subjects of a historical character. While in college he drew some very ludicrous things in watercolors, among them were several in a series entitled a "Buck's Progress," of which Mr. R. H. Dana gives the following description:

"Dr. Harris, Librarian of Harvard College, owns the 'Buck's Progress.' It was suggested by Hogarth, no doubt, and is in three pieces. No. 1. The reddish, lank-haired Buck's introduction to the town bucks at a carousal, in which he appears in the character of a country bumpkin. No. 2. In his room under the hands of his hairdresser; a shoemaker, a very good likeness of old Prior of Newport, who made shoes in Allston's, and, in my school-boy days, for all good Master Rogers's school boarders and most of the rest of the school. He is taking the measure of the Buck's foot, and he, in raising it, has upset a chair and a bottle of wine and a glass, the wine running over. Out of another bottle he is helping himself to a glass of wine. There is a tailor in the scene, and another person untying the Buck's cravat, which, after the fashion of that time, is as big as a hairdresser's towel. No. 3. Midnight fray with the watchman, and, coarsely as they are all executed, done with a good deal of spirit. The moon, just rising behind the lofty buildings which lie in shadow, the light from the lantern in front of the tavern, and shining on the brawlers below, show, even then, when a boy freshman, that he had some notion of the effect of light and shadow. The tall houses in shadow are not wanting in something like grandeur of effect."

"With his intimate friends he used to amuse himself with getting up caricatures and many other odd and humorous things. The southwest room of the old mansion in which he lived was then an unfinished apartment, 'filled in' with brick, and was the scene of a great deal of fine foolery, sometimes to the amusement of the whole family, old and young."

Allston graduated with honor and was appointed poet of his class. His genial nature endeared him to his classmates, by whom he was regarded with that reverent and generous consideration which is the free-will offering to genius. Full of the buoyancy of health and the impetuous ardor of youth, he was in sympathy with the rollicking rashness of the average student, ready for the tricks and sports incident to college life; but never to a degree that obliterated that subtle, indefinable influence which, as a halo, encircles gifted spirits, who, though physically upon the common plane, are, in those higher qualities which make up the essential man, above their fellows. As different associations and interests separated Allston's classmates in divergent walks of life, this sense of his ideal superiority went with them. Evidences of affectionate and high appreciation were constantly given by those who in school or college had enjoyed the influence of his companionship, and in later years the common suffrage found expression in Irving's memorable tribute to his character.

We give here a few of Allston's letters during his college life at Cambridge. The tone of filial regard and affection toward his stepfather, evinced by these letters, shows his own goodness of heart, and the just and kindly nature of Dr. Flagg.

This first, under date of October 21, 1796, was written just after he entered college:

"HONORED SIR: Your kind letter I received a few weeks since, by the way of Rhode Island, added to the pleasure I received from Mr. Avery's letter that you were all well, in hearing from you myself. Perhaps you may think that my long neglect did not deserve even that; but when you consider our retired situation, and the difficulty of knowing opportunities, your goodness cannot hesitate to excuse my silence. Mr. Avery has been so kind as to give me a general invitation to spend the vacation at his house, but the bustle of Boston suits my disposition as much less than I expected, as my situation at Cambridge exceeds it.

"The gratitude which I feel toward you for your paternal solicitude, I hope the future conduct of my life will evince. The Doctor with whom I live has shown a friendship for me that I wish may never be forgotten; tho' the great distance I live from college makes my exercises rather disagreeable, the reflection of my situation makes me forget to complain. In short, I want nothing but your company in Carolina to make a wish vacant.

"Give my sincere love to mamma, and likewise to my sisters, with a kiss for Henry and Toby. I subscribe myself,

Your grateful and affectionate,

" WASHINGTON ALLSTON."

Allston's letters to his mother were less frequent during his second year in college, and their infrequency called forth a remonstrance from his venerated tutor, Mr. Robert Rogers, of Newport. The innate nobility of character which accepts censure without resentment is shown in the following letter, dated October 28, 1797:

"MY WORTHY SIR: Impressed with emotions of the sincerest gratitude, I sit down to acknowledge my obligations to you for the kind letter I have just this moment received from you. Never before have I felt such cruel sensations as I do now from reading those reproaches which are so justly merited by my unpardonable neglect.

"That any of my friends should suppose me capable of one

ungrateful or indifferent feeling toward them is an arrow which could not be inflicted more poignantly in my breast. But I do not, cannot blame anyone for entertaining such an idea of me ; my conduct in that particular has given grounds too specious hardly to admit a doubt in the judgment of the most unsuspicious ; but, as God is my witness, no one has a truer affection for his friends and relatives than I pride myself in possessing. Were it possible that my mother could see and know the inward feelings of my heart, I could wish no other testimony to convince her that the want of affection for her is the last sin which could obtain a residence in my heart. But, however I may deserve any of these reproaches, I cannot omit thanking you for the solicitous advice your kind attention has honored me with.

"It is my greatest misfortune to be too lazy, and by the few mortifications I have already met with on that account I predict many evils in my future life. I have always the inclination to do what I ought ; but by continually procrastinating for tomorrow the business of to-day, I insensibly delay, until at the end of one month I find myself in the same place as when I began it. You, no doubt, will allow all this to be very candid, and that I speak as I should do, but is it not more probable, you will observe, that these professions are good as far as they are professions, but how am I to know you will act up to them unless you practise them? I know it is very easy to promise one thing and do another. We seldom find anyone who is unwilling to acknowledge his faults and promise to reform ; but there are very few who will resist the slightest obstacle or temptation to make good his professions. The most abandoned profligate at particular times will not hesitate to accuse himself of the greatest atrocities, and very frequently resolve to reform ; yet no sooner is he under similar circumstances than we see him plunge as heedlessly into the same vices as if no such resolutions were ever made. But, sir, I assure you this is not, nor, I trust, will be, the case with me. I began to practise before I attempted these. Three weeks since I wrote to mamma, the Doctor, and my sister, some of which letters for length may serve for two or three each. And more, I have made a resolution which I flatter myself I shall be able to maintain, to write to Carolina every month, and, as opportunity offers, send them on. So much, sir, I have troubled you about myself. . . ."

Whether Allston persisted in the resolution formed at this time we cannot tell. It is to be regretted that so few of his letters, especially those written in his youth, have been preserved.

The next in our possession was written after an interval of three years, being dated June 23, 1800. It is interesting in its reference to the Commencement at Cambridge, and his modest entertainment to his classmates, which, in accordance to custom, he felt obliged to give.

" My Honored Sir: Yours of May 19th I have just received. Agreeable to your wish, tho' I have nothing material to add at present, I seize the present opportunity once more to acknowledge the receipt of three separate remittances of one hundred and twenty dollars each. With regard to my expenses at Commencement I cannot make any accurate calculation. It is usual on that day for those who have exercises to perform, generally to give an entertainment, and that entertainment seldom comes short of two or three hundred dollars, indeed some exceed six. But as I have no ambition to shine beyond my abilities, I have thought proper to limit my magnificence to fifty. That sum I hope will enable me to entertain a small party with some degree of elegance; accordingly I propose to invite about twenty gentlemen. As I make no pretensions to gallantry, and am besides intimate with families who are totally unacquainted with each other, whom I should necessarily be obliged to invite, I have thought proper to dispense with the company of ladies. The exercise assigned me for Commencement is a poem ; the subject which I have selected is ' Energy of Character.'

" I look now for Mr. and Mrs. Young, and anticipate much pleasure in returning with them to Carolina. As you are more acquainted with the expense of travelling, I have submitted to you the regulation of that article. Be assured, sir, if I prove extravagant, I shall be more so from ignorance than wilfulness. I am not wholly insensible to the pleasures of the world, therefore shall not be governed entirely by necessity ; but I flatter myself, at least, in being able to restrain their gratification within due bounds. I wait your intended remittance with some degree of anxiety, since the last has not emancipated me entirely from debt, the sums owing, however, are small. My duty to mamma, and remembering me to all, believe me still,

" Your grateful and affectionate

" WASHINGTON ALLSTON."

The last of his early letters is to his mother. It shows that his determination to devote himself to art had strengthened with his years. It was not a whim or a fancy ; it was based in his emotional and intellectual nature. He was born an artist, to paint was with him an instinct, he could not help it, and all influences to sway him from the pursuit of art were as idle wind to the oak.

" NEWPORT, August 12, 1800.

" MY DEAR MOTHER : Yours, dated July 19th, was handed me a few days ago. I should have answered it immediately by post, but hearing of an opportunity by water I have waited till now for that.

" It is needless to express my feelings on account of the Doctor's illness. You know my heart and its numerous obligations to that honored man, and can easily conceive its sufferings. I know not, my dear mother, how it will be in my power to return his services. In all respects and at all times has he acted toward me with the affection of a father; I cannot therefore repay him but with the affection of a son.

"I am now at Newport. The town is crowded with strangers, and gayer than I ever knew it; but I feel so little relish for its amusements that I fancy it will be no great self-denial to comply with your wishes on my return. Be assured, dear mother, your request shall not necessarily be repeated. I will live as 'snug' as you can desire. I feel no curiosity now to visit Charleston, and flatter myself 'twill be no difficult task to keep out of it when in Carolina. I have become so habituated to a country life (for Cambridge is but a rural village) that I shall think myself full happy enough in Waccamaw or St. Thomas.

"It is so long since I have mentioned anything about my painting that I suppose you have concluded I had given it up. But my thoughts are far enough from that, I assure you. I am more attached to it than ever; and am determined, if resolution and perseverance will effect it, to be the first painter, at least, from America. Do not think me vain, for my boasting is only conditional; yet I am inclined to think from my own experience that the difficulty to eminence lies not in the road, but in the timidity of the traveller. Few minds capable of conceiving that are not adequate to the accomplishing of great designs; and if there have been some failures, less blame, perhaps, is to be ascribed to the partiality of fortune than to their own want of confidence.

"In a word, my dear mother, I already feel a fortune in my fingers. With what little skill I possess at present, I am persuaded, did my pride permit, I could support myself with ease and respectability; but I am content to remain poor as I am until painting shall have been formally established as my profession.

I have a few pieces by me which I intend sending on soon by water.

"I write by this to sister Polly, and perhaps a few lines to the Doctor. Eliza, I hear, is quite a belle. As I am a beau, tell her I shall give her a few lessons in the art of heart-catching.

"Remember me to all, and believe me still your dutiful, affectionate son,

"WASHINGTON ALLSTON."

Following is an extract from a letter of Leonard Jarvis to R. H. Dana, Sr., full of interesting details of Allston's college life, and of observations upon his character. Jarvis was a classmate and warm friend of Allston's. He was a man of high character and attained some prominence in public affairs. He was a member of Congress, and associated with Gulian C. Verplank and others in securing for Allston an order from the government to paint pictures for the panels of the Rotunda in the Capitol at Washington, which order though urged upon him Allston declined, for reasons given in his correspondence with the Committee appointed to confer with him on the subject.

"My acquaintance with Allston began with our college life, in August, 1796. It was reported that two South Carolinians had joined our class, and some curiosity was excited as to what manner of men they were. It was at once seen that they had less of the schoolboy or raw student about them, and that they were dressed in more fashionable style than the rest of us. One of the two was Washington Allston, who was distinguished by the grace of his movements and his gentlemanly deportment. His countenance, once seen, could never be forgotten. His smooth, high, open forehead, surrounded by a profusion of dark, wavy hair, his delicately formed nose, his peculiarly expressive mouth, his large, lustrous, melting eye, which varied with every emotion, and complexion of most beautiful Italian cast—smooth and colorless, yet healthy—all blending harmoniously, formed a face which was irresistibly attractive, and which, united with his gentle, unassuming manners, secured him the good will of all his classmates. Those who hated one another most heartily— and there were good haters in our class—and who agreed in nothing else, united in respectful and kindly feelings toward him. He was also a favorite with the officers of the University, for his deportment to them was always respectful and gentlemanly, although a system of constant annoyance to the constituted authorities of old Harvard was at that time quite the vogue. He was not distinguished as a scholar, though he always appeared well at recitations; but his poetical talents and his genius for the fine arts were soon discovered, and gave him a high standing among us. The first indications of his power over the pencil were exhibited in some drawings made for Professor Waterhouse, to illustrate some essay of the professor's, intended for one of his scientific correspondents abroad, and the first lines of his writing which were made public were an elegy, half-burlesque and half-serious, upon the college barber and hairdresser (for in those days of queues and hair-powder and pomatum, such a character did exist), poor Galley, who was found dead one morning upon the steps of the chapel."

" Allston had a room with Wainwright at Dr. Waterhouse's, where he also boarded, on the north side of the Common, and after Wainwright left college, in our Sophomore year, he had a room to himself nearer to the colleges, on the north side of the main road to Boston. It was in a tall, narrow, unpainted, awkward-looking building, opposite the seat of the late Jonathan Simpson. His chamber was on the first floor and on the western side of the entrance, and he boarded, if I mistake not, at Mr. Bartlett's, whose house was on the same side of the road, a little nearer to the colleges. Here he abode without a chum during the remainder of his academic life; but he was by no means left in solitude. Edmund T. Dana and I used to pass a large portion of our time with him. As we both lived at home, remote from the colleges, and had to pass by Allston's room in our journeys to and fro, it was very convenient as well as pleasant to make it a stopping-place. We made ourselves quite at home there; sometimes looking over our lessons, and generally passing there the intervening hour that occurred between lectures and recitations. Sometimes of a cold night, after a visit to our fellow-students (perhaps I had better say our college acquaintances), we would prefer a share of his bed to trudging home. On one occasion Ned and I happened to meet there with the intention of passing the night. We could not prevail upon Allston to determine which of the two should stay, and as neither was disposed to yield, I proposed to Dana, as possession was eleven points in the law, that he who first undressed and got into bed should retain it. He consented to the proposal, and never were garments slipped off more rapidly. Ned beat me by a stocking, so I had to dress myself again and plod my solitary way homeward, of a bitter cold night. There were two closets attached to the room intended for studies. In one of these Allston kept his fuel, and in the other his clothes, his books, and his painting implements and materials. His landlord was a carpenter, by the name of Clark, called by the students Don Clark. This worthy had an exalted opinion of the talents of Allston, and I well remember his remarks upon a picture of Thomson's 'Musidora.' Clark had at times a peculiar simper resembling what I have since seen on the face of that exquisite low comedian, Liston. With this expression, or want of expression, I know not which to call it, playing about his mouth, 'I have seen a picture, sir,' said he, 'painted by Mr. Allston. He has painted a woman, stark naked, going into the water to wash herself. It is as nateral as life. Mr. Allston, sir, is quite a

genius.' The panes in the window of his chamber nearest to
Boston, and fronting the road, our friend had covered with
paintings touched with great spirit. The first was that of a
country fellow walking at the rate of six miles an hour. The
name he gave to this was, 'Walking a Good Stick.' This was
entirely a whim of his own, and it was followed up by other
promptings of his own fancy, or by suggestions made to him by
Dana or myself, until the window was covered with a grotesque
collection of figures which attracted universal attention. It was
high sport to us to see the teamsters on their way to Boston
stopping their cattle and looking up at the window with a
mingled grin of wonder and delight."

"He here gave himself up to painting and poetry; but it
was after a hard struggle that he finally determined to adopt the
former for his future pursuit in life. His step-father, who was
a physician, was earnest with him to follow that profession, and
while filial duty urged him to comply, his genius was drawing
him powerfully in the other direction. He imparted to me his
struggle between duty and inclination, and I advised him not to
hesitate, but to signify at once to his friends his repugnance
to the course which they had pointed out, and his irresistible
bias to the fine arts. This he at length determined to do,
and when the assent of his friends was given he seemed to walk
on air."

"I have never for a moment questioned the judiciousness
of the advice I gave. He was created with a powerful imagination and an exquisite perception of the beautiful, he was
designed by nature for a votary of the fine arts, and in nothing
else could he have excelled; but in these he had only to make
his selection. His strong propension was to painting, but with
the same pains he would have been eminent as a poet or sculptor. In our junior year, a masquerade was got up in our class
in which Allston and I appeared as Don Quixote and Sancho

Panza. I have in later times and in other countries attended at many a masquerade, but never have I seen better masks than those two. Allston carved the heads of the Knight and Squire in wood, upon which he formed masks of moistened paper, which he painted when dry, and they were most exquisite personations of the characters they were intended to represent; they could not have been surpassed in truth of expression. He also made for himself a complete suit of armor from helm to heel of pasteboard, painted to represent steel. In those days he also attempted music, and could make out to scrape a tune upon the violin, but he soon relinquished the bow, being satisfied that he could not excel."

" Before he left Newport to enter college, he was enamoured of the lady who afterward became his wife, and his passion was made known to its object, I think, before he had entered upon his junior year. He had a miniature likeness of her which he had drawn from memory, and many of his amatory effusions of those days were the offspring of his love for this lady. He was fond of writing poetry, and productions of his pen were at times to be seen in the poet's corner of the *Centinell*. On one occasion he sent some lines to that paper which Major Russel declined publishing, because, forsooth, in those days of high political excitement, there was no place for light reading. Our poet and his cronies were very indignant, and Allston revenged himself upon the Goth by sending to him a political article in prose, written in the most bombastic style, and fairly out-Heroding Herod. As he had foreseen, this was published without delay, and we had our joke upon the deficiency of the Major, both in taste and judgment. He copied a part of what he wrote into a manuscript written with a great deal of care and ornamented with a variety of vignettes, for he never for a moment was unfaithful to the pencil. When resting after the composition of a sentence, his pen would often be employed in sketching a head or figure upon the same paper. Even his mathematical manuscript, as well as those of some of his friends, have the marks of his pencil, which he sometimes suffered to run riot in caricature. I can even now call to mind his 'Parabola personified' mechanician drawing up water by the bucketful to set a huge water-wheel in motion ; his God of Day, as gross a caricature of that personage as that of Fielding in 'Tumbledown Dick.' The light of the sun was signified by the glimmer of a farthing candle ; his chariot, a clumsy, two-wheeled cart, and instead of Phelgon, Acthon, and the other fiery steeds, there was a raw-boned Rozinante, 'trotting about as fast as other horses stood still,' driven by a blackguard-looking boy, whom Apollo was telling to 'try to catch the moon.' Under the problem of how to measure the height of an inaccessible object, he had placed for that object a female figure representing Happiness, standing upon the apex of a pyramid. At the annual examination, when the bigwigs of the land were assembled, the mathematical manuscripts of the students were passed in review. Those among us who knew of these decorations watched with some attention to see the effect they would produce. Soon one of the examiners began to chuckle, and he called the attention of another, whose sides began to shake, and so the laughter ran through the conclave, the cockles of their hearts being more rejoiced than they ever had been in the philosophy chamber, as the room was called in which the examinations were held."

"During Allston's college life he was appointed to deliver a poem at the autumnal exhibition of our senior year, which was received with great applause, and during the following winter he was called upon to deliver a poem upon the death of Washington at the University commemoration of that melancholy event. The effect he produced was very great. I have never seen a public speaker whose appearance and gestures were so eminently graceful, and there was a peculiar sweetness and depth and plaintiveness in the tones of his voice. The audience had been cautioned, on account of the solemnity of the occasion, to abstain from the usual tokens of applause, but at several passages they could not be restrained. The murmurs of approbation were evidently involuntary, and the attempts at suppression rendered them still more striking, contrasted as they were with the dead stillness which had generally prevailed, and had manifested unwonted attention on the part of the listeners. The oration that followed, though well written and creditable to its author, was coldly received, and the consequence was that at the following commencement the government of the University took care to place our friend in the order of exercises so far from the orator of the day as not suffer the poem to destroy the oration."

" Allston was fond of reading and writing, but he paid no more attention to our college studies than was necessary to secure a respectable standing. Though not remarkable as a plodding student, he was nevertheless a favorite with the most studious of the class, and, though not given to riot or dissipation, he was equally well regarded by those who were then called 'high fellows.' Indeed it was very remarkable that, without effort, and without derogating in the least from the simplicity and integrity of his character, he should have been such a universal favorite. His favorite reading were plays and romances, particularly romances of the German schools, and he would sup on horrors until he would be almost afraid to go to bed until he had made sure that no goblin was under it or in the closet."

" When he first entered college he was seduced by the tinsel of the Della Cruscan poetry, and I remember his selection of some of Merry's verses for declamation, but he soon abandoned it for the manliness of Churchill. He had also the independence to like the poetry of Southey at a time when the politics of that bard, so different from the sentiments preferred at a later

period by the poet-laureate, had put his writings under the ban
of the arbiters of taste in this country as well as England."

"Though abounding in the intellectual and the ideal, he was
a great stickler for good eating, and it was a red-letter day with
him when that prince of epicures, old Major Brattle, invited him
to dinner. You will hardly credit me when I tell you that one
Sunday, when he had an invitation from the Major, he ate no
breakfast in order that his appetite might be keener and his
relish greater.

"He was, during his college life, a singular compound of diffidence, I might almost say bashfulness, and of assurance, something in the young Marlowe style. At a charity ball, in Boston,
for the benefit of a run-down French dancing-master, where we
did not expect to meet any of our acquaintance, Allston took it
into his head to enact the fop. He was dressed in the very
extreme of coxcombry, and appeared quite at his ease in the
multitude there assembled. Yet in the parlor, and in the company of ladies, he would not be sufficiently at his ease to do
himself justice. While upon his oddities, I may mention that in
the cold nights of winter, not satisfied with the bed-clothes, of
which 'poor Harry had no lack,' he would place upon his bed a
chair or two, in order that he might feel a greater weight upon
him."

"In the year 1798 or 1799 there was a great stir and much
ado about nothing created by Professor Robinson's 'Proofs of
a Conspiracy.' Illuminati and other secret societies were about
to turn the world topsy-turvy. All regular governments were
to be overthrown, and Christianity itself was to be abolished.
While the excitement was at the highest the students of Harvard
were surprised at seeing upon the boards for advertisement in
the chapel entry a summons for the meeting of a secret society,
and while they were seeking to elucidate the mystery, another
paper appeared in the same place solemnly warning them against

indiscreet curiosity, and denouncing the most dreadful penalties against anyone who should seek to lift the veil. This was followed by a second summons in irregular verse, in which all ingredients of a hell broth were made to boil and bubble. All these papers were ornamented with altars, daggers, swords, chalices, death-heads and cross-bones, and other paraphernalia of German romance, which were stamped, not drawn, upon the papers, which besides bore huge seals. All this was the work of Allston and served for a nine days' wonder. Though this was in ridicule of the stuff of the day, yet Allston always belonged to the Federal party, for which, I presume, he had no better reason than Charles V. had for preferring the Church of England to that of Scotland, namely, that it was the more gentlemanly religion. Indeed, he was too far above the worldlings to be able to sympathize in party squabbles, and was too much given up to his imagination to attend much to things of this earth."

" It is only in this way that his ignorance of a large portion of modern history can be explained. Walker, one day, rebuking him for not making himself better acquainted with the affairs of modern Europe, which it was disgraceful to a gentleman to to be in ignorance of, Allston repelled the imputation, and insisted that he was acquainted with history. 'Well,' said Walker, 'what can you say of the Treaty of Westphalia?' 'What can I say?' replied Allston. 'I can say it was a very pretty treaty.'"

"It would hardly be just to try the young men of 1800 by the standard of to-day. Temperance societies were then unknown, very few people were too good to go to the theatre, which at that time was frequented by more than one minister of the gospel; clergymen would dance at private balls, would play at cards, and would even preside over the convivial boards, from which they did not retire until the mirth and fun grew

fast and furious. They would write prologues to plays, occasional addresses for the theatres, and lampoons for the newspapers, and all this without losing caste or giving offence to
their parishioners."

" Allston could hardly be expected to hold back when par-
sons led the way; he loved the festive boards and the social
glass, and was delightful when a little elevated, but I never saw
him 'bitch fou,' as Burns would deem it, or so overtaken as to
forget that he was a gentleman, nor did I ever know him to
drink enough to bring repentance in the morning. He was
also exceedingly fond of the theatre, and he loved dancing, in
which he excelled; but I have no recollection of ever seeing him
take a card in hand. Whatever the religious exercises of the
University may be at the present day, they were at that time
not calculated to encourage religious emotions. Our worthy
president had a wooden face, wore a white wig, and had a
strong nasal intonation, and always repeated the same prayer,
which had nothing to recommend it on the first hearing. What,
then, could be expected of its effect, *milies repetita?* Under
these circumstances it is not to be wondered at that the sum-
moning of the chapel-bell should have been rather irksome, and
I do not believe that among the three hundred under-graduates
of Harvard, in my day, twenty could be found who would gainsay me, and certainly Allston would not have been one of the
score. But I say as positively that I never heard him utter a
sentiment or advance an opinion on serious subjects that in his
riper and more sober years he would have had any occasion to
disavow in consequence of its variance from what religion might
enjoin."

"In my allusion to college days I must not omit to mention
the title of 'Count,' bestowed upon Allston by his two cronies,
in jocular anticipations of the distinctions which were to crown
his genius. To this appellation he would answer as readily as

to his own name, and it was never entirely given up, either in speaking to or of him, by those who had originated it.   He was a member of all sorts of college societies and clubs, one of which was a coffee club, instituted in our senior year, and which survived until he returned to Europe in 1811.   The members had each his nickname, and Allston hitched them into rhyme in a song struck out at heat, which was often sung in full chorus at our meetings.   The rules of our club were, that we have no rules, but to meet every Thursday evening, and have no potation stronger than coffee."

CHAPTER III.

RETURN TO CHARLESTON.—DEPARTURE FOR EUROPE.—STUDENT LIFE
IN LONDON.—DIFFERENCE BETWEEN ALLSTON AND MALBONE.—
ACQUAINTANCE WITH FUSELI.—EXHIBITION AT SOMERSET HOUSE.

Upon his graduation Allston returned to his native State
and took up his abode in Charleston, where his mother resided.
There he painted several pictures. Prominent among these was
one from "Paradise Lost," entitled "Satan Rallying his Hosts."
This picture indicated the steadfast tendency of his mind. He
lived in realms of the highest spiritual thought. The reach of
his imagination was ever toward mystery, sublimity, and the
grandly beautiful. He seldom treated subjects belonging to the
ordinary and familiar walks of life. "Satan Rallying his Hosts"
and "The Handwriting on the Wall in the Palace of the Baby-
lonian Monarch," mark the commencement and close of a series
of pictures, conspicuous as are those of few other men, for attempted delineation in the highest sphere of the emotional and
supernatural. His life-work in art was a kind of pictorial
mythology. His companionship was among the gods. "Uriel
in the Sun" and "Prometheus Bound" were subjects congenial
to his high imagination, but his gentler nature was not less aspiring, and he loved to ascend on "Jacob's Ladder" with the
angels, and lose himself in the dazzling splendor of the infinite.

Of his life in Charleston Allston writes: "On quitting college I returned to Charleston, where I had the pleasure to meet
Malbone, and another friend and artist, Charles Fraser, who, by
the by, now paints an admirable miniature. My picture manu-

factory still went on in Charleston until I embarked for London. Up to this time my favorite subjects were banditti. I well remember one of these, where I thought I had happily succeeded in cutting a throat. The subject of this precious performance was robbers fighting with each other for the spoils, over the body of a murdered traveller. And clever ruffians I thought them. I did not get rid of this banditti mania until I had been over a year in England. It seems that a fondness for subjects of violence is frequent with young artists. One might suppose that the youthful mind would delight in scenes of an opposite character. Perhaps the reason of the contrary may be found in this: that the natural conditions of youth being one incessant excitement, from the continual influx of novelty—for all about us must at one time be new—it must needs have something fierce, terrible, or unusual to force it above its wonted tone. But the time must come to every man who lives beyond the middle age when there is nothing new under the sun. His novelties then are the *refacimenti* of his former life. The gentler emotions are then as early friends who revisit him in dreams, and who, recalling the past, give a grace and beauty, nay, a rapture even, to what in the heyday of youth had seemed to him spiritless and flat. And how beautiful is this law of nature—perfuming, as it were, our very graves with the unheeded flowers of childhood."

"One of my favorite haunts, when a child in Carolina, was a forest spring where I used to catch minnows, and I daresay with all the callousness of a fisherman; at this moment I can see the spring, and the pleasant conjuror Memory has brought again those little creatures before me; but how unlike to what they were! They seem to me like spirits of the woods, which a flash from their little diamond eyes lights up afresh in all their gorgeous garniture of leaves and flowers. But where am I going?"

Among the pictures painted by Allston, previous to his re-

turn to Charleston, was a scene from the tragedy of Borabona.
The grouping of the figures in this picture was of splendidly
dressed tyrants and the slave Selim, surrounded by black mutes,
who were introduced with much effect.   He also designed and
painted several scenes from " The Mysteries of Udolpho," and
one from " The Mountaineers," in which Octavio figured.

He had considerable tact for caricature, and drew one picture
representing his French class seated around a table, except one
boy reciting, the French master holding a pig in his hands and
directing the boy to pronounce " oui " just like the noise made by
the little brute.

Not long before he left school for the University, he painted
a capital likeness of a St. Domingo black boy, who was one of
the house servants.   He was represented with a liberty cap on
his head, ornamented with a tricolored tassel and cockade, holding in one hand a boot and in the other a shoe-brush.   This he
took to Cambridge with him about 1796.

While in college he painted " Damon and Musidora," from
Thomson's "Seasons " (this is not the one mentioned by Jarvis),
and also one in oil of " Octavia."

In autumn, 1800, while in Newport, he painted a portrait of
Robert Rogers, his old schoolmaster, now in the possession of
the Rogers family.

During his stay in Charleston it became so apparent that his
life was to be devoted to art, that all opposition on the part of
his family ceased.   It was arranged that he should pursue his
studies in Europe ; all feeling of aversion to the profession in
which his heart was so engrossed was changed to cordial acqui-
escence ; his patrimony was turned over to him, and every aid
afforded to facilitate his departure for the art centres of the Old
World.

Of the subject of his early life and prospects, Allston says :
" There was an early friend, long since dead, whom I have

omitted to mention, and cannot but wonder at the omission, since he is one whose memory is still dear to me. The name of this gentleman was Bowman; he was a native of Scotland, but had been long settled in Carolina. I believe I was indebted for the uncommon interest he was pleased to take in me to some of my college verses, and to a head of St. Peter (when he hears the cock crow), which I painted about that time. Be this as it may, it was not of an everyday kind, for when I was about to embark for Europe, he proposed to allow me, nay, almost insisted on my accepting a hundred pounds a year during my stay abroad. This generous offer, however, I declined, for having at that time a small income sufficient for my immediate wants, it would have been sordid to have accepted it. He then proposed to ship me a few tierces of rice! That, too, I declined. Yet he would not let me go without a present; so I was obliged to limit it to Hume's " History of England," and a novel by Dr. Moore, whom he personally knew, and to whom he gave me a letter of introduction; the letter, however, was never delivered, as the Doctor died within a few days of my arrival in London. Such an instance of generosity speaks for itself. But the kindness of manner that accompanied it can only be known to one who saw it. I can see the very expression now. Mr. Bowman was an excellent scholar and one of the most agreeable talkers I have known. Malbone, Fraser, and myself were frequent guests at his table, and delightful parties we always found there. With youth, health, and the kindest friends, and ever before me buoyant hope, what a time to look back on! I cannot but think that the life of an artist, whether poet or painter, depends much on a happy youth; I do not mean as to outward circumstances, but as to his inward being; in my own case, at least, I feel the dependence; for I seldom step into the ideal world but I find myself going back to the age of first impressions. The germs of our best thoughts are certainly often to be found there; sometimes, indeed (though rarely), we find them in full flower, and when so, how beautiful to us these flowers seem through an atmosphere of thirty years. 'Tis in this way that poets and painters keep their minds young. How else could an old man make the page or the canvas palpitate with the hopes and fears and joys, the impetuous, impassioned, emotions of youthful lovers, or reckless heroes?"

"There is a period of life when the ocean of time seems to force upon the mind a barrier against itself, forming, as it were, a permanent beach, on which the advancing years successively break, only to be carried back by a returning current to that furthest deep whence they first flowed. Upon this beach the poetry of life may be said to have its birth; where the real ends and the ideal begins."

In May, 1801, accompanied by his friend Malbone, Allston embarked for England. Together they visited the great art galleries of London; Allston was shocked that Malbone had no admiration for the old masters. After viewing the examples of Titian, Veronese, Rembrandt, and others, then on exhibition, he pointed to a portrait by Sir Thomas Lawrence, and said he would rather possess that than all the other pictures of the collection.

To a mind like Allston's, grasping at philosophies, studious of methods, ever striving to understand the principles by which the old masters produced their grand effects; to one who had learned to reverence them as men whose powers had exalted and given them rank as a kind of artistic magi, adepts in the sacred realms of art; to him such want of appreciation was inexplicable, and the more so as Malbone was a man of acknowledged high ability, whose work had delighted him, indeed had largely inspired his own; Malbone's mind was of a different order, one whose inspiration was self-supplied; drawn from within rather than without. Sentimental and impulsive, rather than philosophical and calculating, his works were the result of intuition rather than of study. Viewing genius as the power to remove difficulties in the way of the best results in art, we may say that in some men it is chiefly inspiration, in others study. In some it is intermittent, occasional, and unreliable; in others it is continuous and usually at command, with larger grasp and higher reach. Men like Allston, abounding in both, represent the latter, those like Malbone the former. The spontaneous pleases, the deliberate satisfies.

Genius is strongest when it can brook rules and grow despite educational shackles; when it can conform to conventional methods of training and develop under academic laws. Such was genius in Allston. It could drink culture into itself and expand. The severest schooling but ministered to its outgrowth, as food useful, perhaps necessary, to its full development. Ordinarily culture is a leveller. Now and then a man is found whose individuality is so marked that it cannot be obscured. No degree of culture can make him like any other than himself.

In most cases a student in the atelier of a great teacher becomes a follower, at a respectful distance, of his master. His peculiarities, if he had any, have been so dominated by the stronger genius and higher powers of the teacher that they are buried; they are lost, and he is henceforth only an imitator. Had he not lost his individuality, had his training been confined to that which was best in himself, he would have at least maintained some trace of originality, and a feeble originality is preferable to mere imitation, however trained and polished.

Allston was stimulated by all influences, all schools, all precedents; nothing too large, nothing too small for the grasp and utilizing power of his genius. He was one of those whom nothing can overshadow or reduce to the common level. His first business in London was to prepare himself for admission as a student of the Royal Academy. His first drawing was from the head of the "Gladiator," which gained him permission to draw at Somerset House. He then made a careful drawing of the "Apollo," and submitted it to Mr. West, who was at that time President of the Academy. West was much pleased with the drawing, and assured him there could be no doubt of its acceptance. He speaks of West thus:

" Mr. West, to whom I was soon introduced, received me with the greatest kindness. I shall never forget his benevolent smile when he took me by the hand ; it is still fresh in my memory, linked with the last of like kind which accompanied the last shake of his hand when I took a final leave of him in 1818. His gallery was opened to me at all times, and his advice always ready and kindly given. He was a man overflowing with the milk of human kindness. If he had enemies, I doubt if he owed them to any other cause than his rare virtue, which, alas for human nature, is too often deemed cause sufficient."

Notwithstanding his patrimony, being of an extremely cautious nature, and wishing to guard against the uncertainties of transit from America in those days, and the possible miscarriage of remittances, Allston was anxious to ascertain whether by his work he could make a living in London. Accordingly he showed some of his water-color sketches to a publisher, and asked if they would be salable. The publisher said he would gladly take, at liberal prices, as many as he would furnish. Having thus provided means of escape from possible want, he took lodgings in Buckingham Place, opposite Fitzroy Square, a very low-priced quarter, and entered diligently upon his studies. His efficiency and ability were greatly commended by Mr. West.

On the walls of the Charleston Library Allston had seen engravings from the Boydell Shakespeare Gallery. The "Ghost Scene" in Hamlet, by Fuseli, deeply affected him. On his arrival

Portrait of Benjamin West, President of the Royal Academy.

From the original in the Boston Museum of Art.

in England he sought out Fuseli, who asked him if he was an artist. "I mean to be," said he, "if industry will make me one." "If," said Fuseli, "I have any skill in physiognomy" (Fuseli was a pupil of Lavater) "you have more than industry on your side, but you have come a great way to starve." Allston replied, "I have a certain patrimony." "Ah," said Fuseli, "that makes a difference."

Subsequently, speaking of this interview to an artist friend, he said that Fuseli made a lasting impression on him. To the question, "Why did you not cultivate a man whom you so much admire?" he replied, "Because I could not stand his profanity." One day, in Fuseli's studio, Allston asked him what had become of his illustrations of Milton, engravings of which he had become familiar with in Charleston. Fuseli pointed sadly to a roll of canvas in the corner and said, "They are there." Allston mentioned one of them as having made a great impression on him. Fuseli exclaimed, "No, you don't like that; you can't like that; it's bad; it's damned bad!"

In one of his letters Allston gives this opinion of Fuseli: "It was a few years ago the fashion with many criticising people (not critics, except those can be called so who make their own ignorance the measure of excellence) to laugh at Fuseli. But Fuseli, even when most extravagant, was not a man to be laughed at; for his very extravagances (even when we felt them as such) had that in them which carried us along with them. All he asked of the spectator was but a particle of imagination, and his wildest freaks would then defy the reason. Only a true genius can do this. But he was far from being always extravagant; he was often sublime, and has left no equal in the visionary; his spectres and witches were born and died with him. As a critic on the art, I know no one so inspiring. Having, as you know, no gallery of the old masters to visit here, I often refresh my memory of them with some of the articles in 'Pilkington's Dictionary,' and he brings them before me in a way that no other man's words could; he even gives me a distinct apprehension of the style and color of some whose works I have never seen. I often read one or two of his articles before I go into my painting-room; they form indeed almost a regular course at breakfast."

Sir Joshua Reynolds died before Allston reached London. Allston used to deplore his loss in not having known him personally, for his admiration of Reynolds was unbounded. He had read his lectures, delivered as President of the Royal Academy, and from that fountain of pure English had drunk with wondering delight; wondering that a man so gifted and affluent in the products of his brush should be so surpassingly effective and brilliant with his pen. Contemporaneous and subsequent criticism has sustained this high estimate of Sir Joshua's literary merit. Had his power been expended in more popular work, as in novels, or stories touching the ordinary interests of life, Sir Joshua would rank with the best writers of his time. As Luman Reed, one of the most intelligent patrons of American art, pithily said: "Sir Joshua's lectures are not only instructive to artists, but they furnish rules of life." And when to Sir Joshua's literary attractiveness is added his fascinating power as a painter, it is not surprising that Allston should have said: "Had it been my happiness to have known him, I would, by all means possible to me, have endeavored to ingratiate myself with him."

Before leaving London Allston contributed to an exhibition at Somerset House, of which he speaks thus: "The year 1802 was the first of my adventuring before the public, when I exhibited three pictures at Somerset House—the principal one, 'A French Soldier Telling a Story' (a comic attempt), 'A Rocky Coast with Banditti,' and a 'Landscape with a Horseman,' which I had painted at College. I received two applications for the 'French Soldier,' which I sold to Mr. Wilson of the European Museum, for whom I afterward painted a companion to it, also comic, 'The Poet's Ordinary,' where the lean fare was enriched by an accidental arrest." Allston's versatility is shown in the success these comic pictures made. They must have attracted considerable notice as the biographer of Sir Thomas Lawrence is quoted as saying: "In mentioning American painters it would be unpardonable to omit the broad humor, in the style of Hogarth, in the pictures of Mr. Allston."

CHAPTER IV.

Soon after Allston's arrival in London, he wrote to his friend
Charles Fraser, a young artist in Charleston, the following interesting letter:

"LONDON, August 25, 1801.

"Were it in my power, I would certainly make an excuse for
having so long delayed writing to you; but, as I have none to
make, I shall throw myself on that candor which my short acquaintance with you has encouraged me to expect. You have no
doubt anticipated much, and will, I apprehend, be not a little
disappointed at the account of what I have seen.

"I landed in this country big with anticipation of every
species of grandeur. No city, thought I then, to be compared
with London, no people with its inhabitants. But I have found
London but a city, and its inhabitants like the rest of the world,
much in them to admire, more to despise, and still more to
abhor.

"As to the country, it is beyond my expectation, beautiful
and picturesque; and the appearance of the people, that of
health and contentment; in short, every leaf seemed to embody
a sentiment and every cottage to contain a Venus. But when I
arrived in London, what a contrast! Figure to yourself the ex-
tremes of misery and splendor, and you will have a better idea

of it than I can give you. Scarcely a luxury but you may command here; and scarcely a scene of wretchedness but you may witness at the corner of every street. Indeed, the whole city appears to be composed of princes and beggars. I had no idea before of pride unaccompanied by some kind of merit. But here no one has pride without fortune. Indeed, the most respectable among the middle ranks appear to have no consequence except in boasting of the acquaintance of some one in rank; and among the greater part, so shameful is their venality, they will condescend to flatter the most infamous for a penny.

"It is said in their defence that every man must live, and in so populous a country one must not be scrupulous about the means. But I can conceive of no necessity that should induce a man to degrade himself before those with whom he cannot but feel an equality, and whom he has too frequently occasion to despise. But it is time to conclude with this for I know you must be impatient to read something about the arts.

"You will no doubt be surprised that among the many painters in London I should rank Mr. West as first. I must own I myself was not a little surprised to find him such. I left America strongly prejudiced against him; and indeed I even now think with good reason, for those pictures from which I had seen prints would do no credit to a very inferior artist, much less to one of his reputation. But when I saw his gallery and the innumerable excellences which it contained, I pronounced him one of the greatest men in the world. I have looked upon his understanding with indifference, and his imagination with contempt; but I have now reason to suppose them both vigorous in the highest degree. No fancy could have better conceived and no pencil more happily embodied the visions of sublimity than he has in his inimitable picture from Revelation. Its subject is the opening of the seven seals, and a more sublime and awful picture I never beheld. It is impossible to conceive anything more terrible than Death on the white horse, and I am certain no painter has exceeded Mr. West in the fury, horror, and despair which he has represented in the surrounding figures. I could mention many others of similar merit, but were I particular on each I should not only weary you but write myself asleep.

" Of Fuseli I shall speak hereafter. I have seen but few of his pictures, therefore cannot so well judge at present. They are, however, sufficient to entitle him to immortality. Indeed, his 'Hamlet' alone, were it not for the picture I have just mentioned, would undoubtedly place him in the first seat among the English artists. Another picture also of his that I admire much represents ' Sin Separating Death and Satan.' The attitude of Satan is beyond improvement sublime, and the others are such as none but Fuseli could have painted. In short, it is the only picture I ever saw that was worthy of being joined with the name of Milton. The following are some extempore lines I made on it :

> "Artist sublime, I own thy powerful spell,
>   I feel thy fire, and hear the blasts of hell ;
>   I see thy monster from the canvas stride,
>   While chilly tremors o'er my senses glide ;
>   Thro' heaving throttle vainly gasp for breath,
>   And feel the torture of approaching death.
>   I hear thy Satan's rebel thunders roll,
>   While awful tempests gather round my soul.
>   Convulsive now I lift the admiring eye,
>   And now with horror from his presence fly ;
>   Still in suspense, as laboring fancy burns,
>   I hate, admire, admire and hate by turns.

" Opie comes next in rank ; as a bold and determinate delineator of character he has not a superior. He is surpassed, however, by Northcote in effect. But that is a subordinate excel-

lence. Indeed, were it not the English artists might well stand
in competition with many of the ancient masters. You have
seen a print from Northcote's 'Arthur.' The original, I must
own, is a beautiful thing. But Opie has painted the same subject, and I assure you the two pictures will not bear a comparison. You may think I exaggerate when I say the head of
Arthur is the divinest thing I ever beheld. But I assure you
it is no less. His Hubert I do not like, it is not equal to
Northcote's. But his two villains are such as the devil nour-
ishes in the cradle. They have murder written on every feature ; and I cannot but think that Opie, like Salvator Rosa,
must have lived among banditti to have so admirably portrayed
them.

"Are these all? you will ask. All indeed, I assure you,
that are worth mentioning. I had forgot, however, the portrait
painters. The two first are Lawrence and Sir William Beechy,
but even Lawrence cannot paint so well as Stuart ; and as for the
rest they are the damnedest stupid wretches that ever disgraced
a profession. But I do not include the miniature painters ; that
is a line I am but little acquainted with, therefore I am not able
to judge. As far, however, as my judgment extends I can pronounce Mr. Malbone not inferior to the best among them. He
showed a likeness he painted of me to Mr. West, who complimented him very highly, 'I have seldom seen,' said he, 'a
miniature that pleased me more.' I would mention also some
compliments which he paid me, but I should blush to repeat
what I cannot think I deserve.

"Your friend White I like very much. He has a spice
of literature about him which makes him not the less agreeable
to me, who am about (*mirabile dictu*) to publish a book. By
the by, how long do you suppose Trumbull was about his 'Gib-
raltar?' It is truly a charming picture ; but he was a whole
year about it, therefore it ought to have been better. I have no

idea of a painter's laboring up to fame. When he ceases to obtain reputation without it, he becomes a mechanic. Trumbull is no portrait painter. By this picture alone he has gained credit. But it is indeed credit purchased at a most exorbitant interest.

"I have lately painted several pictures; but am now about one that will far surpass anything I have done before. The subject is from the passage of Scripture, 'And Christ looked upon Peter.' It contains twenty figures, which are about two feet in height, on the whole making the best composition I ever attempted. The two principal groups are Christ between two soldiers, who are about to bear him away, the high priests, etc., and Peter surrounded by his accusers. The other groups are composed of spectators, variously affected, men, women, and children."

"Next week I shall apply for admission into the Academy. The very first figure that I drew from plaster, Mr. West said, would admit me. It was from the 'Gladiator.' He was astonished when I told him it was my first, and paid a compliment (too pretty to be repeated) to the correctness of my eye. He also observed that I not only preserved the form, but, what few artists think of, the expression of my subject. You see by this account that I am not very modest. Indeed I despise the affectation of it. But my principal motive in being thus particular is to encourage you by proving that much greater men than either you or I were once no better than ourselves. And could I convince you, by flattering myself, of the dignity of your powers, I would boast as much again. Believe me, sir, it is no proof of vanity that a man should suppose himself adequate to more than he has already performed. Confidence is the soul of genius. Great talents to a timid mind are of as little value to the owner as gold to a miser, who is afraid to use it. Great men rise but by their own exertions. It is the fool's and the child's pusillanimity alone that are boosted up to fame. How are we to learn our own powers without a trial? Accident will, indeed, sometimes discover them; but are we all to wait for accident? No, sir; the principle of self-love was implanted in us to excite emulation, and he violates a law of nature who yields to despair without a previous trial of his powers. A little seasonable vanity is the best friend we can have.

"Not that silly conceit founded on adventitious advantages, which exalts us but in our own imagination. But I mean the confidence which arises from a determination to excel, and is nourished by a hope of future greatness. The great Buffon thought there were but three geniuses in the world—two besides himself. And what was the consequence? His application was indefatigable. He was a genius and ought to surpass other men. He did surpass them. Cæsar, giving an account of his conquest, said, 'Veni, vidi, vici.' No man, perhaps, had so great an opinion of his own strength, and no man was capable of more. When a man is thus confident he is not to be discouraged by difficulties. But his exertions rather strengthen as they increase. It was a saying of Alcibiades, and I believe a very just one, that 'When souls of a certain order did not perform all they wished, it was because they had not courage to attempt all they could.'

"Why, then, my friend, should you despair? You have talents; cultivate them—and it is not impossible that the name of Fraser may one day be as celebrated as those of Raphael and Michael Angelo. Resolve to shine, and, believe me, the little crosses of to-day will vanish before the more substantial joys of to-morrow.

"In the meantime let me advise you to beware of love. Love and painting are two opposite elements; you cannot live in both at the same time. Be wise in time, and let it not be said, when future biographers shall record your life that, 'Mr. Fraser

promised much, his genius gave symptoms of expansion beyond
mortality, but love, alas! untimely love had set a seal upon his
fame. His soul, which was just about to grasp a world, is now
imprisoned within the bosom of a girl.'

" ' Where now are those mighty schemes which were to elevate him to the summit of fame ? Where are those characters
which were to inscribe the name of Fraser on the front of time ?
Alas! a woman's tears have washed them from his memory.
No longer is he anxious to be distinguished from the crowd ;
no longer does the spirit of Michael Angelo point the way to
heaven ; he is blessed with a smile from his mistress, his ambition is contented ; he seeks no other heaven than the bed of
roses on her bosom.'

" No, Fraser, let this not be said of you.   Love in its place I
revere ; but it is not at all times to be indulged.   There are many
beautiful girls in Charleston, but Raphael and Michael Angelo
are still more beautiful than they.

"Believe me, with sincerity, your friend,

"WASHINGTON ALLSTON."

In this letter to Fraser, Allston's characterization of the majority of portrait painters in London is very remarkable. "They
are the damnedest stupid wretches that ever disgraced a profession." This rather profane expletive might pass unnoticed from
an ordinary man, but from Allston it is a surprise. From his
most intimate friends, and from the whole range of his correspondence, if we except this letter, we can discover no instance
where his sense of propriety seems to have been off guard. We
may conclude from this that the intimacy between Allston and
Fraser was so close as to obliterate barriers of ordinary circum-
spection. It would be interesting to know more of one who
could find his way through all defences to the inner life and
thought of his friend.

Two other interesting letters, written from London to his friend Knapp, we give below:

" LONDON, July 28, 1803.

" DEAR KNAPP: The relief of confession is always so great that I know not whether we do not frequently what is wrong for the pleasure of acknowledging it, as an epicure will often go without food for the increasing gratification of his appetite. At least so I am willing you should account for my neglect. Besides, I may also lay claim to another motive—the pleasure of undeceiving a friend where circumstances may have induced him to doubt our attachment. But, however agreeable the last may be, I cannot assign it here as a serious motive, for in that case I should suppose you (which I am far from thinking) both ignorant and suspicious of my character. My silence, I dare say, you will attribute to laziness, and you know me too well to expect that I shall deny it; you will therefore excuse me if I do not attempt a thorough vindication.

" Your letter, by Wyre, I have received. You complain much of stagnation, but the activity of thought you display in describing your situation goes very little toward convincing me that your complaint is serious; and unless I should consider you as one of those unfortunate gentlemen who fancy themselves oysters, while they are reasoning like philosophers, I must still hold to the opinion that you were possessed of the same feelings, that you are the same acute observer, and the same poet, as when I left you. Your observation about critics may not be confined to America. I have found it applicable more particularly in London. There are indeed a few daring spirits who judge for themselves; but of the few who dare, there are still fewer whose judgment is sanctioned by their candor or their taste. It is sufficient, however, to be received that an opinion is pronounced with boldness, as every one is willing, when done, to reverence what he had the courage to attempt.

"Neither do I think it should be confined to London. For when we reflect that to judge with propriety the critic should be enabled to incorporate his mind with his author, it is not so wonderful that so few should be fond of, as that so many should be capable of, judging anywhere. I hope, however, you were not led to the observation alluded to under any apprehension for yourself. If you were, I take the liberty to say you were wrong; for an original genius will command attention at least, if not admiration, among any people; and that such is yours you will not think it flattery if I declare. This critical timidity I apprehend, will continue to increase in every society where the literary condidates are themselves afraid. When a man undertakes a great design, and expresses a doubt whether he shall be successful, we are always ready to commend his modesty; but we lose that admiration of his powers which a proper confidence will never fail to inspire. Let modesty be considered in an agreeable light, but only as a buoy on the ocean of literature, to warn each adventurer of the wreck beneath it. By you, my friend, it always has been, and I hope always will be, considered as the most graceful ornament of private life. I only request that you would lay it aside in the literary world.

"I have made these observations under a persuasion that you will aspire to salute the great toe of the holy Pope Apollo, or, in other words, that you had either begun or intended to begin a poem. You will do right not to neglect your profession. But you should never forget what you owe to the future fame of your country; you should never forget that the muses who nursed you and watched round your cradle are now mystically anticipating the future reputation of their favorite, and though they behold the scythe of Death level him in his course, still hoping to enjoy the never-dying glory of his labors.

"You were so good as to give me some advice in your last, for which I thank you. This you may consider only as a return. But I offer it with sincerity; and would urge it with effect, if it should be necessary. Your powers, my friend, are such as heaven has bestowed on few; and you have already given no little promise that they were not given in vain; let not that promise be forgotten, or ever hereafter remembered with regret. What think you of a poem in the manner of Spenser? It is not a popular mode of versification, and the simplicity of his style (at least as much as Beattie has adopted) is admirably suited to the wildness of Indian story. Not that I would have you imitate him in preference to writing from yourself, for your own style has a decided character, and one that I should be sorry you should change; but I mean only that you should write in the same stanzas and adopt some of his words. However, in whatever metre, in whatever words, I beg you will write. I have not forgotten your 'Wacoon chanting from some viewless cliff.' By the by, I never answered your poetical letter which I received last winter. My reason is my hearing afterward you had sailed for Europe.

"Mr. Derby, who will take charge of this letter, goes sooner than I expected, so I will break off here and write in a few days in continuation. I go to France in about two months."

"LONDON, August 24, 1803.

"DEAR KNAPP: As I promised you a letter in continuation of my last, I will resume a subject in which I feel no little interest. The high opinion I entertain of your talents may be an excuse (if you should deem one necessary) for my boring you to exert them. Do not suppose I think you wanting in confidence or enthusiasm, as a man of genius I know you possess them both; but you may, probably, weigh too scrupulously the effect of your labor in America. It is, therefore, that I would urge the exertion of your powers—of powers capable of the sublimest flights in the regions of fancy. If you will not write for yourself, at

least write for your country; and should the critics attack you,
answer them in the language of Euripides, when the Athenians
criticised him, ' I do not compose my works in order to be corrected by you, but to instruct you.'

"I do not see why every author is not adequate to the judging of his own performance. Surely the mind which is capable
of conceiving a great plan may also possess an equal power to
analyze its principles. The affection which parents feel for their
offspring I know is opposed to it; but without the severity of
Virgil, a father may obtain a temporary ignorance of his child by
sending him away. Then it may be urged a return would naturally increase his affection. True; but the same novelty that
displays the accomplishments will discover the defects of his offspring. Strong memories stand likewise in the way of this; but
Pope says men of genius have short memories. Whether true or
false, I will not undertake to determine. I am satisfied to answer
that very retentive memories have been rare, and many geniuses
have been remarkable for their absence; besides, a man of great
memory can never be alone; he is always in company with the
thoughts of other men.

"In reply to all this, you will naturally ask what I have done.
I cannot answer that I have done anything, but I mean to do
something. My profession will always be painting, but I have
not serenaded the Muses so many cold wintry nights for nothing; they shall grant me a favor before I die. The ' notable
plot for a tragedy,' you allude to, I have with many alterations
completed. The dialogue, however, is still unfinished. But I
resumed it not long since, and have advanced in it considerably,
so that I hope, ere many moons, the voice of Melpomene will
decide its fate. I will quote from it an address to the moon,
by the principal female character. She is destined to move in a
conspicuous sphere, and I intend her to represent the combination of a masculine mind and an ambitious spirit with vehement

passions, nor yet destitute of feminine delicacy.   Ambition, however, is her predominant feature.   How far the address is in
character, I leave you to judge.

'TO THE MOON.

' Olympia, pale queen of mystery, I hail thy beams.
   Now all is dark save here and there to view,
   Where mid thy dim and solemn empire rise
   Vast rocks and woods and towers and gorgeous towns.
   So o'er the shadowy regions of my soul
   Hope's mystic rays reveal the dusky forms
   Of Fancy's wild creation.   To thy power,
   O potent sorceress, I yield my soul.
   Watch o'er my thoughts and round my glowing brain,
   While darkness veils in dread sublimity,
   Pour thy majestic visions ; for to thee,
   Alone to thee, belongs the mighty charm
   That swells the heart in towering confidence,
   Scorning the coward prudence of the world
   To meet the vast conceptions of the mind.'

" I believe it has been the case with many who have conceived great plans, which have been rendered abortive by the
opposite opinions of those they live with, that they only wanted
the confidence which solitude inspires to carry them to perfection.   I speak of all plans, whether good or bad.   A man in
society and a man alone are two different beings.   It is unfortunate, however, for the world that so many have not felt the want
of this solitary confidence.   It would be a curious speculation to
calculate the mischief that many villains would make were they
not restrained by the fears awakened by virtuous examples.   I
will quote one more passage by the same character, simply as
expressive of the same energy.

" She replies to the Prince, who is her lover and hints
at making her his mistress.   Her indignation is not more in-

spired by love than ambition, for her principal object is his throne.

> .   .   .   .   .   'to purchase love?
> Oh, blasphemy to love. As soon, mean reptile,
> Mayst thou purchase life and bribe the worms
> That revel in thy grave their feasts forego,
> And weave their volumes into flesh again.'

" The second line, you will perceive, is defective in measure, but it will be corrected in due time. I have not time to add another line. You will excuse my abrupt conclusion, and, believe me, your friend,

" WASHINGTON ALLSTON."

CHAPTER V.

After a comparatively brief stay in London Allston, accompanied by Vanderlyn, went to Paris. It was during the exciting
period of the wars of Napoleon. Here he became a constant and
diligent student in the galleries of the Louvre.

Never before, never since, has there been gathered into one
collection so many masterpieces of art as were to be seen in the
Louvre when Allston and Vanderlyn visited it. These trophies
of Napoleon's conquests throughout Europe were the best works
of the greatest masters. Subsequently many were returned to
their rightful owners, and still the exhibition of the Louvre is
justly considered the finest in the world. In his "Lectures on
Art," Allston writes of the impression made upon him by this
splendid collection as follows:

"Titian, Tintoret, and Paul Veronese absolutely enchanted
me, for they took away all sense of subject. When I stood before
'The Peter Martyr,' 'The Miracle of the Slave,' and 'The Marriage of Cana,' I thought of nothing but the gorgeous concert of
colors, or rather of the indefinite forms (I cannot call them sensations) of pleasure with which they filled the imagination. It
was the poetry of color which I felt, procreative in its nature,
giving birth to a thousand things which the eye cannot see, and
distinct from their cause. I did not, however, stop to analyze

my feelings—perhaps at that time I could not have done it. I
was content with my pleasure without seeking the cause. But
now I understand it, and think I understand why so many great
colorists, especially Tintoret and Paul Veronese, gave so little
heed to the ostensible stories of their compositions. In some of
them, 'The Marriage of Cana,' for instance, there is not the
slightest clue given by which the spectator can guess at the subject. They addressed themselves, not to the senses merely, as
some have supposed, but rather through them to that region (if
I may so speak) of the imagination which is supposed to be under the exclusive dominion of music, and which, by similar excitement, they caused to teem with visions that 'lap the soul in
Elysium.' In other words they leave the subject to be made
by the spectator, provided he possesses the imaginative faculty ;
otherwise they will have little more meaning to him than a calico
counterpane.

"I am by nature, as it respects the arts, a wide liker. I cannot honestly turn up my nose even at a piece of still life, since,
if well done, it gives me pleasure. This remark will account for
otherwise strange transitions. I will mention here a picture of a
wholly different kind, which then took great hold of me, by Lo-
dovico Carracci. I do not remember the title, but the subject
was the body of the Virgin borne for interment by four apostles.
The figures are colossal; the tone dark, and of tremendous depth
of color. It seemed, as I looked at it, as if the ground shook
under their tread, and the air were darkened by their grief.

"I may here notice a false notion which is current among
artists, in the interpretation they put on the axiom that 'something should always be left to the imagination,' viz., that some
parts of a picture should be left unfinished. The very statement
betrays its unsoundness, for that which is unfinished must necessarily be imperfect; so that, according to this rule, imperfection is made essential to perfection. The error lies in the

phrase, 'left to the imagination,' and it has filled modern art with random flourishes of no meaning. If the axiom be intended to prevent the impertinent intrusion of subordinate objects (the faults certainly of a mean practice), I may observe that the remedy is no remedy, but rather a less fault substituted for a greater. Works of a high order, aspiring to the poetical, cannot make good their pretensions unless they do affect the imagination; and this should be the test—that they set to work, not to finish what is less incomplete, but to awaken images congenial to the compositions, but not in them expressed; an effect that never was yet realized by misrepresenting anything. If the objects introduced into a picture keep their several places as well in the deepest shadow as in the light, the general effect will suffer nothing by their truth; but to give the whole truth in the midnight as well as in the daylight, belongs to a master."

It is doubtful whether the Gallery of the Louvre was ever more faithfully studied than by Allston. He devoted himself almost exclusively to the old masters, toward whom his allegiance never wavered.

Vanderlyn, his most intimate friend during his stay in Paris, was the protégé of Aaron Burr; he distinguished himself by his celebrated picture of " Marius amid the ruins of Carthage," and his beautiful rendering of " Ariadne." For the former, which was exhibited in Paris, he was awarded a prize medal.

While in Paris Allston's remittances failed, and he had his first experience in pecuniary embarrassment. Vanderlyn assured him that he could arrange for his relief. " How ? " asked Allston. " I can swear to your financial soundness," was the reply. Vanderlyn went to his tailor and stated the case so effectively that the tailor told Allston to draw on him for whatever he needed. He drew for a thousand francs, and shortly after refunded the money, and further, to discharge the obligation, ordered two suits of clothes.

In character and methods of art it would be difficult to find two men more dissimilar than Vanderlyn and Allston. Vanderlyn, with many fine traits and eminent ability as an artist, grasped only the external and obvious. Facts ; truth, however barren or angular, was the prime object of attainment with him. Imagination was bridled and curbed by a stern regard for the obviously true. He might conceive and plan, but he would paint only that which he could see with his physical eye. Even the ruins of Carthage must be constructed from the remains of Greek temples, and in miniature proportions placed in his studio before he would attempt to paint his great picture. He lived in the outer, and had but little communion with the purely ideal. His intellectual powers, though large and vigorous, seldom waited upon his emotions. With Allston, emotion aroused and fired imagination, and intellect, though ever present in large measure, was tempered and mingled with the emotional. The one was altogether practical, matter of fact; the other dreamy, thoughtful, eccentric, and full of the adventuring spirit of genius.

Allston travelled to Italy through Switzerland, drinking in, with ever-increasing delight, the beauties of the scenery in the vicinity of the Swiss lakes and in the Alps. Few of the letters written at this time have been preserved, but from one of these we quote :

"The impressions left by the sublime scenery of Switzerland are still fresh to this day. A new world has been opened to me, nor have I met with anything like it since. The scenery of the Apennines is quite of a different character. By the by, I was particularly struck in this journey with the truth of Turner's Swiss scenes—the poetic truth, which none before or since have given, with the exception of my friend Brockhedon's magnificent work on the passes of the Alps. I passed a night and saw the sun rise on the Lake Maggiore. Such a sunrise ! The giant Alps seemed literally to rise from their purple beds, and putting on their crowns of gold to send up a hallelujah almost audible."

In Italy Allston stopped first in Sienna, to acquaint himself with the language before going to Rome. He visited Venice, and spent a year studying and painting in the galleries of Florence; he went to Rome in March, 1805, and there became imbued with the spirit of the old masters. Michael Angelo's forms and Titian's color found a response in his own ideals of majesty, harmony, and beauty. But they found in him an individuality that, while it could be strengthened and impressed, could not be obliterated or overwhelmed. He painted himself, inspired by the Italian masters, and the result was a new manifestation. He studied with all the powers of his mind, intent upon understanding the methods of his great prototypes in art, and it is not too much to say that he exhibited more of the spirit of the best old masters than has been shown by any student of modern times. He studied pictorial anatomy diligently, modelled in clay, and never ceased his practice in drawing.

He thus expresses his reverence for the old masters:

"It is needless to say how I was affected by Raffaele, the greatest master of the affections in our art. In beauty he has often been surpassed, but in grace—the native grace of character —in the expression of intellect, and, above all, sanctity, he has no equal. What particularly struck me in his works, was the genuine life (if I may so call it) that seemed, without impairing the distinctive character, to pervade them all; for even his humblest figures have a something, either in look, air, or gesture, akin to the *venustas* of his own nature, as if, like living beings under the influence of a master spirit, they had partaken, in spite of themselves, a portion of the charm which swayed them. This power of infusing one's own life, as it were, into that which is feigned, appears to me the sole prerogative of genius. In a work of art, this is what a man may well call his own, for it cannot be borrowed or imitated. Of Michael Angelo, I do not know how to speak in adequate terms of reverence. With all his faults (but who is without them) even Raffaele bows before him. As I stood beneath his colossal prophets and sybils, still more colossal in spirit, I felt as if in the presence of messengers from the other world, with the destiny of man in their breath, in repose even terrible. I cannot agree with Sir Joshua that 'The Vision of Ezekiel,' of Raffaele, or 'The Moses,' of Parmegiano, have anything in common with Michael Angelo. Their admiration of Michael Angelo may have elevated their forms into a more dignified and majestic race, but still left them men, whose feet had never trod other than this earth. The supernatural was beyond the reach of both. But no one could mistake the prophets of Michael Angelo for inhabitants of our world; yet they are true to the imagination, as the beings about us are to the senses. I am not undervaluing these great artists when I deny them a kindred genius with Michael Angelo; they had both genius of their own, and high qualities which nature had denied the other."

Toward the end of the year Allston was joined by Vanderlyn, and they were the only American students in Rome. Of his fellow-students and comrades, and of distinguished foreigners resident in Rome at that time, Sweetser, in his "Washington Allston," says: "Vanderlyn has told us how he and Allston, Turner, and Fenimore Cooper, frequented the famous Caffè Greco, the resort of the northern barbarians in Rome for so many decades. There, too, were to be seen Thorwaldsen and Cornelius, Anderson and Louis of Bavaria, Flaxman and Gibson, Shelley, Keats, and Byron. Thorwaldsen could hardly have been a student with Allston, as some assert, for he had been in Rome eight years when the latter arrived, and had already won rich pecuniary rewards and the praise of Canova. Nevertheless he was a friend of the American artist, and often in after-years pointed to him as a proof that the loftiest abilities were indigenous to the Western world.

" Another group of eminent persons then living in Rome, and accessible to the young Carolinian, was gathered around William von Humboldt, the Prussian ambassador, and Alexander von Humboldt, who had just returned from his travels among the South American Andes. The Danish envoy, Baron von Schubert, and the Neapolitan envoy, Cardinal Fesch, were also members of the artistic society of the city. Madame de Staël was living there at the same time, also A. W. von Schlegel and Sismondi. During this period the city was continually menaced by the armies of Napoleon, which had occupied several of the papal provinces."

Samuel Taylor Coleridge, Washington Irving, and Washington Allston, met the first time in Rome in 1805, and soon became intimate. They were young men diverse in temperament, in character, and in pursuits; having little observable similarity, save in the healthful vigor of early manhood, yet attracted to each other by a moral magnetism, such as binds together kindred souls despite the varying circumstances and influences of life. Different, yet inseparable, these young men traversed the streets of the " Eternal City." Could their conversations, as from day to day they wandered in and about Rome, be recalled and written, we should unquestionably have a record of great interest, rich in poetry, in philosophy, and historic truth.

Doubtless much of the subject-matter of those conversations in and about Rome would, through Coleridge, have found its way to the public, but for an unfortunate incident in connection with his return to England, in the summer of 1806. He had intended to go by way of Switzerland and Germany, but being somewhat apprehensive of danger on account of the movements of the French troops, took the precaution to ask the advice of Ambassador von Humboldt; he advised Coleridge to avoid

Bonaparte, who was meditating the seizure of his person, and had already sent to Rome an order for his arrest, which was withheld from execution by the connivance of the good old Pope, Pius VII., who sent him a passport, and counselled his immediate flight by way of Leghorn. Accordingly he hastened to that port, where he found an American vessel ready to sail for England, and embarked. On the voyage they were chased by a French sail; the captain, becoming alarmed, commanded Coleridge to throw his papers, including his notes on Rome, overboard.

As Traill, in his "Life of Coleridge," informs us, "The animosity of the First Consul was directed against Coleridge in consequence of the statement of Mr. Fox in the House of Commons, that the rupture of the peace at Amiens had been brought about by certain articles in the *Morning Post*. These articles were written by Coleridge, and, as his biographer remarks, in answer to a certain writer in *Blackwood*, "There is certainly no reason to believe that a tyrant, whose animosity against literary or quasi-literary assailants ranged from Madame de Staël down to the bookseller Palm, would have regarded a man of Coleridge's reputation as beneath the swoop of his vengeance."

It cannot be doubted by those who know Coleridge's high appreciation of Allston, that in those manuscripts, lost through the fright of the captain, there were many allusions to the seven months of daily intercourse with a spirit so in accord with his own in its culture, and in poetic and philosophic thought; we cannot but think that in his impressions of Rome, Coleridge would have risen to the height of his finest efforts. He was at his best; he had reached the maturity of his intellectual power; although he had commenced the fatal habit which a few years later was so painfully evident, it had not yet become apparent even to his companions. It had made no visible inroads upon his body or mind. Relieved as he was of financial embarrassment by a certain though small annuity, with the invigorating influence of change of scene, change of air, and inspiring companionship, we are justified in believing that the lost notes would have added an important contribution to the scanty exhibitions of his best. One whose work was so often fragmentary and incomplete, one so irresolute and inconstant, in a career so brief could ill afford to lose any work performed under stimulation so auspicious, in the zenith of his powers.

No inconsiderable influence must have been exerted by Coleridge, Irving, and Allston upon each other during their intimacy in Rome. The character of each must have been to some extent moulded by the others. Doubtless they were beneficiaries all; fine natures, cultivated as they were, have much to give and are always ready to receive. Perhaps none received more than he gave, so balanced were they in natural gifts and qualities. Of Coleridge, however, it may be said that his nature had in it more of the aggressive than belonged either to Allston or Irving. He was the senior and, in a sense, the primate; the leader and chief speaker of the trio. It may indeed be questioned whether there has ever lived his superior in the oral use of language—in captivating fluency and brilliancy of speech.

In a conversation with Mr. Albert Mathews, of New York, S. F. B. Morse, referring to the fluency for which Coleridge was so celebrated, said: "When Leslie and I were studying under Allston, Coleridge was a frequent, almost daily, visitor to our studio. For our entertainment while painting, we used to arrange in advance some question in which we were interested, and propound it to Coleridge upon his coming in. This was quite sufficient, and never failed to start him off on a monologue to which we could listen with pleasure and profit throughout the entire sitting." His mind was exhaustless, and his power to interest was always at command.

Allston said : " To no other man do I owe so much intellectually as to Mr. Coleridge, with whom I became acquainted in Rome, and who has honored me with his friendship for more than five and twenty years. He used to call Rome ' the silent city,' but I could never think of it as such while with him, for meet him when and where I would, the fountain of his mind was never dry, but, like the far-reaching aqueducts that once supplied this mistress of the world, its living stream seemed specially to flow for every classic ruin over which we wandered ; and when I recall some of our walks under the pines of the Villa Borghese, I am almost tempted to dream that I have once listened to Plato in the groves of the Academy."

Allston loved the classic beauty of Greece in her sculptured forms. He partook of the spirit of the men who reared her temples, and chiselled her immortal statues. The chaste dignity, the purity, and elegance of the Doric ; the ornate simplicity of the Corinthian and Ionic, appealed to him as to one educated in the schools of Phidias, Myron, and Polycletus, in the splendid era of Pericles. No child of Attica was ever more sensitively alive to the pure, refining, and inspiring influences of her marble forms. The tendency of his mind was toward the statuesque, simple, majestic, beautiful, ornate without filigree, rich without an intimation of the sensuous or voluptuous. To the ordinary observer, the Farnese Hercules is a grand statue of the demigod of Greece, exceedingly impressive in its semblance of majesty and power. To him it was the immortal offspring of its author. It had survived the rise and fall of nations. It was immortal, he said, because of its integrity to the highest principles of art, which made it the embodiment and visible image of truth. It was something more than an exaggeration of the human form. Though of mortal mould, it possessed more than mortal powers, and he tells us that while standing before it he felt its essential life, as if he were in the presence of a superior being.[1]

The Apollo Belvedere, to many who view it, is an extremely graceful figure, with faultless proportions, of a young man with his left hand extended, holding a bow, while his right hand, which has apparently just left the string, is near his hip—nothing more. To him it was immeasurably more—more, we might almost say, than its author intended. In speaking of this statue, Allston says: "In this supernal being the human form seems to have been assumed as if to make visible the harmonious confluence of the pure ideas of grace, fleetness, and majesty; nor do we think it too fanciful to add, celestial splendor, for such in effect are the thoughts which crowd, or rather rush, into the mind on first beholding it. Who that saw it in what may be called the place of its glory, the Gallery of Napoleon, ever thought of it as a man, much less as a statue? But did not feel, rather, as if the vision before him was one of another world— of one who had just lighted on the earth, and with a step so ethereal that the next instant he would vault into the air. If," he continues, "I may be permitted to recall the impression which it made on myself, I know not how I could better describe it than as a sudden intellectual flash filling the whole mind with light and light in motion. It seemed to the mind what the first sight of the sun is to the senses, as it emerges from the ocean; when from a point of light the whole orb at once appears to bound from the waters and to dart its rays, as by a visible explosion, through the profound of space."

The charge that Coleridge endeavored to draw Allston from his love of Greek art has, we think, no sufficient foundation, though in conversation upon the comparative beauties of Greek and Gothic styles, he once said to Allston: "Grecian archi-

---

[1] Lectures on Art, p. 99.

tecture is a thing, but the Gothic is an idea." And then added: "I can make a Grecian temple of two brick-bats and a cocked hat." Unquestionably he preferred the Gothic, for obvious and sufficient reasons.

The Gothic in its richest development was the outcome of the Middle Ages. Its composite beauty grew and expanded under the encouragement and patronage of the Church; it was the outgrowth of that ecclesiasticism which appealed to the religious sentiment through visible forms. As thus, a part of the Church, Coleridge loved and revered it. To him the Gothic was Christian; the Greek, Pagan. In commending the Gothic, he seemed to feel the enthusiasm of one who was contending for the supremacy of the Christian faith.

It were unjust to suppose that Coleridge was insensible to Grecian beauty; Plato and Socrates could charm his intellect, but Christ and the Church captivated his heart and soul. Monuments of Greek art appealed to his sense of beauty and gave him pleasure, but the Gothic touched his sense of worship, and revealed to his chastened imagination a higher beauty; to him the one was earthly, the other heavenly.

CHAPTER VI.

Irving's influence was genial and beneficent in all directions.
His admiration for the young artist was true and profound.
Allston's studio was to him a temple wherein was enshrined the
purest spirit of art, and to it his emotional nature paid daily
homage. So engrossed was he in this worship, that at one time,
as he tells us, he seriously contemplated devoting himself to art
as his pursuit in life; but encouragement in the direction of a
literary career finally prevailed. Whether the world has lost by
his decision, who can say? Allston was his ideal of a true artist
in character and attainment, and it is not strange that Irving's
imaginative and fervid nature should have inclined him to enter the path to fame in which his friend was making so great
progress.

Speaking of Allston, he said: "The pleasure he derives
from his own thoughts is so great that he seems to forget that
there is anything to do but to think." In this brief sentence we
have the key to Allston's inner life and character. His mind,
filled with images of beauty and constructive plans, did, as it
were, feed upon itself, apparently well satisfied in reverie to
while away the hours that might have been devoted to more
tangible work. When the creative power of imagination is so
great as to construct a world for itself from which all that is of-

fensive is excluded, and where only forms of beauty enter, it is but natural to forget and neglect the outer and material, the present, tangible, and hard world in which we struggle for existence. We can hardly blame him for preferring to dream his time away in that which was to him a real Elysium, rather than cope with adversity in the business and turmoil of ordinary daily life. We should not conclude from this, however, that Allston was an idler; nothing could be further from the truth. The charge of idleness has been made as accounting for the comparatively small number of pictures left by him. We shall consider this charge further on.

The following sketch by Irving, published with his " Miscellanies," is a tribute so beautiful and comprehensive, that were nothing further written of Allston, this alone would embalm his memory in the best literature of the day. It is so admirable and interesting a vindication of our purpose in this biography, that we give it in full :

" I first became acquainted with Washington Allston early in the spring of 1805. He had just arrived from France, I from Sicily and Naples. I was then not quite twenty-two years of age, he a little older. There was something, to me, inexpressibly engaging in the appearance and manners of Allston. I do not think I have ever been more completely captivated on a first acquaintance. He was of a light and graceful form, with large blue eyes, and black, silken hair waving and curling round a pale, expressive countenance. Everything about him bespoke the man of intellect and refinement. His conversation was copious, animated, and highly graphic ; warmed by a genial sensibility and benevolence, and enlivened at times by a chaste and gentle humor. A young man's intimacy took place immediately between us, and we were much together during my brief sojourn at Rome. He was taking a general view of the place before settling himself down to his professional studies. We visited together some of the finest collections of paintings, and he taught me how to visit them to the most advantage, guiding me always to the master-pieces, and passing by the others without notice. ' Never attempt to enjoy every picture in a great collection,' he would say, ' unless you have a year to bestow upon it. You may as well attempt to enjoy every dish in a Lord Mayor's feast. Both mind and palate get confounded by a great variety and rapid succession, even of delicacies. The mind can only take in a certain number of images and impressions distinctly; by multiplying the number you weaken each and render the whole confused and vague. Study the choice piece in each collection; look upon none else, and you will afterward find them hanging up in your memory.

" He was exquisitely sensible to the graceful and the beauti-ful, and took great delight in paintings which excelled in color; yet he was strongly moved and roused by objects of grandeur. I well recollect the admiration with which he contemplated the statue of ' Moses,' by Michael Angelo, and his mute awe and reverence on entering the stupendous pile of St. Peter's. Indeed, the sentiment of veneration so characteristic of the elevated and poetic mind was continually manifested by him. His eyes would dilate; his pale countenance would flush; he would breathe quick, and almost gasp in expressing his feelings when excited by any object of grandeur and sublimity.

" We had delightful rambles together about Rome and its environs, one of which came near changing my whole course of life. We had been visiting a stately villa, with its gallery of paintings, its marble halls, its terraced gardens set out with statues and fountains, and were returning to Rome about sunset. The blandness of the air, the serenity of the sky, the transparent purity of the atmosphere, and that nameless charm which hangs about an Italian landscape, had derived additional effect from being enjoyed in company with Allston, and pointed out by him with the enthusiasm of an artist. As I listened to him and gazed upon the landscape, I drew in my mind a contrast between our different pursuits and prospects.   He was to reside among these delightful scenes, surrounded by masterpieces of art, by classic and historic monuments, by men of congenial minds and tastes, engaged like him in the constant study of the sublime and beautiful.   I was to return home to the dry study of the law, for which I had no relish, and as I feared, but little talent.

"Suddenly the thought presented itself: 'Why might I not remain here and turn painter?'   I had taken lessons in drawing before leaving America, and had been thought to have had some aptness, as I certainly had a strong inclination, for it.   I mentioned the idea to Allston, and he caught at it with eagerness. Nothing could be more feasible.   We would take an apartment together.   He would give me all the instruction and assistance in his power, and was sure I would succeed.   For two or three days the idea took full possession of my mind; but I believed it owed its main force to the lovely evening ramble in which I first conceived it, and to the romantic friendship I had formed with Allston.   Whenever it recurred to mind it was always connected with beautiful Italian scenery, palaces, and statues, and fountains, and terraced gardens, and Allston as the companion of my studio.   I promised myself a world of enjoyment in his society, and in the society of several artists with whom he had made me acquainted, and pictured forth a scheme of life, all tinted with the rainbow hues of youthful promise.

"My lot in life, however, was differently cast.   Doubts and fears gradually clouded over my prospects; the rainbow tints faded away; I began to apprehend a sterile reality; so I gave up the transient but delightful prospect of remaining in Rome with Allston and turning painter.

"My next meeting with Allston was in America, after he had finished his studies in Italy, but as we resided in different cities, we saw each other only occasionally.   Our intimacy was closer some years afterward, when we were both in England. I then saw a great deal of him during my visits to London, where he and Leslie resided together. Allston was dejected in spirits from the loss of his wife, but I thought a dash of melancholy had increased the amiable and winning graces of his character. I used to pass long evenings with him and Leslie; indeed Allston, if anyone would keep him company, would sit up until cock crowing, and it was hard to break away from the charms of his conversation. He was an admirable story-teller; for a ghost story none could surpass him. He acted the story as well as told it.

"I have seen some anecdotes of him in the public papers, which represent him in a state of indigence and almost despair, until rescued by the sale of one of his paintings. This is an exaggeration. I subjoin an extract or two from his letters to me, relating to his most important pictures. The first, dated May 9, 1817, was addressed to me at Liverpool, where he supposed I was about to embark for the United States.

"'Your sudden resolution of embarking for America has quite thrown me, to use a sea phrase, all aback. I have so many things to tell you of, to consult you about, etc., and am such a sad correspondent, that before I can bring my pen to do its office, 'tis a hundred to one that the vexations for which your advice would be wished will have passed and gone. One of these subjects (and the most important) is the large picture I talked of soon beginning; the Prophet Daniel interpreting the handwriting on the wall before Belshazzar. I have made a highly finished sketch of it, and wished much to have your remarks on it. But as your sudden departure will deprive me of this advantage, I must beg, should any hints on the subject occur to you during your voyage, that you will favor me with them, at the same time you let me know that you are again safe in our good country. I think the composition the best I ever made. It contains a multitude of figures, and (if I may be allowed to say it) they are without confusion. Don't you think it a fine subject? I know not any that so happily unites the magnificent and the awful. A mighty sovereign surrounded by his whole court, intoxicated with his own state, in the midst of his revellings, palsied in a moment under the spell of a preternatural hand suddenly tracing his doom on the wall before him; his powerless limbs like a wounded spider's shrunk up to his body, while his heart, compressed to a point, is only kept from vanishing by the terrified suspense that animates it during the interpretation of his mysterious sentence. His less guilty, but scarcely less agitated, queen, the panic-struck courtiers and concubines, the splendid and deserted banquet - table, the half - arrogant, half - astounded magicians, the holy vessels of the temple (shining, as it were, in triumph through the gloom), and the calm, solemn contrast of the prophet, standing like an animated pillar in the midst, breathing forth the oracular destruction of the Empire! The picture will be twelve feet high by seventeen feet long. Should I succeed in it to my wishes, I know not what may be its fate; but I leave the future to Providence. Perhaps I may send it to America.'

"The next letter from Allston, which remains in my possession, is dated London, March 13th, 1818. In the interim he had visited Paris in company with Leslie and Newton; the following extract gives the result of the excitement caused by a study of the masterpieces of the Louvre.

"'Since my return from Paris, I have painted two pictures in order to have something in the present exhibition at the British Gallery; the subjects, "The Angel Uriel in the Sun," and "Elijah in the Wilderness." "Uriel" was immediately purchased at the price I asked, one hundred and fifty guineas, by the Marquis of Stafford; and the Directors of the British Institution, moreover, presented me a donation of one hundred and fifty pounds, as a mark of their approbation of the talent evinced, etc. The manner in which this was done was highly complimentary, and I can only say it was fully as gratifying as it was unexpected. As both these pictures together cost me but ten weeks, I do not regret having deducted that time from the "Belshazzar," to whom I have since returned with redoubled vigor. I am sorry I did not exhibit "Jacob's Dream." If I had dreamed of this success I certainly would have sent it there.'

"Leslie, in a letter to me, speaks of the picture of 'Uriel Seated in the Sun:' 'The figure is colossal, the attitude and air very noble, and the form heroic without being overcharged. In the color he has been equally successful, and with a very rich and glowing tone, he has avoided positive colors which would have made him too material. There is neither red, blue, nor yellow in the picture, and yet it possesses a harmony equal to the best pictures of Paul Veronese.'

"The picture made what is called a 'decided hit,' and produced a great sensation, being pronounced worthy of the old masters. Attention was immediately called to the artist. The Earl of Egremont, a great connoisseur and patron of the arts, sought him in his studio, eager for any production from his pencil. He found an admirable picture there, of which he became the glad possessor. The following extract is from Allston's letter to me on the subject:

"'Leslie tells me he has informed you of the sale of "Jacob's Dream." I do not remember if you have seen it. The manner in which Lord Egremont bought it was particularly gratifying—to say nothing of the price, which is no trifle to me at present. But Leslie having told you all about it, I will not repeat it. Indeed, by the account he gives me of his letter to you, he seems to have puffed me off in grand style. Well, you know I don't bribe him to do it, and if they will buckle praise upon my back, why, I can't help it! Leslie has just finished a very beautiful little picture of Anne Page inviting Master Slender into the house. Anne is exquisite, soft, and feminine, yet arch and playful. She is all she should be. Slender, also, is very happy; he is a good parody on Milton's "linked sweetness long drawn out." Falstaff and Shallow are seen through a window in the background. The whole scene is very picturesque and beautifully painted. 'Tis his best picture. You must not think this praise the "return in kind." I give it because I really admire the picture, and I have not the smallest doubt that he will do great things when he is once freed from the necessity of painting portraits.'

" Lord Egremont was equally well pleased with the artist as with his works, and invited him to his noble seat at Petworth, where it was his delight to dispense his hospitalities to men of genius. The road to fame and fortune was now open to Allston; he had but to remain in England and follow up the signal impression he had made. Unfortunately, previous to this recent success, he had been disheartened by domestic affliction, and by the uncertainty of his pecuniary prospects, and had made arrangements to return to America. I arrived in London a few days before his departure, full of literary schemes, and delighted with the idea of our pursuing our several arts in fellowship. It was a sad blow to me to have this day-dream again dispelled. I urged him to remain and complete his grand painting of 'Belshazzar's Feast,' the study of which gave promise of the highest kind of excellence. Some of the best patrons of the art were equally urgent. He was not to be persuaded, and I saw him depart with still deeper and more painful regret than I had parted with him in our youthful days at Rome. I think our separation was a loss to both of us—to me a grievous one. The companionship of such a man was invaluable. For his own part, had he remained in England a few years longer, surrounded by everything to encourage and stimulate him, I have no doubt he would have been at the head of his art. He appeared to me to possess more than any contemporary the spirit of the old masters;

and his merits were becoming widely appreciated. After his departure he was unanimously elected a member of the Royal Academy.

" The next time I saw him was twelve years afterward, on my return to America, when I visited him at his studio at Cambridge, in Massachusetts, and found him, in the gray evening of life, apparently much retired from the world, and his grand picture of 'Belshazzar's Feast' yet unfinished. To the last he appeared to retain all those elevated, refined, and gentle qualities which first endeared him to me. Such are a few particulars of my intimacy with Allston—a man whose memory I hold in reverence and affection as one of the purest, noblest, and most intellectual beings that ever honored me with his friendship."

CHAPTER VII.

The following letter was written to Allston, by Coleridge, on
June 17, 1806, while he was en route for Leghorn:

"MY DEAR ALLSTON: No want of affection has occasioned
my silence. Day after day I expected Mr. Wallis. Benvenuti
received me with almost insulting coldness, not even asking me
to sit down, neither could I, by any inquiry, find that he ever returned my call; and even in answer to a very polite note inquiring for letters, sent a verbal message that there was one, and
I might call for it. However, within the last seven or eight
days, he has called and made this amende honorable; he says he
forgot the name of my inn, and called at two or three in vain.
Whoo! I did not tell him that within five days I sent him a
note in which the inn was mentioned, and that he sent me a
message in consequence, and yet never called for ten days afterward. However, yester evening the truth came out. He had
been bored by letters of recommendation, and, till he received a
letter from Mr. M——, looked upon me as a bore—which, however, he might and ought to have got rid of in a more gentlemanly manner. Nothing more was necessary than the day
after my arrival to have sent his card by his servant. But I
forgive him from my heart. It should, however, be a lesson to

Mr. Wallis, to whom, and for whom, he gives letters of [introduction].

"I have been dangerously ill for the last fortnight, and unwell enough, heaven knows, previously; about ten days ago, on rising from my bed, I had a manifest stroke of palsy along my right side and right arm; my head felt like another man's head, so dead was it, that I seemed to know it only by my left hand and a strange sense of numbness. Violent attempts to vomit, each effort accompanied by involuntary and terrific screams. Enough of it, continual vexations and preyings upon the spirit. I gave life to my children, and they have repeatedly given it to me, for, by the Maker of all things, but for them I would try my chance. But they pluck out the wing-feathers from the mind. I have not entirely recovered the sense of my side or hand, but have recovered the use. I am harassed by local and partial fevers.

"This day, at noon, we set off for Leghorn; all passage through the Italian states and Germany is little other than impossible for an Englishman, and heaven knows whether Leghorn may not be blockaded. However, we go thither, and shall go to England in an American ship. . . .

"My dear Allston, somewhat from increasing age, but more from calamity and intense [painful] affections, my heart is not open to more than kind, good wishes in general. To you, and you alone, since I have left England, I have felt more, and had I not known the Wordsworths, should have esteemed and loved you first and most; and as it is, next to them I love and honor you. Heaven knows, a part of such a wreck as my head and heart is scarcely worth your acceptance.

"S. T. COLERIDGE."

The foregoing letter is interesting as indicating the great physical suffering endured by Coleridge. He seemed peculiarly sensitive to pain, both bodily and mental, and one can hardly condemn the use of opiates in a case like his. Doubtless he struggled to resist the control of the narcotic which brought immunity so desirable, and moral delinquency cannot be justly charged to any habit growing out of, and continually induced by, the impulse to escape pain. With Coleridge this impulse was so recurrent that the drug might well have been regarded by him as necessary medication. It is unjust to accuse such a man of the habitual use of opium, simply from a love of its pleasing, dreamy influence.

Two years after Coleridge was in Leghorn, Allston himself was there. He was now twenty-eight years old. His studies and travels had given breadth and finish to the abundant gifts wherewith nature had endowed him. Few, if any, were better qualified to teach or practise art. Writing to Vanderlyn, from Leghorn, he concurs with him about a certain picture then on exhibition in Rome, and makes very clear an important distinction between that which can be taught and that which cannot. He virtually insists that the most important and effective part of a picture is that which nature alone teaches. Much may be learned of man, but more is given by nature. Teaching is but the directing of faculties already possessed. The amount of the natural gift measures and foretells the degree of attainment possible to the pupil.

He says: " Your observations on the famous picture which made such a noise at Rome are exactly such as I expected from you. If you think it any compliment, I give them my approbation, which I conceive may be readily honored, from my little knowledge of art and greater knowledge of man—both of them convincing me of the impossibility of effecting at will a total change of style no less than of manners. Depend upon it, no man who possesses from nature a true feeling for color could ever have prevailed on himself to live to the age of forty in total neglect of it. The first may teach a man to draw a correct outline—I mean after a model; may teach him to put figures together so they may appear neither awkward nor embarrassed; to dispose of light and shadow so as to correspond with common reason; but to the last alone is reserved the province of feeling and expressing the beauty of form, of painting the soul, of giving life and motion to a group, and expression and harmony and magic to the mystery of chiaro-oscuro."

The troublous times in Europe, the disturbances of war, which had driven Coleridge from Rome, began to alarm American citizens abroad, and Allston felt that he must return to America while he could escape possible forced detention. His heart influenced him strongly to the determination to return, but little was required to make him believe in accordance with his wishes, for apprehensions enforced by the affections grow rapidly. Toward the end of the letter quoted above, he says:

"Perhaps you will be surprised to find me so soon on my way home. The truth is, the situation of my country, as it now respects Europe, makes me apprehend a loss of our neutrality. Perhaps I look too far; but a man who is expected home by his bride is not likely to risk so much as one who is so occupied by the whole sex together as to think of no one in particular. I therefore thought it prudent, though six months before it may be necessary, to cross the Atlantic while I was permitted. I hope your 'Marius' is safe arrived. My cases are all here, but they will not accompany me. I shall take only 'Cupid and Psyche' and the little 'Falstaff.' What queer times for a painter!"

Coleridge and Irving had left Allston in Rome, and carried his praises with them to London. At a dinner party, where Northcote and Lamb were present, Coleridge entertained the party by a very interesting account of the young American artist whom he had met in Rome. Northcote, who did not enjoy listening to praises bestowed on others, interrupted Coleridge, saying: " I have no doubt this Mr. Allston is a very great artist, as Mr. Coleridge sayes he is, but it is rayther remarkable that we never heerd of him before." Coleridge related this table-talk to Allston on his return to London, much to his amusement. Subsequently, when engaged on his picture of "The Dead Man Revived," which was already highly spoken of in art circles, Northcote mentioned the picture to an artist friend, and asked him if it was really as fine as they said it was. The artist replied that he had seen it, and thought it well deserved all that had been said of it. Northcote rejoined, "Well, then, you think he means to coot me out?" His arrogant and selfish nature could not brook a rival. Upon one occasion, when Allston himself called upon Northcote, in the course of conversation he remarked that he had heard a book recently published by him highly spoken of. "By some artist, I suppose?" said Northcote, sneeringly. "No," replied Allston; "by a literary man." "Ah," said he, in a jubilant tone, "why, you delight me."

Speaking of George the Third, and Sir Joshua Reynolds, his old master, and perhaps the only living artist for whom he had any great admiration, he said that Sir Joshua Reynolds was very little troubled with royal patronage. The King, he said, could not afford to ignore so great an artist as Sir Joshua, and accordingly sat to him for his portrait, but that once was sufficient for the King, as he could not endure the presence of so great a man. Subsequently Northcote himself painted a portrait of the King, and on hearing it complimented said he was glad to have been successful, for he considered George the Third one of the best sovereigns England had produced, for all England required or needed in a king was a figure to put robes on. Northcote did not relish the idea of Allston dividing the palm with him in England; he considered himself as outranking all artists of the kingdom, excepting only his great teacher, Sir Joshua.

In 1809 Allston returned from Europe to Boston. He brought with him the prestige of foreign travel, in those days an important factor in the reputation of an artist. He also brought with him no inconsiderable distinction achieved by his work in England and on the Continent. The great praise awarded him by Coleridge and Irving had found its way across the ocean and prepared a cordial reception for him in Boston, the city of his adoption. Boston was endeared to him by many associations connected with his college life in Cambridge. There many friendships had taken root, and he was held by unnumbered pleasant memories to that home of his early manhood where his happiest years were spent. The rekindling of early friendships afforded him the keenest pleasure. The old road from Boston to Cambridge was picturesque with recollections of the past, and in all directions pleasant greeting welcomed him, attentions were lavishly bestowed, men of fortune and of letters were continually inviting him to their houses, vying with each other in civilities inspired by admiration for the young artist. His works had already given him such notoriety that his promise of fame was beginning to be regarded by Bostonians as the property of his country, a kind of national endowment of which all should be proud.

The regard in which Allston was held for his ability as an artist is not to be accounted for by assuming that there was no one in America to compete with him. There were strong men in art here, even then; Stuart, Vanderlyn, Jarvis, and Trumbull are names of great eminence. They were then at the height of their fame, acknowledged and liberally patronized. It was in the reflex of Allston's English reputation, and in his pleasing personality, that we find the secret of the appreciation in which he was held in Boston at that early day.

During this visit he was married to Miss Ann Channing, to whom he had long been engaged. She was the daughter of William Channing, a lawyer of eminence in Newport, and granddaughter of William Ellery, one of the signers of the Declaration of Independence.   In a letter to his grandfather, her brother, the celebrated William Ellery Channing, thus speaks of the marriage :

" A few hours ago Washington and Ann, after their long and patient courtship, were united in marriage.   Your granddaughter has found, I believe, an excellent husband, one who from principle and affection will make her happiness his constant object. I hope that she will settle at no great distance from us, but we have not yet sufficient taste for the arts to give Mr. Allston the encouragement he deserves."

Miss Channing was thirty-one years of age when she married. She was a woman of pleasing manners and personal beauty. The influence of her life upon her husband was beneficent and wifely.   The effect of her early death was disastrous and irreparable.   But we must not anticipate events which belong to a later stage of our work.

During his brief sojourn in America, on the occasion of his marriage, Allston painted some of his finest portraits, among which was that of his mother, now in the possession of Mr. Cornelius Vanderbilt, whose wife is Allston's grand-niece ; one of his brother-in-law, Dr. Channing, and also his beautiful picture, " The Valentine," painted from a pencil drawing of his wife. Immediately after his marriage he visited his mother, who was at New Haven with her son, his half-brother, Henry C. Flagg, then a student at Yale.   At this period one of his occupations, or, we might say, pleasures, was poetic composition.   His genius overflowed in verse.   The poetic spirit, like the play fund in the child, was natural to him, and not to be repelled.   Indifferent as to the medium, through pen or brush, it constantly flowed.   His poems delighted his friends, to whom he read them, from time to time, as he would show a picture.   In 1811 he was invited to read a poem before the Phi Beta Kappa, of Harvard College, which was highly praised.   His classmate, Leonard Jarvis, in a

Portrait of Allston's Mother.

From the original in the possession of Cornelius Vanderbilt, of New York.

letter to R. H. Dana, Sr., from which we have already quoted, referring to his meeting with Allston on the occasion of this visit, thus writes :

" After we graduated, in 1800, I lost sight of my friend until he returned to this country in 1809. We met unexpectedly on Congress Street, Boston; our greeting was most cordial, and our former intimacy was at once renewed. He soon engaged a room in an old building where the granite erections of Brattle Street now are, which had been previously occupied by Johnson, the portrait-painter. Here he painted a portrait of your brother Edmund,* for which he sat so often and so long that Welles drolly asked him one day whether he did not think such a sedentary life would be injuring his health. Here, too, he painted a sea-piece, and also ' Catherine and Petruchio,' and the ' Poor Author's Visit to the Rich Bookseller.'

" He occupied this room at the time of his marriage, in 1809, and here I found him, on the morning after his nuptials, at his usual hour, engaged at his customary occupation. While he occupied this room, as I had a leisure interval between my transatlantic excursions, I passed much of my time with him, and found him the same unsophisticated, pure-minded, artless, gentle being that I had known at college. He had the same oddities, the same tastes, and the only change I could discover was that his diffidence had increased with his years. I mean his diffidence in the company of ladies, for of his own powers as an artist he never entertained a doubt. It was impossible that he should not be conscious of his extraordinary genius, but he was without vanity or self-conceit. It was about this time that, during a dinner-party at the house of the late Jonathan Harris, the conversation turned upon Allston, and Mrs. Harris produced a miniature likeness of her eldest son, painted by Allston in the earlier part of his college life. It was not without difficulty and

* E. T. Dana.

with reiterated charges to be careful of it that I persuaded the good lady to intrust me with the miniature for the purpose of showing it to Allston. I carried it to his room and told him that a lad, in whom I felt a strong interest, was very earnest to become an artist, but his friends were averse to it, and that I had with me a specimen of his skill which I wanted to show him, and to obtain his opinion whether he thought the lad would ever rise to eminence in the art. After some hesitation he agreed to give me his opinion frankly, and I put the miniature into his hands. I shall never forget his start of surprise, and the queer expression of his countenance as he exclaimed, ' O God!' and then held the miniature in different lights, screwing his mouth about, and turning his head first upon one shoulder and then on the other, in a peculiar way he had when examining a picture. ' Well, Allston, what do you say to it?' ' Why, it is a queer-looking thing! How old do you say he is?' ' About sixteen or seventeen.' ' What are his pecuniary circumstances?' ' Sufficiently prosperous to insure him a good education and give him a handsome outset in life.'

"He still kept looking at the miniature. ' Well, Allston, what is your opinion?' He still hesitated, but at last, by dint of urging, I drew from him that the young man had better follow the advice of his friends, for he did not think it possible that he could ever excel as an artist. I then asked him if he had no suspicion who the young man was. ' No; do I know him?' ' Why, as to that I can't say, for people are not very apt to know themselves.' ' You surely don't mean to say that I ever painted that thing?' ' I do.' ' It is impossible.' ' It is not only possible, but certain. Don't you remember painting a miniature likeness of John Harris while at college?' ' I do,' said he. ' I do, and it begins to come back to me now; but I could not have believed that I ever painted so indifferently. This will be a lesson to me as long as I live never to discourage anyone who thinks he has stuff in him. I know what I am and what I was then, but I can find nothing in that miniature that would lead me to suppose that the person who painted it could ever rise to mediocrity in the art.'"

This brings to mind an incident relating to Stuart Newton during his art studies in Italy. He was drawing from the antique in the school of Bezzoli, at Florence, an artist of eminence under the patronage of the Grand Duke of Tuscany. After Newton had drawn a few weeks in the school, Bezzoli advised him to abandon his purpose of becoming an artist, as he had not the talent requisite to success. Newton withdrew, and in his own room painted a picture and invited Bezzoli to look at it. On examining it Bezzoli expressed great surprise, and remarked that the color was good, that it reminded him of the Venetian school, and, said he, " What puzzles me most is that the drawing is so good." Newton replied : " I cannot see form apart from color." Stuart Newton's career in art was brief. He died at an early age, and left comparatively few pictures, but his work in the South Kensington Museum is quite sufficient to show how mistaken was the judgment of his Tuscan teacher.

Jarvis's letter continues: "On my return from Europe, in 1810, I found him in Devonshire Street, about a stone's throw from State Street. He here painted a landscape of American scenery and a sunrise, of which your brother said to me, two or three years ago, in speaking of Allston's love for his bed in the morning, that he had often said that Allston must be a genius, since he could paint what he had never seen. I told Ned that this picture afforded proof positive that Allston had never seen the sun rise, for if he had he would never have painted the reflection of the sun in the water widening as it approached the foreground. In the summer of 1811 our friend left this country and established himself in London, where I had the pleasure of seeing him in the autumn of that year. He was at housekeeping, and I never saw him when he appeared so perfectly happy as then."

In 1811 Mr. and Mrs. Allston, accompanied by S. F. B. Morse, sailed for England. Upon his graduation from Yale College he sought Allston's acquaintance, his taste for drawing and painting inclining him to adopt art as a profession. This inclination was strongly encouraged by Allston, and resulted in Morse's becoming his pupil, and not only his pupil, but his life-long friend and admirer. In one of his early letters to America he writes:

" Mr. Allston is our most intimate friend and companion. I can't feel too grateful to him for his attentions to me ; he calls every day and superintends all that we are doing. When I am at a stand and perplexed in some parts of a picture, he puts me right, and encourages me to proceed by praising those parts which he thinks good ; but he is faithful, and always tells me when anything is bad. It is mortifying sometimes, when I have been painting all day very hard, and begin to be pleased with what I have done, and on showing it to Mr. Allston, with the expectation of praise, and not only of praise, but a score of 'excellents,' 'well-dones,' and 'admirables'—I say it is mortifying to hear him, after a long silence, say, 'Very bad, sir; that is not flesh, it is mud, sir; it is painted with brick-dust and clay.' I have felt sometimes ready to dash my palette-knife through it, and to feel at the moment quite angry with him ; but a little reflection restores me. I see that Mr. Allston is not a flatterer but a friend, and that really to improve I must see my faults. What he says after this always puts me in good humor again. He tells me to put a few flesh tints here, a few gray ones there, and to clear up such and such a part by such and such colors ; and not only that, but takes the palette and brushes, and shows me how. In this way he assists me ; I think it is one of the greatest blessings that I am under his eyes. I don't know how many errors I might have fallen into if it had not been for his attentions."

Six months after Morse and Allston arrived in England, Charles R. Leslie, a young American, full of enthusiasm for the study of art, arrived in London. There he made the acquaintance of Morse, and, with him, became Allston's pupil. Like Morse, Leslie became a student at the Royal Academy, under West. Of Allston Leslie says:

"My first instructors in painting were Mr. West and Mr. Allston. It was Allston who first awakened what little sensibility I may possess to the beauties of color. He first directed my attention to the Venetian school, particularly to the works of Paul Veronese, and taught me to see, through the accumulated dirt of ages, the exquisite charm that lay beneath. Yet, for a long time, I took the merits of the Venetians on trust, and, if left to myself, should have preferred works which I now feel to be comparatively worthless. I remember when the picture of 'The Ages,' by Titian, was first pointed out to me by Allston as an exquisite work, I thought he was laughing at me."

In answer to the statement that Morse was a pupil of Mr. West, we cite the following extract from a letter written in 1813:

"I cannot close this letter without telling you how much I am indebted to that excellent man, Mr. Allston. He is extremely partial to me, and has often told me that he is proud of calling me his pupil; he visits me every evening, and our conversation is generally upon the inexhaustible subject of our divine art, and upon home, which is next in our thoughts. I know not in what words to speak of Mr. Allston. I can truly say I do not know the slightest imperfection in him; he is amiable, affectionate, learned; the possessor of the greatest powers of mind and genius; modest, unassuming, and, above all, a religious man. You may, perhaps, suppose that my partiality for him blinds me to his faults; but no man could conceal, on so long an acquaintance, every little foible from one so constantly in his company; and during the whole of my acquaintance with Mr. Allston I never heard him speak a peevish word, or utter a single inconsiderate sentence. He is a man of whom I cannot speak sufficiently, and my love for him can only compare with that love which ought to subsist between brothers. He is a man for whose genius I have the highest veneration; for whose principles I have the greatest respect; and for whose amiable properties I have an increasing love. . . . You must recollect, when you tell friends that I am studying in England, that I am a pupil of Mr. Allston and not Mr. West; they will not long ask you who Mr. Allston is; he will very soon astonish the world. It is said by the greatest connoisseurs in England, who have seen some of Mr. Allston's works, that he is destined to revive the art of painting in all its splendor, and that no age ever boasted of so great a genius. It might be deemed invidious were I to make public another opinion of the first men in this country; it is, that Mr. Allston will almost as far surpass Mr. West as Mr. West has other artists, and this is saying a great deal, considering the very high standing which Mr. West enjoys at present."

Morse's opinion, given in the above letter, was shared by his fellow-pupil, Leslie, who became a member of the Royal Academy, and rose to high rank among English artists of his day.

Mr. Morse was the founder of the National Academy of Design, and its president for a number of years. In 1866 he purchased Leslie's portrait of Allston, and presented it to the Academy with these words: "There are associations in my mind with those two eminent and beloved names which appeal too strongly to me to be resisted. . . . Allston was, more than any other person, my master in art. Leslie was my life-long friend and fellow-pupil, whom I loved like a brother. We all lived together for years in the closest intimacy and in the same house."

CHAPTER VIII.

PAINTING AND PURCHASE OF "THE ANGEL RELEASING ST. PETER FROM PRISON."—ALLSTON'S SKILL IN PERSPECTIVE.—APPRECIATIVE LETTERS FROM SIR GEORGE BEAUMONT AND THOMAS APPLETON.—CURIOUS FATE OF THE PICTURE.

Allston returned to England under auspices full of encouragement. A new chapter in life had been happily begun. The foundation of a high reputation had been well laid; thoroughness had marked its progress. He had not begun to read before he had learned the alphabet of his art. No royal road had enticed his untrained powers. Hand, eye, and brain, had worked symmetrically up to self-confidence and enviable public recognition, when, in the buoyancy of youth, he made his home with his bride in London. He had not returned to strangers to cope with untried obstacles in that human wilderness, but to friends, admirers, and patrons. Thus, under most favorable circumstances, he entered again upon his career in London, with every promise of success.

One of the first to recognize his genius at this time was Sir George Beaumont. He was intimately acquainted with English art of the time of Sir Joshua Reynolds, and was a liberal patron of artists, down to the time of Haydon. He was himself an amateur painter of marked ability. One of his pictures, that of "The Cynical Philosopher," was owned by the National Gallery. He was a man of high literary tastes; Allston and he became very warm friends.

Allston had already formed a conception of his great picture, "The Dead Man Revived," and had completed a careful study on a small canvas. This so impressed Sir George that, soon after seeing it, he wrote Allston the following letter:

" COLEORTON HALL, ASHBY-DE-LA-ZOUCH, August 21, 1812.

" MY DEAR SIR: Your picture gave me so much satisfaction and so fully answered all the expectations which had been raised in my mind respecting your power, that I cannot refrain from troubling you with a line or two of congratulation; if you accomplish the work with the same happiness with which it is conceived (and I have no doubt upon the subject), I think I may venture to promise you the approbation of all those whose judgments are deserving of your consideration. I could not well judge the effect of light and shadow in the state in which I saw it; but I take it for granted you intend to make it very powerful, having Rembrandt more in your mind than S. del Piombo, with regard to that part of the arrangement. I think large portions of shadow, 'deep, yet clear,' blank almost at a sudden glance, yet broken with nameless tints and mysterious approaches to shape, have a wonderful effect upon the mind in subjects of this elevated description. In this particular Rembrandt is so happy that the little picture of 'The Crucifixion' now before me, makes my very blood run cold, and I have frequently thought, in spite of his Dutch virgins and occasional vulgarities, there is as much of the true sublime in the light and shadow of Rembrandt as in the lines of Michael Angelo. At any rate, it would be well to endeavor to unite excellencies which if brought together would, according to my feelings, delight and astonish the world. With regard to color, I should wish you by all means to avoid a large portion of cold tint, but I am taking liberties which I hope you will excuse for the sake of my zeal, and I will now come to the business of my letter.

"I have a great desire to place a work of yours in this church; there is a place which I think would afford a good light to a picture of small dimensions, a whole length, perhaps something larger. I will now be very open with you. My expenses in building, etc., have been, and continue to be, so very heavy that I cannot afford more than two hundred pounds for this indulgence, and if that sum appears inadequate, I trust you will tell me so with the same friendly spirit which I take the liberty to use.

"If this offer meets with your approbation, perhaps in the course of a month or two you may find time to leave your work for a little relaxation and look at the spot, the more time you can afford us the better. We shall be here till the end of October. We may hope for a fine autumn. I have now taken up much of your time, and will only add Lady Beaumont's best wishes to those of,

"Your faithful and devoted friend,

"GEO. BEAUMONT."

The result of Sir George Beaumont's offer of two hundred pounds for a picture to place in the church he was then building, was a work for which five hundred pounds, even at that time, would have been only a fair price. Sir George expected a comparatively small picture, but many considerations led Allston to increase the size. Among these we may regard as foremost a desire to gratify his friend. The office of the picture, too, if we may so express it, was another important consideration. It was to minister to souls. It was to occupy a prominent place in the little parish church at Ashby-de-la-Zouch. There, as from Sunday to Sunday, the gentry and the working people, with their children, assembled for worship, the angel would greet them and turn their thoughts heavenward. With such possibilities in view, Allston needed no other stimulus to enlist his highest powers, and secure his best work.

The subject was happily chosen, "The Angel Releasing St. Peter"—divine interposition in behalf of the imprisoned—an angel symbolizing the power of truth to emancipate. Allston's religious sensibilities responded to such thoughts till his work seemed radiant with a divine influence.

Martin, the famous painter of grand architectural compositions, was in Allston's studio when he was engaged on this picture, and had just introduced the winding stairway, he asked Martin if he would make a drawing, putting the stairs in correct perspective. Martin assented, but was so dilatory that Allston, becoming impatient of the delay, went on and painted the stairs. When Martin brought his drawing, and found the stairs completed, he carefully compared them with his mathematically accurate lines, and said, "They are so correct as really to need no alteration."

The following letter from Sir George shows his appreciation of the picture:

"MY DEAR SIR: I am just returned from the church, where your picture hangs in full view, and I must say it appears to such advantage that I hope sooner or later you will see it in this light. Some time or other you will perhaps be induced to visit Mr. Wordsworth and your friends in the north, and then you will recollect this place is hardly out of your way.

"Time has mellowed the colors, and the general tone is much improved. Did you not take the idea of the angel's wings from those of the dove? It appears so to me, and I think them most appropriate. The bluish gray suits the picture admirably, and the downy softness of the inside of the wing is excellently described. As to the background of the picture, it is, I think, perfect, the gloom and depth set off the figures to the best advantage.

"To you who have been accustomed to the extended lakes of

America, our comparatively small pools would appear trifling;
still, however, I think you would be much gratified with the
sight of them, for the mountains are high enough to induce the
clouds to repose upon their bosoms, and that is the criticism by
which I judge what is the proper height of a mountain. Those
upon the Wye, although well formed, are not high enough to
produce the most sublime of all landscape effects—the union of
the earth with the heavens. A foggy cloud, shapeless and forlorn, will sometimes drizzle upon them; but I like to see fair,
floating summer clouds arrested in their course, unable to resist
the strong attraction of the mountain.

"I hope your head has not been affected by this last dreary
weather, and equally unpleasant autumn winds; but in spite of
them we were often favored by many magnificent cloud effects,
and as I had a pretty good view from my window, with pen and
pencil I set the weather at defiance.

"Lady Beaumont desires me to thank you for the great pleasure your picture has given her.

"I am, dear sir, your most faithful servant,

"G. BEAUMONT.

"Have you seen Coleridge lately?"

Mr. Thomas G. Appleton, of Boston, while in England, after
Allston's death, visited Sir George Beaumont, and saw this picture, about which he thus wrote to Mr. Dana, Sr.:

"I wish, while the impression is strong upon me, to give
you some idea of Allston's fine picture, painted for Sir George
Beaumont; I have now seen it twice, and the last visit, particularly with a fine morning light, deepened and enlarged very much
my first idea of its beauty. Lady Sitwell, at whose house I have
been making a visit, two days since, drove me over to Coleorton
Hall, where it is—she herself having become interested enough
in Allston to wish to see it. We saw it there to disadvantage,
as the evening shadows obscured it; but yesterday I walked out

to see it again, and found it worthy of Allston in his best days. For myself, I have not seen a picture in England (certainly not of our time) I should prefer to it, and I would gladly exchange all Sir George's other pictures against this one. The picture is not far from the size of 'Jeremiah,' and the figures natural size, apparently. It is hung in a side aisle of a very sweet and graceful church, which stands like a guardian angel to the grounds near the house. Its frame is ungilt, and it is the only picture in the church, so that it rises superior.

"If you were to see these lovely grounds, now classic through many an age of poets, from Fletcher's associate to Wordsworth and Allston, and the meek and simple church, half hid in stately elms, you would, I am sure, think your friend's picture appropriately placed. Yet I wish it were in America, for I really think we are more impressionable than the English by high religious works of art, and it would do more good there than here. The angel stands with feet upon two different steps of a flight of stairs which lead out of the prison, and through the open door of which the angel has come. The angel is perfectly beautiful, the most simply so of all Allston's faces I remember. He expresses perfect happiness, his face is almost expressionless, only a divine necessity of joy shines throughout him,

> . . . . . "'that grace
> So eloquent of unimpassioned love!
> That, by a simple movement, thus imparts
> Its own harmonious peace, the while our hearts
> Rise, as by instinct, to the world above.'

"His nut-brown hair falls in clusters round his head and agrees well with the sweet face. He is clothed all in white, pointing with expanded and radiant hand to the open door, while with the other he invites the astonished saint. The saint's face you know from the sketch in Boston. His whole figure is of that grand mould in which the 'Jeremiah' is cast. A dark purple

The Angel Liberating St. Peter from Prison.

From the original study for the large picture now in the Hospital for the
Insane, Worcester, Mass.

drapery envelops him from below the waist; one hand grasps his chain, while he supports himself with the other, all of which is in deep shadow. On either side the two guards are sleeping profoundly. The architecture I admire more than any in all Allston's pictures. There is a circular flight of stairs winding away into the gloom, while the shadow is relieved from above by a huge disk of moonshine, coming through the grated window in the roof. From all of this you will get very little idea of this noble work, but you may think it better than nothing. I am glad to say the picture is perfectly well-preserved. It is high in a dry aisle, and bids fair to hold its color.

"I have nothing more to communicate at present relating to Allston, as I have not had the good fortune to see any more of his pictures than the 'Peter.' If I should ever visit Bristol, I shall make it a point of looking up his pictures there, of which I have heard some little said since my visit to this country."

The vicissitudes of fortune induced those having charge of this picture, after the death of Sir George Beaumont, to dispose of it to an American gentleman. It was brought to America, and presented as an altar-piece for the chapel of the Hospital for the Insane in Worcester, Mass. It is to be regretted that a work of such beauty and high artistic merit should be so secluded. It is due to the memory of its author that it should be placed where it can readily be seen. It is due to the cause of art culture in America that this, one of the greatest works of America's greatest painter, should be rescued from its present seclusion. As the angel released St. Peter, so let us hope that the pure spirit of love for art will release from its prison this beautiful picture, and place it where its gentle ministry may be more extended; its refining and elevating influence more generally felt and acknowledged.

CHAPTER IX.

While engaged on the " Dead Man Revived," Allston lost his
health from a sufficient and obvious cause. Ambition prompting
and reinforcing his enthusiasm, led him to a continuous violation
of one of the most important laws of health. So engrossed was
he by the great work in hand that he could not, or did not, find
time to care for his bodily nutrition. This went on for three
months, when the limit came, and violated law demanded its
penalty. Alarming symptoms appeared, which his physician in
London failing to remove, it was decided to take him to Clifton
for change of scene and air. In speaking of this illness in after-
years, Allston loved to tell of the kindness of his friends, and
especially of Coleridge, who nursed him with tender and affectionate solicitude. The penalty demanded for his imprudence
was life-long, it was never quite paid till he fell asleep with the
frosts of age upon him. When he was able to return to London
his physician told him he would never again be entirely well.
He said to a friend, some thirty years after this, that, although
he had been tolerably well, he had never experienced an hour of
buoyant health since that sickness.

Leslie was so affected by Allston's illness that he laid aside
his own work and gave his time and attention to him. With

Morse, he accompanied him on the trying journey, which he thus describes:

"I think it was in the summer of 1813 that Allston was attacked with an extremely painful disorder, which, increasing in defiance of the physician to whom he applied, he determined to try change of air. Having often been invited by his uncle, Mr. Vanderhorst, who lived at Bristol, to visit that neighborhood, he and Mrs. Allston set out for Clifton by easy stages, accompanied by Mr. Morse and myself. But Allston became so extremely unwell on reaching Salt Hill, near Windsor, that Mr. Morse returned to London to acquaint Coleridge, who, as you know, was affectionately attached to Allston, with the alarming state of his friend. Coleridge came the same afternoon to Salt Hill with Dr. Tuthill, and they both stayed at the inn with Allston for the few days that he was confined there. As soon as the patient could proceed on his journey, Coleridge and the doctor returned to town, and we travelled on slowly, resting a day at Oxford (from whence he visited Blenheim), and another day at Bath. Poor Allston's sufferings were so frequent and so great that, though he looked with us at the beautiful things we saw, they scarcely afforded him a moment's enjoyment. So excruciating was the pain he felt at times that he compared it to what he supposed a man might feel if the region of his bowels were filled with boiling vinegar. I spent a fortnight with Mr. and Mrs. Allston at Clifton, and had then the pleasure of leaving the latter convalescent, under the care of a Mr. King, a very eminent surgeon, to whom Coleridge had procured him a letter of introduction from Southey. Allston was, however, subject to a good deal of annoyance from Mr. Vanderhorst of a nature to be severely felt in the weak and nervous state to which his acute suffering had reduced him. The old gentleman bore an inveterate hatred to the medical profession and to every class of its members, and it was necessary to keep it a profound secret from him that

Allston was in the hands of Mr. King. This was no easy matter, as Mr. Vanderhorst, who was very kind to his nephew in his own way, visited him or sent to him every day. He frequently sent dishes from his own table, which was a very luxurious one. He believed all that his nephew required was good air and nourishment, and the dishes he sent consisted of rich soups, game, puddings, etc., not one of which the patient, who was then restricted to a water-gruel, was permitted to touch. Allston's gradual amendment was soon apparent to his friends, and it was amusing to see Mr. Vanderhorst taking all the merit of the cure to himself, while the case was in reality a surgical one, and Mr. King was removing some internal obstruction, which caused the pain, by a series of operations, not, I believe, of a very painful nature. 'My nephew would have been dead by this time,' said Mr. Vanderhorst, 'if he had allowed one of those scoundrel doctors to come near him.'

"Never did I witness greater devotion in a wife to a husband than Mrs. Allston's throughout his long and severe trial. He was truly blessed in having a bosom friend, 'An Israelite indeed without guile,' as Cole called her, and he has again, I am told, been so blessed. I remember to have often heard Mrs. Allston speak of her brother, Dr. Channing, before he was known to the world ; 'that little Saint William' was her usual mode of introducing any anecdote of him. When Dr. Channing visited England I had the happiness of seeing him frequently, and one day, at his request, accompanied him to his sister's tomb."

Allston's sojourn at Clifton, during his sickness, was beneficial in many ways ; as a vacation, taking him from his constant brain-work, it was important, probably necessary to his recovery. During his convalescence it gave the much-needed rest which comes from change of occupation. His mind was active, it could not be idle, but it worked on other themes, and with the pen. Different channels of thought, and a different medium for its expression, gave relaxation, helpful and restorative. It prepared his mind for a new grasp of the subject which had so exhausted his vitality and threatened his life. This subject, "The Dead Man Revived," touched his genius on all sides, and taxed his powers to the utmost. It charged his ambition with hope, and rewarded it with encouraging progress at every stage. The design was startlingly dramatic and impressive. Its effect was grand to a degree that placed it beyond the ordinary range of artistic endeavor. For a description in detail, we quote Allston's own words:

"The sepulchre of Elisha is supposed to be in a cavern among the mountains, such places, in those early ages, being used for the interment of the dead. In the foreground is the man at the moment of reanimation, in which the artist has attempted, both in the action and color, to express the gradual recoiling of life upon death. Behind him, in a dark recess, are the bones of the prophet, the skull of which is peculiarized by a preternatural light. At his head and feet are two slaves, bearers of the body, the ropes still in their hands, by which they have let it down, indicating the act that moment performed; the emotion attempted in the figure at the feet is that of astonishment and fear, modified by doubt, as if still requiring further confirmation of the miracle before him; while in the figure at the head, is that of unqualified, immovable terror. In the most prominent group above is a soldier in the act of rushing from the scene. The violent and terrified action of this figure was chosen to illustrate the miracle by the contrast which it exhibits to that habitual firmness supposed to belong to the military character, showing his emotion to proceed from no mortal cause. The figure grasping the soldier's arm, and pressing forward to look at the body, is expressive of terror overcome by curiosity. The group on the left, or rather behind the soldier, is composed of two men of two different ages, earnestly listening to the explanation of a priest, who is directing their thoughts to heaven as the source of the miraculous change; the boy clinging to the young man is too young to comprehend the nature of the miracle, but, like children of his age, unconsciously partakes of the general impulse. The group on the right forms an episode consisting of the wife and daughter of the reviving man. The wife, unable to withstand the conflicting emotions of the past and the present, has fainted; and whatever joy and astonishment may have been excited in the daughter by the sudden revival of her father is wholly absorbed in distress and solicitude for her mother. The young man, with outstretched arms, actuated by impulse (not motive), announces to the wife by a sudden exclamation the revival of her husband; the other youth, of a mild and devotional character, is still in the attitude of one conversing—the conversation being abruptly broken off by his impetuous companion. The sentinels in the distance, at the entrance of the cavern, mark the depth of the picture and indicate the alarm which had occasioned this tumultary burial."

About this picture Leslie writes : " In the preparatory studies he took great pains, for he not only painted a small one of the subject, but he modelled in clay (of small size) the principal figure, over which he cast wetted drapery ; and he also modelled the head very finely, of the size of life. (The cast of the head of the Dead Man was in his studio in Cambridgeport.) These models proved that he might have excelled in sculpture as well as in painting.

" Encouraged by the success West had met in exhibiting large pictures from sacred history, Allston contemplated an exhibition of this picture, and when near its completion he hired a room for that purpose, in Pall Mall. Morse and I were one day with him when he was putting the finishing touches to his work in that room; Allston was called out for a few minutes by a stranger (for he would admit no one but intimate friends), and when he returned he told us that a little, goggle-eyed man, in a shabby black dress, had offered his services to write a paragraph in praise of his picture for the newspapers, having seen its approaching exhibition advertised in them, and had brought the commencement of one, which he read to Allston as a specimen. It ran as follows : 'The venerable President of the Royal Academy has set an excellent example to our artists by selecting the subject for his pencil from the inspired writers, which example we are happy to see followed by his countryman, Mr. Allston. "The Dead Man Revived by Touching the Bones of the Prophet Elisha," what a subject for descriptive painting.' 'But,' said Allston, 'this, sir, would look like a puff.' 'No, sir,' replied the author, 'as it is not written by yourself it cannot be called the Puff Direct, though I own it may be considered somewhat in the light of the Puff Oblique.'

"Allston declined the assistance of the little gentleman, saying he would rather let the picture take its chance with the newspapers, upon which the other entered into a long narrative of his distresses. Allston said : 'Really, sir, I am so poor myself that such a trifle only as I can afford to give, I should be ashamed to offer to a gentleman.' On being assured, however, that the smallest pittance would be thankfully received, Allston put a half-crown into his hand, which was accepted with great gratitude. I think it was by the advice of Sir George Beaumont that Allston gave up his intention of exhibiting the picture himself, and sent it to the British Institution."

Leslie, in a letter to his sister, tells of West visiting the studio. "I believe I mentioned to you before that Allston was about a large picture, 'The Dead Man Revived.' Mr. West called on him the other day to see it, and was quite astonished, 'Why, sir,' he exclaimed, 'this reminds me of the Fifteenth Century ; you have been studying in the highest schools of art.' He added : 'There are eyes in this country that will be able to see so much excellence;' and then turning around he saw a head Allston had modelled in clay from one of the figures, and asked what it was, taking it to be an antique. Allston told him it was one of his, at which, after examining it carefully, he said, there was not a sculptor in England could do anything like it. He did not find fault with any part of the picture, but he merely suggested the introduction of another figure.

"I was never more delighted in my life than when I heard this praise coming from Mr. West, and so perfectly agreeing with my own opinion of Allston. He has been in high spirits ever since, and his picture has advanced amazingly rapid for these two or three days. He intends sending it to the Exhibition of the British Gallery, where it will no doubt obtain the prize."

"The Dead Man Revived" was first exhibited at the British Institution, commonly called the British Gallery, and it there obtained the first prize of two hundred guineas. This was the first important work Allston had ever exhibited. It made a great sensation in art circles in London. It was generally acknowledged to be a work that should rank prominently in the domain of the highest art. Mr. West, expressing his admiration of it, said of Allston, "He has commenced where most of us leave off." When such men as West, Sir Thomas Lawrence, and Sir William Beechy regarded it with admiration, no one could be found to question his right to the general applause which was heard on all sides.

The attention this picture received was extremely encouraging. The praises it called forth were extravagant upon any theory that did not place it upon a par with the works of the old masters. The prize of two hundred guineas it received stimulated Allston's ambition and inspired him with great purposes. It was a voucher for his ability and an encouragement to still greater effort.

The following congratulatory letter from Sir George Beaumont was written just after the exhibition of his picture:

"DUNNOW, January 16, 1814.

"MY DEAR SIR: I am truly sorry to hear your health has been in such a bad state. I hope, however, you will feel the benefit of the air you have inhaled at Clifton more in London than whilst you were upon the spot. This I know is not infrequently the case. I assure you I have been very anxious on your account, and have been prevented from writing only by having by some accident mislaid your letter and not being able to recollect the address. I am sincerely sorry for your sufferings and heartily wish it were in my power to relieve them. I am very glad to hear you have completed your picture, which I have no doubt will do you great credit. I should have been happy to have been in town at the time the arrangement of the British Gallery took place, but I am at present attending Lady Beaumont, my mother, in an illness which has every appearance of ending fatally, altho' she is now somewhat better; this I hope will excuse me for writing in haste. In such an anxious state it is difficult to confine one's thoughts to other subjects. I will therefore only add at present, that I like the subject you mention extremely; it is simple, well known, and capable of a pungent effect, which I would wish you to push to the utmost bounds of propriety.

"I remain, my dear sir, with every good wish, most faithfully yours,

"GEORGE BEAUMONT.

"I shall be happy to hear of the progress of your health, and when you can with prudence attend to a sketch, I should be glad to have it sent here, for my stay at this place may probably be long."

CHAPTER X.

Allston says: " As I returned to London chiefly to finish this
picture ('The Dead Man Revived'), that done, I went back to
Bristol, where I painted and left a number of pictures; among
these were half-length portraits of my friend Mr. Coleridge, and
my medical friend, Mr. King, of Clifton. I have painted but
few portraits, and these I think are my best. So far as I can
judge of my own production the likeness of Coleridge is a true
one, but it is Coleridge in repose ; and, though not unstirred by
the perpetual ground-swell of his ever-working intellect, and
shadowing forth something of the deep philosopher, it is not
Coleridge in his highest mood, the poetic state, when the divine
afflatus of the poet possessed him. When in that state, no face
that I ever saw was like his ; it seemed almost spirit made visible
without a shadow of the physical upon it. Could I then have
fixed it upon canvas! but it was beyond the reach of my art.
He was the greatest man I have ever known, and one of the
best ; as his nephew, Henry Nelson, truly said, 'a thousand
times more sinned against than sinning!'"

There has been a conflict of statements relating to this portrait. By some it is said to have been painted in Rome ; others,
with equal positiveness, assert that it was done in Bristol, after
his serious illness there. Both statements are true, but not of
the portrait in question. The conflict arises from a confusion

of facts. There are two portraits of Coleridge by Allston. The one of earliest date was never finished. It was commenced in Rome, and well advanced, though far from finished, when it was arrested in its progress by Coleridge's sudden departure to England. This portrait is now in Boston, in the possession of Allston's niece, Miss R. Charlotte Dana. It is extremely interesting and does not disappoint the admirers of Coleridge. The Bristol portrait was painted for a friend and ardent admirer, Mr. Wade. He valued it so highly that he wished it kept in his family, and although he assented to the opinion of Wordsworth that it should be placed in some public gallery, he nevertheless gave it, by his will, to a relative, with the injunction that he should not part with it.

During the latter part of Allston's life Wordsworth wrote a long letter to Professor Henry Reed, of Philadelphia, about the final disposition of the portrait, which he thought, in accordance with the verbal assent given by Mr. Wade, should be placed in one of the public galleries of England. Professor Reed forwarded this letter to Allston for his opinion and approval, and Allston replied, in one of the very last letters he ever wrote, concurring in Wordsworth's ideas, and expressing his wishes in regard to an engraver, as the subject of engraving this portrait had been much discussed. It was not till ten years after Allston's death that Mr. Derwent Coleridge, son of the poet, succeeded in obtaining permission to place it in the engraver's hands.

We quote from the London *Guardian* of November 29, 1854:

" Mr. Moxon has published a portrait of S. T. Coleridge, which will be received with great pleasure by the admirers of that celebrated man. It is engraved by Mr. Samuel Cousins, from a picture by the American painter, Mr. Washington Allston, himself a man of great ability, quite capable of appreciating his sitter, and very intimate with him. It is by far the finest portrait of Coleridge in existence, and so much more recalls the power and intellect of his face than any other we ever saw. It was painted when he was forty-two years old, but it retains a great deal of the appearance he presented when we remember him in much later life. We can quite believe what is said of the picture by those who recollect Coleridge when it was painted, that it was at that time an excellent likeness. He is sitting in a room which has something of an antique cast about it, with his hand upon a book, looking upward; the portliness and white hair of middle life have come upon him, but the expression of his face is very refined and beautiful, and the form of his head grand and noble, and exceedingly like the well-known cast of it by Spurzheim. The engraving is a choice specimen of Mr. Cousin's mixed style of engraving, in which almost every effect of color is given by light and shade.

It was no doubt due chiefly to Wordsworth's influence that the original painting was placed in the British National Portrait Gallery where it now hangs. The friendship that existed between Coleridge and Allston at the time this portrait was painted was so sincere and intimate that it was frequently remarked upon by their friends, one of whom, Mr. Joseph Henry Green, writes, in a letter to Richard H. Dana, Sr. :

"Coleridge never failed, when Allston's name was mentioned, to express his high admiration of his genius, both as a poet and a painter, and always spoke most warmly of his character as a man; indeed the name of Allston may be adduced as proof and instance of Coleridge's often-repeated assertion that true genius ever has its taproot in the moral being, and I hold it scarcely possible that Coleridge could have felt the affection, which he undoubtedly did, toward Allston, without having had the strongest assurance of those excellent qualities of the heart, which, whatever sympathy their common tastes and pursuits might have produced, were the real ground of his attachment and undeviating friendship.

Portrait of S. T. Coleridge.

From the original in the National Portrait Gallery, London.

"It is unnecessary to say that Allston cherished similar and responsive feelings toward Coleridge; and how well he had read the character of his admired friend may be best inferred from his masterly portrait of Coleridge; so only could one who knew, and therefore esteemed, the man have portrayed him—with the delicate feeling of his feminine gentleness combined with masculine thought, with the perception of the depth and inwardness of his imaginative meditation—it is not too much to say that it embodies, as far as can be presented to the sense, the character of the poet as 'the philosopher with the seraph's wing.'"

Allston's intimacy with Coleridge was so close as to touch his entire nature, acquainting him with the inner depths of his character. Their mental endowments were kindred. The artist understood his subject as did no other artist of his time. Hence, though frequently painted by others, Wordsworth said of Allston's portrait, "It is the only likeness that ever gave me any pleasure; it is incomparably the finest of the likenesses taken of Coleridge." Nothing can add to such testimony from one who was Coleridge's most intimate friend, and it is a satisfaction to know that this portrait is now to be seen in a permanent exhibition of the portraits of distinguished Englishmen. There the American can point with pride to a work by one of his own countrymen unsurpassed by modern art in the higher qualities of portraiture.

There are but few subjects for portraits that are utterly void of interest to the eye of an artist. But there are fewer still sufficiently beautiful or picturesque to make, without an effort of imagination in arrangement and treatment, a pleasing and beautiful picture. Therefore the majority of subjects must be rendered by a powerful imagination and consummate skill, to produce a pleasing effect, without loss of likeness. There are charming portraits—portraits which never lose their interest for us, portraits of which we never tire—portraits which, like the varying aspects of nature, always repay contemplation with a new pleasure, yet these are in many instances portraits whose originals would be passed by as unattractive and void of special interest. But this cannot be said of the portrait of Coleridge by Allston. In that instance the subject was as inspiring as the portrait is satisfactory and pleasing. "The ground-swell of his ever-working intellect" is felt in the far-off look of his full gray eye, and a sense of thought-movement in every line of his noble face. As a whole it is pre-eminently a portrait of which one never tires. Intellect is the vitalizing power of beauty, and without it forms, though faultless, are not, in the highest sense, beautiful. Allston, it may be said, painted the intellect of Coleridge.

The portrait of Dr. King, Allston mentions as having been painted at the same time with that of Coleridge ; he classes them together in point of merit, giving no special preference to either, yet one is comparatively unknown, while the other is conspicuously historic and prominent among the most famous portraits of England's gifted men.

CHAPTER XI.

After their sojourn in Bristol, Allston and his wife returned to London, renewed in health, full of hope, and confident of success. They rented a house and began their first experience in housekeeping. This important stage in the progress of life, to one of Allston's sensibilities, must have brought happiness peculiar in degree. The basis of his pleasure was broad and all-satisfying. The adjustments of character welding the young couple in bonds of sentiment were perfected. Allston's was an ideal marriage. The benediction of contentment was in his household, because love in its fulness was there; love lightening all burdens, heightening all pleasures. If, in the great world without, trials and disappointment weighed upon his spirit, he could take them to the sanctuary of his home with confidence of relief in sympathy and encouragement. Many things conspired to make auspicious his present outlook. Patronage assured, fame rapidly increasing—the future was tinted with a thousand hues to gratify, to cheer, and stimulate. But alas for the mutability of human conditions! Hardly had the young husband and wife taken possession of their new home when death entered. Within a week the gentle, loving, and loved wife sickened and died. The shock was bewildering, almost stupefying; but when gradually the greatness of his bereavement appeared, it seemed immeasurable and overwhelming. From the greatness of the cause some have assumed what might be regarded as its natural effect, and have reported that Allston was rendered insane by the death of his wife. The report, however, was untrue, as an extract from a letter by Leslie, which we here quote, affirms:

"A biographical sketch of Allston, by Mrs. Jameson, has appeared in the *Athenœum,* in which she repeats (on the authority of Dunlap) that 'a temporary derangement of the intellect' was caused by the death of his wife. This is not true, as Mr. Morse can assure you. He and I were with Allston constantly at that time, and sudden as was the blow, and deeply as he felt it, there was nothing in his manner that for a moment showed him to have lost the mastery of his mind."

The funeral of Mrs. Allston was deeply impressive in its simplicity. Morse, Leslie, John Howard Payne, and Allston were the only persons present, and were the only persons who followed the coffin to the grave. As in thought we picture that scantily attended burial, we are impressed with a feeling of great solemnity. They were Americans, associated by patriotism and kindred tastes ; Morse and Leslie, pupils of the chief mourner ; John Howard Payne, author of that lyric which has thrilled so many hearts with the echo of a universal sentiment for the sweet ministries of home, they were mourners all, touched with profoundest sympathy and solicitude for their friend, the heartbroken husband, as he stood by the grave and gazed upon the coffin and heard the hollow sound marking the solemn words, "Earth to earth, ashes to ashes, dust to dust."   Allston's friends felt that it was not good for him to be alone in his grief-stricken house. Morse and Leslie persuaded him to leave it and take up his lodgings with them. Their proposal was the dictate of a wise and true friendship. Gradually old associations and pleasant companionship dispelled paralyzing grief, and led him from his overshadowing sorrow into comparative cheerfulness.

Allston's love for art was his great solace. As an angel of consolation it ministered unto him by alluring visions; it led him away from himself; it allowed him but little time or thought for musing upon his bereavement and estimating its greatness. He yielded to its blessed influence and was comforted. He realized how great a boon in affliction is agreeable and absorbing occupation. The first picture painted by him after the loss of his wife was the " Cavern Scene from Gil Blas." Many years after, when the exhibition of his pictures took place at Boston, his nephew, George Flagg, expressed admiration for this picture, as the one he preferred to any other in the collection, to which Allston remarked that it was painted while he was in deep affliction, and constantly in tears. His nephew said, " I do not understand how it is possible to paint under such circumstances." " Ah, George," he said, " nothing can prevent my painting but want of money ; that paralyzes me."

We cannot restrain regret that there was mingled so little of worldly wisdom in Allston's character. His generosity made him improvident to a degree that entailed pecuniary embarrassment in his later years. In a letter to Mr. Dana, Leslie writes :

" I do not remember any circumstance during Allston's residence in England that would lead me to think he was ever in distress for money, though it was evident he felt it necessary to live with the strictest economy. But there was one branch of economy he could not practise, and that was economy in charities. The streets of London were then more filled than they are now with objects of real and fictitious suffering, and he could not resist giving to every beggar he met far more largely than any man I ever knew, whose means were so limited. It was vain to tell him how often he was imposed upon by appearances. His answer was, ' It is better I should be imposed on than to miss doing what I can for one real sufferer.' One winter day he brought a wretched-looking woman home with him ; she was barefooted, and had nothing on but a ragged shift and petticoat. Allston clothed her warmly from the wardrobe of his wife, saying he was sure, could she look upon what he was doing from her abode in Heaven, she would smile on him. The next day I saw this woman in the street as ill-clad as when she excited his pity. Allston became well known to the beggars, and was persecuted by letters and other applications from impostors to a degree that made him miserable; and indeed his plagues of this kind so increased that I really think they had something to do in hastening his departure to America."

Allston's classmate, Jarvis, in a letter, part of which forms one of our early chapters, thus writes in reference to his bereavement:

"When I saw him again he was a widower, and I have never witnessed more simple, touching, and heartfelt sorrow. It was in his countenance, in every motion, and in every tone of his voice. Without any of the outpourings of grief, he appeared to be heart-broken. It was the mourning of Allston which could not be understood or appreciated by the herd, any more than they can understand or appreciate what gives the greatest value to his pictures. He repeated to me at this time some beautiful lines, which evidently had originated in the melancholy scenes through which he had passed. This recollection, combined with the sadness of the lines and the touching manner of his recitation, almost affected me to tears. He never made to me any more direct or any other allusion to the loss which he had sustained, nor was it necessary; we saw and felt that each understood the feelings of the other.

"An abiding effect of this loss upon our friend was to turn his thoughts, affections, and desires toward another world, in a greater degree than before. This is the true, and certainly the more rational and natural, explanation of his increased piety. I say increased, because a mind like his could never have been without feelings of reliance upon, and gratitude toward, his Creator, and because I never had, from my earliest acquaintance with him, the least reason to doubt his correctness in this particular.

"I am induced to make these observations from having had my attention called to an anecdote by some scribbler of the *Atlas*, in which Allston is represented as having been irreligious at one period of his life, and as a man who would enjoy a joke at the expense of religious subjects, and who was brought into a religious life by an almost miraculous interposition, which saved him from starving.

"I recollect seeing in some autobiographical sketch of the life of an English fanatic of the beginning of this century, that he found a new pair of breeches by his bedside when his old ones were in a woful plight, and regarded it as a direct interference of Providence. This might answer very well for an inspired or rather a crack-brained cobbler, but would not agree either with the composition of the head or heart of our friend. He had too much humility and too much good sense to convert an ordinary transaction of life into a special interposition of Providence in his behalf, even if it were true that he had ever been in such circumstances of pecuniary destitution, which I may be permitted to doubt.

"Allston never sat in the seat of the scorner, and had always too much good feeling and too much good taste ever to have joined in an atheistic laugh. I would not have you suppose that he was what might be called a serious young man, for I have no reason to think that the subject of religion had occupied much of his thoughts; but I am entitled to deny, from a most intimate acquaintance with him, that he was himself a scoffer or an encourager of scoffing in others. The peculiar cast of his religious sentiment, I have no doubt, might be traced to his intimacy with Coleridge; but this is mere conjecture, for, as our views of religion were not the same, we avoided that, as we did all other topics of conversation on which we knew we could not agree."

When news of Mrs. Allston's death was received by his friends out of London, letters of condolence attesting deep concern and friendship were written by them. Among these we cite one from Coleridge. It should be remembered that this letter was written at a time when views so large and generous toward America were seldom entertained by Englishmen. It was at a time when a sense of mortification at our naval victories was rankling in the English mind. Extreme bitterness toward America was the rule, when the heart and intellect of Coleridge, which dictated this letter, were the exception:

" October 25, 1815.

" MY DEAR ALLSTON : I could have wished to have learned more particulars from you respecting yourself. I have perhaps felt too great an awe for the sacredness of grief, but those of our household know with how deep and recurrent a sympathy I have followed you, and I know what consolation it has been to *me* that you have in every sense the consolation and the undoubting hopes of a Christian. Blessed indeed is that gift from above, the characteristic operation of which is to transmute the profoundest sources of our sorrow into the most inexhaustible sources of our comfort. The very virtues that enforce the tear of earthly regret fill that tear with a light not earthly. There is a capaciousness in every living heart which retains an aching vacuum, what and howsoever numerous its present freight of earthly blessings may be ; and as God only can fill it, so must it needs be a sweet and gracious incarnation of the heavenly ; that what we deeply loved, but with fear and trembling, we must now love with a love of faith that excludeth fear. Love is in God, and God in it.

" From such thoughts none but an abrupt transition is possi-

ble. I pass, therefore, at once, by an effort, to the sphere in
which you are appointed, because highly gifted, to act; and in
this I can but pour forth two earnest wishes. First, that equal
to the best in composition, and I most firmly believe superior in
the charm of coloring, you would commend your genius to the
universally intelligible of your παγγλώσσης τέχνης—Expression.
Second, that you never for any length of time absent yourself
from nature and the communion with nature, for to you alone of
all contemporary artists does it seem to have been given to know
what nature is—not the dead shapes, the outward letter, but the
life of nature revealing itself in the phenomenon, or rather attempting to reveal itself. Now the power of producing the true
ideals is no other, in my belief, than to learn the will from the
deed, and then to take the will for the deed. The great artist
does what nature would do, if only the disturbing forces were
abstracted.

"With regard to my MSS. I had no other wish, and formed
no higher expectation than this: that a copyright, as exclusive as
the American law permits, should be vested in some one bookseller who should have the copy in time enough to get it printed
in America two months before the work could arrive from England; that is to say, have it published in Boston or Philadelphia
at the same time of its first publication in England, and that the
bookseller, in return for the copy and copyright, should secure
to me some portion, say one-third, of his net profits. If this can
be done, I shall think it worth while to continue the transcrip-
tion, though the ultimate profits should be but from £20 to £0
0s. 0d. One volume of 900 pages octavo contains the history of
my life and opinions; the second my poems, composed since
1795, *i.e.*, those not in my volume of 'Poems' already printed.

"In the 'Ode on the Death of General Ross,' if I ever finish
it, I shall utter a voice of lamentation on the moral war between
the child and the parent country, a war laden with curses for un-

born generations in both countries. You may well believe, therefore, that I shall not make myself an accomplice directly or indirectly, by flattery or by abuse, in what I regard as a crime of no ordinary guilt, the feeding or palliating the vindictive antipathy of the one party, or the senseless, groundless, wicked contempt and insolence of the other. Even now it would not be too late, if the spirit of philosophy could be called down on ministers and governments. The true policy is palpable and simple. A child, wearied out by undue exercise of parental authority, elopes, marries with an independent fortune, and sets up for himself. The matter is irrevocable; a reconciliation takes place, and the parent himself is convinced that he had acted tyrannically and under false notions of the extent of his authority, and that in the same proportion his child had acted justifiably. What, then, would a good parent do? Evidently treat the child with the kindness of a parent, but with additional respect and etiquette, as now a householder and himself the master of a family; and this he will show in the character of his messengers, in the style of his letters, etc. But if, in addition to the duties of family love, their two trades or estates played into each other's hands, so that they could not really prosper without increasing their dealings with each other (suppose the father a shoemaker finisher and the son a tanner-currier), then common self-love would dictate the abandonment of every act and impulse of jealousy. Were I Dictator, I would not only send to America men of the highest rank and talent, with more than usual splendor, as ambassadors, ministers, etc., but would throw open not only the West Indies, but the whole colonial trade to the Americans, confident that every new city that would thence arise in the United States would add a new street to some town in Great Britain. Alas! that the dictates of wisdom should be but dreams of benevolence, to be interpreted by contraries. The malignant witchcraft of evil passions reads good men's prayers backward, and I cannot help dreading that the hot heads of both countries will go on to make folly beget folly, both the more wrong in proportion as each is right. How little, then, ought we to value wealth and power, seeing that every nation carries its only formidable enemy in its bosom ; and the vices that make its enemies elsewhere are but the systole to its diastole.

" I have received a most flattering letter from Lord Byron. Should my tragedy be accepted (of which I have little doubt), I shall, God willing, see you about Christmas. Meantime may God bless you and let me hear from you soon.

"S. T. COLERIDGE.

" P. S.—Friday last (20th) my forty-fourth birthday ; and in all but the brain I am an old man ! Such ravages do anxiety and mismanagement make."

CHAPTER XII.

When news of the success of Allston's picture, "The Dead
Man Revived," reached Philadelphia, his friends in that city desired to secure it for the Pennsylvania Academy of Fine Arts.
Messrs. Sully and McMurtrie succeeded in raising $3,500 (a
large sum for a picture in those days) with which they purchased it. This evidence of his fame at home added a gratification to the pleasure he had already received from public
acknowledgment. The kindness and generous appreciation he
had met in England endeared to him the mother country. He
loved to acknowledge the ties of blood existing, despite political
severance and national independence.

"Next to my own," he writes, "I love England, the land of
my adoption. I should, indeed, be ungrateful did I not love
a country from which I never received other than kindness;
in which, even during the late war, I was never made to feel that
I was a foreigner."

The purchase of his picture by the Pennsylvania Academy seemed to impart new life to his patriotism. If, in the
heyday of success in the world's metropolis, he was in danger of
virtual expatriation, the evidence of interest and appreciation
shown by his countrymen in thus securing his picture dispelled

that danger. It doubtless added greatly to the influences which brought him back to a residence in America at a sacrifice that we cannot but regret.

His gratitude and appreciation of the kindness of his friends he expresses at length in a letter to McMurtrie, dated June 13, 1816, from which we give an extract :

" When you first made me the generous offer of taking out my picture, you may remember with what implicit confidence I submitted the entire management and disposal of it to yourself and Mr. Sully. I would not have done this if I had not been fully assured that, whatever might be the event, I should have every reason to be grateful; for, even if it had wholly failed of profit, I should still have felt myself indebted for every exertion that kindness and liberality could make. If such would have been my feelings in the event of a total failure, you may well judge what I now feel at the account of this most agreeable result. I beg you both to accept my warmest and most grateful acknowledgments. The sale is in every respect highly gratifying, both as affording me a very seasonable supply, and on account of the flattering circumstance attending it. I assure you I think most of the honor conferred by the Academy in becoming the purchasers of my work. Will you express to them my sense of the honor done me.

" If I am constrained from various circumstances to disappoint you as to the proposal respecting a picture from my sketch of 'Christ Healing,' I trust you will believe me as sensible of your kindness in making it, as if it had been in my power to comply with it. Upon reconsidering the sketch some months since (though still pleased with the general arrangement), I found the principal incident so faulty and inefficient, and myself, at the same time unable to suggest any one better, that I was forced to come to the resolution of relinquishing it alto-

gether; or, at least, to lay it by for some future and more propitious period, in the hope that my imagination might then supply a more suitable incident. I may here observe that the universal failure of all painters, ancient and modern, in their
attempts to give even a tolerable idea of the Saviour, has now
determined me never to attempt it. Besides, I think His character too holy and sacred to be attempted by the pencil.

"It is the first importance to a large work that the principal
incident should be obvious and striking, leaving no doubt in anyone of its meaning. Now, in the incident I allude to, I have attempted to express the miracle of restored health to a sick man,
and that I have failed of this is certain, because no one who has
seen it (and I have shown it to several) has been able to guess my
intentions. I could easily express disease in any stage of languor
or emaciation, but there would then be no incident—merely a
sick man waiting to be healed—which is but repeating what Mr.
West has already so admirably done. My object was not to treat
the subject thus, but in a different way—that is, to show both
the operation and the effect of a miracle. The blind boy, or,
rather, the boy that was blind (which you may recollect in the
sketch) is, I think, a very happy incident; for the miracle there
is obvious, and clearly explains itself; but as it is a miracle which
has already been wrought it becomes necessarily subordinate.

"Had I been equally successful in the principal object, who
is supposed to be under the immediate influence of the Saviour's
word, I should not only be satisfied, but have reason to think I had
achieved something great. I still like all the rest of the sketch;
but this great and radical defect in it has compelled me to give it
up. But were I even perfectly satisfied with it, I am afraid it
would not be in my power to paint it on a large scale for less than
eight hundred or a thousand guineas, without a loss, as it would
employ me full eighteen months or two years, and in addition to
my present expenses I should be obliged to hire a large room."

"But, though it is not in my power, for the reasons I have above stated, to engage in a large picture from this sketch, I should be most happy to undertake another subject of five or six figures, size of life, which would make a picture about the size of ' St. Peter in Prison,' and this I could do for the sum you mentioned, say five hundred guineas. (By the bye, the ' St. Peter ' employed me more than six months after you left London, instead of two, as I had calculated.) Such a picture I could paint in my present room, and could finish, I should hope, in somewhat less than a year. Should this be agreeable to you, you will say what kind of a subject you would prefer ; I think Scripture subjects, as being the most known and interesting to the world, are the best. Perhaps some splendid subject, uniting brilliancy of color with strong character and expression. Should the preceding meet your views, you have every reason to depend on my best efforts.

"Whenever you send the portfolio of drawings, I will, with pleasure, attend to your request respecting them. Mr. West, who is, I believe, one of the most learned in Europe in these things, will be happy, I am sure, to assist me in assigning to them the names of their proper authors. Since you thus encourage me with the hope of selling the landscape, I will send it out in the course of the summer. I think I gave you a memorandum of the price. I do not recollect whether it was one hundred and fifty or two hundred guineas. If it is worth anything, it is worth two, having cost me four months' hard labor. However, I should be content with one hundred and fifty guineas, provided I get that sum without loss by exchange.

"At the same time I shall send the picture of ' The Virgin and Child,' which, as I know it to be a great favorite with you, I beg you to accept as a small testimony of my esteem. I have lately improved it very much, having repainted the mother's head and the whole of the infant, as well as retouched the background.

" I have sold the 'Gil Blas' to our countryman, Colonel Drayton. A nobleman wished to have bought it, but he was too late. Before you get this, it will have arrived, I suppose, in Philadelphia, having been sent there to the care of Mr. John Vaughan. I have retouched it since you saw it here.

"I do not remember whether Mr. Leslie had begun his 'Murder of Rutland by Clifford,' before you left London. It is now in the Exhibition at Somerset House, and does him great honor. It is very finely conceived, and painted with a powerful hand. The figure of Rutland alone is sufficient to confirm his just pretensions to genius, a word too often misapplied. He possesses the rare merit of combining the excess of imploring terror with uncommon beauty. Clifford is also a fine though opposite character, and the background is managed with great spirit.

"Mr. West has begun, on a grand scale, the subject of 'Death on the Pale Horse.' You must remember well his admirable sketch.

"Begging you once again to accept my best thanks, I remain, dear sir, with great esteem,

"Yours sincerely and obliged,

"W. ALLSTON."

" P.S.—In a letter to Mr. Leslie, Mr. Delaplaine, has done me the honor to inquire my terms for a large picture, fifteen feet, figures size of life. I have requested Mr. Leslie to reply that I could not undertake it without loss, for less than a thousand guineas, which I fear will be a disappointment to him."

When the " Cavern Scene " was finished, Allston exhibited it in a collection in Pall Mall. There it attracted the attention and admiration of Colonel William Drayton, of Philadelphia, an old friend, who had known him in Charleston, just after his graduation. So pleased was the Colonel with the picture that he purchased it at once, without knowing by whom it was painted. Colonel Drayton thus relates the incident:

" Allston wrote me only a single letter on the subject of ' Gil Blas,' with the beauty of which I was so much struck, whilst examining the picture gallery in Pall Mall, that I immediately purchased it, and was exceedingly gratified afterward to learn the name of the artist, of which I had been previously ignorant, its insertion in one of the corners of the piece having escaped my notice."

The " Cavern Scene " was by many considered one of the best in the large collection of Allston's pictures exhibited in Boston. In speaking of this picture he remarked to a friend that no part of it was painted directly from nature. This is another instance and evidence of the remarkable accuracy and memory of his eye.

One day Hazlitt, the author, who wrote so pleasingly on art, and was the most prominent art-critic of his time, asked Allston where he found models for his heads, as he had never seen any like them in the streets of London, remarking that some of them looked like Asiatics. Allston said he did not paint them from models, but from his imagination. Hazlitt gave him a look of incredulity, which seemed to say, as interpreted by Allston himself, " You are the greatest liar I ever met."

The following is another letter to his friend McMurtrie, for whose persistent kindness in the sale of his pictures in America Allston felt under great obligations:

"London, October 25, 1816.

" My Dear Sir : I have at length the pleasure to inform you that, availing myself of your continued kindness, I have shipped and addressed to you the two pictures mentioned in my letter to you of June last, viz., the ' Landscape' and the ' Mother and

Child.' I wish you not to consider it now as the 'Virgin and Child,' but simply as a mother watching her sleeping offspring. A 'Madonna' should be youthful; but my mother is a matron. Besides, there are other reasons, which I have not room to state, that would fix the propriety of the change now made in the title. The first, the 'Landscape,' to be exhibited and disposed of in any way that shall seem best to you. Of the other I beg your acceptance, as a small testimony of my esteem and gratitude. I have a double pleasure in offering this little present, inasmuch as, since retouching, I think it one of my best works, and as I know it will be possessed by one who can truly appreciate whatever merit it may have. It does not always happen that the possessors of pictures are also possessed of taste; and therefore it is a source of no small gratification to an artist to know that his works are cherished by those who will neither mistake nor overlook their excellences, however few or subordinate.

"In my letter of June, alluded to just before, I had fixed the price of the landscape at from two hundred to one hundred and fifty guineas. Upon reconsidering this last price, I think it so low as to be tantamount to a complete sacrifice; I must, therefore, request you not to part with it by any means for less than two hundred guineas. Though I am very much in want of money, I should prefer keeping it all my life to disposing of it at so much below its value. But I commit it to such good hands that I feel perfectly easy as to the event. . . .

"Would it not be possible to obtain an exemption from the duties by means of the Pennsylvania Academy? For I find that all pictures, casts, prints, etc., intended for their use, are now free by law. I think the duties on pictures in America are unconscionable. Here, where they are considered very severe, the highest duty on my largest picture (even of 30 feet) never exceeds eight pounds sterling; for after four feet square the duty does not increase, whatever may be the size.

"My paper will not admit of any notice of the present world of art here. Leslie's picture of Clifford is, I suppose, arrived. I think you will agree with me that it does him great honor. He desires his best regards to you. Pray present mine to Mr. Sully, and believe me, with a true sense of your kindness,

"Sincerely yours,

"WASHINGTON ALLSTON."

CHAPTER XIII.

ALLSTON'S SECOND VISIT TO PARIS, WITH LESLIE AND COLLINS.—
GIFT TO COLERIDGE, AND ITS APPRECIATION.—"URIEL IN THE
SUN" TAKES THE HIGHEST PRIZE AT THE EXHIBITION OF THE
BRITISH INSTITUTE.— LESLIE'S OPINION OF "ELIJAH IN THE
DESERT."—"JACOB'S DREAM."— MRS. JAMESON'S DESCRIPTION
OF IT.—LINES BY WORDSWORTH.

After the sale of his picture, "The Dead Man Revived,"
Allston was induced by his friends Leslie and Collins to accompany them to Paris, to enjoy the galleries of the Louvre. Of
this visit Collins writes :

"It was in the year 1817 that I accompanied Allston and
Leslie to Paris, where we benefited much by having Allston for
our guide, he being the only one of the party who had visited
that city before ; during our stay of about six weeks, Allston
made a beautiful copy in the Louvre of the celebrated 'Marriage
at Cana,' by Paul Veronese, and as Leslie had professional employment in Paris he remained there, and we returned together
to London ; during this visit I had, of course, the best opportunities of becoming acquainted with my friend's real character,
which in every new view I took of it became more satisfactory.
The sweetness and subdued cheerfulness of his temper under the
various little inconveniences of our journey was much to be admired, and his great reverence for sacred things, and the entire
purity and innocence of his conversation, coupled as it was with
a power of intellect and imagination I never saw surpassed.
Blessed be God for these qualities, these gifts more effectual to

the pulling down of many strongholds and vain imaginations on
my part — how then can I be too grateful to Heaven for my
acquaintance with one to whom and to whose example I owe so
much."

The copy of "The Marriage in Cana of Galilee," mentioned
by Collins, was thought to be the best ever made of that greatest
picture of Paul Veronese ; that marvellous work of which Stuart
said, "Were all the pictures in the world destroyed this alone
would be sufficient to restore art."

Upon this occasion he probably painted the picture, of which
Leslie says : "I remember an exquisite pasticcio Allston painted
from part of a picture by Titian ; the subject was the 'Adoration
of the Magi,' and the portion of the picture which Allston imitated rather than copied, contained a white horse, most beautifully colored. He afterward gave this to Coleridge, and the
frequent sight of it continued to delight me many years."

Of this picture Coleridge wrote :

"MY DEAR ALLSTON : The bearer of this is a particular friend
of mine, a German gentleman, of excellent good taste in painting,
and himself a possessor of a very curious collection of the old
Netherland masters. As he was sitting in our parlor talking with
me, he kept his eye fixed on your picture, and at last he said,
'I beg your pardon, but you have a valuable picture of some
Venetian master.' I answered, 'Titian, do you think ?' 'No,'
said he, 'though he has the coloring of several of his early
works, but the outline is too soft for him. He was crisp to a
defect. It is more like a picture of Paul Veronese.'

"He could scarcely believe me when I told him it was yours,
though imitated from an old picture. He is exceedingly desirous
to see 'Jacob's Dream.' You will find him a man worth knowing both in head and heart. When shall we see you ?

"S. T. COLERIDGE."

A lady who had great knowledge of pictures, and had lived and painted for many years among them, wrote Coleridge from Florence : " As to the picture you possess of Allston's painting, I saw the original, a Titian. His copy, if such it could be called, is decidedly one of the most wonderful I ever saw, and has all the spirit and feeling of originality, and the only picture that could be said truly to equal Titian in color ; in fact, Laurent, a famous picture-dealer, who came here from abroad and saw it at your home at Highgate, would not believe it a modern picture, or any other's than Titian's."

Coleridge prized this picture very highly and bequeathed it by will to Mrs. Gillman, in whose family he was a beloved guest for many years before his death. She thus describes it :

" My picture consists of one white horse, in a beautiful position, bending his neck gracefully, and licking himself just above the knee ; its countenance is so pleasant—perhaps, in its way, beautiful. There is a Greek, I believe, standing, his face toward you, with one hand on the saddle. Also a second horse, of which you see only the back part—the rider, who has on a turban and looks like a Turk, sitting on him quite at ease. There are other figures in the foreground, and in the back animals' heads are seen under an open shed, with a sort of penthouse top ; also the figure of an Indian."

This picture was the probable inspiration of a letter from Coleridge to a lady friend, from which we give an extract :

" I will take care, if God grant me life, that my unlucky disposition shall be no injury to Allston. I should have done more, had I not been so anxious to do so much. I could not bear the thought of putting in an ordinary puff on such a man, or even an anonymous one. I thought that a bold avowal of my sentiments on the fine arts, as divided into poetry, first, of language ; second, of the ear, and third, of the eye, and the last subdivided into the Plastic (statuary) and the Graphic (painting), connected, and, as it were, isthmused, with common life by the link of Architecture, exemplifying my principles by continued reference to Allston's pictures.

" This would, from the mere curiosity of malignity and envy, answer our friend's pecuniary interests best. His fame he will achieve for himself, for which he has indeed but one thing to do. Having arrived at perfection—comparative perfection certainly— in coloring, drawing, and composition, to be as equal to these three in his expression, not of a particular passion, but of the living, ever-individualizing soul, whose chief and best meaning is itself, as even in this he is superior to the other artists."

The project mentioned in the above letter was undoubtedly carried out, in a degree, in Coleridge's "Essays on the Fine Arts," published in the Appendix of Cottle's " Early Recollections of S. T. Coleridge."

Encouraged by the generous praise of Coleridge, and invigorated by his trip to Paris, Allston entered his studio in London full of enthusiasm and eager for work. He had commenced his "Jacob's Dream " and several smaller works. Of this time he thus speaks :

" Ah, I was then in health, young, enthusiastic in my art, in a measure independent as to my pecuniary affairs, and I painted solely from the impulse within. I felt that I could do the work of a Titan or a Hercules. But from the moment I felt the pressure of want, and began to look upon my pictures as something I must finish in order to get so much money, from that moment I worked to a disadvantage, and the spirit of the artist died away from me. I never did anything well in my art under the pressure of poverty. I must be free, and feel no motive but such as my subject itself will supply, to work to my own satisfaction and do justice to my art and to my own mind. I painted my pictures of ' Uriel' and 'Elijah in the Desert' in eight weeks, of which I gave five to the ' Uriel' and three to the ' Elijah.'

"'Uriel in the Sun'* is a colossal figure, foreshortened, nearly twice the size of life. I surrounded him and the rock of adamant on which he sat with the prismatic colors, in the order in which the ray of light is decomposed by the prism. I laid them on with the strongest colors; and then with transparent colors, so intimately blended them as to reproduce the original ray; it was so bright it made your eyes twinkle as you looked at it."

In a letter to Washington Irving, Leslie speaks of the impression made on him by this picture as follows: "Allston has just finished a very grand and poetical figure of the angel Uriel sitting in the sun. The figure is colossal, the attitude and air very noble, and the form heroic without being overcharged. In the color he has been equally successful, and with a very rich and glowing tone he has avoided positive colors, which would have made him too material. There is neither red, blue, nor yellow in the picture, and yet it possesses a harmony equal to the best pictures of Paul Veronese. I hope you will be in London ere long to see it."

This picture received the highest prize at the Exhibition of the British Institution, and was immediately purchased by the Marquis of Stafford, who at that time was vice-president of the Institution. This incident gave Allston an opportunity to perform one of those generous acts so natural to his character, which is related by the grateful beneficiary, Brockhedon:

"I do not remember the year when Allston received the first prize of the season for his fine picture of the angel Uriel, at the British Institution. In that year I also exhibited there my large picture of 'Christ Raising the Widow's Son at Nain.' The second premium was awarded to me. The next day Allston called on me and said, with his peculiar delicacy, 'They have given me more and you less than was deserved, and I fear you must be

* Paradise Lost, Book iii.

disappointed in your fair expectations, and may suffer some in-
convenience from their not being realized; for I know that your
picture has been very expensive to you; I do not want all that I
have received, and I shall be really gratified if you will take part
of it, use it, and repay me when you can.' I saw that I should
have wounded his generosity if I had altogether refused it. I
did take a small part, and when I repaid it I acknowledged the
value of its use and his kindness to me by sending to him a
packet of ultramarine, which I had brought from Rome; an
acknowledgment which would have distressed him if I had
offered it in the form of interest for the sum he had so gener-
ously lent me."

Of the other picture, Allston mentions as having painted at
this time, Leslie says: "'Elijah in the Desert' was painted with
great rapidity; I saw it a few days ago and was greatly struck
with its wild grandeur, I cannot conceive the subject to be more
finely treated." This picture was taken to America, but was
afterward sold to Mr. Labouchere, M.P., and brought back to
England.

Soon after the Marquis of Stafford had purchased "Uriel in
the Sun," certain lovers and patrons of English art conceived
the idea of an annual Loan Exhibition, to which they were to
contribute such pictures of the old masters as were in their
possession. This idea met with coldness on the part of the
London artists generally; it was carried out, however, and the
best Flemish, Venetian, Italian, and Spanish masters were
admirably represented. At the opening, Sir Thomas Lawrence was observed to be profuse in his criticisms and fault-
findings, and the artists generally followed his lead. Cuyp
was too hot, Vandyck too cold, Titian, Veronese, Raphael,
Tintoretto, and Murillo were in their way well enough, but, as a
whole, the collection represented a period and progress in art
quite below the modern standard.

In the midst of the general detraction Allston was conversing with a group of gentlemen, and was heard to say, in reference to the pictures: "These suns make our stars hide their diminished heads." To which the Marquis of Stafford, addressing himself to Allston, replied, "You, at least, need not say so."

Allston was in pressing need of money, with no prospect of immediate relief, when Lord Egremont called at his studio intending to purchase his picture "Jacob's Dream." He invited Allston to accompany him to his house and see where it could be placed. Taking him into a room he asked if there was any space suitable. Allston pointed to one where the light would do, but it was not large enough. His Lordship said he would alter it to the required size by removing a door; Allston advised him not to do it as the alteration would injure the architecture of the room. "Then," said he, "I will have it at my country-house at Petworth."

In regard to Allston's religious character much has been said. A very remarkable story is told of him as illustrating the efficacy of prayer. This might naturally have grown out of the incident connected with the purchase of "Jacob's Dream," and the seemingly providential call of Lord Egremont when the artist was in so great need of money. We find no other basis for the story.

Mrs. Jameson describes "Jacob's Dream" in these words: "The subject is very sublimely and originally treated, with a feeling wholly distinct from the shadowy mysticism of Rembrandt and the graceful simplicity of Raphael. Instead of a ladder or steps, with a few angels, he gave the idea of a glorious vision, in which countless myriads of the heavenly host are seen dissolving into light and distance, and immeasurable flights of steps rising, spreading above and beyond each other, till lost in infinitude."

At an artists' dinner in London, at which were present some of the most distinguished painters of the time—Royal Academi-

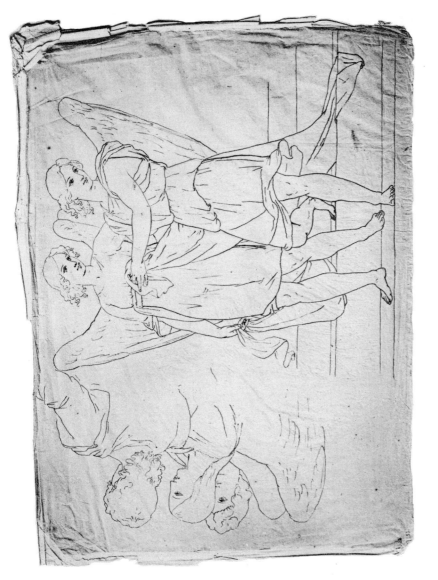

Outline Sketch of Two Angels in "Jacob's Dream."

From the original in the Boston Museum of Art.

cians and others—this picture was discussed. The praises it received were profuse. There was no dissent from the most exalted opinion of its merits. It was regarded as possessing, in a remarkable degree, all the elements required to produce the best effects in the highest range of ideal art. It was declared to be not only the star of the Exhibition, but, in its sphere, the greatest picture of modern times. In conception the picture was really unique. There was in it the self-assertion, the calm assurance of power—power to tread untried fields, to disregard high precedent, and to explore for himself the way of the ascending and descending angels of the patriarch's vision. No one who sees it can fail to observe the peculiar sublimity of Allston's conception. It is remarkable in its departure from the common conventional ladder without violence to the textual authority, and without unduly straining a poetic license. The expanse of golden steps melting into the supernal; the grace of the celestial beings rendered congruous and natural by the easy ascent; the amplitude of space illimitable; the repose of beauty—the lofty expression in every line of the angel figures; the poetry of movement; the spiritualization of familiar forms into images immaculate and heavenly, combine to make it a singularly impressive and beautiful picture.

Not long after Allston's return from England he received a copy of Wordsworth's poem, "Composed upon an Evening of extraordinary Splendor and Beauty," with the accompanying note: "Transcribed by Mrs. Wordsworth, in gratitude for the pleasure she received from the sight of Allston's pictures, in particular 'Jacob's Dream.'" And at the end of the poem was added the following:

"N.B.—The author knows not how far he was indebted to Mr. Allston for part of the third stanza. The multiplication of ridges in a mountainous country, as Mr. Allston has probably observed, are from two causes, sunny or watery haze or vapor; the former is here meant. When does Mr. Allston return to England?

"WM. WORDSWORTH."

The third stanza only need be included here.

> And if there be whom broken ties
> Afflict, or injuries assail,
> Yon hazy ridges to their eyes
> Present a glorious scale;
> Climbing suffused in sunny air
> To stop—no record hath told where!
> And tempting fancy to ascend
> And with immortal spirits blend!
> —Wings at my shoulders seem to play;
> But rooted here I stand and gaze
> On those bright steps that heav'nward raise
> Their practicable way.
> Come forth, ye drooping old men, look abroad
> And see to what fair countries ye are bound!
> And if some traveller, weary of his road,
> Hath slept since noontide on the grassy ground,
> Ye Genii to his covert speed,
> And wake him with such gentle heed
> As may attune his soul to meet the dower
> Bestowed on this transcendent hour!

CHAPTER XIV.

ALLSTON'S FINAL RETURN TO AMERICA.—LETTERS OF EARNEST PRO-
TEST AGAINST HIS LEAVING ENGLAND.—ELECTION AS AN ASSO-
CIATE OF THE ROYAL ACADEMY.—WARM LETTERS FROM
COLLINS AND LESLIE.

To quote Allston's own words: "A homesickness which (in
spite of some of the best and kindest friends and every encouragement that I could wish as an artist) I could not overcome, brought me back to my own country in 1818." Thus
briefly did he touch upon the cause for making, in many respects, the most important move of his life. His career as an
artist culminated at this time. He had painted his portraits of
Coleridge and Dr. King, with other pictures, in Bristol; he had
finished "The Dead Man Revived," "Uriel in the Sun," and
"Jacob's Dream." By these works he had secured substantial
public recognition, having received on several occasions prizes
from the British Institution and the Royal Academy. He had
secured private patronage from distinguished men, connoisseurs,
and lovers of art. Every avenue to preferment in the line of his
profession was open to him; social, literary, artistic distinction;
fame, fortune, academic honors—all invited, all urged him forward. America had furnished men who had figured conspicuously in England and left a lasting record in the annals of
English art, but Allston seemed confessedly destined to surpass
them all. As Morse wrote in a letter given elsewhere, "Mr.
Allston will almost as far surpass Mr. West as Mr. West has

oth'er artists, and this is saying a great deal, considering the very high standing which Mr. West enjoys at present."

It goes almost without saying, to those familiar with his career, that had Allston remained in England he would have succeeded West as President of the Royal Academy. Morse spoke advisedly when he said he was looked upon by his contemporaries in England as the one man capable of restoring the best art of the sixteenth century. Also Leslie, when he said of "Uriel in the Sun," "It is worthy to rank with the best works of Paul Veronese." In accord with this, we find in the author's copy of the "Sibylline Leaves," now owned by the family of the poet Longfellow, on the margin, opposite Allston's poem, "America to Great Britain," the following in Coleridge's handwriting: "By Washington Allston, a painter born to renew the sixteenth century."

In view of these high testimonies from competent witnesses, it is impossible not to feel regret at Allston's return to America. Leslie gives as his belief that one cause for his leaving England was the result of his open-handed charity to the street beggars in London. They made his life miserable by their incessant importunities at home and in the streets. Among other reasons leading to a step so ill-advised we may suggest the encouragement he derived from the sale of "The Dead Man Revived" to the Pennsylvania Academy of Fine Arts; this no doubt strongly influenced his return, but probably that which more than anything else determined his action was the intelligence he received from Charleston about that time, that his patrimony was exhausted. Moreover, his love of country was a constantly stimulating motive. It was an element of power in his ambition and in his work. His first great picture had taken the highest prize at the British Institution. It had won the praises of the best judges of art in London, but it was purchased by his own countrymen. Thus his patriotism probably increased that homesickness which he assigned as the sole cause for a step which proved fatal to the hopes of his friends and brought to an untimely end his great career.

Of his English friends Allston says: " By the English artists, among whom I number some of my most valued friends, I was uniformly treated with openness and liberality. Out of the art, too, I found many fast and generous friends, and here, though I record a compliment to myself, I cannot deny myself the satisfaction of repeating the kind words of Lord Egremont a few weeks before I left England : ' I hear you are going to America,' said he. ' I am sorry to hear it. Well, if you do not meet with the encouragement which you deserve in your own country, we shall all be very glad to see you back again.' I have ventured to allow myself this piece of egotism for the sake of my countrymen, who, I hope, will never let any deserving British artist, who should come among us, feel that he is not welcome. England has never made any distinction between our artists and her own; never may America.

" Among the many persons from whom I received attentions during my residence in London I must not omit Colonel Trumbull, who always treated me with the utmost courtesy. Among my English friends it is no disparagement to any to place at their head Sir George Beaumont. It is pleasant to think of my obligations to such a man, a gentleman in his very nature—gentle, brilliant, generous. I was going to attempt his character, but I will not; it was so peculiar and finely textured that I know but one man who could draw it, and that's Coleridge, who knew him well—to know whom was to honor."

When Sir George heard that Allston was going to leave England he wrote as follows :

"GROSVENOR SQUARE, June 29, 1818.

" MY DEAR SIR : I am very sorry I was from home when you called this morning, and it is with concern I hear of your intention to return to America immediately. I am far from the exclusive wish of limiting the arts to this or that country, for I am convinced the more they are spread the greater degree of emulation will be excited, and the more all the benefits they are capable of giving to mankind will be of course extended, and they themselves will be brought to a greater degree of perfection. But I am convinced you are quitting this country at a moment when the extent of your talents begins to be felt, and when the encouragement you are likely to receive will bring them to perfection, and you would then return to your native country fully qualified to improve and direct the exertions which I am happy to hear are now apparent in America.

"However, whatever you may resolve upon, depend upon this, that you will be attended by the best wishes of both myself and Lady Beaumont that your endeavors will be crowned with all the success they so amply deserve. I am, my dear Sir, with much regard,

" Sincerely yours,

" GEORGE BEAUMONT."

Charles R. Leslie said : " There can be no doubt but that Allston, had he remained in England, would very soon have been made an Academician. The feeling was unanimous in his favor among all the members, at the time when his pictures were seen here. Indeed, I am not certain but that, had he exhibited pictures with us after his departure he might have been elected."

In a letter from W. F. Collard to Leslie, he says : " How many hours have dear Allston and I spent together, both by night and alone in his studio by day, and never once have I quitted him without considering him one of the most benevolent, intelligent, and interesting men I had ever known. There are some, and of the highest class, who are subject to let their imaginations outstrip their industry, and the dreams of their intentions occupy too much of that space which should be covered by prompt exertion. It was from a tendency of this sort that I thought observable in the disposition of our friend that I lamented exceedingly his quitting England; for this is the place where the *furor* of emulation, with its consequent spur to industry, was more likely to be kept up by the antagonism of talent than in his own country.

"The picture which subsequently procured his Academic honors gave him a position from which his ambition would not allow him to recede, and I therefore have full hope that if he had remained here his further efforts would have carried him to that height in his profession to which his rare talents were capable of bearing him, whereas the seating himself down in a more limited sphere, the want of rivalry (which few can bear with impunity), the praise he was likely to receive, and the ease with which he might live, might, I am fearful, prevent the full development of the abilities he so unquestionably possessed."

Irving wrote to Leslie, "I shall try hard to see Allston before he sails. I regret exceedingly that he goes to America, now that his prospects are opening so promisingly in this country. His 'Jacob's Dream' was a particular favorite of mine. I have gazed on it again and again, and the more I gazed the more delighted I was with it. I believe I could at this moment take a pencil and delineate the whole with the attitude and expression of every figure."

Allston says: "Leslie, Irving, and Sir Thomas Lawrence were the last persons I shook hands with before leaving London. Irving and Leslie had accompanied me to the stage, and Sir Thomas, who was passing by on his morning ride, kindly stopped to offer me his good wishes. It is pleasant to have the last interview with those whom we wish to remember associated with kind feelings."

After a very stormy passage the ship which bore Allston to

America arrived in safety. He thus expresses his emotions at that time :

"We made Boston harbor on a clear evening in October. It was an evening to remember! The wind fell and left our ship almost stationary on a long, low swell, as smooth as glass, and undulating under one of our gorgeous autumnal skies like a prairie of amber. The moon looked down upon us like a living thing, as if to bid us welcome, and the fanciful thought is still in my memory that she broke her image on the water to make partners for a dance of fireflies, and they did dance, if ever I saw dancing. Another thought recurs, that I had returned to a mighty empire; that I was in the very waters which the gallant Constitution had first broken; whose building I saw while at college, and whose 'slaughter-breathing brass,' to use a quotation from worthy Cotton Mather's 'Magnalia,' but now ' grew hot and spoke ' her name among the nations."

Immediately after Allston's departure for America he was elected an Associate of the Royal Academy. His friend Collins was the first to notify him of the bestowal of this Academic honor.

"LONDON, November 4, 1818.

" DEAR ALLSTON : From my very heart's core do I congratulate you upon your election as an Associate of the Royal Academy, a circumstance as honorable to that body as to yourself, and of which I received the gratifying intelligence yesterday. I immediately sent to Leslie, who came over out of breath; and all the news I had to communicate to him has, I believe, kept him, to a certain degree, in the same state ever since. Had you been here!—but you will come.

" And now to the fulfilment of your commission, to send all the news I can, to which end I shall give you a succession of such events as may serve to remind you of the ties you have in this country. The letter you sent me at Sir George Beaumont's came during dinner, and I, of course, made Sir George and her ladyship acquainted with that part of it relating to themselves. If I have any knowledge of the human heart, what the two said of you was direct from that spot. May all the success we that day wished you attend your steps.

" With the scenery of the north I am charmed, and, considering the time necessarily occupied in travelling, I have not been altogether idle. Your hints about Coleridge I did not fail attending to. With his wife I am pleased, and his elegant daughter Sara I have made a painting of. She is a most interesting creature, about fifteen years of age, and the parties we occasionally form with these good people, Southey, Hartley Coleridge, etc., I shall not soon forget.

" From Keswick I went to Scotland. After spending ten days in Edinburgh, I returned to Sir George's, and, with himself and Lady Beaumont, visited Ullswater and Ambleside, where we stayed some days with Wordsworth, with whom I am much delighted; and in some of our rambles, when he could have had no motive but that of gratifying his own love of truth, he left me perfectly persuaded that, among all your friends and admirers, you had not a more disinterested one than himself. The kind regards I am desired by Wordsworth, his wife, Southey, and Hartley to send to you, are testimonies of a friendship by no means common, and therefore will have their true weight with you.

" Having now, at the least possible expense of style, told you so much, I have only to assure you of the warm wishes and hopes of all your friends, and (as you already know) of how much I am, my dear Allston, yours ever,

" WILLIAM COLLINS."

" P.S.—I shall expect a letter from you. Come *home* and take your seat at the lectures; have you no *esprit de corps?* I presented your poems to Lady Beaumont, who had never seen them, and I had the very high gratification to hear them spoken of in terms of considerable approbation not only by her ladyship but by Southey and Wordsworth. Southey said that, whatever defects some of them might have, he had no hesitation in saying that they could not have proceeded from any but a poetic mind; in which sentiment he was most cordially supported by Wordsworth, who was present at the time. Fare thee well, God bless you! Write soon. Sir George Beaumont and Wordsworth propose writing to you."

Leslie's congratulations followed closely those of his friend; he thus writes:

"LONDON, November 7, 1818.

"MY DEAR FRIEND: You will doubtless receive by this opportunity various information of your election. You had ten votes out of fifteen. Need I say that all your friends most cordially rejoice at it. I carried the pleasing intelligence out to Highgate the day I heard it, and while I was there Mr. Gillman received a note from Phillips, the R. A., informing them of it as a circumstance that he knew would give them the greatest pleasure. By the bye, Collins thinks that your picture of 'Jacob's Dream' ought now to be exhibited at the Academy, and as he has no doubt you will concur in the same opinion, he intends proposing to Phillips to ask Lord Egremont's permission. He told me last night he had seen Sir George, who had just arrived in town, and who heartily partakes of the general pleasure on your account. He intends writing to you.

"Coleridge is as well as he usually is; Mrs. Gillman is better than usual. When Collins was in Cumberland he made a sketch of Coleridge's daughter, a very interesting girl of fifteen, and it is by far the best portrait he ever painted The sentiment (for in speaking of it I may safely use that hackneyed word) is exquisite. I took it to show Coleridge as one of my own, to see if he would discover the likeness, which he did; a proof that it must be very strong, as he has not seen her for many years and had not the most distant idea that it was intended for her. Coleridge is going to lecture again on philosophy and Shakespeare. Ogilvie is lecturing at the Surrey Institution; Payne has written a tragedy, which has been received at Drury Lane and is to be speedily produced. The story is that of Junius Brutus. Kean plays Brutus. Irving is still in town, and, I believe, intends remaining here. He is occasionally manufacturing. I have not seen Collard since his return, though I have called on him several times.

"I called on Mr. West as soon as I heard of your election, but did not see him; his health is pretty good. If Morse is in Boston tell him I have received his letter of the 8th September, and will answer it immediately. I suppose the Doctor is married by this time; if so, give him my love and sincere congratulations upon the occasion. We are in hourly expectation of the news of your arrival.

"I hope your new title will encourage you to dash on boldly with 'Belshazzar.' Success and every blessing attend you. I have no expectation now of going to America this autumn, and when the spring arrives I shall wish to see the Exhibition at Somerset House, so that it is probable I may not get away till about the time of year you did.

"Yours, with greatest affection,
"CHARLES R. LESLIE."

About this time Allston wrote the following letter to McMurtrie:

"BOSTON, November 7, 1818

"MY DEAR SIR: The enclosed, which was written more than three weeks ago, I have been prevented finishing before this by such incessant engagements and excitements as have left me not one collected hour in which I could calmly sit down to write. I therefore beg you to excuse the delay, and take my wish to have been more punctual for the performance.   .   .   .

" The success I have lately met with in England left me but one finished picture to bring with me, ' Elijah in the Wilderness,' and which, had I remained a few weeks longer, I had the prospect of also transferring to another proprietor. I have brought, however, several others, on the stocks, some of which are considerably advanced, particularly ' Belshazzar's Feast, or the Handwriting on the Wall '—sixteen by twelve in size, which, I believe, is several feet larger than ' The Raising of the Dead Man.' I purpose finishing it here. All the laborious part is over, but there remains still about six or eight months' work to do to it.

" As I get on with it and other smaller works, which I may probably proceed with at the same time, I will take the liberty, occasionally, to drop you a line. In the spring or summer I may not unlikely pay you a visit. I have a great desire to see your city, and the state of Arts there. Though I have not the pleasure of a personal acquaintance with Mr. Sully, I yet so well know him through his friends, and the friendly assistance he, in conjunction with yourself, has rendered me, that I must in a particular manner beg you to present my respects.

" I left Leslie well. He intends embarking for America in the spring. He has lately finished a beautiful little picture, ' Anne Page inviting Master Slender in,' from ' The Merry Wives of Windsor.' It is finely composed, and I thought it his happiest effort.

> " I remain, dear sir, sincerely yours,
>
> " WASHINGTON ALLSTON."

And in a letter dated Boston, December 14, 1818, he writes :

"Mr. Rogers has kindly offered to see to the shipment for Charleston, S. C., of my picture, namely, the large landscape of Swiss scenery, with figures, representing 'Diana in the Chase,' which I sent out from London, to your care, about two years ago. . . . Will you gratify him by showing him your little picture, by me, of 'The Mother and Child?'

"Stuart has painted an admirable portrait of Trumbull, who has had great success here with his picture, having got, in three weeks, seventeen hundred dollars by its exhibition."

CHAPTER XV.

The following letter, dated London, February 6, 1819, from C. R. Leslie, was in reply to his first news from Allston after the latter's return to America:

"My Dear Friend: I received, sometime ago, yours of December 4th, which I must beg your pardon for not answering sooner. I had before received the pleasant intelligence of your safe arrival and cordial reception by your friends. The dangers of your voyage, must, if possible, have given you a keener relish for the endearments of home.

" Five commissions for small pictures ? Bravo! I hope this will last, and I shall hear by the next opportunity that the hospital has engaged you to paint 'Belshazzar' for them. The British Gallery is now open, but Lord Egremont, who is out of town, did not send your picture there. As you are an Associate, all your friends presume you would wish it to be at the Academy, particularly now that Lord Egremont has not sent it to the Gallery. Phillips mentioned it to me, and said he would undertake to ask Lord Egremont.

" They have placed my 'Anne Page' very well at the Gallery, and it has already been highly spoken of by some of the papers ; I have great hopes of selling it. Newton has sent there a very beautiful picture of 'Falstaff in the Buck-basket,' which was mistaken by one of the editors for Stephenoff, and highly praised.

The Exhibition is rich in small pictures. There is a beautiful little sunny gem by Wilkie, of 'China Menders at a Cottage Door.' Two very clever sketches by John Chalon, of Parisian scenes, in which the present French character is admirably hit. A beautiful one by Alfred Chalon, of Molière reading one of his plays to his housekeeper; a very fine group of fighting horsemen by Cooper; a falling figure, foreshortened against a blue sky, by Etty, which in purity and force of color resembles Paul Veronese; a Jew's head, as a matter of course, by Jackson; and though I mention it last, yet very far from least, a magnificent picture of the 'Fall of Babylon' by Martin, which, I think, even surpasses his 'Joshua.' I need say no more. It attracts general admiration, and Sir John Leicester has been to see him on the strength of it. I hope it will benefit his purse.

"I am at present painting a picture on commission for Mr. Dunlop for one hundred guineas. The subject is from the 112th number of the 'Spectator,' Sir Roger de Coverley and the Spectator going to church, surrounded by Sir Roger's tenants. The background is from a sketch of Mamhead Church, I made in Devonshire. It will contain about fourteen principal figures, the largest of which will be about sixteen inches high, the canvas between four and five feet long, and between three and four high. With the sketch, and as far as I have proceeded with the picture, I am far better pleased than with anything I ever attempted before. Collins has very nearly completed a most excellent picture for Sir John Leicester. It is a grander scene than he ever painted before, made up from his Cumberland sketches and the most interesting picture of English mountainous scenery I ever saw. He has introduced a group of figures in his best style, and over the whole picture he has thrown his greatest luxuriance of color and execution.

"I saw Irving to-day. I wish, when you have leisure, you would write to him; he will probably remain in London some

time. By the bye, if you have not already done it, pray write to
Collins. You know he sometimes annoys himself causelessly.
He talks a great deal about you, and is constantly calculating
upon all the chances that may bring you here again. As for myself, I will not engage you to any regular correspondence. Write
often as you feel inclined, and delay it as long as you like, being
to me as assured of one thing, that your letters, whenever they
do come, will be most dearly acceptable to me, who must be ever,
while I have life, yours truly,

"C. R. LESLIE."

The following, from Allston to Verplanck, is dated at Boston,
March 12, 1819 :

" MY DEAR SIR : Pray accept my thanks for your book. I
like it exceedingly, and know not how I could better express my
pleasure in the perusal than by saying that it appeared to me
just what it ought to be; concise, yet eloquent. The character of
Penn I knew but little of, of Roger Williams nothing more than
as the principal founder of the town of Providence ; but Berkeley
had long been a favorite with me, and I was pleased to find his
character so happily touched by your pencil ; it seems to have
been sketched *con amore.* He is one of the very few philosophers whom we can love as well as admire, for, as you well observe, even his most eccentric flights are marked by a moral
splendor. In the character of Las Casas, also, I think you have
been eminently successful. Would not his adventures with a
little embellishment furnish a good subject for a tale ? Perhaps
you will be gratified to learn that your book is also liked by
others ; Mr. Quincy in particular spoke of it to me in high
terms. The *North American* has a review of it, which I understand is quite favorable, but I have not read it. Now that your
pen is resumed, I hope that you will not soon lay it aside. We

want some good books on national subjects, and you have shown yourself equal to the task of supplying them.

"I must not close this without some account of what I am doing. At present I am engaged on two small pictures, which will be finished in a few days. After these I shall proceed with some on commission, somewhat larger, and probably by June I shall be enabled to go on with the large picture I began in England of Belshazzar's impious feast, which I hope to make profitable by exhibition. After that, if it please God, I am commissioned and shall paint a large picture for the hospital in this town, the subject not yet determined, but it will be from Scripture. So you see my friends here are disposed to give me substantial welcome. I had a letter from Leslie lately; I am sorry to find that he does not intend returning to America before this time next year. Have you heard from Irving? I hope before the summer passes to see you in New York. What are the artists there quarrelling about? Certainly not to advance art, or even themselves.

"I remain, sincerely yours,
"WASHINGTON ALLSTON."

In the spring or early summer of 1819, Allston received the announcement that he had been elected an honorary member of the New York Historical Society. The announcement was accompanied by the following letter from Gulian C. Verplanck:

"DEAR SIR: The above has just been handed to me to forward to you, and lest you should think so empty an honor not worth the postage which it will cost you, I take the liberty to fill up the sheet. We had elected Colonel Trumbull one of the Vice-Presidents, in compliment to his talent as an historical painter, and I therefore thought it proper that you should share in the honors, such as they are, of the Institution.

"You suggest Las Casas's history to me as furnishing the groundwork of a tale. I hardly think that he could be made the hero; he might, however, be introduced with great effect, as indeed Marmontel has already employed him in 'The Incas.' Permit me, in my turn, to recommend him to you. What do you think of (as the subject of a small picture) Las Casas reproaching Ferdinand with the personal guilt of the crimes of his soldiers in New Spain, and the monarch conscience-struck and trembling before him? The scene might be either in the midst of the court, which would give room for great variety of expression, or you may presume it to have taken place at a private audience, which will give you a scene like that of Nathan and David, a subject, by the way, which I do not remember ever to have seen managed with much ability. I would not trust to invention for the countenance and person of Las Casas, but would embody him with the form of Fénélon, such as we have him in the better portraits and engravings of him.

"I have a literary plan which I shall embody as soon as I find opportunity and materials. It is a sketch of the literary history of this country, containing notices of the various original works printed here; views of controversies, religious and political; biographical and critical sketches of distinguished literary men, from Cotton Mather and George Winthrop to Barlow and Dwight, with, perhaps, views of the state of eloquence at the bar and in the pulpit, of the public taste and education. The plan is yet very crude, and I do not know whether it will be a memoir to be read before one of our societies or an independent work. If I can get the materials, I have no doubt that I can make a most entertaining book, whatever its real value may be.

"I am sorry to hear that Leslie still lingers in England. I should like to send him and Collins a copy of my 'Historical Discourse,' but I do not know their addresses. I much fear that

Irving will loiter about London for a long time and waste the most useful part of his life out of his proper sphere. I perceive by your frontispiece to the new edition of ' Knickerbocker,' that you have become an accomplice of his in calumniating the fathers of this State, of whose fame I consider myself the champion. The new edition, I learn, is curtailed and corrected, but has no new matter.

"I am, yours very truly,

"G. C. VERPLANCK."

Following is a brief letter from Allston to Mr. McMurtrie :

"BOSTON, April 26, 1819.

"MY DEAR SIR : Agreeably to your wishes I made inquiries of Mr. —— respecting the expense of living in Italy, and he says that a family may live very comfortably in Pisa for twenty-five hundred dollars per annum ; in Florence for less. He has not been in Italy, I believe, since 1816. Probably the expenses may be now somewhat increased, in consequence of the present numbers of English residents. But the English now, I understand, live far less profusely abroad than formerly ; indeed, many go abroad to nurse their fortunes. I do not remember the precise sum it cost me in Rome, but I believe it was somewhere near three hundred pounds sterling per annum, though many that I knew, who were better managers, lived equally well for a third less. I beg you to accept my thanks for your kind invitation ; but I fear it will not be in my power to leave Boston for a year at least, on account of my engagements. . . . My friend and pupil, Morse, is meeting with great success in Charleston. He is engaged to paint the President for the City Hall.

"Sincerely yours,

"WASHINGTON ALLSTON."

Under date of May 15, 1819, Leslie gave Allston a full budget of London art news, as follows:

"My Dear Sir: If I had not lately heard of you by the way of Philadelphia, I should be very uneasy at your long silence. I conclude you must have written and your letters miscarried. In my sister's last letter she tells me Sully has heard that you have taken a painting room for three years, and that the hospital at Boston is going to have your large picture of 'Belshazzar.' I hope this last may be true. I enclose you some notices of the Exhibition from the *Examiner*. Your picture of 'Jacob's Dream' looks beautifully; it is in an excellent situation, at the end of the inner room, opposite the door, and in the centre. It is on a line with the eye. Collins varnished it, with the permission of Lord Egremont. It is very greatly admired, and all your friends wish you could see it there.

"My 'Sir Roger de Coverley' is the most successful picture I ever painted. It has gained me an introduction to Sir George Beaumont, with whom I dined a day or two ago. Sir George and Lady Beaumont talked a great deal in your praise, and seemed to regret very much that you had left this country. Sir George intends writing to you. They are going to make a tour through Switzerland very soon. The success of 'Sir Roger' makes me hope I shall be enabled to live without painting portraits.

"To return to the Exhibition. Wilkie's 'Penny Wedding' is, I think, the best picture he has painted, for color and effect, and equal to any of his others in character and expression. It is painted for the Prince Regent as a companion to his 'Blind-Man's-Buff.' Calcott's 'Rotterdam' is a most admirable picture. I like him better than Turner this year. He has given, what is not usual for him, a very beautiful sky, and has left out those heavy, leathery clouds he used to be so fond of.

"Turner has painted Richmond Hill, and I think has not done justice to the scene. In arriving at splendor of effect he seems to me to be meretricious, both in this and in a picture of an orange-ship striking on a bar. There are, however, in them both very wonderful things, and what no one but Turner can do.

"Poor old Mr. West has been very ill, and is now a little better. He was unable to attend the dinner at the Academy this year, which I believe is the first time he has missed. I have not seen or heard of Coleridge or the Gillmans for a long time. Irving is still in London, and is at present in high spirits; he has just sent off the third number of his work to America. Haydon and Carey have had a violent quarrel. Carey was attacked in the 'Annals of Art,' and he has returned the salute in an octavo volume, identifying Haydon with the 'Annals,' and exposing the whole system of puffing by which Haydon has done himself so much harm. There is some hopes that the attack will do him good. He has not answered it, and there is a probability that he will lay aside the pen for the pencil."

．　．　．　．　．　．　．　．

May 19, 1819, Verplanck wrote from New York to Allston as follows:

"MY DEAR ALLSTON: I have been intending for this last fortnight to answer your kind letter, but I fear you have communicated to me some portion of your spirit of procrastination. You were right in your conjecture of my being the writer of the paragraph alluding to your 'Belshazzar,' but I have no concern with the paper in which it appeared further than that one of the persons most interested in it is a relation of mine, so that I can occasionally make use of the paper for the service of my friends. I send you the article in question, together with another paper containing a witty but malicious attack on our poor little Academy. The Exhibition, however, is better than our maligners have anticipated, as you may judge of from the catalogue which I send you. I think the effect of this Exhibition is very visible in the work of our artists; and in a city of this size a little inquiry always enables us to find some good pictures of the old masters, or great foreign artists, which, while they add to the interest of the collection, do something toward forming the public taste. It is, to be sure, our 'day of small things,' but still, according to the wise man, not to be ' despised.'

"I was glad to hear from you that Irving was not idle, and I have since been enabled to judge for myself how he has been employed. It is a sort of a secret, and if you are not in it, I must not betray confidence. As profit is now essential to Irving, I must bespeak of your *North American* friends the privilege of using their pages in such a way as his friends here may think advisable to promote the circulation and reputation of his production. Do not, however, make this public at present.

"I hope you have not altogether abandoned your plan of visiting us. Perhaps a little excursion up the river might be of use to the artist as well as amusing to yourself (a distinction which I suspect I borrowed from *Mr. Puff* in the 'Critic'). If anything in the way of criticism on our artists should appear in the papers I will send them to you. The *Advocate* has generally something on the subject, and pretty well done, though in a censorious spirit.

　　　　　　　　　　"Yours truly,

　　　　　　　　　　　　　"G. C. Verplanck."

Following are letters from Sir George Beaumont and Leslie to Allston, and from Allston to McMurtrie:

　　　　From Sir George Beaumont to Allston.

　　　　　　　　　　" Grosvenor Square, May 29, 1819.

"My Dear Sir: I feel myself culpable for having so long neglected to thank you for your book of beautiful poems, and expressing my sincere regret at your leaving England. Coleridge, you know, has observed, that every great and original poet must create the taste by which he is to be relished, as far as he is great and original. This is certainly applicable to painters also, and is necessarily the work of time. This state of probation you had passed, and your value would soon have been well appreciated; it was therefore an additional grief to your friends at losing you, that you should leave them at a moment when they delighted themselves at the thought of seeing your labors requited.

"Your picture at the Exhibition looks admirably, and I have heard the Royal Academy much regret your absence, and had intended to elect you a member of their body, and indeed would have done so notwithstanding your absence, could they have received assurance that you meant to return. You will be concerned to hear our valuable and venerable friend Mr. West was so ill it was not in his power to preside at the annual dinner. I saw him day before yesterday, and although I hope he was better he was still very feeble and unable to stand. I believe I have frequently expressed to you my high opinion of his merit, and when we consider the state of art in this country, particularly the time in which he has with such laudable exertion persevered, the greatest praise is due to his labors. Indeed, if we consider the disadvantages of his situation when he first turned his mind to art, we must admit that such a progress, under such circumstances, is not to be found elsewhere in the annals of painting. Without anything to direct his tastes but a few paints, the religion of his parents inimical to his pursuits, I believe about the age of twenty he left America for Italy, and by his astonishing perseverance in about four or five years he produced not only the picture I have, but many others of pure classical merit. Whenever we lose him the arts will experience a severe and almost irreparable loss.

"Our friend Wordsworth has just published his 'Peter Bell,' which has brought all the minor wits about his ears, and although he seems insensible to the hum and venom of these gnats, I own I wish he would reserve these small poems, which afford such scope for ridicule and misrepresentation to injure and traduce him, for future publication, whatever their merits and beauties may be, and every man of feeling will allow them to be great, and come forward with his great works. Yet I have no doubt time will do him ample justice, and although the good his works must effect sooner or later is indisputable, yet I am unwilling the present generation should pass away without receiving the full advantages of his instructions, or he himself pass through life without his due share of fame, and his family lose the profits of his honorable labors. I send you, by the kindness of your friend Mr. Leslie, a copy of 'Peter Bell.' I must add that Mr. Leslie has obtained great credit by his picture of 'The Spectator' at Sir Roger de Coverley's; for character and expression it stands very high indeed. Mr. Collins has introduced me to him, and I find him a most interesting young man, and I hear he is as deserving as he appears to be.

"Your 'Jacob's Dream' looks poetically beautiful, and is highly approved of. Our friend Collins has also excelled himself in a coast scene. Lady Beaumont unites with me in best wishes, and cannot help uniting with them a hope of your speedy return to England. We are to set off this week on a tour to Switzerland, and if health is granted to us we expect great pleasure.

"I hope you found your mother well.

"Ever truly yours,

"G. BEAUMONT."

From Leslie to Allston.

"LONDON, August 6, 1819.

"MY DEAR SIR: I received, a short time ago, yours of June 20th, by the Triton, which gave me great pleasure. I had been delighted some time before by the intelligence of your commission from the hospital, contained in your letter to Collins. In my last I gave you some account of the Exhibition; your picture looked as well as you could have wished. . . . At the close of the Exhibition I saw it safe home to Lord Egremont's. He has hung it up in the large room, the first you enter upstairs. I am sorry I have not by me any criticism on 'Jacob's Dream,' but the one in the *Examiner* is not a good one. I regret also that I have no critique on my own to send you. The Marquis of Lansdowne has commissioned me to make a copy of 'Sir Roger' for him.

"I am at present painting a picture of a party spending a day in the woods, which is a very common thing with the people of the middle class in the summer. They go out in a 'shay cart,' as they call it, take their provender with them, and choose some retired spot, where they dine and drink their tea, and come home in the evening. It affords an opportunity of painting a domestic group with rural accompaniments. I lately spent a fortnight at Epping Forest, and in my rambles I lighted on some parties of the kind I have described, which suggested it for a subject. . . .

"You will have seen, ere this, the two first numbers of Irving's 'Sketch-Book.' We have heard but little of the reception of the first number, but that little is gratifying to himself and friends. He is, in consequence, in very good spirits about it. I wish you would write to him.

.   .   .   .

"I have not seen Coleridge or the Morgans lately, but hope to visit them soon. I have heard that you are making some designs from Sir Walter Scott's novels. They afford excellent material, though the picturesque scenes with which they abound are almost too highly finished by the author to leave anything for the painter to do but merely follow him, which is some disadvantage.

"I send you, by this opportunity, the trees by Lewis, and a little print he has made from my sketch of 'Chinkford Church,' which I believe you did not see. All your friends that I am acquainted with speak of you most affectionately whenever I see them, and desire me to remember them when I write, which I do in a bunch. Poor old Mr. West has been feeble for some time. I called on him to remember you, as you desired, and he appeared much pleased to hear of your welfare. He said the Academy had never done a more proper thing than electing you a member.

"God bless you, says

"C. R. LESLIE."

From Allston to McMurtrie.

"BOSTON, October 30, 1819.

"MY DEAR SIR: So far from having taken any exception to the contents of the letter alluded to in your last, I felt myself in a particular manner obliged for the friendly interest you manifested in it for my professional success; and it was my intention so to have expressed myself in reply, and I should have done so had I answered it when I ought. But while I still beg you to believe me sensible to the friendly motive which advised my sending on the picture of 'Elijah in the Wilderness' for exhibition, I cannot avail myself of the advice. My reason is this: From all my experience in England, both in my own case and that of other artists there, I have always found that every successive exhibition of a picture lessens its chance of selling. Those who would perhaps buy a picture from an artist's room while it is fresh in their minds and unseen but by a few, are apt to look on it with indifference, or at least with diminished interest, when it becomes the gaze of the multitude. It is owing to this that Turner, Collins, and other artists of the first rank in England still retain some of their best works, though painted five or six years ago.

   .   .   .   .

" As soon as I accomplish anything of sufficient importance to describe to you, I will send you some account of it. . . . Want of funds has in some degree retarded me, but I have got agoing again, and shall soon proceed with 'Belshazzar.' Have you any news in the way of arts?

      " I remain, dear sir, with sincere regard,

          " Yours truly,

             " WASHINGTON ALLSTON."

        From Allston to Leslie.

                   " BOSTON, November 15, 1819.

" DEAR LESLIE :

   .   .   .   .

" Your letter by the London packet, together with the prints, has been received. Tell Frank Collins I feel greatly obliged to him for hunting up the admirable print of Lieven's ' Lazarus,' which I value more than I should twenty of Lebrun's battles, fine as they are. Pray say to him that when he has collected for me to the amount of ten pounds, I wish him to stop, until I shall be a little more in cash, when I will write to request him to proceed. Thank him also for the present of his brother's print of the sea-coast ; I am glad to have such a remembrance of the picture, and accept yourself my thanks for the print of your church. I like it exceedingly.

" The critiques on your 'Sir Roger' and my 'Jacob,' from the *New Monthly Magazine*, were republished here before I got

the *Magazine* you sent.   I find, as I supposed, they were written
by Mr. Carey, indeed I thought they must have been by him, as
there is not one of the London picture critics who could have
done them half so well.   Pray present him my best thanks for it.
He has described your picture so well that I could almost copy
it from the description.   I heartily congratulate you on its success, and hope that it may prove a trusty pioneer for you to fame
and fortune.   The last, however, is only dreamt of by young
painters; a dream which becomes dimmer and dimmer as we
advance in life.   But no matter, the art itself has so much intrinsic pleasures for its votaries that we ought to be satisfied if
to that is added but enough of the Mammon to make the ends
of the year meet.   Indeed I often think, with Collins, that if a
painter who really loved his art had, together with fame, as much
wealth as he wished, he would be too happy in this world ever
to be in a suitable state of mind to leave it.   I hope, notwithstanding, that Collins is getting money so as to lay up something
at the end of each year ; for a little more than we have, I trust,
would do neither of us any harm, but everything is for the best
so we do our duty to Heaven.   Tell him I think and talk a great
deal about him (as I do also about you), talk to those whom he
has never seen, but who in feeling an interest in all I love and
esteem, require not the aid of sight to admit him and you among
the number of their friends.

    " How mysterious, when we ponder over it, is this communica-
tion by words, and how real and distinct an image do they create
in our minds of objects far removed, even of those long buried in
the grave, over which centuries have passed.   Indeed so familiar
is the image of Sir Joshua to me, his manners, habits, modes of
thinking, and even of speaking, created by the description of
him, that I feel almost persuaded at times I had actually been
acquainted with him.   What a world is that of thought !   And
what a world does he possess whose thoughts are only of the

Unfinished Portrait of Allston by Himself when a Young Man.

In the possession of R. Charlotte Dana, of Boston.

beautiful, the pure, and holy. How fearful then is his where the vindictive and base and sensual make the sum. 'As the tree falleth, so shall it lie.' . . .

"I write without order whatever comes uppermost, and consequently have left myself too little room to tell you all I wished. I have painted a small picture from Spenser, and a head of Beatrice, both just sold. I shall soon proceed with the 'Belshazzar,' then the hospital picture, and no more small pictures. Morse has spent the summer here, and has just finished a large whole-length portrait of a beautiful girl wandering amid the ruins of a Gothic abbey. 'Tis well drawn, composed, and colored, and would make a figure even at Somerset House. I always thought he had a great deal in him, if he would only bring it out by application, which you will be glad to hear he at length has acquired. Circumstances made him industrious, and being continued, his industry has grown a habit. He leaves town this week for Washington, where he is to paint a whole-length of the President for the City Hall, Charleston.

"I have written to Mr. Howard, the Secretary of the Royal Academy, enclosing to him a paper he sent me for my signature, and have requested him to deliver my diploma to you, which I will thank you to have put into a deal box, and to deliver to Captain Tracy, to bring out to me when he returns. Tell me all about the artists. What is Welles doing? Give my best and most affectionate regards to Irving, and tell him I will write by the next opportunity. His 'Sketch-Book' is greatly admired here. I like all the articles. Above all give my regards to Mr. West, to whom I have written a note enclosed to Mr. Howard.

"God bless you, yours ever,

WASHINGTON ALLSTON."

CHAPTER XVI.

Interesting reference to Allston's work during the years from 1820 to 1824 will be found in the following letters:

From C. R. Leslie to Allston.

"LONDON, March 3, 1820.

"MY DEAR SIR: . . . . . .

"Since my return I have painted a copy of 'Sir Roger' for Lord Lansdowne, and am now engaged on a picture of a citizen and his family 'gypsying' (as it is called), or spending a day in the woods in the manner of gypsys. It contains eight figures, and I hope to complete it for Somerset House.

"Martin has painted a picture of Macbeth and Banquo meeting the witches on the blasted heath; it is as usual tremendously grand. He is now employed on your subject of 'Belshazzar,' making it an architectural composition with small figures, the writing on the wall to be about *a mile long*. Willes has very much improved; he made his *début* this year at the Gallery with his picture of 'Danger,' from Collins's poem. It looks extremely well there. He will exhibit a large landscape at the Academy, which I think will do him great credit.

"My sister sent me, some time ago, a paragraph from a newspaper containing an extremely well-written description of your picture 'Florimel.' It brought it completed before my eyes. I am sure such a subject treated in your way must make an exquisite picture.

"The Gallery is now open, and except in the landscape department I think it one of the best exhibitions I have seen. Newton has there a beautiful little picture of an old man reading some dull book to a young girl, without perceiving that she is fast asleep. The corner of a love-letter emerging from her bodice speaks for itself. It was purchased almost immediately by a Mr. Chamberlain, a perfect stranger to Newton. Wilkie's picture of the 'Interior of a Highland Whiskey Still' is very fine. The master of the place, an old fellow of herculean make and somewhat corpulent, with his kilt and bonnet, and a brace of pistols in his belt, is criticising a glass of the spirits, which he holds between him and the light, half closing one of his keen eyes and smacking his lips with the air of a perfect connoisseur; it is, I think, one of Wilkie's happiest efforts.

"Young Landseer's picture of the two dogs scratching a man out of the snow is the most interesting animal picture I ever saw. One is licking the hand of the man (who appears to be dead or almost so) as if to assure him that help is near, while the other is barking or howling for assistance; in the distance are seen the monks of St. Bernard making their way toward the sound. Cooper has some exquisite little battle pictures. Collins has nothing this year. The little picture I sent of 'Contemplation' is a female figure with a moonlight effect, which I began for *Juliet*, but not thinking when it was finished that it expressed her character I gave it another name.

"Captain Tracy has given us a gleam of hope that we may see you in the course of the summer, though only for a short time. The months of May, June, and July are, in my opinion, worth all the rest of the year in London, and there is every season some additional exhibition of pictures open. There will, this season, be at least five principal private galleries open. Haydon's picture is completed and will be exhibited at Bullock's rooms in Piccadilly. The weather, you know, is always delightful at that time of the year. I am sure, if you can accomplish it, that a visit, if only for the season, to London will do you great good, and that you will paint the quicker and better for it. I hope I need not say what delight it would be sure to give numbers of your friends besides myself. There is one thing, at all events, I think you might do, and that is, if it is quite impossible for you to come yourself, at least send us a picture, which I should think you might borrow from some of your purchasers for the next Exhibition. The voyages are now performed with so much certainty that there can be little risk either in your borrowing or the owner's lending one for that purpose. You are now sure of a good situation at the Academy, and I think it will facilitate your being made an R. A. Let it be something striking, and the larger the better. I hope you will come and bring it with you. If you should be obliged to return again before the Exhibition, you may depend on my taking every care of it, or in case of my absence, which is not likely to occur, Collins, I am sure, will attend to it.

"Collins, Lonsdale, etc., are all well, and all desire to be remembered to you. Irving has published four numbers of the 'Sketch-Book,' with every chance of success as soon as it becomes known, which you know cannot happen all at once here. There have been two most favorable notices of it, with long extracts, in *Blackwood's* and the *New London Magazine*. He is at present in Birmingham, on a visit to his sister. . . .

"I think your patience must by this time be pretty well exhausted by all this chit-chat, which I have run into in the hope that you may pick out of it something to interest or amuse. Be it as it may, all I ask is ample payment in my own coin, and so farewell, my dear sir, till next time, till when,

"Yours as ever,

" C. R. Leslie.

"Mr. Visger is much pleased with your 'Hermia and Helena.' It hangs in his drawing-room, Portland Square, Bristol."

From Allston to Leslie.

"BOSTON, May 20, 1821.

"DEAR LESLIE : So many things must have been done in the Art since you last wrote, that I begin to feel not a little impatient for some account of them ; but as I have so long owed you a letter, I have no right to expect one from you till I pay my debts ; so I must e'en, lazy as I am, write to you.

"Of you and Newton I occasionally hear from such of our countrymen as have met you in London ; but they seldom give any distinct account of what either of you are doing ; of which, however, the newspapers sometimes speak, after their manner, with more conceit of their own judgment than distinctness in their criticism. The last account which I have seen of you in the latter was of your 'Gypsying Party,' which was almost a year back. I am pleased to find that Newton's last picture, 'The Importunate Author,' from Molière, was so generally admired. I can have little notion of the picture, it being a branch of art he has engaged in since I left London. But from the variety of notices, and all favorable, which I have seen of it, I conclude it must have been generally liked by the artists, from whom the newspaper critics, especially when they agree in praising, always take their tone. By the by, have you seen a criticism on Haydon's 'Entrance of our Saviour into Jerusalem,' in an article on the 'State of the Arts in England,' in a late number of the *Edinburgh Review?* The praise it gives, I think just, but cannot say the same of all the censure ; one point, however, in the latter seems well founded—the want of those subtle niceties and inflections in the outlines which make so great a part of the charm in some of the old masters ; it was what I always felt the want of in nearly all the pictures of modern date. With respect to the rest of the review, it is but little better than a gross libel on the English school. The speculations of the writer seem to be

those of a man who, in hunting after originality, runs down a
common thought till it falls to pieces, then putting it again together, and by stitching on the head where the tail was, is astonished to find what an extraordinary animal he has been
chasing. It is a dangerous thing for a writer to think of his own
cleverness when he is engaged in the cause of truth ; the interest
of the cause is too apt to become subordinate to the *éclat* of the
pleader's wit.

"But it is time that I say something of myself. Various circumstances have prevented me from recommencing with ' Belshazzar ' till last September, since which I have, with one interruption, been constantly at work on it. On seeing it at a greater
distance in my present room, I found I had got my point of distance too near, and the point of sight too high. It was a sore task
to change the perspective in so large a picture ; but I had the
courage to do it, and by lowering the latter and increasing the
former I find the effect increased a hundredfold. I have spared
no labor to get everything that came within the laws of perspective correct, even the very banisters in the gallery are put in
by rule. Now it is over I do not regret the toil, for it has
given me a deeper knowledge of perspective than I ever had before, for I could not do that and many other things in the picture, which are seen from below, without pretty hard fagging at
the ' Jesuit.' * I have, besides, made several changes in the composition, which are for the better, such as introducing two enor-
mous flights of steps, beyond the table, leading up to an inner
apartment. These steps are supposed to extend wholly across
the hall, and the first landing-place is crowded with figures,
which being just discoverable in the dark have a powerful effect
on the imagination. I suppose them to be principally Jews, ex-
ulting in the overthrow of the idols and their own restoration, as
prophesied by Jeremiah, Isaiah, and others, which I think their

* A standard work on perspective.

action sufficiently explains. The gallery, too, is also crowded, the figures there foreshortened as they would appear seen from below.

"I have written to Collins by this opportunity, and given him a list of what I have done since I have been here. Among the pictures mentioned I consider 'Jeremiah' and 'Miriam the Prophetess' the best I have done here; the last, I think, is one of the best I have ever painted, in the back of which is seen the shore of the Red Sea, and on it the wreck of Pharaoh's army. . . .

"I have a piece of news for you—no less than that I am engaged to be married. The finishing of 'Belshazzar' is all I wait for to be once more a happy husband.

"Believe me, affectionately your friend,

"W. ALLSTON."

From Leslie to Allston.

"LONDON, August 20, 1821.

"MY DEAR SIR : I received your letter of May 20th some time ago and ought to have answered it earlier. I was not standing on ceremony before I received it, for my friends here would witness for me that I have talked of writing to you constantly for the last six months. Have at you then, without more words.

"I had heard, some time before I received your comfirmation of it, the report of your intended marriage, and also the lady's name, which, by the bye, you do not mention. I am exceedingly anxious to hear more about her. Why did you not give me a description of her in your letter? From her having such a brother as I have often heard you describe Mr. Dana to be, and from the husband she is to have, I cannot but infer the lady to be very superlative. I hope, however, you will give me a particular description of her in your next.

"I am sure the alterations you have made in your 'Belshazzar' must have improved it. A low point of sight is certainly essential to a large picture which must necessarily be hung above the eye of the spectator. The reverse is very injurious to the effect of Raphael's cartoons. I wish very much some of your late pictures could find their way here. The Academy I believe are a little disappointed that you have sent them nothing since your election. Could not some of those you have sold be borrowed for the purpose? There would be scarcely any risk in it. You are remembered here with the greatest admiration by everybody acquainted with art, and your particular friends are all anxious that you should keep such recollections alive. For myself I feel every day more and more what I have lost in you, and I feed myself with the hope that you will one day return to England. I have little prospect at present of going to America.

"You naturally wish to rouse me to do something in the style of art you are fondest of, but I believe I must for the present be contented with a humbler sphere. My inclinations lead me to subjects of familiar life and manners, and what I have done in that way has been more successful than anything else. My last picture was 'May-Day in the Reign of Queen Elizabeth,' which is in some respects an antiquarian picture, as I took pains to adhere as closely as possible to the costume and manners of the time. It contains more figures than anything I have painted. I have sold it for two hundred guineas. I have been lately studying the Dutch school a good deal, and find my fondness for those admirable matter-of-fact painters increase in proportion to my acquaintance with them.

"The Exhibition this year was considered a very good one, though there was nothing of any importance in the historic class, excepting Allan's 'Death of Archbishop Sharpe.' This picture, like all of his, was full of powerful and natural expression. What struck me as its principal fault was a family likeness in

some of the heads, as if he had used the same model too frequently. Wilkie had two small pictures. The one I liked best
was an interior of a cottage in which was a young man writing a
letter to his sweetheart, who was coming in unexpectedly behind
him and blinding his eyes with her hands. He called it 'Guess
my Name.' The expression was excellent, and the light and
shadow quite magical, but the color of the flesh was very yellow
and leathery, a fault he has got into in his late pictures. His
other picture I did not like so well. It consisted of a group of
figures, the principal of which was a baker with a roast shoulder
of mutton on a tray on his head, listening to a young girl who
was seated on a stile reading a newspaper. It appeared that in
aiming to get light in the picture he had run into the error that
Sir George Beaumont complains is so common in the English
school, of mistaking whiteness for brightness. Mulready had a
picture of a boy who had been sent on an errand and had stopped
by the way to play marbles, having set down a young child and
a pound of candles in the sun. A servant girl had detected and
was just about to give him a thrashing. Parts of it were very
fine, but as a whole I did not like it so well as his last picture.
Lawrence quite surpassed himself this year. He sent the whole
length of Mr. West, which he has painted for the New York
Academy. The head of it I think the finest thing he ever
painted. Collins had three very fine pictures. One, a beautiful
thing, of children fishing, with a mountainous background. By
the bye, he was much delighted at receiving your letter, which I
suppose he has answered by this time. He is now in the north
of Devonshire. Newton's picture of 'The Importunate Author'
was very successful. The story was most happily told, and with
great delicacy of humor. An author (not a poor threadbare one,
but a man of fashion, by dress and appearance) had got hold of
a young nobleman by the arm, and was reading with great appearance of self-satisfaction a huge manuscript, while the gallant

was secretly looking at his watch as if he had some appointment which he was anxious to keep, and yet was too polite to interrupt the poet. The dresses were of the time of Louis XIV., and the scene on the terrace in an old-fashioned French garden. He sold it to Mr. Hope, and has painted a duplicate of it for the Earl of Carlisle, and is to make another copy for Mr. Murray the bookseller. Newton has another picture which I think will surpass it. It is a quarrel between fashionable lovers. They are returning miniatures, presents, etc., while the lady's-maid is standing behind the chair of her mistress looking at them. It is the same costume as the other, and the effect of color is very beautiful.

"Irving has returned to London and is preparing another book for the press. His 'Sketch-Book' has made him one of the most popular authors of the day. Coleridge and the Gillmans were very glad to hear that I had got a letter from you, they talk about you very much, whenever I see them, which I am sorry to say is not very often. Haydon has been exhibiting a small picture (for him) of 'Our Saviour in the Garden,' which is the worst thing he has painted. He is going on with the 'Raising of Lazarus.' Mr. West's sons have built a magnificent gallery in Newman Street, and are exhibiting there the principal large pictures of their father. Martin's picture of your subject, 'Belshazzar,' made more noise among the mass of people than any picture that has been exhibited since I have been here. The artists, however, and connoisseurs did not like it much. It was first exhibited at the Gallery, and drew such crowds that they kept it open a fortnight longer than usual solely on account of that picture, and the picture was bought for eight hundred guineas by a speculator, who immediately opened an exhibition of it himself and has made a great deal of money by it.

"Newton, Irving, Willes, Martin, etc., all desire me to remember them affectionately to you when I write. Mrs. Bridgen's family all beg to be remembered, not omitting Betsy, who often tells me I am not half as good as Mr. Allston; indeed she despairs of ever seeing so nice a man again.

"Farewell, my dear sir, and may heaven bless and prosper you in all your undertakings is the sincere wish of,

"Yours affectionately,

"C. R. LESLIE."

From Allston to Leslie. (Extract.)

"BOSTON, September 7, 1821.

"I congratulate you with all my heart on the success of your picture 'May-Day.' The story that we have here is that you sold it for three hundred guineas, and Mr. Sully, who is now in Boston, says it is true. I have seen some account of it in the newspapers; the *Examiner*, however, is the only English one I have met with. I could have wished to have seen a description from a more discriminating critic. I shall not forgive you if you do not give me the 'whole history' of it. Tell me all that the artists have said of it, and others out of the art whose opinion is of value. After your exit, let the next who enters for my entertainment be Collins, and Newton, and Ward's great picture, and Martin and Willes—you must have by this time a vast deal to tell me about them all. By the bye, I saw an account of Martin's 'Belshazzar' in *Blackwood's Magazine*, which I read with great delight, and the more so when it was added to the description that he had not only received two hundred guineas premium from the British Institution, but sold it afterward for eight hundred. I suppose he would not paint fans now unless the sticks were made of gold. It is very delightful to hear of such success of those who really deserve it, and especially when they happen to be those whom we also esteem as men. Tell Martin I would get up before sunrise and walk twenty miles to see his picture, which is saying a great deal for me, who have seen the sun rise about as often as Falstaff saw his knees, and who had almost rather stand an hour on my head than walk a mile.

"As I have given either you or Collins, when I wrote by Captain Tracy, a full account of what I have done, I shall not say any more on the subject at present, except that I am still hard at work on 'Belshazzar,' and shall so continue until it is complete."

From Allston to Leslie.

"BOSTON, May 8, 1822.

"DEAR LESLIE: Accept my thanks for your print of 'Sir Roger,' which I think admirable. The principal group is, I think, the best; Sir Roger's character seems to be exactly hit— and the widow and her children are just the kind of objects to call forth the good knight's kindness of nature; next is the old maid, then the old man and his daughter—though I do not know whether I don't prefer to the former the little old woman a little beyond him; perhaps because she seems more completely than the rest to belong to the last century. I am pleased also with the landscape, the church and effect, in short, I am delighted with the whole.

.   .   .   .

"I congratulate you with all my heart upon your election into the Academy. As to my becoming an R. A., I fear, as you say, that it is hopeless so long as I continue on this side of the water, and, though I still hope to revisit England, it is very uncertain when. Sometime next year, however, if possible, I will paint a picture expressly for Somerset House, as I would not be thought unmindful of an institution in which I feel so strong an interest. By the bye, I cannot help thinking the law that excludes foreigners or artists residing in a foreign country from the honor of membership a very narrow one. No other Academy has such a law. The art belongs to no country. I hope the day will come when that law will be expunged, for I see not any good purpose it can effect. But don't think I feel sore under it, I assure you I do not.

"I would give a great deal to see Etty's 'Cleopatra;' you and Willes have quite made my eyes water with your descriptions of its splendor. I remember his former works well. They generally struck me as falling short of the mark; but nevertheless I used to think that his mark was a good one; he appeared to be in the right road, though he travelled slowly. Ah, the old masters, after all, are the only masters to make a great artist; I mean an original one. For I have rarely seen an artist who neglected them that did not imitate his contemporaries, and often, too, while he was deluding himself with the thought that he was confining his study to nature. When I think thus of the old masters, 'tis only of their language, not their thoughts. I would not have the latter derived from any source but nature.

"We have just heard of the arrival of Irving's 'Bracebridge Hall.' I promise myself infinite pleasure from it. The public here are all agog for it. Irving well deserves all his popularity. If I find a subject in it for a picture, I will make a drawing and send it to him."

From Allston to Leslie. (Extract.)

"BOSTON, July 23, 1822.

"When I tell you that I am still fagging at 'Belshazzar' I believe I shall have told you all. I hope to finish in three months more. That done I must think of painting something to send to the Royal Academy—yet it is not likely that I shall be able to finish anything in time for the next Exhibition.

. . . .

"Tell Irving that I am delighted with his 'Bracebridge Hall,' that is, the first volume, for I have not yet seen the second. Every individual of the family is as well drawn as could be, and I felt as if I had been reading of real people. The 'Stout Gentleman' is exquisite. I felt every drop of rain in it and could smell even the stable-yard; but I was sorry he introduced anything like a *double entendre.* I allude to the landlady's visit to the 'Stout Gentleman's' chamber. Perhaps he did not mean anything more than a kiss to have been given, but some readers would not be satisfied with a kiss. Remember me to him affectionately. I liked also the 'Student of Salamanca.' The procession of the inquisitors with their victim to the stake is terrific. Nothing could be finer than the description of the prisoners and the effect of the whole scene on the multitude; they meet the eye with a horrible breadth."

From Allston to Leslie. (Extract.)

"BOSTON, February 7, 1823.

"DEAR LESLIE: I received sometime since a case containing Wilkie's 'Blind-Man's-Buff,' 'The Rabbit on the Wall,' and Allan's 'Circassians,' together with several smaller prints from your designs from 'Knickerbocker' and the 'Sketch-Book.' There was no note or letter accompanying them, but I concluded that they were from you and for Judge Jackson; so I accordingly delivered them to him, all excepting one of the duplicates from my design of 'Wouter van Twiller,' which I supposed you intended for me.

.   .   .   .

"I was exceedingly pleased with your designs from 'Knickerbocker' and the 'Sketch-Book.' They and 'Sir Roger' show what a stride you have made in *chiaro-oscuro* and other matters. The best, I think, is 'Rip van Winkle' mounting the hill with the ghostly Dutchman. Rip's nether jaw hangs ominously, and his dog has a true eye for a ghost. 'Tis equal to the story, which is saying a great deal. The next best is 'Ichabod Crane and Katrina,' which is exquisite; then the 'Van Corlear's Leave-taking;' but they are all good. I was also pleased with the engraving of my 'Wouter.' The characters are all well preserved, but the composition is hurt by the reproduction. Yet that could not have been avoided, and it looks better reduced than I thought it would. But why did the engraver omit the A. R. A. after my name? If it be not too late, I should like to have it added.

" I have made so many changes in 'Belshazzar' that it is yet unfinished, but they are all for the better. I do not regret the time bestowed on it, especially as I find it at last drawing to a close. I hope to complete it by the end of May. Till then I shall say nothing about it. Morse, I hear, has just finished a picture of Congress Hall, and is daily expected here to exhibit. At odd times I have made a number of compositions, but I have laid them all aside until I finish 'Bel.' The best among them is ' Macbeth and Banquo Meeting the Witches on the Heath,' one of the happiest, I think ; the next is Minna and Brenda on the seashore, from the ' Pirate.'

From Leslie to Allston.

"London, August 18, 1823.

" My Dear Sir: I sit down to perform a promise I made some months ago of writing you a long letter of all sorts of news.   .   .   .

" I did not get my 'Autolycus' finished for Somerset House, and have laid it entirely aside for some time. I have lately been employed entirely on small portraits, *alias* ' pot-boilers.' One of these was posthumous, and from a grandchild of Lord Egremont's. I succeeded to his Lordship's satisfaction, for when I told him my price was twenty-five guineas, he immediately wrote me a cheque for fifty. I am to paint him a picture from ' Don Quixote' of Sancho in the apartment of the Duchess, in which I shall probably introduce a portrait of one of his lordship's daughters.

" By the bye, I remember your telling me of one of them you nearly fell in love with when you were at Petworth, pray which was it ? Lord Egremont talks a great deal of you, and I am sure he would be very glad to see you here again. Phillips says your 'Jacob's Dream' is hung in an excellent light at Petworth and looks very grand. The exhibition at Somerset House is considered rather below par this year. Wilkie is almost the only artist of eminence who is equal to himself. The small, whole-length portrait of the Duke of York is one of the finest things he has ever painted. The Duke is in a blue military surtout over a red coat, sitting at a table reading a despatch. His face is lighted by a reflection from the paper. At his back is a window with a muslin blind, through which the picture is lighted, and under the table at which he sits is an immense black dog. The materials (you will perceive) are of the commonest kind ; yet disposed with so much art and painted with such exquisite truth that it is the most interesting picture in the Exhibition. Lawrence is inferior to himself this year. He has made Lady Jersey (a very unusual thing for him) look like a vulgar trollope. Phillips's whole-length of the Duke of York in his coronation robes is finely managed, but the head, and indeed the whole portrait, is very inferior to Wilkie's. I must go back to Wilkie again, whose other picture I had liked to have forgotten. The subject is a parish beadle putting some vagrants (an Italian musician, his wife and boy, dancing bear, etc.) in the watch-house for having a row at a fair. The subject is an unpleasant one, and the cause for which the poor creatures (foreigners, too) are locked up, is not apparent, so that it becomes an act of sheer oppression on the part of the beadle. It is, however, full of beautiful painting. The Italian woman's head, and a monkey, are perhaps as perfect specimens of imitation as could be produced from the whole range of art. The picture, however, generally considered, is too powerful in light and shade for an out-of-door scene under any circumstances. Fuseli expressed his surprise to Wilkie to see him painting in the 'Caravaggio style,' as he called it. Sir George Beaumont, whom you know is a great enemy of the white school, is delighted with this picture and the Duke of York, and hails them as indications of a reform in art.

"Howard's 'Solar System' is a beautifully imagined picture, and would delight you, excepting perhaps in color. A figure of Apollo forms the focus of light in the centre, and around him are revolving personifications of the planets, receiving light, as they pass, in small vases. Mercury, Venus, Mars, Jupiter, and Saturn are represented by the deities of those names, and the Earth, which is the nearest figure, by a beautiful female in a green mantle, with towers on her head. Her waist is gracefully encircled by the arm of a smaller female, in white drapery, half shaded, with a crescent on her forehead, and receiving light from the sun in a silver vase. Jupiter, Saturn, and the Georgium Sidus are dimly seen in the darker parts of the circle, surrounded by their satellites. The only drawback to this picture is the color, which, though not disagreeable, is far from being as poetical as the conception.

"Turner, in all his last pictures, seems to have entirely lost sight of the 'modesty of nature.' The coloring of his 'Bay of Baiæ,' in the present Exhibition, would have been less objectionable perhaps in Howard's 'Solar System;' but as applied to a real scene, although splendid and harmonious, it is nevertheless a lie from beginning to end. Some people who have been in Italy say it is like the atmosphere there; but if that is the case, Claude, Poussin, and Wilson must have been very bad painters. Calcott is not so good as usual. Constable's 'Salisbury Cathedral' is one of his best pictures. You are much wanted in the Exhibition. The number of historical and poetical pictures is lamentably small, and of that small number very few are good for anything. Haydon is in the King's Bench. It is said he owes ten thousand pounds, and of that a considerable sum is for wine. Sir George Beaumont's picture of 'Macbeth,' which happened to be lent to Haydon for exhibition, was seized with his other pictures, and it is doubtful whether or not Sir George will get it without buying it over again. He (Sir G. B.) has lately made a present of all his pictures to the Nation as a beginning of a public gallery, and it is rumored that the Government is going to purchase the collection of Mr. Angerstein, who is lately dead, to add to it.

" Sir George and Lady Beaumont often talk of you with great regard. He told me he wrote to you some time ago, but is afraid you never got the letter, as you did not answer it. I am sure it would gratify him very much to hear from you and to know what you are doing. Coleridge and the Gillmans are also very anxious to hear from you. They were very much delighted with Mr. and Mrs. Channing. For my own part I was so perfectly acquainted with Mr. Channing by report, before I saw him, that I felt quite like meeting an old acquaintance. The little I saw of him so fully answered to all I had heard—indeed, he exceeded my expectations (and, as you well know, his portrait was drawn for me by a most affectionate hand), that I very greatly regretted I had no longer time to profit by and enjoy his society. He gave me a sermon of his own, the last time I saw him, which I have since read with great admiration. Coleridge was speaking very highly of this sermon a few days ago, at Sir George's, who regretted that he had not known of Mr. Channing's being in London. Irving is still in Germany. Newton is quite well. By the bye, I forgot to mention his picture of ' Don Quixote in his Study,' as among the best in Somerset House.

" I am, yours ever,

"C. R. LESLIE."

From Allston to Verplanck.

"BOSTON, July 2, 1824.

"MY DEAR SIR: I need hardly tell you, late as it is, how much pleasure you have given me by your 'Discourse.' The view you take of the Fine Arts, as connected with the glory and improvement of our country, appears to me both just and important, and I cannot but hope that your strictures on our architecture will have a beneficial effect; at least they ought to produce it, and if read by all future committees whom our good people may appoint to overrule the designs of regular architects, they may possibly influence some sensible bricklayer or baker amongst them, and touch his presumption, to the great saving of his time, and the public expense. I do not know a surer way of teaching our countrymen wisdom than by showing its economy. If they can be made to feel that money is really wasted on such piles as they are wont to cumber the ground with, they will perhaps be less liberal of their advice; and then we may expect some improvement. The finest speculations on taste in the abstract will do little good where so many claim the liberty of having a taste of their own. Amongst all our good qualities, and I am patriotic enough to think that our countrymen have as great a share of them as any people on earth, it must be confessed that modesty as to matters where they have no means of information is not a very prominent one. About what they *do* understand they are as modest as other folks. But *malgré* the inconveniences of this disposition to assume, a good-natured man, perhaps, may see in it only the spray of that spirit of enterprise which has prompted them to dash through every known and unknown sea, to the fame as well as to the solid advantage of our country. But the deviations even of this good spirit must be checked in many things before we can become a refined nation.

"As to the present subject, I think you have applied the

most efficient corrective—I mean where you appeal to our vanity; the contempt of foreigners goes farther even than considerations of economy. A book abused in England, or a building ridiculed by an Englishman, however irritating, does actually open our eyes to their defects. If we were proud, such attacks would only confirm us in what is bad, but we are a vain people, the most malleable of all things ; of course, all the better for hard thumps. But we are not all vain, or all ignorant, and there are very many, I doubt not, on whom the refined and speculative parts of your 'Discourse,' so eloquently set forth, will not be lost. The artists ought to thank you for the dignity with which you have invested their art; and I, for one, not only do so for that and for your kind, flattering compliment to myself, but for the honorable mention of my Sir Joshua ; I call him mine, for I feel as if I had a property in his mind ; *quoad* the painter, he has laid the foundation of my own, most of my speculations are built on it, and it is mine by right of settlement. But I hardly know where I am rambling——

"Mr. Dana was much pleased with your kind remembrance of him, and would, I dare say, send you a message did he know of my writing. If you see Mr. Cooper, pray remember me to him. I was delighted with the 'Pilot;' 'tis a great performance.

"Believe me, dear sir, with sincerest esteem, yours,

"W. Allston."

CHAPTER XVII.

The following elaborate letter concerning the technical methods of Allston's painting, and his views as to the many difficult problems of his art, was written by Henry Greenough in answer to the request of R. H. Dana, Sr., as a contribution to his proposed biography of Allston. It is almost a complete hand-book of instruction for students of painting, and will be found interesting, as well, to those who have but a general interest in the subject:

"In the early stages of my acquaintance with Mr. Allston it was my good fortune to hear him describe his mode of preparing his palette for painting flesh. This led to a conversation on color, in the course of which he explained very minutely his system of coloring. As it was a subject on which he always dwelt with pleasure, and frequently recurred to, I have heard him describe his process some five or six times, very nearly in the same words; but as he often went into explanatory remarks suggested by questions interrupting him, I will endeavor to give the result of these several conversations, using as nearly as possible his phraseology, although the exact order of his remarks may not be preserved.

" ' My present system,' said he, ' is one which I have practised for the last fifteen years, and I may say that I am perfectly satisfied with it, because I know it is capable of producing far greater results than my lifetime will ever enable me to attain. I sometimes vary or modify my process according to my subject, but my general practice is on the same principle.

" ' If, for instance, I have a head to paint, I suppose it to be first accurately drawn in outline and dead-colored with black, white, and Indian red. This dead color I paint solidly, with a good body of color, and in a broad manner, that is, with no hard lines or attention to detail in form or color. The object of the dead color is to give the general effect of light and shade, and the masses, which should be made out accurately; so that in the next stage I shall not be obliged to think whether the eyebrows, for instance, are to be lowered or raised, but having arranged these points, my whole attention shall be given to the coloring and modelling of the head.

" ' For the next painting I prepare my palette thus : At the top I put a good lump of white; next to it some yellow (say yellow ochre, raw sienna, or Naples yellow, according to the complexion I am to paint). Then red (vermilion is the best, but I always put by it some Indian red and lake to strengthen the lowest tints if required), lastly, ultramarine blue, and by the side of it a little black. My palette, you perceive, now has white, black, and the three primitive colors.

" ' By admixture of white with yellow I form three tints of yellow in regular gradation from dark to light, and the same with the red and blue. These I call my virgin tints, and they form a regular scale of four different tints from the lightest down to the crude color. Lastly, I take a little pure yellow, pure red, and pure blue, and mix them to a neutral hue, which comes as near to olive as any of the tertiaries. This is for the shadows. I used formerly to make two olives, one light and one darker, but that is unnecessary; a little Indian red, or vermilion and lake, deepened by black, serves to strengthen the shadows, if necessary, and comes in play to mark the deep shadow of the nostrils, the eyelids, and parting of the lips.

" 'I now take my canvas, on which I have dead-colored my head, and with a large brush, say as big as my thumb, but one which will come to a point, I lay in the shadows with olive, not thin, but with a good, firm body. With this olive I paint over the shaded side of the face; the shadows at the roots of the hair, or where the hair joins the flesh, under the eyebrows, nose, and lips. The half-tints which join the shadows, such as the lower part of the lighted side of the face, and in general wherever the shadow becomes less positive, I go over with olive more lightly.

" 'I then take another brush, such as I used for the olive (for I always keep one brush for the olive and another for the lighter tints) and taking on the end of it a little of the lowest of my three tints, that is, the lowest tint of yellow and white, red and white, and blue and white, I mix them on my palette with my brush only, not grinding them together with my knife, but by a few turns of my brush, mingling them in a light and delicate manner. This broken tint I apply to such parts as join the shadows. In the same manner I proceed with the middle tints, taking a little of each and gently mingling them I paint over all the portions of the face which remain uncovered, with the exception of the highest lights. These I paint over with the three lightest tints, neutralized in the same manner as the others were. My head is now covered, and each of the three colors enters into the composition of the whole. In every part there is a blue, red, and yellow, as there is in flesh, even in the highest light.

" 'I should have remarked that although I use each of the three colors in every part, I still endeavor to keep the character of the flesh. I keep the shadows neutral and the mass of light warm, *i.e.*, with a predominance of reds and yellow, rather than blue. This part of the process will occupy me, say half an hour. I have now not only the effect of light and shade, but the character of flesh, and the parts more accurately made out. It only remains to perfect the local colors and model up the detail. I find, for instance, that my picture has less red in the cheeks than the model has; I dip my brush into one of the virgin tints of red and break it in; if it is too light I try the next lower, and so on. The forehead may not have enough yellow; I break some in until I have corrected the deficiency in general. Wherever I find my picture wanting any color (on comparing it with my models) I touch in that color. It is really wonderful how any color thus broken in will be in perfect harmony, owing to the neutrality of the *impasto*, that is, owing to its being touched into a body of color composed of three colors. It seems like magic, the effect is so strong and so true to nature. When I say that I paint my shadows in flat with olive, you must not suppose that I leave them so; I endeavor to make my shadows as varied in color as my lights and half-tints. To be sure, shadows are generally neutral in color, but if you look at the shaded side of the cheek, for instance, you will perceive red in some parts. You should break in red then, either pure vermilion or one of the lower tints. In fact I modify the whole of my shadows by breaking in pure color—blue, red, or yellow—just as my eyes tell me that either of these colors is wanting.

" ' The only object of the first coat of olive is to lower the tone and neutralize the color of the tints which I afterward break in. And here I would remark that unless the shadows are painted solidly you can never make a brilliantly colored head. It is a very common error that the shadows should be painted thin in order to get transparency. You may get a certain degree of transparency by doing so, but then the whole will want force.

" ' Rubens's method of painting flesh, as described in Field's

work on color, was faulty in this respect, as also in having streaks
of separate colors, which always remind me of a prize-fighter,
who has been bruised black and blue. The fact is, sir, Rubens
was a liar, a splendid liar, I grant you, and I would rather lie
like Rubens than to tell the truth in the poor, tame manner in
which some painters do. His pictures are like the sophistical
reasonings of a liar, to whom you have only to grant his premises
and he will thereon erect a gorgeous fabric, but deny these premises and it all falls to the ground. There is a traditionary saying of Rubens that white is the poison of shadow in painting.
This is nearer the truth in glazing than in the *impasto* or body-
color painting. The *impasto* cannot be true to nature without
the tints are modified by admixture of white. I often touch
into my last glazing even with pure color. In this case it becomes necessary to use tints very low in tone, sometimes even
the crude vermilion, ochre, or blue. Sir William Beechey once
remarked to Gainsborough that he had that day made a great
discovery. "It is one," said he, "which I find enables me to
produce great effects, and in your hands would, I think, work
wonders." "What is it?" asked Gainsborough. "Painting into
glazing, sir," said Sir William. "That is no news to me," said
Gainsborough; "but I thought I was the only man in England
who knew the secret."

"'This is a digression, however. I was speaking before of
painting in body colors. It is very important in covering the
head, as I have already said, when you mix the three tints to do
it lightly with your brush only. The modern Italians mix their
pearl tints with the palette-knife, which is death to all brilliancy
of color. It makes mud of the tints at once. They no longer
sparkle to the eye, but become flat as stale beer. By mingling
them lightly with the brush, you make a neutral tint of ten
times the force of one ground up with the knife, and if you were
to take a magnifying-glass and examine the tint you would find

small particles of pure color which give great brilliancy. You must have observed the difference in lustre between silks woven from different-colored threads and those dyed with a compound hue. A purple silk woven of two sets of threads, one blue and the other red, cannot be matched by any plain silk-dyed purple. The first has a luminous appearance like the human complexion. This luminousness is the grand characteristic of flesh. It is what Titian calls the "luce di dentro," or internal light. When I first heard that expression of Titian's it opened to me a world of light. It is common with painters to talk of the transparency of flesh; it is not transparent but luminous. When I was in Paris, a student, Hazlitt (author of " Conversations with Northcote "), was there painting a copy from Titian. We were examining the texture of the color, and he remarked upon the singularly varied character of the tints. " It looks," said he, " as if Titian had twiddled his colors." I don't know whether this expression strikes you as it did me. To me it is very expressive, and first gave me the idea of catching up each of the three colors and merely twiddling them together instead of grinding them with the knife.

" ' I always endeavor to finish my *impasto* in one day. With ordinary diligence and success this may be easily done.' A friend who was present here expressed great surprise at the idea of a head being painted in one day, so as to be ready for glazing the next; meaning, of course, a highly studied head and not a mere sketch. Mr. Allston replied : ' Oh, yes, even a portrait (supposing it to have been already drawn and dead-colored previously) might be painted in one day, that is, the face alone, the hair could be painted separately as well as the dress, background, and accessories. At all events, if I were a portrait-painter I would make the experiment. I would devote great attention to making a careful and correct outline and dead-color, but afterward, instead of taking several short sittings, I would complete the *impasto* in one long sitting, and glaze afterward. If on a review of my work I find any part incorrect, or which does not satisfy me, I go over the shadows and the half-tints, in such parts as I wish to repaint, with a thin glaze of olive, very slightly, and touch into it. There is no difficulty in matching the lights, but it is very difficult to paint over your shadows and half-tints, unless you prepare an olive glazing to touch into.

" ' When my head is ready for glazing I give it a general glazing a day or two previous to finishing it. I mix asphaltum, Indian red, and ultramarine to a neutral tint, and with this I just tinge some megilp—the least in the world—just enough to discolor my megilp a little; this serves to lower the tone of my picture a mere shade and give harmony to the colors. I add to the megilp some japan gold size, which serves to make it dry firm and enables me to work it over the next day, wiping out or painting over as I please. When this is dry I prepare some megilp with asphaltum, Indian red, and blue of a deeper tint, as before, only I put little or no japan in, as I wish to prevent its drying too soon. The neutral tint mixed as I have described is what I call "Titian's dirt." With this I go over the face, strong in the shadows and lighter in the half-tints; with a dry brush or rag I wipe off the glazing or weaken it as I wish, and in this way model up the general form and detail. This part of the process is very much like water-color painting, only that water colors dry several times during the process, but here the paint is left moist. If any part seems weak in color I paint in pure color, either red, blue, or yellow, as the case may be.

" ' The effect of glazing is to deepen the tone. You may paint a bit of canvas over with a solid body of ivory black, which one would suppose is as black as paint can represent, but let it dry and then by repeated glazings of asphaltum and Prussian blue over a portion of it, you will deepen the tone as much as to make your first coat of black look like slate-color by the side of it. The variety of hues producible by glazing is infinite, and yet the modern Italians, and, in my time, the French, were utterly ignorant of it. When I was in Rome a German professor of painting asked me what colors I used. My colors, he said, looked like what the old masters used. I told him that I used the ordinary colors, sold by the color-men there, but that the effects he spoke of were produced by *vellatura* (glazing). Happening to have by me an old palette on which some colors had become dry, I took some megilp, asphaltum, and lake, and passed over some dry vermilion and showed him how much it deepened the tone; then with asphaltum and blue I glazed over some yellow and produced a beautiful green, and so with several other colors, which seemed to astonish him like a trick in jugglery. "Aha!" said he, "I have often heard of *vellatura*, but never knew what it meant before." I don't relate this anecdote as redounding to my credit at all, as I did not invent the system, but brought it with me from England.

"'The French, I am told, have already greatly improved in color of late years. When I was in Paris they knew nothing of glazing. I was making a study from a picture of Rubens, one of the Luxembourg collection, and was preparing my picture as I supposed the original to have been prepared, that is, instead of painting up my effect at once, I had painted certain portions different in actual color, to be modified afterward by glazing. I was somewhat annoyed in the course of my work by observing that the French artists were deriving great amusement from my picture at my expense. They frequently watched my progress and tittered together in groups. Some of them went to Vanderlyn (who was then in Paris) and told him there was a countryman of his in the gallery whom they pitied very much; I was in a sad mess, they said, and evidently didn't know what I would be at.

"'It happened, however, that one morning when I had commenced my preparation for glazing, and had commenced glazing a part of my picture, a Roman cardinal and his suite was passing through the gallery. You are aware that among the Italian clergy are many men who, having great learning and taste, devote much of their attention to the study of the fine arts, and become, in fact, much better judges of art than the present artists; not studying the art professionally, they do not, like the artists, become blinded by prejudices in favor of this or that system, but judge by the effects. As this cardinal was passing by me he stopped and examined my work with evident interest. He asked me of what country I was, where I had studied, etc., and ended with a compliment. "Monsieur," said he, "vous vous entendez; je vous en fais mes compliments." ("I see, sir, you understand what you are about; accept my congratulations.") I don't hesitate to repeat this compliment, because I considered it as paid to the English school of color, where I had learned this process, and when some of the Frenchmen afterward made me the *amende honorable* for their previous rudeness, I disclaimed the merit of the compliment for the same reasons?

"Mr. Allston one evening commenced a conversation on the subject of backgrounds, by remarking that he had been exceedingly amused that day by an anecdote of a young painter, who, understanding literally Sir Joshua Reynolds's precept, that the painter should on the background disperse all the treasures of his palette, actually compounded with his palette-knife all the odd tints which happened to remain on his palette, and having plastered on this muddy compound, really fancied that it gave a harmony to his picture! 'All that Sir Joshua meant,' said he, 'was that the colors of the head or figure should be somewhere repeated, otherwise it would be a spot in the picture. Sir Joshua was the last man to grind his colors together. A background should be painted, however, with a solid body, whether in a portrait or landscape. If the background of a portrait, for instance, instead of being painted solidly, be washed or glazed up strongly, it will come forward too much, and the head will appear embedded into it ; a thin pellicle of glazing, just enough to give harmony, is sufficient. I had an opportunity of testing the truth of what I say on a large scale. I was painting my large picture of the "Angel Delivering St. Peter from Prison." My figures were all drawn and dead colored ; I had made out the lines of the architecture and washed in the background with umber ; this gave me my effect of light and shade, and served to prevent any uncovered canvas from disturbing my eye while painting my figures. I then finished my figures, and Mr. Leslie happening to see the picture in that stage, I remarked to him, that, according to Mr. West's theory, I ought not to touch my background again. Mr. West had at that time a theory (which I think he must have adopted late in life, as his early practice does not savor of it at all), that "*if you once lose the ground of your canvas in the background, it is not within the reach of art to supply the loss.*" "Now," said I to Leslie, "I think I can prove to you that this is an error ; I will paint over this background a new one which will make it as flimsy as a gauze veil." Accordingly I prepared my palette with a variety of tints mixed with white, and painted over a small portion, say about half a yard. I then retired a short distance to observe the effect. To my great dismay, I found it looked weak and chalky to the last degree. I had used, as I thought, very strong color, and yet, by the side of the glazed portions even vermilion and white looked like slate color. A new thought struck me. I became convinced that my principle was right, but my palette was in this case wrong. I swept it clean of the tints I had prepared ; I took off a pint of paint, and then took a bladder of pure yellow ochre and emptied it upon my palette ; for my red I ground two whole papers of pure vermilion, and so with all the colors I wanted, with the exception of ultramarine ; to give body to that I added

The Stoning of St. Stephen.

From the original sketch in the possession of Jared B. Flagg, of New York.

a little white; this was the only color I used with any white. I then went to work again, and with these pure colors—blue, red, and yellow—I painted away fearlessly and found the result just as I had anticipated. I found that with this strong color I could match my glazed background perfectly; it was already made out, in lines, form, and chiaro-oscuro, and all I had to do was to match as I went on. The prison-walls were illuminated by a supernatural light, and the focus of it was on the walls behind the angel. I there used almost pure yellow ochre, and in order to make the lights upon the nailheads of the door, I was obliged to use *pure Naples yellow and vermilion.* When I had done about half of it, I compared the two portions, the old with the new; why, sir, the stones of the wall in the glazed portion looked as if you could blow them down with your breath. I completed the whole of the background in that day, and never had occasion to retouch it, except to give it one general wash of thin as-phaltum glazing. Sir George Beaumont, in a letter to me, speaking of the background of the picture, said, "the back-ground is perfect," and *I think I may say to you that it was as perfect as anything I ever painted or ever shall paint.'*

"This last remark was made in so modest a manner that I felt that the enthusiasm of his manner was all for the art, and that there was no *personal feeling* in it. It was like the enthusi-asm of a chemist in describing a beautiful result of some darling experiment. Mr. Allston then paused a moment and added, 'It was a happy accident, sir.' As if desirous of disclaiming all glory *for himself.*

"Subsequent to the conversation in which Mr. Allston ex-plained his mode of painting flesh, he observed that to a certain degree he practised the same system in painting other sub-stances. 'I paint even my pebbles and rocks on this system, always putting in the high lights with three colors. Any pict-ure in which the high lights are so painted, with the local color true to nature, and the reflexes appropriate to the subject, must be pleasing to the eye; whether the composition of colors will be harmonious is another affair. Field's work on the "Harmony of Colors" is a very scientific and profound book, but I have lately seen a little unpretending book, called "Hay's Harmony of Coloring for Interior Decorations" [since Allston's death it has been favorably reviewed in the *Edinburgh*], which exhibits many important truths in so plain and practical a shape as to make it a most useful work to any artist.

"'I remember receiving a visit from Field when I was in London, and his remarking upon my picture of "The Sisters" [now owned by Mr. Alexander] that it was painted exactly in accordance with his theory of color. I was not then aware that he was preparing a work on the subject, or I should have liked to compare notes with him. I have a rule for composing which sometimes is of use, and it is, I think, less complicated than his; as near as I can explain, it is this: I have, for instance, a figure draped with a compound hue, say a drab; to paint drapery for the next figure I should choose a drab also, but make the predominant color a different one. If the first figure was draped with a yellowish drab I would take a reddish drab for the next, and then a bluish drab, by which means I obtain harmony and melody together. White drapery I paint precisely as I paint flesh, that is, with three tints—blue, red, and yellow—on a very light key of course, and touching pure white into the lightest parts. I have a different process for painting such portions as are represented in large masses all in the light. In such cases in nature the mass of light strikes the eye as all white, and yet on inspection the eye detects often a great variety of tints. To produce this effect I model up my drapery with umber and white, making out the folds and different planes by weakening or strengthening the tints with umber. When this is dry I go over it with pure white, thinly, loading the lights alone with a heavier body of paint. At the proper distance the under shades will show through and diversify the surface, and yet it will appear to be all white. This is characteristic of Titian's white, and generally puzzles the copyists to imitate it. If any portions require deeper shadows than can be given in this way, I then touch them into the white with my three tints, of a tone sufficiently low to produce the desired effect.'

"It becomes a question of considerable interest how far the principle of the last described process was applied by Mr. Allston in his landscapes and other pictures. It would seem to be the key to many of those mysterious effects in which he is unsurpassed by any artist with the exception of Titian—those effects in which he combines breadth of style with the most scrupulous attention to detail. In his picture of 'The Troubadour' [now owned by Mr. John Bryant, Jr.], for instance, every one must be struck with the relief and true modelling of the limbs of the figure, and yet upon close examination they appear painted with a color so uniform that it seems a mystery how such relief can be given by so little variety of tint, were they not first painted with strong variety of light and shade, and then painted over with a tint nearly uniform, through which the under shadows show and give the necessary variety. In the background of the same picture there is another instance of the same effect in color as well as chiaro-oscuro. The marble boy holding a vase on the garden wall is relieved, not only by light and shade, but by opposition of the colors of the sky ; and yet on inspection it is difficult to select a variety, either of tint or hue, sufficient to produce the effect which we see at a distance. One thing is clear, that Mr. Allston did not always trust to mere body-painting and glazing for his effects, as will appear by his own description of another effect.

"He was one evening describing different effects in painting, when I remarked that I had been always struck by the lumi-

nousness of his skies and truth of tone and color of his mountains; that in his mountains he produced an effect which I did
not remember to have seen given by any other painter. 'A
mountain at a great distance,' said I, 'sometimes is so deep-
toned and intense in its color that any tint of blue which will
match it seems to be so strong as to bring it directly into the
foreground, and yet, sir, you contrive to give the deep tone and
keep your mountains at any distance you please. Besides this,
you give a certain mellowness of tone which I can only describe
by saying that your mountains look as if one could with a spoon
help himself easily to a plateful. This idea struck me in your
Alpine scenery, but more particularly in the "Spanish Girl," now
owned by Mr. Clark.'

"Mr. Allston replied, 'I am glad you liked *that* picture, for
I thought I had been happy in that very effect, and I will tell
you how I painted it. I first conceived the process when studying Mount Pilot, in Switzerland. I painted the mountain with
strong tints of pure ultramarine and white of different tints, but
all blue. Then to mitigate the fierceness of the blue I went
over it, when dry, with black and white, and afterward with Indian red and white, not painting out each coat by the succeeding one, nor yet scumbling, but going over it in parts as seemed
necessary. You know that if you paint over a red ground with
a pretty solid *impasto* you get a very different effect of color
from one painted on a blue or yellow ground. Whatever be the
color of the ground it *will* show through and have its effect on
the eye, unless with *malice prepense* you entirely bury it with
opaque color. In this way I went over that mountain, I suppose, *at least twenty times*, and that is the secret of the diapha-
nous effect which you mention.

"'If I wish to paint a clear blue sky, of a warm and brilliant
tone, I dead-color it with orange, grading my tints from deep
orange at the top down to light yellow on the horizon, just as if

I were going to paint an orange sky instead of a blue one. When this is dry, I then paint a sky over it of pure blue and white, grading my tints from dark to light as before, the orange underneath modifies the blue just enough to prevent its looking cold. I finally give it a slight glazing of umber, asphaltum, or any neutral color, which not only gives harmony and atmosphere, but takes away the appearance of paint.

"'The process by which I paint foliage was the result of accident. I was painting a landscape in which a large tree was the most prominent feature. When I had given it the finishing touches, I found that the tree was flat and opaque; the air did not circulate through the leaves and branches. It was a case in which I must "*either make a spoon or spoil a horn,*" for the picture was good for nothing unless I could remedy this defect, and I resolved on a bold experiment. I took pure yellow ochre and dotted leaves all over it wherever I wished the branches to come forward. This gave my tree the appearance of having had a shower of yellow ochre from a dredging-box. When it was dry I gave it a thin glaze of megilp and gold-size, just tinged with asphaltum, and found to my surprise that these last touches were, by the glazing, so assimilated to the former painting that no one could have discovered that they were not painted at one and the same time. I afterward took asphaltum and blue and varied the light and shade of the masses by glazing. I found that by the thinnest possible glaze over any portion I could throw it back and in the deepest shadows; I found that a deeper tint of asphaltum and blue gave just the effect of deep shade— it was just like painting with dark air! The result was that my tree was now better than any I had previously painted, and from that time I reduced the process to a regular system in painting my trees, and even my plants, in the foreground. I paint in the forms of my plants with yellow ochre, Naples yellow, and ultramarine, and then glaze and touch into my glaze. This gives form, light, and shade, and the color of plants; everything but texture; to give this, I finally give them a thin glaze of yellow ochre, which adds the texture also.

"'For glazing foliage and such parts of my picture as I wish to glaze over several times in the same day, I employ a vehicle which I much prefer to megilp, and which would seem to be very nearly the same thing as is said to have been used by Correggio. I mix spirits of turpentine and Japan gold-size in a wine-glass, say half and half, or one-third gold-size and two-thirds spirits of turpentine. This furnishes a very delicate and ethereal medium for my glazing colors, and dries very soon, enabling me to go over my picture a great many times without clogging my canvas with oils and resins.

"'Speaking of vehicles and mediums for color, reminds me of an experiment I tried in my picture of "Elijah in the Desert." My colors were prepared in dry powders, and my vehicle was *skim-milk;* with this I moistened my powdered colors and mixed them of the same consistency as oil colors. My canvas had an absorbent ground, and my colors dried nearly as fast as I could paint. When I had completed my *impasto,* I gave it a coat of copal varnish, and while it was fresh touched into it with transparent oil colors, and afterward glazed it in my usual manner. The picture was finished in an inconceivably short time (although I put into it as much study as in any other), owing to there being no delay from complicated processes. And it was the most brilliant for tone and color I ever painted. Although the experiment succeeded so well in London, where the milk is so bad that it goes by the name of "sky-blue," I have never felt at liberty to try it again, since my return to America. I am confident, however, that great results might be brought about by it.'

"I was one evening present at a conversation between Mr. Allston and a young artist, in the course of which he made several remarks which strike me as worthy of preservation in connection with his art. After some compliments and an assurance (which must have been in the highest degree encouraging, coming from such a source) that he was in the right road, Mr. Allston continued : 'I have frequently been told by friends of yours, sir, that they were *afraid* you were running after the old masters. Now if that frightens them, I *would make every hair on their heads stand on end !* for you may depend upon it that you cannot go to better instructors for your art. From them you will learn the language of your art, and (will learn) to see nature as they saw it. You will understand, of course, that I am not recommending you to *imitate*, but to *study*, them. By studying their works you will imbibe their spirit insensibly ; otherwise you will as insensibly fall into the manner of your contemporaries. The *old* masters are *our* masters, and there is hardly an excellence in our art which they have not individually developed. With regard to preparatory studies, I should warmly recommend your devoting a portion of every day to drawing ; for this reason, that if an artist does not acquire a correct design *while young*, he never will. Sir Joshua Reynolds always felt conscious that his powers were very much limited and his works incorrect for want of the *early habit* of drawing. A painter may be blest with every gift of nature, but unless he has acquired the art of design he can never *express himself.* If you would not be tormented by a consciousness of having noble and beautiful conceptions to which you cannot give birth, you must give much of your time to drawing. For this purpose I should recommend a course of study *somewhat different from what is generally pursued.* I would devote my attention principally to outline. It is perhaps well enough to learn how to make a finished drawing, but when you have once done that, your time had better be spent in making drawings of the figure in highly studied outline only. My own practice is to make a finished outline always before touching the brush to canvas. I

draw the outlines of such figures as I intend to drape, making
out the figure as nicely as if it were to be painted naked. I take
a large, rough piece of common chalk, which makes a broad mark,
and then with my finger or a bit of bread I can rub out a portion and thus get a *little more* or *little less* much better than by
using a fine point. When I have arranged the contour of my
figure or head I trace the final outline with umber. I would
recommend your studying your outline as highly as if it were
not to be disturbed, but when you paint use your *brush as freely
as if you had no outline to go by*. This is the only way to avoid
the hardness of effect which is apt to arise from a close study of
the outline. I frequently paint my figures over the outline and
let my background encroach upon the contour of the figure again
several times in the course of the painting.

   " 'The process of shading with chalks or pencils is, more
strictly speaking, painting, but it is painting with the very worst
of materials. I know of no better exercise in drawing than the
study of Flaxman's " Illustrations ; " and I would make it a rule to
copy two or three figures from them every day. This, of course,
I recommend as an initiatory study. After you have acquired a
readiness of giving the air and spirit of the figure, preserving the
proportions, you will then have recourse to nature and the antique with great advantage. The drawings of the old masters,
which are now preserved with so much care, are almost all studies
in outline and pen sketches. I cannot see how the modern devi-
ation from this practise can be attended with any good. I would
adopt for my motto that of Tintoret, "The design of Michael
Angelo, with the coloring of Titian." But I would modify it by
substituting the design of Raphael for Michael Angelo's, for
Michael Angelo's style of drawing was mannered, peculiar to his
individual nature and intellect, while Raphael's was truer to nature and more suitable to form a school of drawing.

   " 'Be industrious and trust to your own genius ; *listen to the voice within you*, and sooner or later she will make herself understood, not only to you, but she will enable you to translate her language to the world, and this it is which forms *the only real merit of any work of art.*   An artist must give the impress of his own mind to his works or they will never interest, however academically correct they may be.   If you work in this spirit you will often find yourself working for months and months without effecting your purpose, and at last some accident or chance touch will produce an effect which something within you will immediately recognize as true.'

   " Mr. Allston here read the following sonnet, in which he embodied the above ideas.   It forms one of the highest specimens of poetry connected with art :

Sonnet on Art.

O Art, high gift of Heaven ! how oft defamed
When seeming praised !   To most a craft that fits,
By dead prescriptive rule, the scattered bits
Of gathered knowledge ; even so misnamed
By some who would invoke thee ; but not so
By him—the noble Tuscan *—who gave birth
To forms unseen of man, unknown to earth,
Now living habitants ; he felt the glow
Of thy revealing touch, that brought to view
The invisible Idea ; and he knew,
E'en by its inward sense, its form was true ;
'Twas life to life responding—highest truth !
So through Elisha's faith the Hebrew youth
Beheld the thin, blue air to fiery chariots grow.

[This sonnet, I think, adds great force and meaning to the above remarks.]

   " ' I sometimes think that to an artist great riches would be-

---

* Michael Angelo.

come valueless; he would have no occasion for them. For myself I can truly say that I have no pleasures out of my art. Of
late years my health has obliged me often to relax my efforts,
and I sometimes accept invitations to dinners, or social meetings with my friends, to divert my mind, but I generally submit
to it as if a tooth were to be drawn. I often wish I could live a
thousand years to enable me to execute all my designs, for it
seems [and here he laughed very merrily at his own enthusiasm]
as if time is only valuable to be employed in painting and all
objects only useful as they are good to be painted.'

"I remember a few remarks of Mr. Allston's made upon
different pigments, which, although not generally interesting,
might perhaps be worthy of being preserved in a note. Speaking of white-lead, he lamented bitterly that the manufacturers, in
endeavoring to obtain great purity of white had ruined the body
of this most useful pigment. 'I very much prefer white-lead to
Cremlitz white or silver white. I do not care so much about the
extreme whiteness as the opacity. Nowadays they have almost
entirely purged all body from it to make it pure. It looks beautifully white, but you might almost as well paint with snow! Brilliancy of color depends more upon the opacity of the lights than
the transparency of shadows, because the proportion of shadow to
light is but small. It was a false idea of Rubens, *that white is the
poisoner of shadow*, and that saying of his has, I fear, led many
astray. I introduce white always into my shadows, for, although
I prepare my shadows first by laying them in with olive, I
always break in tints compounded with white. Sir Joshua Reynolds did not like vermilion, but he was obliged to come to it at
last, and those pictures which he painted with vermilion are the
only ones which have stood the test of time. I contrive to give
my vermilion the *spunk* of lake by touching in blue (ultramarine)
even in the red of the cheeks; not by painting with it so as to
leave it apparent, not by mixing it with the red, but with a deli-

cate touch, as it were, fusing them together. Whenever I use lake I add a very little vermilion to give it body.

" 'Raw sienna and burnt sienna are very powerful colors, but require to be used with great care; they are such *stainers*—so little produces such strong effects. There is nothing like raw sienna for painting the lights of gold, when mixed with white. Naples yellow makes *brass*, but not *gold*. I painted my vase of gold in "Belshazzar" in this way; for the reflexes I was obliged to mix Indian yellow and vermilion to avoid the use of red-lead, which changes color with time. Prussian blue is a most useful color for glazing. With Prussian blue and asphaltum you may, by repeated glazings, get any depth of tone you wish. If desirable, you can get a warm tone from them by adding good madder lake. If Prussian blue did not change in hue it would be the best color for skies; it is nearer to sky-color, when fresh, than ultramarine, but changes directly. But of all colors the most unexceptionable is ultramarine. I remember reading of Van Dyck's having received a present from some prince of *twenty pounds* of it! I think that for that moment I *envied* Van Dyck more than if I had heard of his receiving as many thousand pounds sterling.'

It is difficult to speak of the character or works of Mr. Allston without seeming to run to excess in eulogium and superlative praise. I leave to an abler hand the pleasing task of tracing the perfection of his intellectual and religious nature and content myself with giving my humble testimony in favor of the graceful dignity, the refined elegance, and benignant urbanity of his manners. In this respect he was the perfect model of a gentleman. Etiquette of the most approved mode, and conforming to the strictest rules of conventionalisms at upon him like an easy, familiar garment; while it fitted him to mingle with the noble and refined, it was never felt to be oppressive by those of the most simple and homely breeding. Envy, malice, and detraction alone felt rebuked by his presence. It was impossible to converse with him without being made to feel that his mind, by nature benevolent in the highest degree, had been, by religious culture, so chastened and purified as to elevate him beyond the influence of petty passion and weaknesses. He seemed, like a superior being, to sit in sunshine above the clouds and storms which, alas! but too often overshadow the children of this world.

"As an artist it is not easy to compare him with those who have enjoyed the same degree of reputation. Combining as he did the excellences of all the old masters he still kept free from their individual defects. He seems early to have adopted Tintoret's idea of forming a perfect school of art, and has certainly succeeded better than any painter since the time of Raphael in analyzing the processes of the old masters and making them subservient to the embodiment of his own conceptions. He was a thorough proficient in every branch of art; not only drawing his figures with the most academical correctness, but even modelling his forms with great mastery in order that beauty of form and delicacy of organization, the highest excellence of sculpture, might in his works be superadded to painting.

"Of his proficiency in the sister art, sculpture, I remember several specimens, in particular a clay model for the head of the Prophet Jeremiah, of the size of life, and a colossal foot which he had occasion to introduce in one of his large pictures. The last, from its masterly style and exquisitely idealized form, might well be mistaken for a cast from the antique.

"In speaking of his contemporaries he was most liberal of praise, awarding to each the highest degree of merit to which he considered him entitled. If he had occasion to speak of defects, it was evident that he did so from a regard to truth, and that it gave him no pleasure to dwell upon them. He had a familiar maxim, which seems to have been his guide in speaking of works of art, that it is an easy matter to find fault, but to praise judiciously requires an intimate and extended knowledge of art.

" The old masters were to him the patriarchs of the painter's religion, of whom he always spoke with reverence, and to whom he looked for lessons in the practice of his art. Had he ever spoken slightingly of them or let drop one word from which we could infer that he would detract from their reputation, we might hesitate to assign him a place among them ; if it be true, as has been asserted, that Michael Angelo ever spoke disparagingly of the Greeks, it must raise a doubt whether an incapacity to appreciate them must not rank him their inferior. But if genuine unaffected modesty is a sure proof of real merit, the name of Allston must one day take a high rank, even among the *Old Masters*."

The following letter was written by Allston to H. Pickering, as a memorandum of general and specific counsel for the painter Thomas Cole, then a young artist on the eve of departing for study in Europe :

"BOSTON, November 23, 1827.

" MY DEAR SIR : To be of service to young artists of merit has at all times been to me a pleasant duty; I need hardly say, then, that in serving any friend of yours I shall find real pleasure. Therefore I most cordially comply with your request. As the limits of a letter, however, will not allow me to offer more than a few general hints, I beg that what I have to say may be considered merely as such, and that some allowance may be made for the want of connection. The narrowness of my limits must be my apology for abrupt transitions.

" As you have not mentioned for what part of Europe your friend intended to embark, I suppose you have left it to me to advise on this point. If so, I want to recommend his going first to England, where I would have him remain at least half the time he proposes to remain abroad. The present English school comprises a great body of excellent artists, and many eminent in every branch. At the head of your friend's department he will find Turner, who, take him all in all, has no superior of any age. Turner's 'Liber Studiorum' would be a most useful work for him to possess. I venture to say this without having seen it, but coming from *him* I know what it must be. There are many other admirable landscape painters whom I could also name, but your friend will hear of them before he has been long in London. I advise this disproportionate stay in England because I think it important that the *first bias* he receives should be a good one, inasmuch as on this not a little of the future tone of his mind will depend. This bias (in art as well as manners) is taken from the living, whether we choose it or not; and to impart a true and refined one, together with sound, practical principles, I know no modern school of landscape equally capable with the English; in my judgment it has no living rival; many of them having attained to high excellence, and all knowing, even those who cannot reach it, in what it consists. On quitting England a short time may be spent in France, two or three months in Switzerland, and the remainder of the time in Italy. It is hardly necessary to lay out any plan for your friend when he visits these countries, as he will be enabled to form one more suited to his peculiar wants by the advice of artists recently returned from the Continent, whom he will meet in London.

"You say that your friend is a passionate admirer of nature. Let him never lose his love for her. This may perhaps seem to him impossible. But there are artists, as well as connoisseurs, who, as Sir Joshua Reynolds says, 'have quitted nature without acquiring art.' To avoid this the young artist should study nature and pictures together; he will find they mutually reflect light upon each other. By studying the works of other men we are in effect appropriating to ourselves their experience;

in this way we may be said to multiply our eyes and to see a thousand things that might otherwise elude us; in studying nature we are enabled to separate, in art, the true from the factitious; thus we become learned in both. In no other way can a sound critic be formed, much less a sound artist. As every artist must begin by taking things on trust, it is of the last importance that he does not misplace his admiration, for it is not so easy to unlearn as it is to learn. Hence I would advise the student to select his models from among the highest. In imitating these no doubt the difficulty will be greater than if he felt he followed those who seem nearer to himself; but high attempts have this double advantage, that they make us better acquainted with what we *cannot*, as well as what we *can* do. Nor is the former an unimportant piece of knowledge, if we have but the courage to meet it; it is profitable in more than one sense; since the very process by which we attain to it strengthens our powers in having tasked them to the utmost. If many men fail from attempting too much, there are also some who owe their want of success to having attempted too little. For I believe it to be no less difficult for a great mind to excel in trifles, than for a narrow mind to produce a great work. I would therefore recommend it to your friend to place at the head of his list Claude, Titian, the two Poussins, Salvator Rosa, and Francesco Mola, together with Turner and the best of the modern artists, whom I cannot be supposed as meaning to exclude after what I have already said of the English School. I would have him study them all, and master their principles and examine their masses of light and shadow and color; observe what are the shapes of these, and how they recall and balance each other; and by what lines, whether of light, shadow, or color the eye travels through the pictures. Among the painters I have mentioned (with the exception of the two Poussins) no two styles will be found to have the least resemblance, yet they are not more unlike than nature often is at different times to herself. It is for the sake of the difference that I recommend them ; as the exclusive study of any one of them, though by the brightest intellect, would never make even a tenth-rate Titian or Claude, much less an original painter.

" Every original work becomes so from the infusion (if I may so speak) of the mind of the artist, and of this the fresh materials of nature alone are susceptible. The works of man cannot be endued with a second life, that is, with the mind of another ; they are to another as air already breathed. It is this imparted life which we call genius ; we know not how communicated, or what it is, but the spirit within us discerns it in an instant, whether in a picture or poem, and we pity, love, admire, or give the reins to the mind to travel where it listeth through the nameless regions of reverie. It is not unusual for young artists to be startled at the depth of tone and the powerful chiaro-oscuro of the old masters, and to think them exaggerated, if not unnatural. But the old masters were not only true, but in their best works express the highest truth, such as nature reveals only to a gifted few. Their effect may be called the poetical moods of nature, occurring rarely, and only known to occur in poetical minds. Sir Joshua has the same thought somewhere, though he has expressed it better. I think it is Young who says, ' an undevout astronomer is mad.' This may also apply to the painter. It has been my happiness to know many artists who were no less estimable for their moral and religious characters than distinguished for their genius. I hope your young friend may be added to their number. He has chosen a profession in itself innocent, if properly pursued, that is, for its own sake, in a high degree elevating. Indeed it seems as if no one could truly love nature without loving its divine author, who in all his works, even in the terrible, if rightly understood, no less than in the beautiful, speaks only in the language of love.

"I feel assured that to you I need not apologize for these concluding remarks; when we hear of a young man of genius, it is natural to wish him a happiness proportioned to his endowments. I remain, my dear sir, with the highest esteem and respect, sincerely yours,

" WASHINGTON ALLSTON."

Following is an extract from a letter by Allston to John Greenough, written in 1827 :

"I am glad to hear that you are devoting your time to drawing. No reputation, however high during the artist's life, will survive it, except he be a first-rate colorist like Sir Joshua. But great as he was, and you know my admiration of him, I still think he would have been ten times greater had he known how to draw; for he had both character and expression, and only lacked the higher invention because he wanted the means of embodying his conceptions. His capacity for inventing showed itself in his backgrounds and his chiaro - oscuro, and it would have been equally rich, I have no doubt, in form, had he been equally master of that.

"I am persuaded that anyone may learn to draw accurately if he will only be patient and peg for it. To draw finely, that is with grace and beauty, is another thing. This requires vigorous genius, but no one can know if he has this genius until he has first fagged to acquire accuracy. I am myself too much fagged with my day's labor, or would willingly fill this paper, so I must bid you good-night. God bless you.

" WASHINGTON ALLSTON."

CHAPTER XVIII.

From Allston's return to Boston, in 1818, to 1827, he kept
up his correspondence with Leslie, to whom he revealed himself
with confidence and affection. After 1827 intervals between his
letters to Leslie began to lengthen, and he wrote more frequently
to Gulian C. Verplanck, of New York, and John F. Cogdell, of
Charleston, S. C. Cogdell was a young artist friend for whom
Allston seemed to have the warmest regard. He wrote to him
with openness, as to a younger brother. This feeling as of
kindred, was shared by Allston's mother, who said she regarded
Cogdell as a son.

In his correspondence with Leslie, Verplanck, and Cogdell,
running from 1818 to 1843, Allston gives us a record, from which
had nothing more been preserved, we would be able to form a
clear estimate of his character. These letters need no word of
comment or explanation, and we give them with confidence that
they will be found extremely interesting :

From Allston to Cogdell.

"BOSTON, July 1, 1826.

"DEAR COGDELL: I suppose you know that I am not formed
for being a very frequent correspondent. I must acknowledge
that I am not. Perhaps, however, were the number of letters

known which I write in the course of a year, I might not be
thought quite so sad a one. That I write many letters, then,
supposes many correspondents, which is indeed the case—in
Europe as well as here. When this is considered, together with
the little leisure which my arduous profession leaves me, I feel
very sure you will allow much for me.

"When I wrote the passage which you quote from my letter
in your last, I sincerely entertained the hope it expressed; but
it was grounded on the contingency of my possessing the health
and ability requisite to complete the work on which many other
of my hopes have been raised. And I failed from the want of
both. In addition to other calamities I was taken from my labors
two months at one time by a severe attack of influenza. Indeed
it is no exaggeration to say that I have lost, by illness and bad
weather, more than four months since October. You tell me
very kindly to keep up my spirits; I thank you. It has been no
easy matter to do so, I assure you. Were nothing at stake, at
least were the stake any other than it is, I should count these
interruptions and delays as nothing, for I may say from experience that I am patient of toil and obstacle; but when the thought
crosses me of how much is depending on my present labor, I
have need indeed of all my philosophy to keep in heart. Affliction and various misfortunes have long since taught me the duty
of resignation. I may say that I have been inured to disap-
pointments; not that I do not keenly feel them, but that I have
learned to submit to them, and it is well for my present work
that I have been, requiring as it does not only all my faculties
but their free exercise. I cannot say, however (though proof
against absolute despondency), that I have always been able to
sustain that entire self-possession so essential to their freedom.
I could not always drive from me the benumbing, anxious
thought; it would come in the midst of my work; and there have
been times when it has fallen upon me like the gigantic hand in

the 'Castle of Otranto,' as if it stretched forth from my picture, and was about to crush me through the floor. This may seem strong; but if you ever felt the 'sinking of the heart,' when in the midst of a work, on the success of which your all depended, and that success, too, depending on a thorough self-possession, you will not think it too strong. This may in part account for my doing and undoing and doing again what, in happier moments, I might have done at once. But this is to me a reluctant subject, and I will spare you as well as myself. And it is better that I say no more about my picture until I can have the pleasure of telling you that it is finished. This, however, I may allow myself to say now, that I have never been so well satisfied with my labors as within the last three months. My health is so much improved that I work eight or nine hours a day.

"My friend Mr. Amory has informed me that you had remitted to him, while he was in Philadelphia, the amount of your subscription, for which I beg you to accept my thanks. I shall not, however, appropriate it to my own use until 'Belshazzar' is ready for delivery to the subscribers. In the meantime Mr. Amory, who is so kind as to act as 'Bel's' treasurer, has placed it to your account, and considers it on interest, for which he will account to you on the completion of the picture, when I receive the principal.

"I have been much gratified by your remarks on my picture of the 'Dead Man' at Philadelphia, and I thank you heartily for the praise bestowed, which is high enough, I am sure, to have satisfied me, had my pretensions been much greater. My recollection of the picture is now so indistinct that I should not venture, were I so inclined, to controvert the few objections you have made. It is most probable, were I to see it again, I should agree with you in all, with one exception, and I have no doubt I could point out many faults which your partiality has overlooked. The exception alluded to is to the remark of the heads

*Dead Man Revived by Touching the Bones of the
Prophet Elijah.*

From the original in the possession of the Philadelphia Academy of Fine Art.

of the two Feretrori being two small. Whatever of style the character of the design may possess is owing, I think, to this proportion. It is grounded on a sound principle extracted from the study of the antique and the old masters, particularly the latter. Michael Angelo owes much of his grandeur to this principle. He has pushed it indeed much farther than I should dare to follow it. I have been much struck, however, with the justness of your objection to the introduction of the wife of the reviving man; it is so just that were I to compose the subject again I should omit her. The incident (her fainting) is dramatic, and as such does not harmonize with the miracle, which is epic.

"Sincerely yours,

"W. ALLSTON."

From Allston to Leslie.

"BOSTON, November 9, 1826.

" DEAR LESLIE : I write you again, and yet not with the intention of fulfilling my long-made promise of a long letter. But I know you will readily forgive the delay when you shall hereafter learn the cause. I have had many things to depress me, and to indispose me for writing about myself. I could never see the benefit, either to ourselves or our friends, of talking about our misfortunes; so I make it a rule to spare both parties by holding my tongue till I can use it to a more useful or pleasurable purpose. I trust, however, that the difficulties under which I have so long labored will soon be at an end, and leave me in a condition to play the part of Hero to a letter, with some pleasure to you and without pain to myself. But all this between ourselves, and—I will add—Collins, to whom I wish you to assign it as the cause of my not writing him, telling him at the same time that I will make him ample amends when my bright day comes.

"My purpose in writing to you now is to ask your good office in behalf of a most valued friend, one who has been to me a friend indeed, and to whom I could render no service that would make me less a moral debtor. Kindness when disinterested can never be repaid, and such has his been to me. This preface might perhaps seem to announce a more important service than the one I would here render Mr. Amory; but I could not forbear saying what I have, or indeed adding, *malgré* the occasion, that he is one of the few men who would find it impossible to make you feel 'gratitude as a *brother*.' But to the point: Mr. Amory has shipped by the Plato, for Liverpool, three pictures, which will be sent to Messrs. Baring & Bates, London, for sale. Now, the favor I have to ask you is to go and look at them, and if they please you, to make favorable mention of them to such gentlemen, should you know any, as you may think likely to become purchasers. In making this request Mr. Amory would not for the world wish you to utter a syllable in their favor unless you liked the pictures; nor would I propose it on any other condition. All we ask is your unbiassed opinion, and good word, if favorable and if the opportunity occur to speak it. This being premised (as the lawyers say) I may now give my opinion, but I give it without even the wish that it should affect yours, however confidently I speak. The Claude is genuine; I have no doubt of it whatever. No other man ever painted such an atmosphere as is there. Of the Salvator Rosa—I have too little acquaintance with Salvator's hand to say whether it is by him or not. But if it is not by him it must be an original by some other master; it does not look like a copy. But by whomsoever it may be, I think it a very fine picture. And so it seems to have been thought by others, having been sold many years since in Paris for two thousand dollars, and at a time when the English were not there, and of course money more scarce. It went thence to Switzerland. The Backhuysen, so far as I am acquainted with the master, appears to be genuine. And this, too, if not a Backhuysen, I would venture to say is no copy. These pictures, before they came into Mr. Amory's possession, belonged to Mrs. Amory's uncle, who lived many years in France, and I believe died there. You will no doubt remember Mrs. and Mr. Amory in London. They well remember you.

"And now accept my congratulations on the birth of your son and heir; I hope he will inherit (if your modesty will allow me to say it) both your virtues and genius. At any rate, he may the former, as he will have the advantage of his father's example; and should that only fall to his lot, better that than only the latter, for goodness before greatness every wise man must wish in those he loves.

"I enclose a letter to Mr. Howard requesting him to transfer to you one of the tickets to which I am entitled as an associate; the other I have asked him to give to Collins. Though it is but a trifle yet I know he will accept it as a mark of my continued regard, which I can assure him has not abated an atom, in spite of time and distance.

"I have not seen Dr. Channing for a fortnight; he has been in the country."

From Allston to Cogdell.

"BOSTON, June 21, 1827.

"DEAR COGDELL: I have just heard of your arrival in New York, and I send you these few lines to bid you welcome by anticipation to Boston, for now, that you are so near, I cannot doubt that you intend to favor us with a visit. As I am so much in arrears to you in letters, if my apologies were in proportion I fear I should have little room for anything else were I to attempt them now, so, as I hope soon to have the pleasure of seeing you, I shall defer them till then. In the meantime, to take something from my apparent remissness, I must tell you that I sent you (in a letter to my mother), some time since, a message respecting your bust of Dr. Holbrook, which I desired her to tell you I thought did you great credit. I may now add that I consider it, for a first attempt, a very remarkable performance, and one which gives assurance of future excellence. With some practice and a little hard fagging (you know my doctrine, that nothing is to be done without it), I think you will be able safely to sign yourself sculptor. What particularly pleased me in the bust was the strong, marked character, which satisfied me, though I have never seen the living original, that it must be an excellent likeness. Next to that was the truth of the several quantities, a particular in which most beginners are mainly lacking. As to the faults, they are such as proceed from inexperience, and which time, of course, will soon enable you to correct. *I pede fausto.*

"I suppose you have heard of our Exhibition here. As I am so large a contributor, I suppose I must be careful, in speaking of it, to except my own works. This, however, I need not be scrupulous about in writing to you, who I know would never suspect me of self-praise. The Exhibition, then, has surprised everybody, myself among them. I assure you that I have seen worse in London. And what has also been an agreeable matter of wonder is the astonishing success it has had with the public. Day after day and week after week it has been thronged to a most delightful degree of annoyance—delightful, at least, to the astonished artists, to whom it might well have been *jam jam*, but never *satis*. I have seen no account of the Exhibition at New York. I hope it has been as successful a one. The receipts here have been upward of three thousand dollars. I saw, however, a very handsome notice of my friend Morse's address. Pray tell him to send me a copy of it by you."

From Allston to Leslie.

"BOSTON, August 12, 1827.

"DEAR LESLIE: This will be handed to you by Mr. John Greenough, with whom (if he is not already known to you), I beg to make you acquainted. He has had the advantage of a liberal education, and you will find him one of cultivated mind, and of good taste in letters, which, though it does not qualify a man to judge of pictures, much less to paint, must still be a matter of no small moment to a young artist, inasmuch as refinement in things even minutely connected with it, will render him less liable to contract vulgar or narrow views of art. He that has elevated views on one subject which he has cultivated, is not likely to form mean ones on any other to which he may give his mind. In the truth of this I know you will agree with me, and also in the opinion that no artist of real eminence can be found of vulgar taste, even on subjects wholly foreign to his art.

. . . .

"Ever truly yours,

"WASHINGTON ALLSTON."

From Allston to Verplanck.

"BOSTON, January 31, 1828.

"MY DEAR SIR: I read your book, 'Evidences of Revealed Religion,' with more than pleasure, I trust with spiritual profit; many of your arguments appeared to me new; the whole, I thought cogent and eloquent. As to the dedication, I could wish I had better deserved it; at any rate, I am grateful for its kindness.

"Your kindness is indeed unremitting, for I have again to thank you for your letter of the 9th, enclosing the report of the 'Debates.' Will you do me the favor to present my best acknowledgments to Major Hamilton for the very kind and flattering notice with which he was pleased to honor me in his eloquent speech in Congress.

"You will probably soon meet in Washington with a young sculptor and friend of mine, Mr. Horatio Greenough, who has a letter to you from Mr. Dana; he was educated at our college, and has passed two years in Italy, which, from ill-health, he was obliged to leave in the commencement of a career of no common promise. It is his intention, however, to return thither, when his purse will let him, and I think I hazard nothing in saying that, before many years, I shall look for his station among the very first in his art. He has genius, harmony, and modesty. The last, I would fain believe, is always the natural shadow of the first. At least it follows his genius like one of the quiet backgrounds of Van Dyck. He is, besides, a gentleman, not merely in manners, but in that better quality which does not meet the eye. Indeed I esteem his character as a man no less than I admire his genius as an artist. I feel sure you will be pleased with him. His main object in visiting Washington is to model a bust of the President. His likenesses are very striking, as he works with as much facility as a painter, indeed more, as he suffers the original to walk about while he is working, which a painter could not do. I hope he will find many others to model, as I know that his purse is not over heavy. Lest others, however, should mistake him for a mere sculptor of busts, I may here observe that he is not confined to portraits, but has studied and is qualified to shine in the highest branch of his art, the inventive; an evidence of which we have in his 'Dead Abel,' an original, full-sized statue, which he brought home from Italy, a figure of beauty and truth, and such a *first work* as I have never before seen.

"Believe me, ever truly yours,

"W. ALLSTON."

From Allston to Cogdell.

"BOSTON, March 21, 1828.

"DEAR COGDELL: I received your letter of the 8th inst. at a late hour last evening, and proceeded to answer it without delay; though I fear that on the point on which you are so desirous of having my opinion I cannot reply with that decision which long experience has enabled me to exercise on questions relating to my own branch of the art. It is certainly true, as you observe, that more expression is given to the eye by carving the retina, and yet it is not practised by the moderns, any more than by the ancients, except in portraits. In this branch it was sometimes practised by the Greeks, especially those who flourished under the Cæsars; of this I remember an instance, in the head of the Emperor Lucius Verus. But why it should be confined to portraits I confess I can see no good reason. Yet the sculptor might be able to assign a very satisfactory one. Indeed, on reflection, I cannot but think they are governed in it by some sound principle, as otherwise the practice would not have been so universal; for I cannot call to mind an example to the contrary in any ancient statue not professedly a portrait. I state this candidly, lest my own inability to account for it should seem to incline me to justify a departure from it. But, though the question may be said to lie out of my peculiar province, and is consequently one on which I should speak with diffidence, there is yet a general (maxim) principle, applicable to all arts, or rather, I should say, essential to their successful cultivation, concerning which I feel no such distrust, namely, that if the peculiar process or mode by which we propose to produce a desired effect be the suggestion of a strong impulse, it is better to risk it than to follow the prescription of any authority however high. It is only (if I may be allowed the phrase) by thus acting out themselves that men of genius originate new modes of excellence and widen the sphere of intellect. The very difficulties which an untried course presents are but so many additional stimulants to invention, which often grows, like the fabled salamander, after six years unsuccessful heating of the furnace, out of the fire of the seventh. When our rule fails it is time enough to adopt that of others. We shall adopt it then with more advantage from the conviction that ours was insufficient. But I should be slow to give up any strong impulse, in anything relating to the art, until it had proved its own insufficiency. I would first give it fair play, and convince myself before I deferred to the judgment of others. Many an artist has drawn the world after him by resolutely following the path which it had predicted would lead to nothing, or worse than nothing. Two painters, and one of them no less a man than Tintoret, advised Ludovico Caracci to give up painting for some other employment more suited to his abilities; but Ludovico knew what was in him; he persevered and became the founder of the great Bolognese School.

"If I have expressed myself with sufficient clearness you will perceive that the result of these remarks is intended to confirm you in the mode you have chosen to treat your subject, that is, to express the retina. If you do it to satisfy yourself, I think I may venture to say that you will be more likely to please others than if you followed mere authority without conviction. When it is finished let me know, without reserve, what you think of it yourself. I am glad to find you persevere, and congratulate you on your success in General Moultrie's head. By the way, J. R. Smith has lately published a very valuable work on what he calls 'Picturesque Anatomy,' exhibiting the skeleton through the muscles. It is copied from the work of an old Spanish painter; and though the outlines are in bad taste (which is the fault of the original) it is the best treatise for an artist I have seen. I will send you a copy by the first opportunity by water.

"As for myself, I am well at present. But I have been far otherwise, having had, by the blessing of Providence, a narrow escape from death — so near that the doctor said had he been fifteen minutes later I should have died. I was poisoned by eating partridge. God bless you.

" Your sincere friend,

" W. ALLSTON."

From Allston to Cogdell.

"BOSTON, August 3, 1828.

"DEAR COGDELL: It was my wish to have written to you long ago, but many things have prevented me; among others not the least has been low spirits, for I have had much to depress me. For this last reason I doubt not you will readily, and as you always do, kindly excuse the delay. It has been in this, as in many other instances, no slight aggravation of my depression that it unfitted me for answering those calls of friendship and duty which I most anxiously desired to fulfil. But I never like to speak of my low spirits, and always avoid it, unless the occasion makes it necessary. Such an occasion seems to me the present; and I mention it that you might know why I have so long delayed telling you how much I like your last work, the bust of General Moultrie. Though I expected considerable improvement on your first effort, I found it very much to exceed my expectation, and most heartily do I congratulate you on your success. I can feel no doubt as to the strength of the likeness, though I knew not the old patriot; I feel assured of it from the strong individual character it possesses—speaking to the spectator in the language of a peculiar mind. In this you have effected the chief purpose of the sculptor's art, without which the most expert management of the material, or the most elaborate finish, is but the triumph of the craftsman. Character, character in your art as well as in mine, is that which shows the artist, since it is the fruit of the intellect, not of the hand and eye, which we may often see trained to a high degree of skill, with but small aid from the head. Hogarth used to complain bitterly of the engravers whom he occasionally employed to assist him, some of them his superiors too, in the mechanical part, though not to be named with him in mind. 'Hang your beautiful lines,' he would say; 'give me character, if you do it with a hobnail.' He often obliterated weeks of their fine work without compunction. I think it is hardly necessary for me to say ' Go on,' for you ought now to feel confidence in yourself. If you have it not, I hope my sincere testimony will impart some. For as confidence in a weak mind must always, from increasing its weakness, end either in vanity or despair, so in a strong one will the want of it render its very strength abortive. And I doubt if as many men have not failed from distrusting as from overrating their powers. Let me therefore urge you to rely on the strength which you have shown you possess, as one of the essentials of success.

"You have probably heard of our friend Stuart's death. He had been breaking above a year past, and he seemed to have been aware for some months before that he could not survive long. The art as well as his country has suffered a loss in him that will not soon be supplied. The infirmities under which he labored, even during the last ten years of his life, though they kept him poor, did not however, as his later works bear witness, extend to his mind. His mind indeed was vigorous to the last, and his bereaved family have this consolation, that he has left nothing in his Art, old and infirm as he was, to take from his great name. 'Tis, alas! the only consolation he had it in his power to leave them, for they are quite destitute. But they have not been without sympathy from the people of Boston, who have got up an exhibition of such of his works as could be collected, for their benefit; in addition to which they have opened a subscription for the purchase of his ' Head of Washington,' at two thousand dollars, for the Athenæum. If your Annual Exhibition were profitable (which I think I understood you to say it was not) I should propose you granting them the benefit of a week or two during your next season. I wrote a short notice of Mr. Stuart, which was published in the *Boston Daily Advertiser* of July 22d; if it has not been copied in your

papers you will probably meet with it at some of the newspaper offices.

"Ever your friend,

"W. Allston."

From Allston to Cogdell.

"Boston, December 21, 1828.

" My Dear Cogdell :

[Portion referring to C.'s recent visit to Boston has been
omitted.]

" I should have liked to have talked with you whole days
about the art, and to have hunted up together every picture in
the town and neighborhood, but of that pleasure, as well as
many others, I was constrained not to think, being then (as I
still am) 'Belshazzar's' slave, as much so indeed as the Genie was
to Aladdin's lamp; I wish I could add with equal power to perform my master's behests; but the painter's magic, as long experience has taught me, is no 'hey, presto,' work. Indeed it is
work—that is, labor, though of the brain, yet labor, which makes
it, as the world might think, no magic at all. This truth would
perhaps have been received by me with an ill grace some twenty
years ago, if at all, by a youthful brain full of magnificent proj-
ects. I thought then, and I suppose like most young artists, that
I had only to dream dreams, and the hand would immediately
embody them; and so it did after a fashion, that is, it put something on canvas, which, by the help of another dream, I made
to resemble the first. But a man who follows up making dreams,
like him who follows up any other (intellectual) manufacture,
soon comes to have a larger apprehension of his business; he
also sees clearer as well as farther every time, every day; what
was before simple becomes complex, what seemed one, a thing
of many parts, all having relation one to another, and each to
the whole; what was apparently plain and easy, intricate and
subtle; in short, the changes stop not till he seems, as it were, to

see quite another thing, and with other eyes. But does not his power increase with his knowledge? Certainly. Yet his labor at the same time accumulates, since his knowledge only informs him that he has more to do. Thus must it be with every artist, if he is not content to repeat himself. If he have a true love of excellence, and the pursuit of it be his real object, he will find it (I should think) impossible to huddle one defect for the sake of sparing himself labor. And if his aim be excellence, though every day makes it more distinct, yet every day also shows its attainment to be more arduous. A sanguine youth may here ask, 'Who then would be a painter?' That same youth, if he have the courage to grow old in his art, might hereafter answer, 'Himself.' For he would then have learned that to overcome a difficulty is to create a pleasure. To advance is a law of the mind; and (so its object be innocent) every obstacle removed clears away a step nearer happiness. To labor, then, is both natural and desirable, and wise, since a wise Providence has so ordained it. What artist would complain of labor? Not I, for one. As it respects the pleasure in my art, I certainly appreciate the moral value of labor too well to complain of it. And yet this one picture, on which I am now employed, has caused me many and many an anxious day. And why? Because on this alone depends so much besides fame. For on this alone has for many years depended the long-hoped for meeting with a good mother and so many other dear relatives. But do not think I am repining, deeply anxious as I have felt, and still feel; I may grieve, but not repine. It becomes not a man of sense nor a Christian to repine at what he cannot help. I have been long schooled to patience and submission; I endeavor to practise them as Christian duties. I am doing my best, and this sustains me, and with Heaven's blessing I look forward to a happy conclusion.

"Your account of Mr. West's picture, as well as I recollect

it, seems to me very just; and I perfectly agree with you in your criticism of the figure of the Saviour. Yet Mr. West has only added one to the uniform failures of all his predecessors. It is, indeed, as you have truly said, ' a face no mortal has ever or can ever portray.' And it is one which I have long since resolved never to attempt. I sincerely thank you for the kind feeling manifested in the concluding remarks of your letter. What I have to say on the subject I must defer till I have the pleasure of seeing you in Charleston, which I still hope for this winter, though it will be much later in the season than I had calculated; for ' Belshazzar,' though near a close, is still unfinished in spite of all my efforts.

"Believe me, with sincerest respect and esteem, truly yours,

"W. ALLSTON."

From Horatio Greenough to Allston.

"FLORENCE, November 17, 1829.

. . . .

"I have tried the receipt you gave me for a palette, and hope one day to arrive at proficiency enough in painting to paint a portrait for my amusement, now and then; but let me protest that of all subjects which I have ever attempted to understand, color is the most subtle, unattainable, and incomprehensible, and by long examination I think I have found that comparatively few pictures are colored. Even those of name, some are drawn in chiaro-oscuro with paint, somewhat approximating in its general tint to seem so. Others are painted in downright light and shade with a little tinge of color glazed into them. Almost all seem to have had a conventional palette, which is too partially or generally reasoned to embrace the variety of nature, or to render her delicate distinctions. Titian is my man, and some of the Dutchmen, too, please me quite as much. There is a picture in the Flemish room, by Giorgione, of Venus on a car with Love by her side, and several marine deities about her, which is one of the most luxurious bursts of light and color that ever feasted the eye—such a union of brilliance and harmony as really surpasses, I think, everything Italian I have seen.

"I found my way the other day to a chamber in the gallery, which seemed to me worth all I had yet seen, 'twas filled with Venetians—Titian, Paul V., Bassano, Giorgione, etc. What brilliancy is there! What music of color! What grandeur of masses! I know not how it is, but it is only when I see a picture of one of these men that I forget my own art and long to be a painter."

"FLORENCE, April 18, 1829.

"I would give more for one impression than for three unanswerable arguments on a question of art, for words are clumsy things after all. I remember that when with you once at Cambridge I asked your opinion on some doubtful point relating to art, and that you said an answer to my question would cost you at least three cigars.

"Sure am I that it would require that number to fit me to describe to you my gratification on reading the verses you wrote on my groups, which lately reached me in a letter from my brother Harry. I believe, my dear sir, that gratified vanity was not the foremost or strongest of my pleasures, for your verses were as far from being addressed to minds of that class as my composition was from being adapted to their tastes."

From Leslie to Allston.

"41 PORTMAN PLACE, EDGEWARE ROAD,
"LONDON, February 17, 1830.

"MY DEAR SIR: I don't know whose fault it is that our correspondence has suffered so long an interruption. But I am willing to take any share of the blame you will lay on me provided you will be quick in bestowing it, and indeed the dread of it is not very great, knowing as I do how gently you deal with all who deserve blame. Our friend Morse, during the short visit he paid to London on his way to Italy, was unable to execute a little commission for you and desired me to attend to it. On receiving the twenty pounds from Brockhedon, and telling him that you wished me to purchase an ounce of ultramarine with part of it, he insisted on sending you some, of which he brought a large quantity from Italy. I have handed fourteen pounds to Greenough, and have six more remaining till I hear from you what I am to do with it.*

" In the hope of provoking a retaliation in kind from you, I have a mind to give you a full account of myself. Here I am, then, with a wife and three children (one boy and two girls) living in a home but two doors from one that was inhabited by my father and mother thirty years ago, when I was an urchin. I take my boy, Robert, who is my eldest, a walking by the Paddington Canal, where my father took me when about his age, to see the men digging. One of my sisters came from America in the same ship with Morse, and is living with us.

"I am now painting a picture from the 'Merry Wives of Windsor,' in which I have introduced nearly all the characters. I imagine them to be assembled after dinner at *Mr. Page's* house, who, you remember, had invited them to make up the quarrel between *Falstaff* and *Shallow*, over a venison pasty. *Falstaff* will be flirting with the two ladies, and *Slender*, seated sheepishly by *Anne Page*. *Mr. Page* is offering the latter some ale from his best silver goblet, by way of making him feel at home. Behind *Falstaff* are *Pistol*, *Nym*, and *Bardolph*, laying their heads together, and perhaps plotting some new roguery. Beyond them are *Sir Hugh Evans* and *Shallow*. The dinner is

* Dana appends to this the following note: " John Greenough was in London and extremely poor and Allston, at this time suffering deep distress of mind for want of money, and paralyzed in his art by it, could not resist disposing of that which, if sent home to him, would have been at least a momentary relief."

just removed, and on a side-table are the 'pippins and cheese,' of which *Sir Hugh* makes mention in the play. I hope to get this picture ready for the Exhibition, and if so I shall have been quicker with it than anything I have painted. I believe I have lost at least half my life in making alterations in my pictures, most of which were perhaps mere changes and additions without being improvements. My wife and children are powerful persuaders to a more rapid course of proceeding.

"You will be surprised to hear that although I have had constant employment for the last fourteen years, I am as poor as when you were here. I am not more extravagant, and my expenses are only the necessary ones of my family. I believe, however, I can paint better and quicker than I ever could, and I have a prospect of doing something by publishing prints of my pictures. I now feel as if I was really in earnest and all my past life but a dream. I sigh in vain over time lost in all sorts of trifling, and make sturdy resolutions to go on vigorously, and, as I hope, in the right path for the future. When I recur to our former intimacy, I feel sure it is to you I owe my first relish for all the best qualities in Art. Many of your maxims that I was not capable of comprehending when I heard them, now come home to me with the fullest conviction of their truth. I wish you were here, and I cannot but think you will come ; I think also you would now be appreciated and patronized. I hear but little of you from Americans who come here. They all describe you as living very retired. They agree in the account that you have painted many small pictures and that you have sold them all advantageously, but that your large 'Belshazzar' is still unfinished. I have no doubt you have painted twenty fine pictures on the canvas of that one. What a pity they could not be separated. I dare say you might finish it as well in three days as in three years if you would have the resolution. I wish you would, and then come immediately to England. With the exception of Mr. West and Sir Thomas Lawrence I believe you were not much acquainted with the principal artists here. You would now be, and I am sure you would enjoy their society as much as I do.

"I need say nothing of the death of Sir Thomas Lawrence, of which, I dare say, full accounts have reached the American newspapers. His loss is much felt in the immediate circle of his friends who well knew the great kindness of his heart. I remember well his passing by on horseback just as you were stepping into the coach to leave London. The farewell you took of each other was forever ; ours, I trust was not. Whenever you come you will find all your friends, who may be left, unchanged, I assure you. I do not think there is a man on earth for whom Coleridge has a higher regard than he has for you. Lord Egremont speaks frequently of you. He says he thinks there is more of the spirit of Raffaelle in your ' Jacob's Dream ' than in any picture he knows of painted since his time. Pray remember me kindly to Mr. Channing, who, I now hear, with great pleasure, enjoys perfect health. I have his essays on Bonaparte and on Milton, both of which I read with the greatest pleasure and admiration of his talents and of his heart.

"My wife, who feels as if she knew you, begs me to offer her best respects to you, and I am, dear sir, yours ever,

"C. R. LESLIE.

"P.S.—I ought to tell you that the *Anne Page* in my picture is painted from Mr. West's granddaughter, whom you must remember as a beautiful child of thirteen or fourteen. She is now married to a Mr. Margany, and is still very handsome."

CHAPTER XIX.

During the year 1830 an interesting correspondence passed
between Allston and Gulian C. Verplanck, in relation to pictures
for the Capitol at Washington. Verplanck was a man of letters, and was a conspicuous figure in public life when politics
and gentlemen were allied. He was Chairman of the Committee
of the House of Representatives on Public Buildings. He
wished Allston to fill, by pictures of suitable subjects, two of the
panels in the Rotunda of the Capitol, and accordingly obtained for
him from Congress an order to paint them. The many advantages secured by such an order, especially for one in need of
money, must have been very tempting to Allston, and from the
stand-point of ordinary men it is difficult to understand how he
could refuse it.

In declining the distinguished honor conferred by assigning
so large a space for his work in the Rotunda, Allston shows the
largeness of his generosity and his freedom from all selfish influences. He recommended, as his substitutes, Morse and Vanderlyn, and with no half-hearted commendation, but in terms of
cordial approval, as men competent to execute the work. Among
his reasons for declining to paint the pictures for the Government
was his inexperience in the line of subjects to which he might be

restricted. But he had said, that though unused to battle-pieces, he sometimes thought he would like to try his hand at one in which he could introduce Indians, with their picturesque costumes, and we are inclined to think that had it not been for the unfinished condition of " Belshazzar," he would have overcome his objections and undertaken at least one of the panels.

From Verplanck to R. H. Dana.

" WASHINGTON, February 17, 1830.

" MY DEAR SIR : I have this moment written to Allston about a picture for our public buildings from his hand, which, as Chairman of the Committee on Public Buildings, I hope to be able to get ordered by Congress, and passed in our general bill for the buildings, etc., without any flourish, or limiting him to any subject of the day. I hope he will answer me without delay, and I must rely upon you to make him do so.

   .   .   .   .

" Before I leave Congress I trust to do the state some service by reducing the magnificent uselessness of our hall, and leaving it to my successors in a state where common-sense can be spoken and heard, and where a shrill voice or else the lungs of a Stentor will not be the chief requisites of a Congressional orator. In other words, I am very busy in studying both the theory and practice of acoustics, for the purpose of improving the hall, and I am convinced that such a reform would do more for the legislature, as well as its taste and eloquence, than any law or constitutional amendment. I feel that I cannot fill my sheet with anything worth reading, and having begun with the benevolent intention of making you act as Allston's flapper, according to the Laputan usage, must end by again urging upon you that duty.

" Yours truly,

" G. C. VERPLANCK."

From Allston to Verplanck.

"CAMBRIDGE, MASS., March 1, 1830.

"MY DEAR SIR: I did not get your letter of the 17th ult. until the night before last (Saturday), and I shall endeavor, agreeably to your wishes, to answer it in a business-like manner, though I have, I fear, but little of that laconic spirit, so essential to it, which I used so much to admire in our excellent friend S. Williams, of Finsbury Square. Without more flourish, then, you could not desire to be more heartily thanked than I thank you for this additional instance of the friendship with which you honor me. These are not words of courtesy, but of grateful truth, and yet I fear there are certain formidable, and to my present apprehension, insurmountable obstacles to my profiting by your kindness. The subjects from which I am to choose, you say, are limited to American History. The most prominent of these, indeed the only ones that occur to me, are in our military and naval achievements. Herein lies my difficulty. I will not say that I doubt—I know that I have not—any talent for battle-pieces; and, perhaps, because they have always appeared to me, from their very nature, incapable of being justly represented; for, to say nothing of the ominous prelude of silent emotion, when you take away the excessive movement, the dash of arms, the deadly roll of the drum, the blast of the trumpet, forcing almost a heart into a coward, the rush of cavalry, the thunder of artillery, and the still more fearful din of human thunder, giving a terrific life to the whole—and all this must be taken from the painter—what is there left for his canvas? It seems to me (at least in comparison with the living whole) *caput mortuum*. All these things, and indeed much more, can be made present to the imagination by words. In this the poet and historian have the advantage of the painter. I know not where, even among the

great names of my art, to look for anything like the living mass
of one of Cooper's battles; there are besides many circumstances
connected with these subjects, such as monotony of color, of costume, of form, together with a smallness of parts (ever fatal to
breadth and grandeur), that make them, at least to me, wholly
untranslatable in the painter's language. The monotony of color
alone would paralyze my hand. Such being my opinion, you will
easily believe that I could have no hope of succeeding in subjects of this nature. Indeed I know from past experience that I
must fail when the subject is not of myself, that is, in relation
to the powers of my art, essentially exciting. In a pecuniary
view it has been, perhaps, my misfortune to have inherited a
patrimony, since it has lasted only just long enough to allow my
mind to take its own course till its habits of thought had become
rigid and too fixed to be changed when change was desirable.
To be more intelligible, having in the commencement of my art,
and for the greater part of my subsequent life, only the pleasure
of its pursuit to consult, I of course engaged in nothing which
had not that for its chief end—the realizing of my conceptions
being my chief reward; for though the pecuniary profit was always an acceptable contingency, it was never at that time an exciting cause; so far from it, that I have in some instances undertaken works for less than I knew they would cost. As an artist
I cannot, in spite of many troubles, regret this freedom of action,
since I feel of such that I owe to it whatever professional skill I
may possess. But of late years, since the source of this liberty
has been dried up, and the cold current of necessity has sprung
up in its stead, I have sometimes, as a man, almost felt the possession to have been a misfortune, for necessity, I find, has no inspiration; she has not with me even the forcing power. Willingly, most willingly, would I have been driven by her, but it
seems that at my age it cannot be; my imagination has become
too fixed in its own peculiar orbit to be moved by anything ex-

trinsic.   In other words, it seems to me almost morally impossible to compose, much less to finish, a picture where the subject
does not afford pleasurable excitement.   I trust you know me too
well to doubt my patriotism because I cannot be inspired to
paint an American battle.   I yield in love of country to no man ;
no one has gloried more in the success of her arms, or more sincerely honored the gallant spirits whose victories have given her
a name among nations.   But they need not my pencil to make
their deeds known to posterity.   Could I embody them as they
deserve, or even make others feel what I have felt, as the fame of
them came to me across the water, while I was in kind, hospita-
ble Old England (for such, even while a foe to my country, she
ever was to me) ; could I send that hearty breeze from our gallant native land to their hearts, there would be no lack of inspiration.   I would invest them with the grandeur of my art, or touch
them not.   But the power is not mine.   I know you will not
doubt the sincerity of this conviction, but you will better estimate the strength of it when I add that at no time would the
commission you propose be more acceptable to me in a pecuniary
view than at present.

"But may there not be some eligible subject in our civil history ?   For myself I can think of none that would make a picture ;
of none, at least, that belongs to high art.   But such a subject
might possibly have occurred to you.   If so, and I find it one from
which I can make such a picture as you would have me paint,
both for my own credit and that of the nation, be assured I will
most gladly undertake it.   I am persuaded, however, that you
will agree with me in this, that no consideration of interest
should induce me to accept any commission from the Government
that will not tax my powers to their utmost.   My best, indeed,
may be all unworthy, but less than that my country shall not
have.   In the meantime, that is, till a practicable subject is
found, I must beg you to suspend, if such is in progress, 'the

order for a picture.' You will readily appreciate the motive for this request, namely, to avoid the censure which the good-natured world are ever too disposed to bestow on all those who seem wanting to their own interests. I know the world too well not to foresee that it would do me essential injury were it known that I declined such a commission. They would not understand the impracticability I have stated, were they even made acquainted with it. Neither would they believe how grievous to me was the necessity of declining it.

" There is another class of subject, however, in which, were I permitted to choose from it, I should find exciting matter enough, and more than enough, for my imperfect skill, that is, from Scripture. But I fear this is a forlorn hope. Yet why should it be? This is a Christian land, and the Scriptures belong to no country, but to man. The facts they record come home to all men, to the high and the low, the wise and simple; but I need not enlarge on this topic to you. Should the Government allow me to select a subject from them, I need not say with what delight I should accept the commission. With such a source of inspiration and the glory of painting for my country, if there be anything in me, it must come out. Would it might be so! But let us suppose it. Well, supposing such a commission given, there's a subject already composed *in petto*, which I have long intended to paint as soon as I am at liberty—the three Marys at the tomb of the Saviour, the angel sitting on a stone before the mouth of the sepulchre. I consider this one of my happiest conceptions. The terrible beauty of the angel, his preternatural brightness, the varied emotions of wonder, awe, and bewilderment of the three women, the streak of distant daybreak, lighting the city of Jerusalem out of the darkness, and the deep-toned spell of the chiaro-oscuro, mingling as it were the night with the day, I see now before me; I wish I could see them on the walls at Washington.

"Now as to the price, should such a dream, I will not call it hope, be realized, it would be eight thousand dollars, which I believe was the price given to Colonel Trumbull for each of his pictures. I should not indeed refuse ten thousand, should Uncle Sam take the generous fit upon him to offer it; but eight is my price for that particular composition, which would consist of four figures, seven feet high; the picture itself (an upright) twelve or thirteen feet high and ten or twelve wide. Were I to undertake a larger composition from another subject, and of the dimensions of Colonel Trumbull's, which I think are eighteen by twelve, the price would be then ten or twelve thousand. I fear this last sum would frighten some of your grave members; my conscience would, however, be quite safe in making the demand, were it even more. And I think I have already given the world sufficient proof that I am not mercenary.

"Pray do not let any part of this letter get into print. I beg you will not think from anything I have said that I intend any disrespect to the painters of battles, or that I would underrate such pictures; I meant only to express my own peculiar notions of them as picturable subjects, *quoad*, myself. There are many of deserved reputation which show great skill in their authors; and among those of modern date it would be unjust not to mention, as holding the very first rank, Mr. West's ' Wolf,' and the ' Death of Warren and Montgomery,' and the ' Sortie,' by Colonel Trumbull.

"Truly you might say, our good friend's laconic mantle has not fallen on the writer of this epistle; I believe if I could write shorter letters I should be a better correspondent, but I have not the secret.

"Ever most truly yours,

" W. ALLSTON."

From Verplanck to Allston.

"WASHINGTON, March 9, 1830.

"MY DEAR SIR: Your letter only convinces me the more that we must, if we can, have one specimen of 'high art' on the wall of the Capitol. By American history mere revolutionary history is not meant. To Scripture I fear we cannot go in the present state of public opinion and taste. But does our ante-revolutionary history present no subject? The 'Landing of the Pilgrims,' a threadbare subject in some respects, has never been viewed with a poet's and painter's eye. What think you of that, or of any similar subject in our early history? Your townsman, Dr. Holmes, has recently published a very useful, though not important, book of 'Annals.' A hasty glance over the first volume of this would perhaps suggest some idea. If not, I still fall back upon the 'Pilgrims.' I have read your letter to Colonel Drayton, who fully agrees with me in honoring your feeling upon this subject, and still wishes to call upon your services in embellishing our national annals. Emulating our friend Williams, not from choice, but from the wish not to lose the mail, I will not turn over the leaf.

"Yours truly,
"G. C. VERPLANCK."

From Allston to Verplanck.

"CAMBRIDGEPORT, March 29, 1830.

"MY DEAR SIR: Your two letters, of the 9th and 12th, have, as the business phrase is, duly come to hand; as you full well know that I cannot be insensible to such persevering kindness I will not trouble you with a repetition of thanks, but proceed to answer them in as business-like a way as I can.

"To the first subject you propose, 'The Landing of the Pilgrims' (not unpicturesque), I have a personal objection. It has already been painted by an old friend of mine, Colonel Sargent, a high-minded, honorable man, to whom I would on no account give pain; which I could not avoid doing were I to encroach on what, at the expense of several years' labor, he has a fair right to consider as his ground. I do not like rivalry in any shape, and my picture on the same subject would seem like it. Indeed it would give me no pleasure to beat anyone. Nor do I consider this business of 'beating' as having any natural connection with excellence of any kind, which, to be such, must be intrinsic and independent of comparison. Nature never made two minds alike; and if the artist, whether poet or painter, has any of the *mens divinior*, with the power of embodying it, his production must have a distinctive excellence which not a hundred bad or good ones by another can either increase or diminish. I know this is not the doctrine of the reviewing age, but I believe it to be true, nevertheless. Moreover, I doubt if competition was ever yet the cause of a great work. It is the love of excellence in the abstract, and for itself, that alone can produce excellence. And I believe that Raffaelle loved Michael Angelo because he thought him his superior for that excellence which he could not reach himself. There may indeed be clever imitations, got up under more ignoble impulses, a kind of second-hand originality, as Edmund Dana calls them, that might pass for it; nay, the world is full of them, mocking each other, and sometimes mocking at, and how bitterly.—But here I am wandering off, like *Tangent* in the play, I hardly know where. After this excursion I will not trouble you with my objections to the other subject, the 'Leave-taking of Washington,' lest I have no room for one of my own choosing, which I should be glad to have you approve, namely: 'The First Interview of Columbus with Ferdinand and Isabella' at court after the discovery of America,

accompanied by natives, and so forth, exhibited in evidence of
his success. As you have read Irving's book it is unnecessary
for me to describe the scene. Here is magnificence, emotion,
and everything, the very triumph of 'matter' to task a painter's
powers. The announcement and the proof of the birth of a New
World. This is not thought of now for the first time. I have
long cherished it as one of the dreams which the future, if the
future were spared to me, was one day to embody. But to business; the size of a picture from this would be not less than eighteen feet by twelve, perhaps twenty by fourteen; and the price
fifteen thousand dollars. As to its class, I know not what subject
could be said more emphatically to belong to America and her
history than the triumph of her discoverer. We, who now enjoy
the blessings of his discovery, cannot place him too high in that
history which without him would never have been. Besides, the
beautiful work of Irving has placed him as the presiding Genius
over the yet fresh, and, we will hope, immortal fountain of our
national literature; the fame of which Columbus was so long de-
frauded is now restored to him, and it will endure, at least with
every American heart. Pray excuse my heroics, I did not mean
to get into them. May I venture to suggest one popular hint.
The subject is from an American book, and a book, too, that any
country might be proud of. Now I am going to take a liberty,
for which, I feel assured you will not require any apology. Could
not a commission also be given to my friend Vanderlyn? He is
truly a man of genius, who has powers, if opportunity is given to
call them forth, that would do honor to his country. His
'Ariadne' has no superior in modern art; his 'Marius,' also,
though not equal to that, is still a noble work. Some persons
have unjustly censured him for not having painted many such
pictures. The wonder to me is how, circumstanced as he has
been ever since I have known him, he could have attained to the
knowledge and power in the art which those works show him to

possess. For, I say it not in friendship, but in simple justice, Vanderlyn is a great artist. I have known him for many years, in France and Italy intimately, and I never knew the time when he had not literally to struggle with poverty ; the process of procuring his daily bread stifling powers that, if allowed freely to act, would have filled Europe with his name. I fear that, like the subject of my last letter, he finds no inspiration in necessity. Let his country now call his genius forth, I know he will do her honor. With this opinion of him I need hardly say that my own commission would be doubly welcome, should I hear at the same time that an equal commission was also given to Vanderlyn. And if Uncle Sam's generous mood would incline him, too, to commission Morse and Sully, I should then be thereby delighted. Morse I consider as a child of my own, and you know what I think of him. The quickening atmosphere which he is now breathing in Europe, will open some original and powerful seeds which I long ago saw in him. I am much mistaken if he has not that in him which will one day surprise. And Sully has historical powers, already proved in his ' Crossing the Delaware,' of no common order.

"I am much gratified to learn the interest which Colonel Drayton does me the honor to take in my behalf. I knew him some years since in London, and I have met few persons with whom I have been so much pleased on so short an acquaintance. Pray present him my respects and thanks. Should the commission be given I hope they will not limit me as to time, as I have several engagements that must previously be fulfilled. My interest would, of course, preclude any unnecessary delay.

" Faithfully yours,

" W. ALLSTON."

From Verplanck to Allston.

"HOUSE OF REPRESENTATIVES, May 29, 1830.

"MY DEAR SIR: We (that is our Committee) had determined to try the taste and liberality of Congress by recommending an appropriation for a picture from you on your terms and choice, restricting you only to American History, in which Columbus would, of course, be included; but, unfortunately, for the present our bill for the improvement of the public buildings has been crowded out by the press of other business, and must lie over till next winter.

"Though our proposed alterations in the buildings are important both to comfort and taste, there was nothing pressing in the bill now passing, and I only regret the delay on your account. Next winter we shall have the opportunity of taking up the bill early, and I hope with better success. But the extent to which Congress will go in these matters depends much on accidental circumstances.

.   .   .   ."

June 1, 1830, Allston married Martha R. Dana, daughter of the late Francis Dana, Chief Justice of Massachusetts, and cousin on the maternal side to his first wife. He thus announces the event to his friend Cogdell:

"CAMBRIDGEPORT, June 8, 1830.

"DEAR COGDELL: My patriarchal courtship is at length ended, and I am now a happy benedict, and I know not what I could do better than to bestow on you some of the spirits which the occasion inspires. I was married on Tuesday last at Cambridge, which we left immediately after the ceremony for our present habitation and home. It is a snug, commodious little mansion, prettily situated in a retired part of this village, and commanding a pleasant view of the adjacent country, taking in a part of the river and a picturesque little pine wood, which used to be the favorite haunt of my younger days, to which I used to saunter after college hours, and dream sometimes of poetry, and sometimes of my art. These youthful associations have an indefinite charm peculiarly pleasant to me at this time ; they seem to bring together the earlier and later portions of my life, mingling them as it were into one, and imparting to the present some of that eloquent quiet of the past which my nature has always most loved. You may well suppose that such a home, with the woman of my choice, must have no ordinary value in my eyes, after the restless, wandering Arab life which I have led for the last ten years.

" Though circumstances have thrown me upon the world for so large a portion of my life, and obliged me to mix so long in its gay and busy scenes, it has seldom, if ever, afforded me any real enjoyment. Not that my disposition is solitary ; on the contrary, it is inherently social ; for the truest enjoyment I have ever known has been in that which has been reflected back to me from those I love—only to be found in the domestic circle, and among a few personal friends. Nothing like this can the world give—nothing but a poor substitute of idle ceremony and heartless show. What are called its pleasures are none to me, nor can they be deemed such even by a man of the world till they stimulate the mind into an artificial state ; that passing off, they are pleasures no longer, but vanish like inebriating illusions, while their places are filled with weariness or disgust. But the sober pleasures of home, taking their source in virtues consonant to our moral nature, have no other condition for their fruition and permanence but equal virtue in the receiver as in the giver. If they fail then of being realized, it is because we are unworthy of them.

" I will not attempt to describe my wife to you ; I will only say, that in the excellence of her disposition, cultivated intellect, sound religious principles, and practical piety, I have a prospect of as much happiness as anyone may look for in this world.

. . . .

"I sent you, as I mentioned in the letter to my mother, through some of your correspondents, several messages respecting your 'Modestia,' saying how much pleased I was with it. I may now more particularly say that I think it superior in execution to your preceding works, as it ought to be. You have well expressed the character, or rather, I should say, embodied the sentiment. There is nothing assumed or theatrical in it, but it is natural and delicate, and does great credit to your invention. There is a remark, however, that I will make which may be of use to you in future subjects of this class, viz., the bridge of the nose is too thin, and the chin too large, for beauty, according to the antique—at least, *secondo il mio gusto*. The folds of the drapery are also too small—what the artists call 'cut up.' But when I say that upon the whole I prefer the old general, you must not think I am disparaging this last work; I mention it merely as exemplifying what I observed in a former letter—that elegance of execution is no match for force of character. The 'Modestia' is certainly the superior in execution, but it is the personification of an abstraction, and therefore but indirectly, and by an effort of our mind, appealing to our sympathies; whereas the other, as the image of an actual, living being comes home to us at once, and produces its effect (as in nature) before we know why. . . . .

"Believe me ever your sincere friend,

"W. ALLSTON."

Allston now settled down to his life as an artist and a married man in the village of Cambridgeport. A few years before his death he moved from the small inconvenient house he had occupied since his marriage, into a new and larger one within the same enclosure with his painting-room. This was his only change of place from the time of his second marriage till his death.

The peculiarities of his uneventful life in Cambridgeport might be termed picturesque; and, so far as observed by his neighbors, they rendered him an object of interest and respect. His dignity and refinement of manner were so tempered with gentleness that the common people accosted him with freedom, though always deferentially. He retained many of the habits formed during his residence abroad. It was his custom to turn night into day, a custom noticeable as far back as his boarding-school life in Newport. Mr. Rogers, the school-master, on his nightly round to see that the lights were out and the boys in bed, would always find young Allston sitting up deeply interested in some book. This tendency to late hours followed him through life. He seldom went to bed before two o'clock in the morning. He would usually rise at about ten, make an elaborate toilet, and then prepare his breakfast, which consisted of the strongest coffee and some slight relish, like a bit of salt fish or ham, and an egg with bread and butter. He never altogether gave up his bachelor habits, and would allow no one to prepare his breakfast or his bed but himself.

Immediately after breakfast he would light his cigar and take some book on art, which he would read for a while in preparation for his painting. About one o'clock, he would enter his studio, put down his pitcher of drinking-water which he always brought with him through the streets from his house. Making out his palette occupied him not less than half an hour, as he had always a system of tints to mix and spread out on a scrupulously clean, large mahogany palette. Then he would take out his picture, place it on the easel, light his cigar, and sit down in front of it, seemingly wrapped in pleasing anticipation of what he expected to do. It is obvious that, with this deliberate preparation, his hours for work in winter were few. After painting he would carefully clean his palette and return to the contemplation of his picture, which would continue generally until quite dark. Then with his brushes and pitcher in his hands, he would start for his house; and so abstracted was he frequently, that upon reaching it, he would return to see whether he had locked his studio door.

After readjusting his toilet, he would enter the dining-room, which was also his sitting-room. There he would usually find some friend or friends whose intimacy rendered invitations superfluous, with whom he would spend an hour or more in cheerful conversation, and the enjoyment of a well-provided and tempting table, on which there was always sherry wine.

He was quite an epicure, and at times greatly enjoyed describing dinners in Paris, the memory of which seemed to delight him. The cloth removed, the wine would be replaced on the table, the cigars lighted, and reinforced occasionally by a few friends dropping in, the night's conversation would continue. About nine o'clock tea, toast, cake, and preserves would be served. The following characteristic letter to John Knapp, Esq., indicates the informal, and yet epicurean, nature of these occasions:

" CAMBRIDGEPORT, February 23, 1831.

" DEAR KNAPP : As we suppose you have by this time finished preparing for the press, the journal of your voyage to the Island of Formosa or Natchitoches (the public are divided as to which, though they have no doubt you have been to one or the other place), Mrs. A. and myself would be happy to have your opinion on a haunch of Yankee venison at five o'clock on Friday.

" N. B.—Mr. Hastings and Mr. E. T. Dana, who will be present, are also very curious (at least I venture to think so) to hear your opinion; especially as to how it compares with the foreign venison which you have doubtless met with in your travels. A bed is provided for you in which you may rest after the labors incident to so important a decision.

"Ever faithfully yours,

"W. ALLSTON."

There are but few surviving who can recall these entertainments, but all who can, recur to them as unique. Art, science, and literature—all current interests of the day, political, theological, social; history and philosophy; adventure, romance, works of fiction, the dramatic and comic; ghost stories, legends, and myths, gave occasion and theme for the most interesting conversations.

As a young man Allston acquired a great love for smoking, which ministered so pleasingly to his dreamy moods that he was wont to say that, next to his religion, his cigar had been his greatest consolation. The mantel-shelf in his painting-room was fringed with cigar-stumps. He would frequently stop his work, light one of these stumps, and smoke while contemplating his picture, then carefully lay the stump in its place and resume his work.

His courteous and kindly nature emboldened his neighbors to consult him freely on all questions of taste. On one occasion, just before dinner, the bell rang and the servant opened the door to two old women, who had called, as they said, to ask Mr. Allston's opinion about some samples of calico; his wife stepped to the door, and told them that they must call at some other time, if they would see Mr. Allston, for he had no taste then for anything but his dinner. Mr. Allston was at the head of the stairs, and hearing the conversation, went down, patiently examined the samples, and gave his opinion.

G. L. Brown, the landscape painter of Boston, made a very fine copy of a Claude in the Louvre, which was purchased by the

Boston Athenæum. Allston pronounced it the best copy of Claude he had ever seen. Some gentlemen, hearing of this high commendation, said to Brown, " If you can get Allston to put that in writing, you can raise all the money you need." He obtained the written statement, and as a result, was sent to Europe to make other copies. This good fortune gave Brown great encouragement. It enabled him to spend several years abroad, and did much to establish his reputation. The unselfish side of Allston's nature was continually manifesting itself. One evening he heard an alarm of fire; going to the street, he saw the flames in the direction of the Poor House. Remembering that an old woman, who was formerly a beneficiary of Mrs. Allston, was then an inmate of the institution, he at once started off to the rescue. Soon after his tall and distinguished figure was seen with the old pauper woman leaning on his arm, walking through the streets of Cambridgeport. Arrived at the gate, he led his charge into the house, and with that courtesy of manner which knew no distinction of caste, or time, or place, introduced her to Mrs. Allston, saying he had brought her a guest. The scope of his kindness was all-embracing. His whole nature was infused with love, and its natural expression was loving interest for all. He used to say that there was no face so deficient in beauty that he could not see in it something beautiful, and so also he could discover something divine, a kindred divinity in every human soul.

Soon after Allston's marriage to Miss Dana, he was told that Miss Merriam, of Newport, daughter of an Episcopal clergyman, censured him for leaving the Episcopal Church, of which he was a member, and going with his wife to the Congregational Church, to which she belonged. This report seemed to impress him deeply. He said, " I should like to see Miss Merriam. I have something to say to her, which may enlarge her views of religion; I am neither an Episcopalian nor a Congregationalist, I endeavor to be a Christian." His philosophical and analytical mind went to the essence and root, the underlying principle of Christianity. He was a Catholic in the largest sense of that large word; from the informal ritualism of the Quaker to that of the Romanist, with all its impressive ceremonial, in whatsoever church or society the spirit of Christ was acknowledged as the supreme guidance—by each and all he could be claimed as a member. He might accept creeds, or formulas, or theologies; he might localize his worship so that men would call him Churchman or Dissenter; but his religion, so full of love and reverence, could be designated by no narrower term than universal, all-embracing, Catholic. This Catholicity could be predicated of him not only in religion, but also in art. Speaking of his preferences in regard to schools and methods, he was wont to say, as before quoted, "I am a wide liker." This was certified by his kindly bearing. Young artists went to him confident of a gentle and encouraging reception. His criticism was always mingled with cheering words to strengthen and guide the young aspirant aright in the difficult ascent to excellence. Thus, his manner invited the inquirer for truth in art and artistic methods, and from his presence none went empty away.

Jeremiah Dictating his Prophecy of the Destruction of Jerusalem to Baruch the Scribe.

From the original in the Art Gallery of Yale College.

CHAPTER XX.

THE "JEREMIAH."—ITS EXHIBITION IN BOSTON.—LETTERS OF 1830
TO 1832, TO McMURTRIE, VERPLANCK, AND COGDELL.

During the latter part of the year 1830 Allston worked on his
picture "Jeremiah," of which he writes to McMurtrie : "I have
now considerably advanced, a picture, figure larger than life of
'Jeremiah,' which I shall describe to you in my next, it will be
finished in a month. I should not have undertaken it, but that I
was obliged to leave Boston just as I was going to proceed with
'Belshazzar,' on account of an epidemic that prevailed near my
painting-room and made it dangerous to remain there. I have
therefore spent the latter part of the summer in Cambridge,
where I began this picture. The picture of 'Jeremiah,' I think
for its materials one of the grandest compositions I have made."

In December of the same year McMurtrie writes : "I have
lately seen an account of your last picture of 'Jeremiah.' Do you
intend we shall see it in Philadelphia? If you do, I entreat you
will allow me to use my best endeavors to promote your views in
this quarter."

This picture was sold to a Mr. Ball, and first shown gratuitously to visitors, in 1831, at Miss Catherine Scollay's residence in
Boston. Allston's friends advised him to prevent this, and desired him to consent to their making application to Mr. Ball to
allow its being exhibited for money. This he declined, through
extreme delicacy, thinking it might lead Mr. Ball to suppose he
was not satisfied with the sum paid, when he himself had fixed
the price and named the subject. Dana says : "Through whose
instrumentality the exhibition was brought about I do not know,"

and he continues, " What Mrs. Jameson says of want of height
in the canvas of ' Jeremiah ' may in some degree be true, but I
suspect that the impression made upon her was from the lowness
of the room in which she saw it, rather than from want of height
on the canvas.

" I should hardly with her call Jeremiah's beard flowing, for
though somewhat long, it was also rather crisp, I think. ' Wide
eyes glaring on the future ' hardly hints their marvellous expression. ' The head of the scribe looking up and struck with a
kind of horror, finer still '—is in my mind an entire mistake of the
expression. She speaks of the relief of the jaw ; how people's
talk of this mere mechanical excellence used to vex Allston ! "

The following notice of " Jeremiah," published in the *Boston
Daily Advertiser*, September, 1830, gives a good description of the
picture.

" I have been to see Mr. Allston's picture of ' Jeremiah.'
The room was perfectly still, for I was the only visitor. The
Prophet seemed lost in mysterious communion with the divine
Being. There was an elevating and solemn impression made upon the mind by this visible yet silent operation of divinity which
no language of poetry ever gave me a sense of. Never did I feel
so distinctly the nigh approach of a heavenly power, or contemplate the inward emotions of the soul so entirely abstracted from
all that is bodily. Jeremiah is a gigantic figure ; yet you do not
think of him as such, and his size only makes upon you an impression of power in perfect agreement with his supernatural
mission, and the sublime energy and resolution shown in the
character of his attitude and countenance ; the eyes are conceived
in high poetry. He is looking beyond all earthly things, into
the infinite distance, and the invisible is made visible to him.
Yet there is an abstracted inwardness of thought in them, intent
upon the workings of the prophetic spirit with which he is filled.
There is a majestic repose in the whole figure, and the right

hand raised, while the elbow is resting on a projection of the prison wall, seems about to move at the first word of prophecy. His head is in a fine style of sublimity, the temples and forehead are marked with clear, eloquent veins. Over all this grandeur is thrown a calm awe which takes from it everything earthly.

"Baruch is in natural contrast, seated lower and at a little distance from the prophet, full of youthful beauty, and the inclination of the body so graceful and easy! With the innocent expression of his countenance is mingled a reverence, at the same time you perceive that he is expecting the words of the prophet. These are the only figures in the picture, except the sentinel in the distance; they are in the court of the prison—the long galleries, flights of steps, and arches of which are in fine perspective. The walls along the passages are colored with great truth, and there cannot be anything better than the daylight shining upon them. The anatomy of the figures seems perfect. The raised arm and fore-shortened foot of the prophet, the out-turned foot and right hand of the scribe, all difficult to draw, are to my eye without a fault. The prophet's beard and Baruch's hair and neck could hardly be surpassed for beauty and truth. The drapery is finely folded, perfectly easy and negligent, without anything slovenly. We have had nothing to compare with this picture for color. It is all harmony, and so rich and deep that the eye bathes in it. The simplicity and unity of the picture are very obvious, no theatrical effect is aimed at; I wish I felt at liberty to tell Mr. Allston how grateful I am to him for having shown me one of the prophets of old, and for having sent me away a more thoughtful and religious man."

The following letter is from Allston to McMurtrie:

" CAMBRIDGEPORT, May 27, 1831.

"MY DEAR SIR: I have just received your letter of the 19th inst., and agreeably to your request I sit down to reply without delay. I regret, however, that it is not in my power to give you available information on the subject of your inquiries. I have but a few weeks since been established in my new painting-room, which I have built in this place. 'Belshazzar' has been rolled up and reposing in a packing-case for more than three years, in consequence of my former large room in Boston passing into the hands of a new owner, who has converted it into a livery-stable; since which I have been compelled to work in a small chamber where I have been employed altogether on small pictures. 'Belshazzar' will still remain for some time to come in its case— some embarrassing debts and my immediate necessities being the cause. I must be free in mind before I venture to finish it. I trust, however, that the time will not be very long. Your room which you mention must be a noble one. I wish there was such a one in each of our large cities. It is a great desideratum with me, as I mean hereafter—that is when I once more become *free*, and should Providence grant me life—to confine myself chiefly to large works.

"I suppose that you know that I have become a benedict. I have been married about a year, and this village is now my home. It is about two miles from Boston, where I can be at any time, by means of an hourly stage, in twenty minutes. I am in better health, and certainly in better spirits, than I have been in ten years. Believe me, my dear sir, with undiminished regard, sincerely yours,

"WASHINGTON ALLSTON."

Allston's interest in younger artists is attested anew in the following entertaining letter to Cogdell:

"CAMBRIDGEPORT, July 25, 1831.

"DEAR COGDELL: I mentioned in my last letter to my mother, of the 4th inst., that a subject for your chisel had then just occurred to me, which I did not name to her, thinking you would be more gratified to have it directly from myself. The subject is Hagar and Ishmael, when the latter is about (apparently) to expire from thirst in the desert. The moment I have supposed is just before the appearance of the angel, when she is taking the last look of her son, previous to the passage where she says, 'Let me not see the death of the child.' Gen. xxi. 16. I think a very beautiful as well as touching group may be made of this. The head of the child resting on the lap of the mother, who is kneeling and slightly bending over him, with the head only, not the body; as the more erect position of the body, contrasting with the inclination of the head, would correspond with the mixed emotion, or rather conflicting thoughts, within— the agony in the thought of seeing him die, and the thought of lessening it by the cruel alternative of leaving him.

"I will mention another subject which also occurs to me as not unsuitable to sculpture, 'Hermia and Helena,' from Shakespeare's 'Mid-Summer Night's Dream,' in whom the singleness and unity of friendship is beautifully illustrated. They are described as animated by one soul in their affections, employments, and amusements; working together on one sampler, like two twin-cherries growing on one stalk, etc. Perhaps you will find some passage in the play that would suggest the action. I certainly should not recommend the sampler, which must be, to say the least, but an awkward thing to represent in sculpture. I painted this subject when in England, and not thinking it essential to adhere to the letter, instead of the sampler I made them reading together from the same book. I endeavored to give the spirit, which is all I would recommend to you in naming the subject. With the book, I think they might make a beautiful group in sculpture.

. . . .

"In a letter to my mother, I expressed my regret in being unable to think of any subject for you, and referred you to the catalogues of the Royal Academy and other London exhibitions, as most likely to furnish you with one. My mother was at the time at Waccamaw, but this I did not then know.

"Will you tell my mother that my nephew, George Flagg, arrived here a few days since. He is a fine, manly little fellow. It will gratify his grandmother to know that Mrs. A. and myself are quite delighted with him. He carries with him in his delicate and modest manners the appearance of having been well brought up, and I find him more intelligent and mature in mind than I should have expected in one of his age. So far as I can now judge, he has every quality to make a fine artist.

"I suppose you have learnt through the newspapers, that we have had an exhibition here of a group in marble, called the 'Chanting Cherubs,' by Mr. Greenough, of Boston, who is now in Florence. It is one of the most beautiful groups in modern art, judging of it not as the work of a young man, but as one of matured powers. I think it places the author of it, if not among the first, certainly above the second-rate sculptors of the day. But when I consider his youth, or rather his limited experience, I have no scruples in predicting his speedy elevation to a pedestal among the very first. In addition to a brilliant, versatile genius, Greenough possesses the advantage of a thorough liberal education. He was educated at our college, and was not idle when there, making himself ere he left it a good classical scholar. In general acquirements also I believe there are few young men in our country who surpass him.

"George speaks highly of your bust of Dr. Elliott; he says it is considered the happiest of your works. I hope you will be tempted by one of the subjects I have proposed, to show what you can do in a work of imagination. If you do not already possess them, I should recommend your sending to England for the compositions of Flaxman, the sculptor, from Dante and the Greek poets. They are all in outline and are worthy of the best age of art. I have three volumes of them. They ought to be in the library of every artist, whether sculptor or painter. The whole of Flaxman's works, I think, may be had for about twenty pounds sterling. I am now in my new painting-room, which I believe has not its superior in Europe. At present I am painting a picture for a gentleman of Carolina.

"Believe me ever faithfully your friend,

"WASHINGTON ALLSTON."

The following note from Verplanck to Allston testifies to the latter's success in his friendly efforts in behalf of Vanderlyn.

"WASHINGTON, February 21, 1832.

"MY DEAR SIR: Knowing the pleasure it must give you to be informed you have rendered an important service to a friend, I enclose you a paper containing our little debate about employing Vanderlyn, and I can assure you that the testimony to his merit which you enabled me to give was what decided the question. The picture would otherwise have been left to be a job for somebody or other, according to accident or interest. Vanderlyn understands that, limited only to Stuart's head, he has *carte blanche* to give us a magnificent picture. He will visit Boston to copy the engraved head. In the meantime the debate alone is a happy thing for him which, I trust, he will take advantage of.

"We have also given your friend Greenough an order for a pedestrian marble statue of Washington, limiting him only to the Houdon face and leaving him free as to everything else. We have an excellent committee on this subject, and I hope to see our Rotunda adorned by your pencil, and others worthy to associate with you under these auspices.

"Yours truly,

"G. C. VERPLANCK."

The following long letter, full of excellent criticism and advice to his young friend, is particularly interesting in the part that relates to "Belshazzar," giving as it does Allston's own feelings about the picture.

Allston to Cogdell.

"CAMBRIDGEPORT, February 27, 1832.

"DEAR COGDELL: It gives me great pleasure that I can bestow sincere praise on your group of Hagar and Ishmael. It is decidedly your best work, and much exceeds what I had expected; it really does you great honor. And though it has many faults, they are by no means of a kind to outweigh its merits. The attitudes of both mother and child are well conceived, and they group well together. Perhaps, however, the group might have been improved had the boy's body been a little farther off, and his head resting where it is. I think it would have presented a better profile view. But its chief merit lies in the general conception and the expression; which are certainly the principal points in a work of art. It has indeed great power of expression. The helpless extremity of the son is very touching, and his physical suffering is affectingly contrasted with that of his mother. She seems to have just said, 'Let me not see him die,' and to be taking a last look; the deep, silent maternal agony of that look is of no common order. The calmness of her action, too, is finely conceived; it is the effort of one who strives not to look into the fearful future; who stands on the brink of an abyss into which she must fall, but will not look. This is indeed great.

"Now (as I suppose you will wish me to do) I will point out the faults, but you must not be frightened at the list, since they are only the faults of inexperience. The principal defect is in the disposition of the drapery, the lines of which are too often repeated, and too abrupt; that is, the folds are too small and cut up, instead of being large, varied, and flowing. The horizontal lines also across the mother's body have an ill effect, and disturb the action of the limbs, which should always in sculpture be indicated, however faintly, by some slight correspondence in the folds that drape them. The next is the costume. The puffs on the arms and the folds on the breast are modern. The sleeves should have been plain—so the drapery on the chest. The right shoulder of the boy is out of its place; it could not be so far projected without dislocation, or breaking the clavicle. The protrusion of his tongue is not in good taste, for though this may be physically true of one dying of thirst, it is one of those unpleasant truths that should be avoided in art. Then you should have given him more beauty—I mean of face. The mother's leg is a little too short. Of the defect of her raised arm I say nothing, it having been injured, as you mentioned, in the casting. These faults, however, as I have already observed, are the faults of inexperience, and such as more practice and the study of good models would very easily enable you to avoid. I would recommend your procuring prints from the antique bas-reliefs of Greece and Rome; the Admiranda Romanorum of Santo Bartoli, and Lope's Grecian Costume. The first perhaps could not be had except from Italy; the last you will get from England. These would be of great use to you as to costume as well as for other things; a week's study of them would let you into the whole mystery of sculpture drapery.

"Now, after this praise, will you allow me, my friend, to say a few words of a prudential nature. Do not let it tempt you to give up a certainty for an uncertainty. I say this because my nephew informs me that when he left Carolina, you talked, as he had heard, of going to Italy, to make art your profession; if so, you must of course give up your office at the Custom

House, which, if I understand you aright, is now your principal
means of support. You remember that some years ago you applied to me for my opinion on this subject, and that I made no
reply, and for this reason (which I supposed from your subsequent letters you understood), because I shrunk from the responsibility. But I ought not to have shrunk from it; my conscience soon told me so; and I had made up my mind to give
it without reserve and should long since have given it, had I not
concluded, from your continued silence on the subject, that you
had given up the intention. I will, however, no longer delay
this discharge of my duty; and do it now the more readily, as
after the high praise I have bestowed on your last work, you
cannot impute it to any doubt of your talents. What I am
about to say, however, I do not give in the shape of advice; for
I as much dislike giving advice as asking it; and I never ask it
in my personal concerns, except in some extreme case, where I
find it impossible to decide for myself; and such have very
rarely occurred. I shall merely express my opinion on the subject, leaving you to weigh it as you think fit, and to decide for
yourself.

"If by making the art your profession you are to depend on
it as the means of support for yourself and family, I cannot but
think that you look to a very precarious source. What may be
the prospects of employment from private individuals you can
judge as well as I, and I no better than you, for I can have no
definite knowledge as to it unless I were myself a sculptor. It
has often, however, been doubted by Greenough's friends here,
notwithstanding the high and general estimation in which he
stands as well for his private character as for his talents, whether
he will be able to support himself in Boston from private employment alone. And if Boston cannot afford him sufficient, I
know not in what other city of the Union he can expect it. His
resource, they think, must be at Washington, in works for the

Government, or in Europe. Indeed, it seems to be the opinion of most persons that I have heard speak of the subject, that employment for the General Government is the only hope for a sculptor who is to live by his profession in our country. And whether it is that people have been but little accustomed to it, or from some other cause, so far as I have observed, the interest taken in sculpture is by no means so general as that taken in pictures. Then the prices which a sculptor must charge, even to defray his expenses, are such as very few in our country are either able or willing to give for works of art. So I do not see much prospect even of a bare support, unless he is content to confine himself to busts that are portraits. But even supposing there were sufficient demand for sculpture, are you prepared to coin your brain for bread—at all times and under all circumstances, of depression, of illness, and the numberless harassments of unavoidable debt? To produce an original work of the imagination, requiring of all human efforts a pleasurable state of the mind, with a dunning letter staring you in the face? With an honest heart yearning to give everyone his due, and an empty purse, I know from bitter experience that the fairest visions of the imagination vanish like dreams never to be recalled, before the daylight reality of such a visitor. Poverty is no doubt a stimulus to general industry, and to many kinds of mental effort, but not to the imagination; for the imagination must be abortive—is a nonentity—if it have not peace as its immediate condition. Pictures that would have otherwise brought me hundreds, not to say thousands, have crumbled into nothing under its pressure, and been thrown aside as nothing worth. I say these things not querulously (for I have an utter dislike to all complaining, and never allow myself in it), but that you might know what it is to be an artist by profession, with no other income than the product of the brain—which, to be at all available, must at least be at peace. And I give them in their naked reality solely from a conscientious regard for your peace and happiness as a man. The love I bear my art you well know; no one could love it more; and I have given proof of it in the sacrifice I have made to it of my fortune. And yet, with all this love, which I still bear it, I thus speak of it as a profession. Because I must speak the truth. But, understand me, when I speak of it thus as a profession, it is when that profession is associated with poverty. With a competence, however small, so it be sufficient to secure me from debt, from demands that I cannot satisfy when due—then, of all professions, it is that which I would still choose. But debt is slavery. And his mind must be free who aspires to anything great in the art. If you have a competence, then I should say, as I once said before your unfortunate loss of property, follow your inclinations. But your case is still a happy one, though art is not your profession; for it may still be your employment; and it is the employment, after all, in which its pleasure consists; this I firmly believe. Your office allows you, I suppose, the half of each day to yourself, and secures to you the means of devoting a moiety of the year to the pursuit of the art, in the way you like best, and independent of the world. Ah, that word independent has a charm which I well know how to value, from having known its reverse. But I still have hope, and I look for repossession of it yet.

"In your letter preceding the last one there was a passage, toward the conclusion, which gave me more pain than, I am sure, you would willingly have afflicted; and I should have felt it most deeply had I not ascribed it to inadvertence, and to your not having considered the full import of certain expressions. I am certain you would not have written them had you reflected a moment on the construction they might bear. The passage is this: Speaking of the 'Belshazzar,' you say: 'Your picture ought to have been delivered years ago, and that hundreds near me think so, though they do not say it, lest they should wound

me;' and you advise me 'to think of this matter with serious-
ness.'

"Now, my friend, I do in my heart acquit you of all intention of giving me pain; for you immediately add 'that it is not
in your heart to wound me;' I fully believe this. But let me
ask you one question. Do you believe that it has been in my
power to finish 'Belshazzar?' Your words 'ought to have been
delivered years ago' certainly imply the affirmative; consequently, that it is still unfinished is because I would not finish it,
when I might if I had so chosen. If this were the case, I could
not be (what I know myself to be) an honorable man; for I have
repeatedly declared it to be my earnest intention and desire to
finish it as soon as it was in my power. Then you advise me to
think of it seriously. Does not this imply that I have intentionally neglected it? Certainly it seems to; for how else could I
need to be reminded of so important a contract; that could not
have been put aside in the memory, except intentionally. It
was this that hurt me, that anyone should think that I could, yet
would not, fulfil a solemn contract; that I had neglected the performance of it as soon as it was in my power, and needed to be
reminded of my duty. But this, as I have before said, I am
sure you never could have meant. No, Cogdell—I say it not in
pride, but in the simple consciousness of integrity—I am one of
the last men in the world to whom such moral delinquency can
be justly imputed. And (though I sincerely believe that you do
not require such assurance) I here assure you, on the word of a
gentleman, and what is more, of an honest man, that it has not
been in my power to finish 'Belshazzar,' and that it still remains
in its case from absolute necessity. Ever since I entered into
the contract with my subscribers it has been my paramount object to fulfil it; all my efforts in subsequent works have had that
for their ultimate end; to extricate myself from embarrassments.
(Here is a sample: It was but four days after the receipt of your

letter, to which I am now replying, that I received a letter from a collecting attorney requiring payment of a debt of more than seven hundred dollars, and all the money I had was five dollars and a quarter.) Over my wife's property I have no control, that being in the care of trustees, and her income seldom exceeds four hundred dollars; which (as repeated experience has taught me) rendered it morally impossible for me to do justice either to myself or my subscribers. I have had no other view in anything I have done; and my personal history, were it known, would bear me out in this to the letter.

"But no one has a right to inquire into my private troubles; I trust my word is sufficient. I will only add that, though the efforts alluded to have not effected their end so soon as I had allowed myself to anticipate, they have yet released me from some of my sorest difficulties. In plainer words, I am getting out of debt. Some heavy and importunate debts, however, still remain: and these I am daily laboring to discharge as I have the others; that done I shall be free. And it is my fixed resolution not to touch 'Belshazzar' till I am so. Should I attempt it now, it would be to no purpose, except perhaps, to ruin it. If labor could have done it, the mental as well as manual labor already bestowed on it were sufficient to have completed five such pictures. I alone know what I can and cannot do. 'Tis only with a free mind that I can do justice to my engagement.

"With respect to remarks on me by the world, I shall endeavor to bear them with what philosophy I can muster. I have lived long enough to know that, let a man act as conscientiously as he will, he will not escape censure. But my private affairs surely are no concern of theirs. I am not a pensioner of the public. Do not then trouble yourself to 'defend me.' All that I would have anyone say in my behalf (if indeed anything) is, that in a life of more than fifty years I have never wronged any man out of a dollar, and that I do not intend to do it now. I hold myself amenable only to my subscribers, and none of them, to my knowledge, have complained. Should anyone of them, however, think himself aggrieved, feel impatient, or be from any cause dissatisfied with the delay, I would most cheerfully, and without an unpleasant feeling, release him from his engagement ; and if it be one who has advanced his share, I will repay it with the interest, as soon as in my power, from the proceeds of my present labors. I speak in sincerity, when I say that I would most willingly do this, and without a particle of resentment. Nay, I should even take it as a kindness, if there be any so disposed, that he or they would consent to this course, since it would be to me a great relief ; for I have never ceased to regret that I ever allowed myself to receive any advance on the picture.

" It has always, from the first, been my intention on delivering the picture to pay the interest on every advancement. No one has ever yet lost a quarter of a dollar by me, and if my life and health are spared no one ever shall.

" Should you see my mother, give her my love and tell her that I intend to write to her in a few days. George is getting on as well as could be wished in Boston. Pray tell his grandmother that he comes out very often to see us. He is one of the finest boys I have ever known ; everyone loves him. Mrs. Allston unites with me in best regards to Mrs. Cogdell and yourself.
"I remain sincerely your friend,
" W. ALLSTON."

The following is from Verplanck to Allston :

"FISHKILL LANDING, July 25, 1832.

" MY DEAR SIR : I send you a New York literary paper containing Mr. Livingston's official letter to your friend Greenough on the subject of the statue of Washington. You must allow that our Committee on Public Buildings at Washington (that is to say, your friend Jarvis, your neighbor Gen. Dearborn, and myself, for the others cared little about the matter), if we have not done much, have done well what we have done in employing your friends Vanderlyn and Greenough, and on liberal terms. I was two or three days in New York last week, on my return from Washington, and found it in a melancholy state. The chief ravages of the cholera are as yet confined to the most worthless and minor part of our population, yet there are many exceptions which spread alarm, and the stagnation of business brings great distress on the industrious poor. The character and habits of those upon whom the disease has mainly preyed upon, however, gives me great hope that it will not spread its devastation unduly throughout our country. It is still a terrible calamity. Irving was with us at Washington and looks wonderfully well, indeed quite unaltered since I saw him in England in 1817, though changed to those who recollect only his sallow and thin American face. He is now wandering about among his friends in this State, and I hope soon to see him again."

CHAPTER XXI.

We have in the subjoined letters a communication between a
committee of three gentlemen of Charleston, S. C., and Hon.
Edward Everett, of Boston, in reference to securing an historical
picture from Allston. Mr. Everett, in a letter to R. H. Dana,
relates his part of the transaction as follows :

"LONDON, August 30, 1843.

"DEAR SIR: I received this morning your letter of the 14th
inst., and I cheerfully comply with your request. . . . Some
ten years ago, I think it must have been, I received a letter from
Charleston, S. C., requesting me to apply to Mr. Allston to paint
an historical picture for an association in that city.

"The subject of the picture was to be the unfurling of the
American flag by the United States Minister at Mexico, from
the window of his house, when he was about to be attacked by
an armed mob. The picture was to be one of the largest size,
there was no limitation of price, and I think it was mentioned
as a circumstance which might have its effect in inducing Mr.
Allston to undertake it, that it was for his native city.

"I waited upon Mr. Allston, at Cambridge, to communicate
to him the purport of the letter, which he received with courtesy. He excused himself, however, from undertaking the commission upon these grounds: that he felt it his duty to devote

his time as exclusively as possible to the great work that he had
so long had on hand ; the other, that, even if he felt at liberty
to begin another large picture, the subject of the proposed work,
which was of the nature of a battle-piece, was a branch which he
had not cultivated, and did not feel prepared to undertake.   I
do not remember going a second time to Cambridge, though I
may have done so ; or I may have mentioned the subject again
to Mr. Allston, on meeting him elsewhere.   This is all I can
recollect with distinctness on the subject.   Of course, I cannot
contradict the statement of any gentleman who has a clear
recollection of any additional facts as coming from me.   I am
pretty sure the application was first made to Mr. Allston, by
means of a letter to me.   I think it was a year or two before I
was Governor.   It proceeded from a gentleman of the 'Union
Party,' of which General Hamilton was not a member.   It was,
I understood, intended for a public use General Hamilton
would not, at that time, have been disposed to promote.   .   .   .
The picture being for a specific purpose, there was of course no
discretion as to the subject.

"My recollection of Mr. Allston's manner, when I waited
upon him, is, except as I have described it above, indistinct.   He
may have spoken with earnestness and emphasis, though I think
that was not his habit ; but there was nothing in the proposal to
affect him disagreeably ; it seems scarcely possible that he, the
mildest and gentlest of men, could have received it in any other
than a mild and gentle manner.   .   .   .   No man regarded Mr.
Allston with warmer admiration than myself ; no one out of his
family circle more tenderly cherishes his memory.

"I am, dear sir, very respectfully yours,

"EDWARD EVERETT."

It is notable that the communication was not made directly
to Allston, but through such a man as Mr. Everett, who was

shortly after elected Governor of his State. There was doubt
as to whether Allston could be induced to undertake the work,
and as Mr. Everett was an influential friend, the committee had
recourse to him, as one who would present their commission
with the best prospect of its acceptance. This solicitude on the
part of the committee indicates the success awaiting Allston,
and that he might have been free from pecuniary embarrassment
but for 'Belshazzar.' Following is the letter of the committee:

"CHARLESTON, April 9, 1833.

"DEAR SIR: The enclosed statement concerns the circumstances under which our national flag was unfurled by the
American Ambassador at Mexico. It is intended that they
should furnish material for a national painting; the object is to
spread before the eyes of our countrymen, and particularly of
the rising generation, the unseen but highly moral protection
afforded by a great, because united, people. Though it is difficult for the mind to calculate the value of the Union, yet the
hand of a master may successfully exhibit, at a single glance,
that national protection, which, like the pressure of the atmosphere, though omnipotent and powerful, is neither seen nor felt.
The sectional excitement at present existing among the States
obliterating national feelings, these must be revived; the arts
are powerful in their operation, and lasting in their effects. We
must have national paintings, national songs, national celebra-
tions to excite and perpetuate national enthusiasm. The flag
of every country is its emblem. It should command respect
abroad, adoration at home. The man who loves and reveres not
his country's flag is prepared to violate her laws, and destroy
her Constitution. It is our object to have the Star Spangled
Banner portrayed in the act of overawing, in a foreign land, an
infuriated and lawless soldiery; and of protecting from revolutionary violence the objects of political hatred. To have this

scene engraved is also our object. That the flag of our country may wave in every house, in every cottage, even in every log-house beyond the mountains. That our children may learn before they can read, to love and reverence the emblem of our country's power, and may realize that it is their guardian and protector, not only on their native soil, but in a land of strangers.

"It is particularly wished that the painting and engraving should be finished at the shortest time consistent with their proper execution. You will therefore confer a favor by informing us whether you can undertake to carry our wishes into effect within that time, and on what terms. If you can also engage to have the painting engraved you will oblige us, at an early day, with your views upon the subject.

"Respectfully, your obedient servants,

"WILLIAM DRAYTON,

"D. E. HUGER,

"BENJAMIN F. PEPOON,

"*Committee.*"

The chairman of the committee, Mr. William Drayton, was the gentleman who purchased Allston's picture of the "Cavern Scene from Gil Blas," in London, in 1814. Allston's reply was as follows:

"GENTLEMEN: Your letter was handed me a few days since by the Honorable E. Everett. It has caused me both gratification and regret. To be thus remembered by gentlemen of my native State awakens many pleasing sensations within me, mingled with sorrow for the sad occasion which has induced you to honor me with the proposed commission. Strong as my attachment is to the State of my birth and childhood, I entirely sympathize in your feelings of pride and patriotism toward our common country; and I see also, as you must, that the safety and dignity of each individual State depends upon the union of all.

"There is no act of my life that would give me such heart-felt satisfaction as that of having done something toward strengthening the patriotism of my countrymen, and arousing once more in them the feeling that we are one people.

"I am, however, gentlemen, compelled to forego this, and to decline the commission with which you have honored me. I have imperative engagements upon me that must be fulfilled; and I could not, without absolute injustice, enter upon a work so important as that proposed by you, till those are completed for which I have some time stood pledged. While I deeply regret that it is out of my power to comply with your wishes, I doubt not that there are others at liberty, who can carry your wishes into effect, and while they accomplish something for the Union, will add to the fame of our country in the fine arts.

"With great respect, gentlemen,

"Your obedient servant,

"WASHINGTON ALLSTON.

"In sending the enclosed you will permit me to say it is my request that it be not published; not because I shrink from any odium which the declaration of my opinion respecting the present state of our country might bring upon me, but from an aversion which I have had ever, of unnecessarily appearing before the public.

"Though my lot in life has been cast in other lands, I have never forgotten that of my birth. I cannot therefore but attach a peculiar value to any mark of regard from that portion of my country; and I beg to repeat to you individually, that I do most sincerely appreciate it in the present instance. And allow me, sir, also to say, that it adds not a little to my gratification to find myself indebted for this valued distinction to one, among others, whose personal acquaintance, though short and long past, still retains a pleasant freshness in my memory."

An interesting suggestion in regard to the influence of water-color practice on Turner is contained in the following letter to Sully:

"CAMBRIDGEPORT, April 11, 1833.

"MY DEAR SULLY: Your letter on Haydon's picture, which I saw extracted from *The National Gazette*, does you honor both as an artist and as a man. The 'Entrance into Jerusalem' is indeed a magnificent work of art. Where the excellence is of so high an order, and the beauties so numerous, I should think myself but poorly employed were I disposed to dwell on its faults. I could overlook them all for the sake of its merits. 'Tis a glorious picture! If Mr. McMurtrie (to whom I beg to be particularly remembered) should write to Haydon, pray ask him to let Haydon know how much I admire it.

"Pray, have you ever painted a picture from the water-color sketch which I so much admired? I mean the 'Mother and Child.' If you have not and intend it, will you allow me to advise your copying the sketch as closely as possible as to the color. I think you will be surprised to find how transparent and silvery an exact imitation of it in oil will be. I am certain that Turner, perhaps also Calcott, owe not a little of the richness of their tone to the circumstance of their having commenced as painters in water-color. The foil of the white paper to which their eyes were accustomed, was the secret. To imitate this in oil requires not merely a high key-note, but a powerful impasto and great clearness of tint. Should you make the experiment, let me caution you against improving on the sketch; if you do, I venture to predict that your labor will be lost. Try to hit the precise tone, especially in the shadows.

"Your sincere friend,

"W. ALLSTON."

The following brief letters from Allston to Cogdell, written at this time, show characteristic traits of the writer:

" CAMBRIDGEPORT, October 9, 1833.

" DEAR COGDELL: I have been thinking of writing to you for several days past to thank you, as I ought long since to have done, for your bust of Mr. Elliott. I suppose you know it was exhibited in the Athenæum Gallery; it was well placed on a table in the centre of the room. I beg you now to accept my best thanks for it. It is a work that does you great honor. In execution it is much superior to your preceding models; and I should think, from its strongly marked character, it must be an excellent likeness.

" I sent you lately, in a letter to my mother, a message concerning it, together with my thanks, that it has been much admired by those I have heard speak of it, and those good judges. What do you say to my presenting it to the Athenæum? I mean in my name. You must not think that I do not value it by my making this proposal. I make it because I think it will be of more advantage to you there than in my room, where few people will see it. A work of art always tells better (to use a cant, but expressive, word) in a public institution than in a private house. This proposal here brings to mind a plan you some time since mentioned respecting your marble bust of Washington, when completed; that you wished it presented to the Athenæum in my name. When you consider that a marble bust is a thing of no trifling value, would it not come with a better grace from the artist himself? I think it would; and be better received; and so think two of my friends on whose judgment I rely. If you think otherwise, however, I will with pleasure do as you wish.

" I have had a pleasant visit from Fraser; he brought with him several landscapes that do him honor. I do not think Miss

Gibbs would be willing to let 'Jeremiah' go to Charleston; she declined lending it a second time to the Athenæum.

" Your sincere friend,

" W. ALLSTON."

" CAMBRIDGEPORT, October 25, 1833.

" DEAR COGDELL : I thank you for your kindness to my mother, of which she made grateful mention in her reply to my last letter. I beg you also to accept my thanks for your kind invitation to me. But you are little aware what an impossible thing you propose when you speak of my passing the winter in Charleston; I am not master of my time, nor indeed of anything else, nor shall I be until I have discharged all my obligations. It is always a painful thing to me to speak of my personal concerns; indeed I never allude to them if I can avoid it. So I will spare both you and myself the unpleasant subject. All I can therefore say is, that I regret I have not the power to accept your friendly offer.

" I was glad to hear that White had got a comfortable place in the Custom House. His friend Dana and myself were greatly disappointed in not finding a sale for his picture. We were about to get up a raffle for it when we found even that avenue closed to us; for it seems that the State Legislature had passed a law last winter against lotteries of all kinds, specifying even raffles.

" Your sincere friend,

" W. ALLSTON."

On the occasion of Leslie's brief visit to this country, Allston wrote him the following letter of welcome:

" CAMBRIDGEPORT, November 6, 1833.

" DEAR LESLIE: As I suppose you well know, increase of years has failed to impress me with a better sense than I formerly had of the charms of letter writing, and I do not mean to

Dido and Anna.

From the original sketch in the Boston Museum of Art.

write a letter now. But I cannot deny myself the gratification
of sending you a line, to congratulate you on your safe arrival
and to welcome you among us. I have no friend to whom I can
more heartily say, right welcome. Pray present my best regards
to your wife and children, whom I am predisposed to like on
your account, and whom I have no doubt I shall like when I see
them on their own. My wife, who better knows you by your letters, than yours can me by mine, joins me in this. I regret that
a visit now to New York is to me among the minor impossibili-
ties : for gold I have none, and all the silver I have is on my head.

> "Faithfully yours,

> "W. ALLSTON."

In December, 1833, Allston wrote in a letter to J. Mason :
" I have just had a pressing demand made on me by my coal
merchant, and a smaller one, equally as urgent, both together
amounting to about one hundred and fifty dollars, which I wish
to settle immediately, but which I have no means of doing until
Mr. Phillips's picture is finished. Do you think that your
brother Powell, who is agent for Mr. P. during his absence in
Europe, would feel at liberty to advance that sum out of what
would be due on completion of the picture ? "

Concerning this and other pressure of the kind upon Allston,
Dana makes the following memoranda : " 'The Angel over Jerusalem' was, I think, the picture he was painting for Mr. Phillips ;
if it was not that, it was the 'Death of King John.' Mr. P. had
at a former time, when Allston was greatly pressed, let him have,
I think it was $500, and Allston was to paint him a picture
when he could. No one knows the misery of mind this whole
affair cost him, nor the time it lost him. I have a perfect conviction that it hastened his death, that what he then endured
stimulated his disease. What wretchedness have I witnessed
when he was struggling to go on with it, and from distress of

mind could not. 'Isaac of York,' belonging to the Boston Athenæum, he painted in a very short time, I forget how many days. Allston said also that he hit upon the name of the picture after it was painted. From Allston's letter to Mason, I gather that it was sold to the Athenæum very soon after it was finished. The Committee of Fine Arts, Athenæum, afterward applied through William T. Andrews to know whether Allston would consent to have 'Isaac of York' engraved by young Morse, of Boston.

"What was the sum he first set upon his exquisite picture of 'The Troubadour,' I forget, but no one was found with taste enough to purchase it at the time. In the letter to Mason of December 27, 1833, he says: 'Should anyone now offer me $300 for "The Troubadour," I would sell it for that sum. I have, however, given up all hope of selling it, so that I cannot be disappointed if it does not sell at this price.'

"Two months later he wrote again to the same gentleman, 'I am so much pushed that I have come to the conclusion to lower the price of "The Troubadour" to $280, and if that can't be obtained to $250, but am resolved to keep it if that cannot be obtained. Please do not delay to offer it for the lowest sum if the first cannot be obtained, as I am so sadly pressed.'

"Distress for money at last drove him to part with it for $70 or $80."

This letter from Allston to his classmate, Leonard Jarvis, then a member of Congress, upon the subject of Greenough's design for his statue of Washington to be placed in the Capitol, contains suggestions and opinions interesting to artists, and especially sculptors.

"CAMBRIDGEPORT, June 19, 1834.

'DEAR JARVIS: I have received yours of the 6th inst., and thank you for your considerate kindness in leaving me to reply to it or not, as I like. This is indeed a kindness to one who has about as much sympathy with letters (when he has to write them) as a mad dog with water. On this occasion, however, it is my duty to write.

" You have described the design of the statue so minutely, that I think I can form as accurate an opinion of it as if I had the drawing before me. I agree with you in every particular of your criticism ; and so does E. T. D. and R. H. D., to whom I showed your description. We were all three struck, as you were, with the inappropriateness of the raised arm. We were also of the same mind respecting the idealizing of Washington. Now, how to unidealize, without changing the present general design, *hic labor*. It can, however, be done ; but it must be done by the artist himself—nay it should not be done by any other person ; and I am the last man who would dictate to a brother artist ; neither my principles nor disposition would allow me to do it, especially to one of Greenough's genius. All that can be done, or at least that I am willing to do, is to throw out suggestions, leaving the adoption or modification of them entirely to him. This appears to me not only the most delicate, but indeed the only efficient, course, for no man of genius ever worked successfully from the mere dictation of another. He must coincide with and enter into the spirit of the change proposed, or his work will not be of a piece. Should Greenough so enter into it, and there is no reason to suppose that, weighing the objections to his present design, he will not, I have the most thorough confidence in his success.

" As the opinion of the world, that is, of the competent judges in it, seems to be pretty nearly balanced on the subject of costume—as many preferring the ancient as the modern, I shall offer no advice on this point, and for two reasons : first, because I would not take upon myself the responsibility of deciding for another artist on a subject where good judges disagree, and secondly, because Mr. Greenough has already decided for himself. I will, however, standing neutral on this question, make a general remark or two, on both that may be of use in either case ; the subject being the statue of *any* distinguished person, of or near our own time. Supposing the ancient to be adopted, all minutiæ and peculiarities belonging to a particular age or country—in other words, whatever tends to remove the subject from his own age to another, should, I think, be avoided. To adopt a distinction of Sir Joshua Reynolds, it should be clothed with drapery, and not in an antique dress.

" The Greek and Roman helmet, cuirass, etc., also, from the peculiar manner in which it is folded, the Roman toga, belong to what is here meant by dress. If the modern be adopted, though it must, *as modern,* be of necessity identified with our own age, it should still be of so general a character as not to fix the mind upon the *fashion* of any particular time in it. Under the head of fashion I would class bag-wigs, wigs, queues, frizzed hair, flapped waistcoats, bag-sleeves, etc.

" How far the ancient costume may be adopted without impairing the individuality of the subject, is more than I can say : that can only be shown by the skill of the sculptor; as to the other question, how the *prescribed* and scanty form of a modern dress can be managed with grandeur, that also must be left to his skill. The general objection of artists to the modern dress is its meagreness, as not admitting of those masses so essential to a grand effect. In general this is true, but there are some exceptions ; for instance the military cloak, which, without violation of its character (I use this word technically) may be used for all the purposes of drapery, admitting of equal breadth and mass with the ancient mantle. But the costume in the statue of a great modern seems to me essentially secondary. The character of the man is, and should be, the principal thing. If this be true, it necessarily limits the artist in his conception. Whatever ideas he may have of grandeur or majesty, if they do not belong to his original, they can have no propriety in his statue. He depends on his subject for all the grandeur that is admissible. But if his subject should happen to be of mean appearance? There is then but one alternative, to make the best of a mean person, or not attempt it; for a noble figure would not represent that person, but his proxy.

"In the present case, however, the artist has no such difficulty to contend with, for his original (I mean Washington) was not only great in mind, but of a noble countenance and majestic stature. Perhaps in all history a grander subject for a portrait statue could not be found; for what attitude could be too dignified, what air too grand for Washington? Dignity and majesty were his personal attributes. With a slight modification, I do not see but that the present attitude which Greenough has chosen might be retained with propriety. Bating the raised arm, it seems to me (as you have described it) a dignified one.

"My notion of the statue of a great modern who has actually lived, is, in a few words, this: It should not bring the person before us as an active agent, but simply as the man whose deeds and virtues have passed into history, and who is already known to us by his deeds and virtues. To this effect, the most perfect repose seems to me essential in Washington, especially (no conscious action should break it), whose name alone fills the mind with his history. If any man can be said to repose in the fulness of his glory, it is he; for nothing in his great mission has been left imperfect; all has been done, and is in the past. We need alone the man as a visible object of our love and veneration.

"Should this notion be approved and adopted by Greenough, there needs but a slight alteration, as I have already observed, as far as concerns the attitude, to realize it; and that is (the alteration) to give rest to the uplifted hand and arm. I mean to bring the hand down, so as to rest on some part of his person, or on the chair. I know not that the hand which holds the sword need be altered, but I doubt the propriety of the antique sword. A scroll would answer for the composition quite as well, besides being more appropriate. Here I beg it to be distinctly understood that I abstain, for the reasons given, from any decision respecting the costume. If, however, the present be retained, I am clear that the breast and arms should be draped; which might well be done by a close tunic with sleeves.

"If you have not already done so, I beg you will show to Mr. McLane that part of my first letter relating to 'Medora.' And, since he is pleased to attach some value to my opinion, I wish you also to say to him that, notwithstanding the objections to the present design, I have no distrust whatever in Mr. G's ability to produce a statue that will do honor to the country. The classic atmosphere in which he has so long lived has, perhaps, and very naturally, biassed his judgment in this instance; but that he can conceive equally well in another way I have no doubt; and that, when he shall have distinctly understood what is desired, he will so modify his design as to give satisfaction, I have the most entire confidence. I know Greenough well, and if I know what genius is, he possesses as much of it as any sculptor living. His natural powers are of no common order, and he has cultivated them by a severe course of study. He is no tyro, nor random flourisher, but a well-grounded scholar in his art. To this I shall only add, that I have been conscientious in every word I have written. On such an occasion I would not give my best friend one tittle more of praise than he deserved. You say that as a work of art the 'design' is worthy of praise, etc. I should have been disappointed if you had not found it so, still more if you had not liked the 'Medora.' I particularly request that this letter may not be suffered to get into the newspapers. I have no objection that a copy of this letter be sent to Mr. G., but it must be sent entire and verbatim, and provided that he be informed that it is done with my consent."

CHAPTER XXII.

In Dunlap's "History of the Arts of Design," published in 1834, we have sketches of lives of American artists up to that time. This book, though defective in many respects, and open to criticism, is, nevertheless, a valuable contribution to the history of art in America. Among its salient points are statements and inferential allusions giving color to accusations of idleness which, with no foundation in truth, were made against Allston. Allston, by request, contributed much interesting material for the sketch of his life, and had Dunlap added nothing to that material, we should have all that need be in a book purporting to give nothing more than brief outline biographies. When the book appeared, Allston was much disturbed by its statements and inferences touching his personal habits. In a copy of Dunlap's work, presented to Allston by the author, was recently found the subjoined portion of the "rough" of a letter, written in vindication of himself against the unjust allusions referred to. We give it without the slightest revision or alteration :

"*Mem. wrote to Mr. Dunlap, March 20, 1835.*"

"At present I will only point out one—the only important one—which is contained in the last paragraph but one, which contains but only two grains of truth ; namely, that I smoked

and sat up late ; the rest, that is, what is supposed to have been
connected with these habits, is not true. You must not think
that I am here wincing at the mention of my faults. I know
that I have faults enough and to spare, and what is more, I have
long learned to bear the mention of them. But the fault imputed to me by *inference*, in this paragraph, is really not mine.
The passage which I allude to as giving a false impression of me
is this : 'that the time he threw away in smoking his cigar, and
delighting his friends with conversation and delightful stories,
should have been employed in keeping up by a succession of
efforts the name he had obtained.'

"Now, the inference drawn from this is, that I was an idler,
wasting my time in company continuously. I cannot take that
to myself. I was then, and am still, a very different man. Next
to what is vicious, there is no character more offensive to me, or
one that I would most strenuously avoid realizing in my own
person, than a company-loving idler. So far from wasting time
in company, my friends both in England and here have often
complained that I did not go into it enough. I would not be an
excuser of late hours. My late hours were spent not in company,
but in solitary study : in reading, often in sketching, or in other
studies connected with my art.

"As to general company, it always was and is to this day irksome to me. And though I take great pleasure in the society
of my friends, my visits among them have always been rare, and
from choice. Nay, it is the very rareness of these visits that
sometimes makes them so pleasant—bringing out what is most
pleasant in myself. Strangers who have seen me with my
friends, and observed the zest with which I enjoyed conversation, have probably been misled by it, and set me down as one
who must needs prefer it to labor. You, indeed, have judged
me truly when you say that such 'minds are never idle.' Without assuming the compliment implied, I may say that mine is so

constituted that I could not be idle for six months and continue sane. Either that or my hands are always at work.

"But much as I love the interchange of mind with the literary and intellectual, still more do I love my art. I have never found the labor in it irksome, though often plied in misery and *abortive:* for when I have been most wretched, and consequently working to no purpose, it has still been to me an unchangeable friend. Although it is not natural for any man to *desire* the exposure of his faults, yet I am not one who would *gainsay* what is true, though it be against me."

At the Ferme St. Siméon, at Honfleur, France, a favorite summer resort of artists, the celebrated Charles Daubigny was met by a young American art student, in whom he became sufficiently interested to correct his work from time to time, giving him valuable instruction. By this unsolicited and kindly attention the young painter was much gratified. The *maîtresse du logis* had from year to year solicited each of her artist guests to leave a memento of his visit in a sketch on one of the panels of her doors. In this way she had made her house uniquely pictorial. When the great landscapist became her lodger, she ventured her usual request that he would at his convenience decorate one of the door panels of her best room. Daubigny cheerfully consented. The young painter determined if possible to be present at the painting. Accordingly he began to sketch a landscape from an open window of the room which was to become famous. One morning, quite early, while the student was at his work, Daubigny entered with his box of materials, laid it upon a table, took a chair, and seated himself before the blank panel. The young American, it is needless to say, was all expectation; the time he had looked forward to with the greatest pleasure had arrived; he would now see the great artist paint, and try to learn something of his method. But his patience was to be sorely tried, expectation was to wait long upon gratification. Still Daubigny sat silently contemplating the blank parallelogram till breakfast, the mid-day meal, was announced. That over, he returned and quietly seated himself as before. The young student now thought his opportunity had surely arrived, and under cover of serious occupation to prevent suspicion that he was merely a looker-on, seated himself at his post and apparently became absorbed in his own work. Again the hours passed slowly by, with no movement on the part of the master to reward the student's vigil.

The stimulating hope of the morning was fading with approaching twilight, the shadows were lengthening, hardly an hour of daylight remained, when, rising from his chair, Daubigny took his palette and brushes in hand and began to paint. The work was rapid: every touch told with precision and power. The picture had already been painted in his thought. All that he was now doing was to place it before his eye; this he accomplished almost as speedily as the paint could be made to cover the panel. Dexterously the masses were laid in, and forms developed, till in a short half-hour, shorter than the young student had ever passed, the work was completed—a landscape full of beauty; a memento of a great artist; an enduring joy for the inmates of that rustic rendezvous of painters.

Shall we call Daubigny an idler because he could sit so long absorbed in his own thoughts, and devote but thirty minutes of an entire day to tangible work? Pictorial results may represent or indicate the work of genius, but they do not measure it. We may not estimate as an element in the production of his work the preparatory, severe study by which Daubigny's skill was attained; but we must consider the long hours of his quiet thinking, on that day of the panel painting, as entering into and giving value to his work.

The picture occupied him an entire day, albeit he painted but thirty minutes. The hard work, if we may so call it, was not confined to the painting : it was in the arrangement, construction, and complete development of the picture in his mind. Had he reversed the order of his work, and commenced painting before thinking, he might have become involved and occupied several days with a less felicitous result. His genius was of that strong kind that can create mentally, and as it were, finish his picture before beginning it. This faculty is evidence of the highest genius. Ordinarily, men—and men of great ability—need an objective starting-point, something visible to build upon ; something to suggest something more. The higher genius works as by an inspiration from the inner to the outer, from thought-work to hand-work.

Pleasure is tinted with a hue of sadness as we recall the scenes of more than fifty years ago in that modest house in Cambridgeport, where Allston lived. It is sad that the veil of time should bury with the evil of the past its pleasures and its beauties. No day laborer was ever more regularly at his post than was Allston at his work. He was one of the most industrious of men. For over thirty years, after his sickness in Bristol, without an hour of full health, disheartened at times by stress of pecuniary embarrassment, he labored with great persistency, and produced pictures which, could they be collected for exhibition, would form an array that would do credit to the industry of any man, even though he were not laboring under the discouragement of want of money and ill-health. He sacrificed himself to conscientious labor. He was imprisoned in a sense of duty and constant necessity. It seems a reproach to humanity that such a man should have been so embarrassed. That this was felt by many of his personal friends, is shown by this extract from the Memoranda of R. H. Dana, Sr. :

" Captain Hamilton, in his work upon this country, questions Allston's genius on the score of its being slowly productive.

The captain should not have published such a remark before being possessed of the facts, and after that he would hardly have done it. In this off-hand way, which merely clever men have of speaking of men of genius, they harm themselves, as it serves to dull their apprehensions of the infinite superiority of genius and the essential difference between it and mere talent. Besides, it weakens that reverence which it is beneficial to ordinary minds to feel for it. See his many designs and outlines, which show how active and productive was his imagination.

" Dr. Channing had right views with respect to Allston. He considered that what was done for Allston was done for art, and for the world, and that for ages to come; that it was not helping a certain individual of the name of Washington Allston, who would by and by die and be forgotten; he did not look upon it in the low way of charity or alms-giving, but as wealth contributing to the realizing of that without which wealth degenerates into a vulgar drug, and man fails of rising to refinement. These views he many times expressed in earnest conversation with me. He felt that to any effectual purpose Allston should be made comfortably independent in his circumstances. I had previously written to Dr. Channing on this subject, and upon the little good that would arise from just keeping such a man's chin above water, instead of taking him fairly out of his seas of troubles, and standing him upon his feet on dry land.

"Morse had the same views, and told me that he once said to Dr. Channing, ' Ask gentlemen what they would do for Raffaelle, were he sent back to earth in his vocation, and that, let them do for Allston.' If one man ever loved and reverenced another, Morse loved and reverenced Allston. He told me that when he found he was likely to succeed with his magnetic telegraph, and had the expectation of realizing a tolerable fortune from it, he had determined to set Allston free and enable him to give himself to his art, working simply from love of it, adding that he would have done it in such a way that it should not have given Allston a moment's painful feeling.

"The very distress which debt and embarrassed circumstances throw the mind into, leads it involuntarily to find ease in forming the most improbable schemes for relief, about which few can believe it is really in earnest. Upon a severe affliction taking place in Allston's family, he said with deep emotion to my son, 'What a blessed thing it is for a man to have work to do in a time of affliction. One may paint with tears in the eyes—but to paint under debt!'

"It used to be one of my dreams, that should God bestow a fortune upon me, one of the first things I would do would be to free Allston from all his pecuniary obligations, make arrangements for his current expenses, so that he should have no more anxiety on that head, furnish him with a man to attend to his brushes, palette, and all such matters, and aid some clever young artist, who might relieve him of much labor on his pictures, improve himself by doing all that work on the pictures which did not require the master's own hand. The simple presence of a human being with him would, unconsciously to himself, have had a kindly, healthful influence upon him; while his being there as his familiar assistant, would have prevented any disturbing effect upon his mental processes.

"But Morse and I have been waked, and behold it was a dream. No, I at times dream still, childish as it may seem, and fancy myself about doing, what in my case I then knew would be almost an impossible thing, and on which Death has now set its seal, making it an entire impossibility; and yet it a little eases the aching of my heart at times to be thus the child still; and may I not then dream? Rather, will not minds have an intuition of other minds, mental images as they are mentally projected?'"

Social duties and advantages were neglected by Allston because the stern necessity for work was upon him and his conscience held him to it inexorably. Mind or body, or both, must yield to the unbroken routine of labor under the hard conditions placed on him. This routine would have been unbroken, had not the charm of his personality, which drew about him of an evening a delightful companionship, brought occasional relaxation.

CHAPTER XXIII.

LETTERS FROM 1835 TO 1838.—ALLSTON TO COGDELL, COMMENTS
ON ART.—CORRESPONDENCE BETWEEN ALLSTON AND THE CON-
GRESSIONAL COMMITTEE.—FINAL DECISION NOT TO ACCEPT THE
COMMISSION GIVEN HIM BY THE GOVERNMENT.

The first of the following letters to Cogdell has an interesting allusion to certain drawings from the old masters, which Cogdell had sent him, and the second refers again to Dunlap's paragraph intimating that he might have been of more industrious habits:

"CAMBRIDGEPORT, March 9, 1835.

"DEAR COGDELL: I have been intending to thank you by letter for your kind present of the drawings of Cork. I was about to begin an apology for not acknowledging it sooner; but I have made so many apologies on the score of letter-writing, during half a century, that I think I may well be excused making any more for the rest of my life. Be assured, however, that though so late in its acknowledgment, I have not been the less sensible either to the beauty of these remarkable drawings, or to the kindness of the donor.

"I had no difficulty in recognizing among them the hands of several of the old masters, especially Raffaelle, Correggio, and Titian. Of one or two, indeed, I doubted for a moment whether to ascribe them to Rubens or to some high Venetian colorist; but a little reflection convinced me that these also were in too pure a *gusto* for the Flemish school; so I set them down as Tintoretto's. The beautiful drawing which you presented to Mrs.

Allston (who begs me to express her thanks for the gift), there can be no doubt, is from the delicate hand of Carlo Dolce. Several of them, however still remain unexamined in their cases; for, as they are too good to be enjoyed alone, I never open them but when the pleasure can be shared by some particular friend. The most remarkable peculiarity of these drawings, and that which particularly struck me is this: that they not only satisfy you with their own beauties, but they set the mind to work, in conjuring up visions of its own, a true test of genius in art. There are indeed some other drawings of Cork, as, for instance, those of the Holland and Cognac schools, which seem to have a similar quality; but it is only the property of repeating themselves, or rather of doubling their own images to the eyes of the spectator. But no such vulgar effect can in any degree be possible of these ideal drawings. The associate forms they suggest are essentially poetical—not a reproduction, a mere *alter et idem* —but a progeny; the probable taking birth from the actual, and from the probable the possible. In a word, I know not to what more analogous I can liken their effect than to those natural visions at daybreak, which the sun reveals to the earth, when he opens the lids of a thousand sleeping flowers, that look up to him in return, blushing to find themselves so happy and beautiful."

"CAMBRIDGEPORT, May 18, 1835.

"DEAR COGDELL: I wrote you last on March 10th. A day or two after I received a letter from Mr. Ticknor, mentioning the arrival of your bust of Scott. On the same day I wrote to my mother, and requested her to inform you of its arrival, and to say that I would go and see it as soon as the nature of my labors would allow me a day for that purpose. I did not get into Boston as soon as I wished or expected.

"Mr. Dunlap has been led into an error by some person who could not have known me except by hearsay, in the account given of me in the last paragraph but one in his biography of me. Two small items in it only are true—the rest have no foundation. My evenings were spent not in the way supposed, but in solitary study, among my books and sketches. There is no character, not in itself vicious, that I despise more than a gossiping idler. Besides, the pencil is in my hand daily, and excepting the Sabbath, or when precluded by business, has been for years. I shall request Mr. Dunlap to correct this in his second edition. Do not let this which I now write get into the newspapers. I am not blaming Mr. Dunlap, who has been most liberal to me of praise, and who meant to be impartial, and who, no doubt, thought the account he received correct. Besides, I have a sincere esteem for him, and would on no account hurt his feelings by any indirect correction of it. I intend, when I have time, writing to him on the subject. In the meantime I would not have this false impression remain with my friends at a distance. . . .

" Your sincere friend,

" W. ALLSTON."

The following correspondence relates to the project that Allston should paint a picture for one of the panels of the Rotunda of the Capitol at Washington:

" CAMBRIDGEPORT, June 24, 1836.

" DEAR JARVIS: I have just received your letter of the 18th inst., informing me of the passage of a bill by Congress for supplying the vacant panels in the Rotunda with pictures by American artists. For your friendly intention in my behalf I beg you to accept my best thanks; but I regret to say that, under present circumstances, it is not in my power to profit by them. I had anticipated this contingency, and had long since deliberately made up my mind on the subject. I am not a free man, nor shall I probably become one in less than three years; for after the completion of ' Belshazzar' (which I expect to resume in a few weeks) I have several other pictures engaged, which I am bound in honor to finish before I undertake any new work.   An expected picture at an uncertain time is an incubus to my imagination ; I have therefore, under this feeling, declined five commissions within the last eighteen months.   Could you know but the twentieth part of what I have suffered from the (compelled) delay of ' Belshazzar,' you would readily believe that my peace of mind requires me to withstand the present temptation, for temptation it certainly is ; but he is safe who knows when he is tempted, seeing the end in the beginning.   Were I free from my imperative engagements nothing would delight me more than to fill one of the panels of the Rotunda.   It has often been a pleasant dream to me ; but I am not my own master and must dismiss all such dreams.

"I would not recall, much less repeat, the many injurious speeches that have been made about me for not finishing this picture, though it was a private affair, with which the public had nothing to do.   Even some who professed to be friendly could not forbear a hard word.   I do not, however, believe there was any ill-nature in this ; but words, if unjust, may be hard without ill-nature.   I never quitted 'Belshazzar' at any time but when compelled to do so by debts, contracted while engaged upon it, and which I could discharge only by painting small pictures ; many of which, from being forced work, cost me treble the labor and time they otherwise would have done, and consequently left but a pittance of profit ; nay, some hardly enough to cover their expenses, and of course without the means of returning to the larger work.   You know that I have been unremitting in my labors.   For years the Sabbath was the only time that I have been absent (except on business) from my painting-room, and I never sit there with my arms folded.   That I have not brought more to pass was because I was like a bee trying to make honey in a coal-hole. But, thanks to some noble-hearted friends, those dark days are now past. They have taken me out of the squirrel cage; my foot no longer falls in the same place, but every step I take carries me onward. By the assistance of these friends my mind is now at ease; but it would not long continue so were I to accept the commission which your friendship has so kindly labored to procure me. If in a private affair the public would reproach me for not performing an impossibility, they can hardly be expected to be more considerate when every man in the country might claim to be a party. 'Will he never finish that picture for the Government?' might be asked from Castine to St. Louis. No money would buy off the fiends that such words would conjure up. I am now an old man, and am besides too infirm of body to bear these things as some might; they would soon wear away the little flesh I have. A regard for my peace, therefore, will compel me to decline the Government commission should it be offered me.

"But I must wind up this long epistle by again expressing my grateful thanks for your kindness, which I trust you know I most sincerely feel, though for the reasons assigned I cannot avail myself of it as you had hoped. That it might not be thought (from ignorance of my motives) that I had carelessly 'thrown fortune from me,' I wish you to show this letter, in confidence, to Mr. Preston. I have written freely to you, as an old friend, what I could not have written to him, and it will save me the awkwardness of a more formal exposition of the reasons for declining the honor which the Committee would confer on me. Pray present my respects to Mr. Preston.

"Give my best regards to Greenough, and tell him that I shall be right glad to see him.

"Your old and faithful friend,

"W. ALLSTON."

"Washington, July 4, 1836.

"Dear Sir: The Joint Committee of the two Houses of Congress, appointed for the purpose of contracting with one or more competent artists for pictures to fill the vacant panels of the Rotunda of the Capitol at Washington, have directed us to inform you of their wish for two of the productions of your pencil.

"The only restriction in the choice of the subjects would be that they must be approved by the Committee and that they must serve to illustrate some events, civil or military, of sufficient importance to be the subject of a national picture, in the history of the discovery, or settlement of the colonies which now constitute the United States of America, of the separation of the colonies from the Mother Country, or of the United States prior to the adoption of the Federal Constitution.

"You would be left free with regard to the time when the pictures should be finished; the compensation will be liberal, and the payments made in proportions to suit your convenience.

"Permit us to assure you of the personal gratification we derive from being the organs of this communication, and to express the earnest hope that neither your inclination nor engagements will prevent your acceptance of the commission.

"We remain, very sincerely,

"Your obedient servants,

"G. C. Verplanck,
"L. Jarvis,
"J. Q. Adams,
"*The Committee.*"

Reference to this project is also made at the end of the long letter from Leonard Jarvis to R. H. Dana concerning Allston, dated Surry, Me., February 12, 1844, from which we have already quoted a number of times in the foregoing pages. It is as follows:

"One thing more and I will bring my prosing to a close. In 1835 and 1836 Congress came to the determination to have the vacant panels of the Rotunda of the Capitol at Washington occupied with pictures according to their original destination. J. Q. Adams, one of the Committee to whom the charge was intrusted, proposed that Allston should be the artist employed. To this proposition our friend would not listen for a moment. He considered that it would be a grievous wrong to his brethren of the palette, and he finally declined any share whatever in the commission. His reasons were that he was bound in honor to complete the 'Belshazzar' before he should undertake another large picture, and this would require time; that if he should accept, every one would think they had a right to inquire into the progress of his work, and this very circumstance would impair his efficiency; that the reproach to which he would be subjected for not advancing like a house painter, though undeserving of notice, would wear upon his spirits and would finally destroy him. He preferred being a free man to being the slave of a multitude. He nevertheless relinquished the offer with great regret, for he had long before selected a subject for one of the panels, on which he loved to expatiate. It was Columbus on his return from the discovery of the Western World presenting to Ferdinand and Isabella the results of his voyage. He thought this subject included all the requisites for a noble picture. I am sure it would have been if executed in the manner in which he proposed to treat it."

Following are several letters to Cogdell containing allusions of interest to art, study abroad, Cogdell's own work, the afterward celebrated landscape painter Thomas Cole, to Powers, and to the more personal matter of the writer's own health, already at this time seriously compromised :

"CAMBRIDGEPORT, October 18, 1836.

"DEAR COGDELL: I have the pleasure to acknowledge the receipt of your kind letter by Mr. Gilman. And I thank you for not noticing my long silence. This is as it should be ; for it shows that you are willing to take me as I am, which all friends should do as to one another in this imperfect world.

.   .   .   .

"Your project of visiting Italy I hope may be realized. I shall rejoice to hear that you are able to accomplish it ; for, as I observed to Mr. Gilman, I believe it would add ten years to your life, not only by the advantage which a change of climate would be to your bodily health, but by the renovation which that delightful country, with its thousand monuments of human genius, would produce in your spirit. You will, no doubt, when there, become more than a mere traveller and spectator. Surrounded as you will be by the finest works of art, I dare say that you will not be in Rome a month before you are hard at work, up to your eyes in clay. With the excitement that must there meet you at every step, you, I am sure, will not be content with simply looking. You will find yourself growing younger in body and more elastic in mind, and I should not be surprised if the consequence prove a development of powers of which you are now unconscious. The lives of Claude and the French sculptor Falconet (the colossal bronze statue at St. Petersburg of Peter the Great is by F.) show that genius may take a start at any period of life. Claude did not touch a pencil till he was forty, and, as Sir Joshua Reynolds well said, ' We are more likely to have another Raffaelle than another Claude.' Up to the same age Falconet was a common laborer in a sculptor's studio. He could then neither read nor write, and was withal one of the multitude. But the genius which nature had given him suddenly, but secretly, became ' A presence ' to his mind ; and he began to develop it by stealth in his scanty portions of leisure ; nor was he suspected of genius till it came before the public in full growth. But he did not stop here. The rank to which his art had raised him made him feel the want of education, which the same energetic industry soon also enabled him to supply. So that he not only learned to read and write his own language in a manner becoming to a gentleman, but finally mastered both Latin and Greek. I mention this not as a parallel case to yours, for you not only have had the advantage of an early liberal education, but are already advanced in the art. I have only cited it to show that where genius exists it is never too late, while the other faculties remain, to bring it forth. Of the existence of this you have already given proof; and I have now only to wish that you may be placed in circumstances where it may have free scope and come to maturity. To this end, and I suppose you will agree with me, ease of mind as regards pecuniary matters is essential. As the love of gain never yet made a true artist, while it has marred many, so do I believe that no genius ever fully developed under the pressure of want. I call that want which involves obligations that we are unable to discharge, which to the honorable mind (next to the companionship of vice) is one of the ills of life most difficult to bear up against.

"I will furnish you with letters, when you are ready to depart, with great pleasure, to some who are among my most valued friends, in Rome, Florence, and London, each of them eminent artists, whom you will find also excellent men. Shall I introduce you to them as an artist, or as one who cultivates the art for his amusement? . . .

"I remain, your sincere friend,

"W. ALLSTON."

"CAMBRIDGEPORT, December 15, 1837.

"DEAR COGDELL: I wrote to my mother in October, well as I can recollect on the 27th, when I begged her to thank you for the kind letter which you wrote me at her request to inform me of my poor brother's death; the melancholy intelligence was

rendered still more affecting by having to communicate it to my
brother Henry, whom I had not seen for years, and who arrived
on the evening of the day I received the letter.   The misfortunes of one of his amiable and gentle disposition, while they
saddened our recollections have still more endeared to us his
memory.   What a strange power has the mind!   I can look back
over an interval of more than forty years, and see him as he
was when a baby in the nurse's arms.   And more mysterious
still, I can connect the countenance of the nervous, laughing
child with the mild, yet grave face of his middle age, feeling,
too, that they are one and the same.   How clearly does this
speak to us of the imperishable identity of the soul through all
physical mutations ; for it is the soul and not the outward form,
which we now recall, and recognize, unimpaired by time.

"I have already, in the letter alluded to, thanked my dear,
good mother for her kind prescription, which I shall certainly
try if I am again attacked in the way I described to her, and I
don't doubt I shall find relief from it.   But temporary relief is
all I can expect from any medicine, as my medical friend in England long ago assured me.   My complaint had even then become chronic ; and he told me then I must compound for being
an invalid all my life. . . .   But I am quite content that
it should be so ; my blessings have been more than I deserve ;
and for my present portion of health I am still most thankful.

·   ·   ·   ·   ·   ·   ·   ·

"I am glad to find you have resumed the pencil.   Not that I
would have you abandon the chisel, but it is better to have two
kinds of agreeable employment than one.   It has struck me that
your group of 'Hagar and Ishmael' transferred to canvas would
make a fine picture.   If you think so, allow me to make a few
suggestions as to the color, which should be strong, but simple,
say red and blue—the tunic red, and a blue mantle.   I do not
recollect if the boy has a tunic ; if he has, I would have that

white. And let the foreground be of a strong, reddish earth, with gray stones; the scene is a rocky desert, rather flat, with mountains, seen over a plain, at a great distance, and the horizon marked by a strip of light under a murky sky—you may remember my criticism on Ishmael's tongue. It should not be seen in the picture, I am sure. It would be offensive. Let the mouth be half open. Be sure you retain the expression of the mother; it was very fine. If you think with me as to the choice of color for the picture, I would recommend for the tunic Venetian red for the lights, and Indian red and black for the shadows, which you may glaze, if you wish to enrich it, with lake and asphaltum; never use vermilion in draperies, it is a flat color.

". . . You will have a visit from my nephew, George Flagg, whom I am sure you will like. I write by him to my mother. He left us about two hours ago for Carolina, by the way of New York. You will receive this by mail. It will probably reach you by the time he arrives.

" Believe me, ever your sincere friend,

"W. ALLSTON."

"CAMBRIDGEPORT, October 21, 1838.

"DEAR COGDELL: It was my intention to have answered your kind letter of September 14th before this, but I have been prevented in various ways. I wrote to my mother on September 30th, and was just about to conclude it when yours was brought to me from the post-office. Believe me, my friend, that I thank you from my heart for all your kindness to my dear mother, and no less for the past than for this last instance of your friendly disposition. Nor is she unmindful of it, as she speaks of you always with the greatest affection, calling you sometimes her son Cogdell. It is needless to tell you how sincerely I rejoice at the intelligence of your letter concerning the pension to my mother. Added to her small income, it will, I trust, make her declining years more comfortable than they have been of late. I have much doubt whether any claim on account of my father's services will be allowed, as they were those of a partisan officer in Marion's regiment. I may be mistaken, but I have always understood that the partisan officers served gratuitously, in which case the Government may deny the legality of the claim. Old Judge Watys, who was his brother officer, used to call him the 'young captain,' and always spoke of him as a gallant officer. I have often lamented that there is no portrait of my father. I think it the duty of all parents to have their portraits painted for the sake of their children. The portrait which I painted of my mother before my second visit to Europe is to me invaluable. It was then considered an excellent likeness, and such, too, I consider it. I never seized a more characteristic expression and that of a strong mind and ardent feelings. My friend Coleridge, who saw it in England, admired the character as belonging to no common woman, in which I think he judged truly.

.   .   .   .

"You told me you had commenced 'Hagar and Ishmael,' but had been obliged to lay it aside on account of the sickness and hot weather. I hope that the more cheering days of the coming winter will enable you to resume it. If you preserve the expression of your modelled group, you will not fail of making a picture of deep interest. There are few subjects so limited in composition, so naturally adapted to awaken general sympathy; but it is one in which, from the very circumstance of its simplicity everything depends on the expression. I use this last word in its ordinary sense, as relating solely to the figures— their air, attitude, and faces. This you have already in the modelled figures, and this would be enough if transferred to canvas. But there is another kind of expression which I hope you will endeavor to add—that of elements; to make them, as it were in sympathy with the human emotion. In this consists no small portion of the poetry of our art, and this is expressed in the character—that is, the forms, tone of color, in short, the general effect, of the scenery. I remember one of Rembrandt's finest pictures owing its whole sublimity to the background alone. Rembrandt, as you know, had no excellence in form, though no one ever surpassed him in expression, even in its widest sense; for he was a poet in all else. The picture I allude to is 'Jacob's Dream,' which consisted of only three figures, Jacob and two angels; the figure of Jacob about six inches in length, asleep on the ground, and nothing better than a drowsy Dutchman; but the angels, which were only two inches in height, and of course too small to indicate more than the general air, were from the skill with which they expressed that air, in the remote distance more like angels than anything I have seen on canvas. And they owed this to the background, the midnight sky, the fathomless darkness—I might almost say the permeable pitch— in which they moved, while the two hardly visible lines of light which formed the ladder seemed to sway with the night-breeze. Nothing could be more simple than these few materials, yet he did contrive to make out of them one of the sublimest pictures I know.

.   .   .   .

"Cole, of New York, whom I believe you know, had a very beautiful landscape in the last Athenæum Exhibition called 'A Dream of Arcadia.' Powers, a young sculptor from Cincinnati, is going to do great things in his art, if I mistake not. He is now in Florence. I saw him before his departure and felt assured of his success. He is no common man."

CHAPTER XXIV.

Mrs. Jameson, the well-known writer on art, when in this
country, visited Allston. The following extracts are from her
beautiful memoir of him, published in 1844 :

"About two years before his death there was an exhibition of
his works in Boston, an exhibition which, in the amount of excellence, might well be compared to the room full of Sir Joshua at
the Institution last year. Those who have not seen many of
Allston's pictures will hardly believe this ; those who have will
admit the justice of the comparison—will remember those of his
creations, in which he combined the richest tones of color with
the utmost delicacy and depth of expression, and added to these
merits a softness and finish of execution and correctness of drawing—particularly in the extremities—which Sir Joshua never
attained, nor, perhaps, attempted. When I have thought of the
vehement poetical sensibility with which Allston was endowed,
his early turn for the wild, the marvellous, the terrible—his nervous temperament, and a sort of dreaming indolence which every
now and then seemed to come over him, I have more and more
deeply appreciated the sober grandeur of his compositions, the
refined grace of some of his most poetical creations, the harmonious sweetness which tempered his most gorgeous combina-
tions of color, and the conscientious, patient care with which

every little detail is executed ; in this last characteristic, and in the predominance of the violet tints in the flesh and shadows, some of his pictures remind me more of Leonardo da Vinci than of Titian or Reynolds. His taste was singularly pure, even to fastidiousness. It had gone on refining and refining ; and in the same manner his *ideal* had become more and more spiritual, his moral sense more and more elevated, till in their combination, they seemed at last to have overpowered the material of his art, to have paralyzed his hand.

" As Allston's works were in accordance with his mind, so, to complete the beautiful harmony of the man's whole being, were his countenance, person, and deportment in accordance with both.

" When I saw him in 1838 I was struck by the dignity of his figure and by the simple grace of his manners ; his dress was rather careless, and he wore his own silver hair long and flowing ; his forehead and eyes were remarkably good; the general expression of his countenance open, serious, and sweet ; the tone of his voice earnest, soft, penetrating. Notwithstanding the nervous irritability of his constitution, which his dangerous and prolonged illness in 1811 had enhanced, he was particularly gentle and self-possessed."

The hanging and varnishing of the pictures in the Allston exhibition above referred to were intrusted to his nephew and pupil, George W. Flagg. One day, while overlooking the work, Allston called his nephew's attention to the clouds in the upper part of the picture of " The Dead Man Restored," and said he thought they were good. His nephew replied that he liked the painting of them, but thought the effect of the picture as a whole would be finer if the mountain peaks were relieved against a plain blue sky. To this Allston said, " No ! " But the next day he said to his nephew, " You were right." This conclusion so far emboldened the young man that he ventured further and remarked that he thought the eye of the spectator wandered too much between the upper and lower groups, and that it would be better if the lower group were more strongly painted, so as to draw attention immediately to the dead man, upon whom it was intended that the interest should chiefly centre. Allston shook his head and again said, " No, I cannot agree to that," and went out. The next day he came and said, " I have been thinking over your criticism, and have come to tell you that you were right, and could I afford it I would take a canvas and paint the picture anew upon your two suggestions." The incident certainly shows very strikingly the frankness of Allston's nature and his magnanimity, for it should be remembered that his nephew was at that time a mere neophyte in art, having neither experience nor reputation entitling his opinions to special consideration.

It was to his mother that he first wrote of the success of this exhibition, and in the following terms, which show a touching filial interest and affection :

" CAMBRIDGEPORT, July 14, 1839.

" MY DEAR MOTHER : I have been waiting for the arrival of sister Polly before I answered your last letter. . . . I am much disappointed that she could not come on while my exhibition was open, but it closed last Wednesday, the 10th inst. The exhibition was extended a month beyond the time originally intended, and it was felt that it would be trespassing on the liberality of the owners of the pictures to ask a further extension, especially as there must necessarily be a continued risk from fire. It would have been a great gratification to me had one I love so dearly as my sister seen these fruits of so many years' labor. There were forty-five pictures at the opening of the exhibition, to which two were afterward added. There were several others in different parts of the country that could not be

Swiss Scenery.

From the original in the possession of Thornton K. Lothrop, of Boston.

obtained. This number was anything but expected by the public; and when they took into account their elaborate finish, many could not help expressing their surprise at my industry.

" This was *one*, at least, of the results of which I felt sure ; and I feel a satisfaction that I am no longer misjudged in this respect. I am now and ever have been, since I made my art a profession, a hard-working man, and as much so from inclination as from necessity ; for the law of my nature impels to employment. I cannot choose but work, sick or well ; indeed six months idleness would soon upset me. But these are by no means all my works, as some of the newspapers have imagined ; the pictures which I left in Europe, though fewer in number, would make a larger exhibition.

"I cannot speak in terms too grateful of the kindness of the people of Boston on this occasion ; more especially of my immediate friends, the gentlemen of the committee, who conducted the exhibition. It was originally proposed by *them*, and *they* asked of the proprietors the loan of the pictures ; I did not solicit one, nor, indeed, would it have become me to have done so.

" I have not yet learned what are the profits, and shall not know, perhaps for days, until all expenses have been paid. The expenses, it is supposed, will fall little short of $900, for besides room-rent, doorkeepers, packing, transportation, etc., there was the insurance. As well as my friends can now guess, the net profits will amount to about $1,500.

"You say in your last letter that you hope I will take good care of the money I get from this exhibition. I have for many years been in the habit of economizing with what little I have had, and I could not (even if I felt inclined, which I am far from feeling) be profuse with this, for it will nearly all go immediately to my creditors ; I shall reserve only barely enough to live on.

"Many people who have seen these pictures think I ought not to be poor ; but my pictures are in truth the cause of my poverty; they would not be what they are (at least what the public are pleased to consider them) without the time and labor they have cost me; and the greater part of them have not more than paid their expenses, some not that even. I do not say this, however, repiningly. I have long ago discovered that mine is not a money-getting art, and have been content with it nevertheless. I never could make it a trade; no picture ever went out of my hands that was not, for the time being, as good as I could make it; and the consequence has been fame and poverty. Well, be it so; the fame gratifies those who are dear to me, and the poverty I can bear.

"As you wish to see some of the 'handsome things' that have been said of me, I will send you in a day or two a few papers, and more by sister Polly. Had it been possible, my dear mother, for you to have seen this Exhibition, it would have given me more pleasure than all the praise I have had. I should then have doubly felt that fame was worth more than money. I believe if I had none who loved me I should care little for fame. I could not say so, however, of my art, for that I must love under all circumstances.

.   .   .   .

"That heaven may ever bless you is the constant prayer of

"Your affectionate son,

"WASHINGTON ALLSTON."

In the presence of the writer, Allston was requested to sit to Clevenger, the sculptor, for his bust; but he refused, saying, that while he was pleased to have his works seen and admired he had no wish to be seen himself. Subsequently, however, he did sit to Clevenger, and to his nephew just mentioned. The portrait painted by the latter at that time is engraved as the frontispiece to this biography.

The circumstances of his sitting, in violation of his expressed disinclination to do so, reveal the tenderness of his nature. His aged mother, then residing in Charleston, S. C., had long been anxiously hoping for a visit from him. Upon being told by a friend who had recently seen him that she must not expect him to visit her, as he was physically unable to endure the journey it would involve, she wrote to her grandson, George Flagg, requesting him to paint his portrait and send it to her. The letter was an exceedingly affectionate one. George gave it to his uncle, who took it to his room and carefully perused it. Its tender expressions of love, setting forth the yearning of her mother's heart to see him before her departure, which was so evidently drawing near; her gentle repining and implied reproach, that he had so long absented himself from her; all this was so charged with pathos that he could not withstand its appeal. He returned the letter with the remark, "I cannot refuse that." Accordingly he sat to Flagg and Clevenger, at the same time, in his studio at Cambridgeport.

"CAMBRIDGEPORT, December 5, 1839.

"DEAR COGDELL: By the brig Josephine, Captain Charles Smith, you will receive two boxes, containing each a plaster cast of my bust; one for my mother, and the other for yourself, of which I beg your acceptance as a small token of my regard. The bust was modelled for the Athenæum, at the request of the trustees, by Mr. Clevenger, a young artist from Cincinnati, whom I consider as one giving evidence of no common mind. He has been passing several months here, previous to his departure for Italy, where, if I mistake not, he will produce a 'sensation.' He has every quality to make a great artist; and what is still better, adorn a great artist, for he is modest, amiable, and single-hearted, loving his art for its own sake, and finding his highest pleasure in its labors. It is delightful to meet with such a man. I know not when I have met, as in him, so beautiful a coincidence of simplicity and power—one of the few whom the world would have great difficulty in spoiling; for his love of fame, if I understand him aright, is not mere thirst of praise, right or wrong, but the purer desire of sympathy, which, if ever realized, is both the best reward and excitement of genius. He is a man, in short, whom, if you knew, I am sure you would like with no ordinary liking.

"I suppose you already know, from my letter to my mother, written about a fortnight since, that the 'King of Babylon' is at last liberated from his imprisonment, and now holding his court in my painting-room. If you have not seen the letter I would refer you to it for the particulars. As the time approached for opening the box in which the picture had lain for so many years, I could hardly suppress some sad misgivings as to what time and confinement had done to it. And you can well imagine my delight on finding it without a crack or stain; only two small places on some subordinate heads being rubbed in the unrolling. But I find I am only repeating what I said in the letter to my mother, so I will end by saying that I feel that in returning to my labors upon it as if I had returned to my proper element. By the way, I must caution you not to heed anything which you may see in the newspapers concerning this picture. They have already begun in New York to fabricate the most fantastic paragraphs about it. A writer in one paper says that he was present at the unrolling, that it is already finished and will be exhibited in a few days; the paragraph, too, purporting to be an extract from the letter of a Boston correspondent. The writer adds, 'In my next I shall give you a description of the picture ! ! !' Now the whole of this is a sheer fabrication. The only persons present were four workmen and my brother-in-law, who came to assist in the unrolling and raising it on the easel, but who would not look at the picture, as he said that he did not wish to see it until it was completed. About fourteen years ago I remember that the newspapers amused themselves pretty much in the same way, but I made up my mind then to take no public notice of these fabrications, nor shall I now, as there would be no end to it. I am determined that the public shall not know anything about 'Belshazzar,' how long I expect to be still employed upon it, or anything else. When he is ready to make his *début* I shall announce it myself. I do not now admit even my friends into my room—so nobody can know anything about the picture.

"You will perceive by the bust that time has laid his finger on me since you saw me. My friends here think it could not be more like me; as well as I know my own face so think I."

· · · · · · · ·

"CAMBRIDGEPORT, January 12, 1840.

"MY DEAR COGDELL: Your letter of December 28th has given me a shock which I had vainly thought I was prepared for; but I found I was not. The advanced age, together with the increasing infirmities of my poor mother had long since warned me that she could not long remain in this world; and I had endeavored to prepare myself for this inevitable and afflicting event. Yet it came upon me with all the force of an unexpected blow. She is gone and I shall never see her more; never till we meet in heaven, which, God grant, I may through His grace be permitted to do. Her image is ever before me, with all the mother's tenderness, with the same benignant expression as when I last parted from her, as fresh as if it had been but yesterday. And I thank God that such is the impression left in my heart; it is a great comfort to me. But this is but secondary to the inexpressible comfort which I feel in the deep conviction of her present happiness, which her true and ardent piety, her perfect Christian resignation (of which I have long been assured in her letters) all confirm beyond the shadow of a misgiving—she is now with her Saviour. There is no consolation for the bereaved like this. Nor indeed can there be any other to a believing Christian. In the midst of her troubles, which I know have been many and hard to bear, this has always crossed me as a cheering thought in her behalf, that my mother was a Christian, and then I felt sure that, happen what might, she would be supported through it. I can now think of her as my blessed mother, numbered with the 'just made perfect,' where there is no more sorrow, no more trouble. I would not exchange this conviction for all the wealth and honors which the world could offer.

"I cannot tell you, Cogdell, how I loved my mother; she herself never knew all the love I bore her. She was the constant object of my daily prayers. And, though separated for so many years by most trying and adverse circumstances, she was never a day out of my mind. But, dear, blessed mother, we shall meet at last, I trust, in another and better world.

"And now, my friend, I know not in what words to thank you for the feeling manner in which you have made your melancholy communication. But your own kind heart will tell you all I would say, not only for this last act of friendship for me, but for all your past devoted kindness to my beloved parent. God bless you for both. While you mourn with me, even as a brother, you have the consolation of knowing that, to her last breath, she loved you as a son. Whenever you were mentioned, which was almost in every letter for the last years of her life, she always spoke of you with the deepest affection. She seemed never weary of repeating your kindnesses, and I never shall forget them.

· · · · · · · ·

"Boyhood.

"Ah, then how sweetly closed those crowded days!
The minutes parting one by one like rays,
        That fade upon a summer's eve.
But O, what charm or magic numbers

Can give me back the gentle slumbers
  Those weary, happy days did leave,
  When by my bed I saw my mother kneel,
And with her blessing took her nightly kiss ?
Whatever time destroys, he cannot this ;
  Even now that nameless kiss I feel.

" WASHINGTON ALLSTON."

" CAMBRIDGEPORT, January 31, 1841.

" MY DEAR COGDELL : I have been long wishing to write you, but, to say the truth, my head has been utterly barren of subject-matter for a letter. I remember one of Cowper's most agreeable letters was merely to tell his correspondent that he had nothing to say ; and though it was literally about nothing, he continued to make it as brilliant as a soap-bubble reflecting all the colors of the rainbow. Would that I had his epistolary talent to make this so too, for my object in now taking up the pen is simply to say the same thing. But as I have not his talent I can only state the plain matter of fact. There is little occurring in this sublime porte at any time, least of all at this season, and what does occur is not worth noting. Indeed I am in a manner out of the world here, more especially in the winter, though not quite three miles from Boston.

" About once or twice a month I have a visitor thence to pass an evening with me, and this is pretty much all that I get sight of from among the busy throng that is moving around me. But this I always thankfully consider as something between charity and a windfall. My own visits to town are very rare, seldom exceeding a dozen in the course of the year—for a visit there always costs me a day, which I can ill afford. As I formerly said that I did not intend to give any account of 'Belshazzar' until it was finished, I shall only say now that I am hard at work on it—and on nothing else. I remember once telling my mother that no picture ever went out of my hand that

was not as good as it was in my power to make it, for the time
being.   Neither shall 'Belshazzar' leave my room until I have
done my best on it.   This is not the way, some artists might
warily think, to get rich.   I knew that, however, more than
twenty years ago; yet I have never swerved from this course;
for it is better to be poor in a course which I know to be honorable, than to be rich in any other.   This, with the love of my
art, has for so many years enabled me to endure poverty without
repining.

My best regards to Mrs. Cogdell, and, believe me, my kind-
hearted friend, ever affectionately,

"WASHINGTON ALLSTON."

"CAMBRIDGEPORT, March 24, 1841.

"MY DEAR COGDELL: Did I not know your unwearied benevolence I should fear to tire you out on the subject of my late
letters; but as I feel assured that the interest you have taken in
the matter is no less from your humanity than to serve your
friend, I shall make no apology for these additional lines.   Soon
after my last letter to you I sent an abstract of its contents to
my brother William at Newport, and I herewith transcribe the
following extract from his reply:

"'Your letter, my dear brother, was received in course, after
which I lost no time in writing to my sister (extracting word for
word what you wrote me on the subject), who will direct my
nephew, J. A. Allston, who is, jointly with Mr. Cogdell, I suppose, my attorney in the matter which now seems to distress you
so much; and I notice, as I hope feelingly, your observations
respecting the slaves inherited from our grandmother.   I agree
with you that they should not be separated if possible, having
formed family connections with Mr. Belin's people, nor be sold
to be carried out of the State.   The price it seems was fixed at
$550 by the court, which directed them to be offered to Mr.

Belin, and being more than he was disposed to give, would it not be well to sell him yours at such a rate as to induce him to take the whole? I only suggest this to you, as by so doing all the slaves might be benefited by your intentions, and Mr. Wigfall and Henry be satisfied. As for myself (although you well know that I am in a manner penniless and without a profession) I would make any reasonable sacrifice which the case may require. My views are well known to my sister.'

"Now, my friend, I will most gladly adopt the course suggested by my brother, that is, let Mr. Belin have my share at such a rate as may induce him to take the whole; indeed to effect this desired object he should have my share on any terms. But as Mr. Belin might not, even in this case, like to make an offer from himself, I will here propose terms, namely, $100 for each of the slaves of my fifth part. And the affair might be easily managed in this way. Let the whole sixteen be rated as the court has already decided, at $550 each; my fifth part of the proceeds, say three (as to the fraction I give it in) slaves, would then be $1,650. Well, instead of paying me this sum for my fifth, let him pay me but $300. And, moreover, let this contract be entirely private between you and him. I wish no one to know anything about it, for it's nobody's business but mine. Also, in respect to the payment, let Mr. Belin name his own terms of credit.

"I have only to add that you must not think in the offer here proposed I am making too great a sacrifice. No, my friend, and I assure you, on the word of a gentleman and a Christian, were the sum in question ten times greater, I would gladly relinquish it to effect the desired object. It has not cost me one moment's hesitation, I consider it in fact no sacrifice at all, for it will give me peace, which is a treasure far above gold. And at this time especially do I need peace of mind, in order to do justice to the important work on which I am engaged. You will therefore, I trust, consider yourself fully authorized to make the proposed private contract with Mr. Belin.

"My best regards to Mrs. Cogdell. God bless you and yours.

Yours affectionately,

"Washington Allston."

The prints referred to in the following letter from Allston to McMurtrie were a set of Burnet's etchings from Raphael's cartoons. The Inman print was an engraving from the portrait of Bishop White. The "one exception" among the engravings from Allston's own pictures we do not know.

"Cambridgeport, June 15, 1841.

"My Dear Sir: I received your letter of the 11th of May, nearly three weeks since, but delayed answering it until the arrival of the box of prints, which has just reached me. For this most acceptable present I beg you to accept my best thanks. They remind me of the spirited etchings of Piranesi, and give more of the character, expression, and general spirit of the cartoons than any finished engraving I have seen of them. They are such as I think must have pleased Raphael, had they been done in his time. Hogarth used to say to the engravers whom he occasionally employed to assist him, 'Give me my character, if you do it with a hobnail;' often obliterating weeks of their fine work without compunction. I wish I could say that the prints which have been engraved from my pictures had anything like the truth of these admirable etchings; but I have been particularly unfortunate for (with one exception) neither my character, expression, nor effect is to be found in any of them; that from 'Jacob's Dream' gave me an immediate fit of the heartburn, which did not leave me for a whole day. It was engraved for one of the London Annuals, by a person who seemed to have had as little notion of the character of the picture as of the human figure.

"I think you are quite right in the opinion that your son should master the elements of our art in the outset. If he does not possess himself of them now, whilst he is young, he will find it hard, if not altogether impracticable hereafter when he shall become aware of his deficiencies. Let him think no time misspent which he devotes to the human form; tell him to fag at it until he can draw it with as much ease as he can write; he will then be able to realize his most poetical conceptions—but not until then.

"The great fault in discipline among our young artists is in their beginning to 'make pictures' too soon; to make a *whole* before they are acquainted with *parts*. It is an easy matter to produce a pleasing effect, either in color or chiaro-oscuro, but not quite so easy to guess right as to form; and he can do no more than guess who attempts it without knowledge. There are hundreds of artists in every age who pass a long life in producing striking effects without an atom of truth in a single component part. Above all, let his progress be *with knowledge*, for only this can secure an artist from the impertinence of ignorance; from being either irritated or disheartened by false criticism. In a word, let him love his art for its own sake, not for the contingent applause, and he will not be satisfied without a thorough mastery of its principles as well in their minutiæ as their leading points.

"As to Dusseldorf, where you propose sending your son, I can express no opinion; indeed, I have been so long from Europe that I know not which is now the most eligible school for a young artist. I have reason, however, to think highly of the present German school, from what I have lately seen of some of their works, having been honored with a very magnificent present from Count Raczynski, of Berlin, consisting of his own valuable work on German art, together with numerous prints from the productions of various living artists of Germany, among the principal of whom are Cornelius, Kaulbach, Schnorr, Bende-mann, and others, whose names I cannot at this moment recall. These specimens certainly place the German school very high, especially in purity of taste.

"I am much pleased with the print from Inman; it is a rich composition. If I may be allowed a critical remark, I should say that the quantity of *dark* is too great; there is consequently not enough of middle tint. But this I apprehend is the fault of the engraver; I daresay the picture is different in these particu-lars. Were the engraver here with his plate he could easily *scrape* down some of the darks so as to remove the objection.

"You have probably had from Dr. Channing, or others, some account of my late Exhibition, where I had the gratification of refreshing my affection for your little 'Mother and Child,' for the loan of which I now send you my thanks. The kindness of my friends, both abroad and at home, on this occasion, is one of those pleasant things to think of in my old age.

"You mention having the great picture of kind, good Mr. West now with you. There are heads in that picture equal to Raphael. Nothing can surpass the High Priest and many others. The Penitent Thief has a sublime expression.

I remain, dear sir, with unabated regard, yours,

"WASHINGTON ALLSTON."

The following letters to Cogdell contain interesting details of a rather more than usually personal character:

"CAMBRIDGEPORT, November 14, 1841.

'MY DEAR COGDELL: Before this letter reaches you, you will probably have received a little volume which I have just pub-lished, and of which I beg your acceptance; I have sent one also to our friend White. They were shipped yesterday, by my publishers, Messrs. Little & Brown, of Boston, to the care of Mr. Samuel Hart, bookseller in Charleston. This book ' Monaldi ' (as I have stated in a prefatory note), was ready for the press as long ago as 1822, but having been written for the periodical of a friend, which was soon after discontinued, it was thrown into my desk, where it has lain until the present time. In the note I add that it is now published, not with the pretensions of a novel, but simply as a tale. My friends have for years past repeatedly urged me to publish, but for various reasons, which some perhaps would think no reason, or at least insufficient, I had kept the work by me so long that, in fact, I became quite indifferent whether it ever saw the light or not.

" Our excellent friend White has, I hope, received permanent benefit from his journey to the North. This visit was a most agreeable surprise to us. It is a pleasant thing in this mutable world to meet with a friend who retains in his old age the warmth and kindly sympathies of his youth. His old friend Mr. Dana felt no less pleasure than myself at the meeting. The meeting of three old men, who have been friends for forty years, is not an every-day occurrence. We were much pleased with his wife. I had another unexpected, as well as most gratifying, visit from my cousin, Dr. Edward Mitchell, whom I have not seen since we were schoolboys forty-six years ago. He was then a slender, delicate child, now a stout, robust man; I a young dandy, sporting three silk waistcoats, according to the fashion of the day, now a person that ought to be venerable, and am indeed—so far as snowy locks can make one so. We might well have marvelled at the metamorphoses of time, and yet, though I am no longer a dandy, I do not find that all my youthful feelings have passed away. In regard to some of these I cannot admit that I am a day older. Should you see Dr. Mitchell, give my regards to him, for he is a worthy, good man; and tell him how much pleased I was with his visit. He was much esteemed by my mother.

"It is but a few days since I left a sick-room. I was brought down by a severe inward cold that threw my whole system out of order. But thanks to my physician, through a kind Providence, I am again well and strong enough to pay continuous court to the King of Babylon.

"Mrs. Allston unites with me in best regards to Mrs. Cogdell and yourself.

"Yours affectionately,

"WASHINGTON ALLSTON."

"CAMBRIDGEPORT, December 5, 1841.

"MY DEAR COGDELL: I have received your letter of November 26th, containing a copy of the account of Mr. Laurens, the Master in Equity. In reply to your question, whether I gave my consent in writing to my mother when she sold the negroes of the life estate to Dr. Mitchell, I answer that I did. My mother asked my consent, as one of the heirs, and I gave it without a moment's hesitation, most willingly; and I beg that this letter may be considered as confirming it.

"I think I acquainted you in a former letter of my noble-hearted sister, Mrs. W. A. Allston's generous offer of her share of the inheritance from our grandmother to be divided between my brother, William M. Allston, and myself; and I have the impression also that at the same time I informed you that, in reply to her, I declined receiving any part of it, and begged her to give the whole to William. With respect to this matter, I have only to add that I still hold the same mind. And (if this letter is, as I hope sufficient authority) I hereby relinquish, in favor of my brother, William M. Allston, all that my sister, Mrs. William A. Allston, may have either given or bequeathed of her share of our grandmother's inheritance to me. You will therefore, my friend, if said share of my beloved sister be set apart for my brother and myself, consider it all as his, and remit it to him accordingly when it shall have come into your hands.

"I had received, as you supposed, before your letter reached me, the intelligence of my sister's death; her son John's letter was received on the 20th of last month. Ah, Cogdell, she was a woman of ten thousand, in mind and heart both. Well, it cannot be a great while before I shall be called to follow her. I have often of late thought of that inevitable hour, that sooner or later must come for me, as well as for those I have loved and lost. This dear sister is now, as I believe, with her Saviour, for she was a Christian, and died in a Christian's hope. From my heart do I feel for her husband, a noble, high-minded man, every way worthy of such a wife. I have written to him, and I trust that my letter may not be wholly without comfort to him, at least after the first shock from such a bereavement shall have been mitigated by time.

"My dear Cogdell, with my whole heart do I reciprocate your kind wishes in my behalf. Mrs. Allston joins me in best wishes to Mrs. Cogdell and yourself.

"Yours affectionately,

"WASHINGTON ALLSTON."

CHAPTER XXV.

During the last years of his life Allston's letters show an unabated interest in the subjects that had been his constant preoc-
cupation, and as searching and sapient comments on them as in
his earlier days. We give herewith one to Count Raczynski, the
Polish writer on art, author of the "History of Modern Art in
Germany," and Prussian Ambassador at various courts:

"CAMBRIDGEPORT, March 6, 1842.

"MONSIEUR LE COMTE: For the gift of your valuable work
on 'Modern Art,' together with the prints from German artists,
which you have done me the honor to present me, I beg you to
accept my best thanks.

"Permit me, sir, to say that I was most agreeably struck
with the pure taste which everywhere pervades your volumes;
and as one who loves his art, and therefore interested in whatever tends to elevate its character, I sincerely hope that the
sound criticisms they contain will be felt and appreciated in
other countries besides Germany. And I cannot doubt that
such will be the case wherever your work is known; at least
with those who acknowledge in art a higher end than mere
gratification of the senses.

"The prints which accompany your books give me a high

opinion of the present German school. I was particularly pleased to notice in most of them so pure a taste in form, and in all the entire absence of the theatrical and fantastic in composition; even where some of the subjects might have tempted the artist to extravagance I found nothing to revolt me, as 'overstepping the modesty of Nature.' Indeed one of the most remarkable instances I have ever met of this rare discretion is in Kaulbach's 'Combat' in the air between the Huns and Romans; though in the highest degree visionary, the improbable is yet so tempered by the true that the imagination does not doubt it for a moment. Only a genius of a high order, a master of the poetic nature of the imaginative possible, could have produced such a work. I know nothing in modern art which I would place before it; no dream ever brought with it a deeper faith, and I longed, as I looked on it, to take the hand of the artist and express to him my admiration. It is not to the purpose to say which of the artists appeared to me the best; but I cannot forbear mentioning, as among the first, together with Kaulbach, Cornelius, Bendemann, Schadow, Schnorr, and Meyer. To these, were it necessary, I might add several other names not unworthy to be classed with them.

"For the kind notice with which you have been pleased to honor me, in your account of American artists, I beg you, sir, to accept my respectful acknowledgments. I have the honor to be, Monsieur le Comte,

"Your obliged and obedient servant,

"WASHINGTON ALLSTON."

Renewed testimony to Allston's anxiety to finish his "Belshazzar" is furnished incidentally in this letter to McMurtrie:

"CAMBRIDGEPORT, June 23, 1842.

"MY DEAR SIR: I have received your present, the sketch of 'Prometheus,' by Mr. West, for which I beg you to accept my

thanks.   But I am sorry to say that it is not in my power to send
you such a drawing as I could wish ; I can only send one or two
pencil sketches—hardly worth your acceptance, except for the
good-will that accompanies them.   I hope, however, to be able,
at some future time, to add something better.   Though I have
a very considerable number of sketches, they are, for various
reasons, such as I could not well spare, being for the most
part compositions on large mill-boards, or on canvas, for future
pictures, with some few that I wish to preserve as memoranda of former works.   On paper I have rarely sketched of
late years.

"Perhaps no artist has been more careless than myself of
his sketches, the greater part having been lost, destroyed, given
away, or otherwise disposed of, years ago.   I have often of late
regretted that I took not better care of them.   The pencil
sketches referred to, being small, I will enclose within the leaves
of a volume which I published last summer, and of which I ask
your acceptance.   The book was first published in Boston, but
the copy I send you is from the London edition of it, which I
have just received.

"I very much regret that it is not in my power to avail myself of your friend's wish to possess a picture by me ; my engagements being such as to oblige me to decline any commissions, which I should have been otherwise glad to undertake.
Besides 'Belshazzar,' on which I am now exclusively employed,
and shall continue to be until it is completed, I have already engaged pictures enough to occupy me many years (perhaps more
than I can expect to live) ; the picture you refer to in your letter
has been sold several years since.   I suppose it is the one which
Coleridge named 'The Sisters,' and which Sully (it being a favorite with him), may have described to you.   One head in it—
as to air and colors, but not in character or head-dress—was imitated from the picture by Titian, called his daughter holding up

The Sisters.

From the original in the possession of Thornton K. Lothrop, of Boston.

a casket. The other figure, with the rest of the composition, choice of colors, etc., was mine. . . .

"Believe me, dear sir, with unabated regard,

"Sincerely yours,

"WASHINGTON ALLSTON."

A letter, dated July 4, 1842, from Cambridgeport, to Cogdell contains the following:

.   .   .   .

"I congratulate you on your present prospect of visiting Italy. And I have no doubt that the new spring it will give both to your mind and constitution will add many years to your life, and that they will be happy ones I venture to predict; for with health and competence (even though it be barely sufficient to secure one from the slavery of debt) what is to prevent a pleasurable flow to time in the free pursuit of our most innocent art?

"Your promised introduction to the Pope, in presenting him with the portrait of Bishop England, I should think must be of great advantage to you. As to the glowing works of art by which you will be surrounded in Rome—they will breathe new life into you. Even at this distance of time I live upon them in memory. In that 'Silent City,' as my friend Coleridge used to call it, were some of my happiest dreams; for they were the dreams of youth, to which even the then gorgeous present was but a dark foreground to the beautiful and dazzling distance of the future. And though my approaches to that future have uniformly caused it to fade more and more into the common daylight, laying bare to the senses the illusions of the mind, yet I do not regret that I once so dreamed of it; since I have only, as if reversing a telescope, to look back into the past, even from my present foreground, matter of fact as it is, to see the same delightful, though imaginary distance—dimmed, indeed, because diminished, but still the same. The visions of the past are not always lost to us; they may become less defined, but they do not all vanish; and I have still enough of them (thank Heaven!) to call up at will, to embellish, as it were with pleasant pictures, the homely walls of the immediate reality. No, whatever changes have fallen to my lot, I cannot regret these illusions; my youth was one, if I may so express it, of intense life, and the mere memory of it were sufficient to keep me from repining.

.   .   .   .

"Ever, affectionately, your friend,
"WASHINGTON ALLSTON."

In the year 1842 Allston's picture of "Spalatro" was exhibited in South Carolina. Of this picture his friend Charles Fraser said: "Of all his pictures I give 'Spalatro' the preference. Once seen, it can never be forgotten; the scene is one of terrific interest, and the murderer appears to tremble; the flame and light from the lamp are perfect." To the *Magnolia*, a literary magazine, formerly published in Charleston, Fraser contributed the following, September, 1842:

"'A scene from Mrs. Radcliffe's "Italian,"' by W. Allston. We have heard this (save the mark!) called a 'pretty picture. We do not think it is so, and we are sure that the unsuspecting artist never dreamed that it would be so considered. If high-wrought delineation of character; if the personification of the vilest impulses that agitate the heart and distort the features; if depravity stamped by nature on every trait, and nurtured in deeds of violence and bloodshed; if the contortions produced by a terror-stricken conscience, in every limb and joint and sinew and extremity, from the crown of the head to the very toenail, as seen in the faltering figure of 'Spalatro'; if the stern unpitying fixedness of the man who grasps the dagger, and points the way to his sleeping victim; if the midnight gloom of a dungeon, made visible by the glimmering of a little lamp, with its associations of hopeless suffering; if all these brought together with the matchless skill of the artist, and embodying to the eye what had been before only unveiled to the imagination, if these constitute mere beauty, then indeed might we pronounce this a 'pretty picture.'

"But we apprehend there is something more than beauty in it; a charm in which art itself is hidden, and which makes us forget the pencil in its creations. No painter could have produced such a picture without a profound knowledge of human nature, without being able to trace to their deepest recesses the springs of conduct, and without a philosophical knowledge of their influence on the actions of men. In a word, we know of no picture ever painted in this country that has concentrated in a greater degree the delight and admiration of the intelligent. Its execution is in Mr. Allston's peculiar style of high finish; his maxim is, that as nature is nowhere found slovenly and negligent, the art that professes to imitate her should be elaborate in its process, and never fall short of its object from want of care. We never see, therefore, what is technically called *handling* in his pictures, but his effect (and in this he never fails) is made out by study and diligence. One remark more, and that is the magic effect of the lamp, which seems to flicker before the eye. The lights on the figures and surrounding objects neither take from its brilliance nor lose any of their own distinctness."

To Cogdell, September 26, 1842, Allston writes:

"MY DEAR COGDELL: I have this day received your letter of the 20th inst., and thinking you might wish an immediate answer to your question, 'Whether I had surrendered to my brother, William M. Allston, my part of my late sister's portion of the inheritance from our grandmother, which she had destined for my brother and myself,' I lose no time in replying that I had. Soon after the death of my mother, my sister wrote to me particularly concerning the inheritance referred to, and expressed her intention to divide her portion of it between my brother and myself. In my answer to this letter, after thanking her for this generous proffer, I declined accepting any part of it, and begged her to give all she intended for me to William, as he had children and I had none, besides, that I had a profession, whilst he was without one. I wrote you also to this effect, so that your impression respecting it is correct.

"As to strangers meddling with your private concerns, that is a penalty which every man at all known to the public must inevitably incur. I not only hear, but am doomed to read, accounts, both of what I have done and am doing, as new to me as they would be to my antipodes. And nothing is more common than to hear opinions ascribed to me which I never expressed, and could not entertain. Indeed I have had so much of this kind of gossip circulated about me that I have become quite callous about it, giving it no heed, especially as I ascribe it rather to idleness than ill-nature. I sometimes say to my friends that if I wanted to learn what I was going to do next, I had only to ask the first stranger I should meet.

"I have at last, in my old age, got into a house of my own, built from the proceeds from the sale of land which but a few years ago rented for no more than $250. Having the control over the design, the house was constructed not only according to my notions of convenience and comfort, but in some degree to suit my taste. It is somewhat in a different style from our dwelling-houses here, and I should not have been surprised if much fault had been found with it by others; but people seem to be generally pleased with it. At any rate it has one great advantage, it is but fifty feet from my present painting-room.

"Mrs. Allston joins me in best regards to Mrs. Cogdell and yourself.   Ever affectionately yours,

                                   "WASHINGTON ALLSTON."

The subjoined letter, dated October 11, 1842, to Leslie, was one of the writer's last to his friends oversea:

"Dear Leslie: This will be handed you by my friend Mr. Albert G. Hoit, whom I beg to introduce to you as one whom I highly esteem both as a man and an artist. It is Mr. Hoit's intention to visit France and Italy as well as England. But his time abroad being necessarily limited, his stay in London will of course be short. If you will favor him with such facilities as may be in your power for seeing various works of art in London, especially such as are not open to the public, you will much oblige an old friend.

"Mr. Hoit having obligingly offered to be the bearer, I take this opportunity to send you a volume which I published last year. I send one also to Collins, and one to Mr. Green, the Professor of Anatomy to the Royal Academy. I knew Mr. Green when in London, and I show him this mark of respect as the friend of Coleridge, and as one whom I know Coleridge to have held in high estimation. In an eloquent work of Mr. Green, 'The Hunterian Oration,' which I have lately read, I think (but am not certain) that F.R.S. was affixed to his name in the title-page. If so, will you add these letters where I have written it, on the blank-leaf of my book.

"I was very ill, so as to be confined to my chamber, the greater part of last winter, and continued very feeble throughout the spring and summer; but, thank Heaven, I have now regained sufficient strength to proceed in good heart with my labors. I would tell you more about myself, but that Mr. Hoit, to whom I shall leave it, will be able to say more for me than I could put into a letter. Do not, however, follow my example when you shall feel inclined to write to me, but tell me all about yourself, the more minutely the better, and all about your wife and children, to whom, though I have never seen, yet, as parts of yourself, I must send my regards.   To Collins remember me most affectionately.   Though a poor correspondent, or rather, no correspondent, I am not, therefore, forgetful of my friends.   You would hardly believe it, but it is a melancholy fact that I write hundreds of letters to strangers, persons whom I never saw. And why?   Because their letters must be answered, else I have no peace with a gentleman's conscience!   You will think, perhaps, that I fully console myself for this infliction by deducting what I owe to my friends.   Be that as it may, I believe they all understand me, and do not measure my regard by the length or frequency of my letters.

"I remain, dear Leslie, your unaltered friend,

"WASHINGTON ALLSTON."

As connected with the foregoing, it is perhaps worth while to give this extract from a letter from Hoit to Allston, dated London, November 14, 1842:

"Samuel Rogers seemed gratified to hear from you, and said it gave him pleasure to show his collection to any friend of yours; and he went with me from basement to attic, pointing out to me every picture and object of *virtù* with all the activity and enthusiasm of the first love of art in a boy. . . . I agree with you in your high estimate of Stoddard.   After seeing Rogers's Titian, 'Christ and Mary in the Garden,' I perceive now, more than ever, how perfectly you have been imbued with the spirit of the masters of that age, and how little of it there is in the present English school."

Following are such portions of two of his latest letters to Cogdell, to whom he always wrote very intimately, as are of public interest:

"CAMBRIDGEPORT, April 15, 1843.

"MY DEAR COGDELL: . . . Greenough, as I take it for granted you know through the newspapers, has long been returned to this country. He is still in Washington, seeing, I suppose, to the erecting of a new building for the proper exhibition of his statue. I hear he was absolutely startled at the appearance it made in the Rotunda; the shadows falling so perpendicularly as almost to obliterate the features, and otherwise misrepresent the whole figure. I hope the new building to which it is to be removed, and which will probably be erected under his superintendence, will be such as to do it justice, as it is a work, according to the testimony of several competent judges who saw it in Florence, that undoubtedly does him honor. When he intends returning to Italy I know not. He being out of the question, there are only two persons left to whom I can give letters, Clevenger and Kellogg, who are both now in Florence. I am not sufficiently acquainted with Powers to add a letter to him, but Clevenger's introduction to him will serve you quite as well. Clevenger's marble bust of me, which he made for the Athenæum, so far surpasses the cast that, without impairing a jot of the likeness, you would hardly know it to have been done from it; it is an exquisite work.

"As the time draws near for your voyage, I suppose your enthusiasm must be pretty near boiling-heat. Ah, my friend, that is the true country for art, and it is a proud thing for America that in art she is now so well represented there.

"Ever affectionately your friend,

"WASHINGTON ALLSTON."

"CAMBRIDGEPORT, June 29, 1843.

"MY DEAR COGDELL:

.   .   .   .

"You ask if I think your visit to Italy will have the same effect on you now, as I formerly supposed it would. I see no reason for changing my opinion; for, though some ten years have been added to your age, you are by no means beyond the age to feel the influences of a happier and more congenial employment, and a finer climate; you will profit by them, I doubt not, both in body and mind. I have no doubt, were all circumstances propitious to my revisiting Italy, that the change of scene as well as the climate would add vigor also to me, could I bear the voyage, which I could not, as the motion of the vessel would soon increase the chronic complaint which has so long afflicted me to a degree of torture.

"As I have never been in correspondence with Thorwaldsen, I could not with any propriety write an introductory letter to him; but I am happy in being able to procure you letters to our consul, Mr. Green, and to Crawford, the sculptor, from a friend of mine in Boston, who is an intimate friend of both those gentlemen, either of whom will make you acquainted with Thorwaldsen, as they are both well known to him.

"Poor Legaré! You must, no doubt, as well as myself, have been deeply affected by the news of his sudden death. One of the highest intellects and the most noble-hearted statesmen has been lost to his country. The death of no public man for many years has been so universally lamented; even his political opponents seem to have forgotten their party feelings in the general sorrow. Judge Story pronounces him one of the most learned jurists of his time. And certainly he has not left a more accomplished scholar behind him. He had many and thorough friends here, in whom his high principle, no less than his extensive attainments, had won a confidence that connected him with the future welfare and honor of our country. But if he has been taken away from the hope of his friends, and in the midst of his usefulness, it is no slight consolation to them that he was cut off also in the flower of his integrity. He has left a great name; but what is far better in his case, a good name.

"Mrs. Allston joins me in best regards to yourself and Mrs. C.   Believe me, ever affectionately yours,

"WASHINGTON ALLSTON."

The last letter Allston wrote was to Mrs. Channing, the widow of William Ellery Channing, and most of it is given herewith:

" CAMBRIDGEPORT, July 4, 1843.

.   .   .   .

"I never could write a letter at the time it ought to have been written; and this answer to yours, I fear, forms no exception. In addition, however, to the exhaustion caused by the excessive heat of the weather, I may plead, as some excuse, that I have been troubled of late by a wearing, dull pain in my side, which makes writing more than usually fatiguing to me; occasionally it becomes very acute, so much so indeed as to force me, while painting, to suspend my labors until the paroxysm is past.

"With respect to the portrait I had promised,* my necessities compel me to say that it will be wholly out of my power to undertake it with any hope of success until I shall have completed 'Belshazzar.' My friends, I have reason to think, are not aware how much depends on this work, which has so long and anxiously employed me, and which has so often been suspended, but never voluntarily. But, I trust, you will understand it, when I add (to say nothing of present embarrassments) that to this source alone can I look for the means of discharging obligations that have weighed upon me for years. Besides, there is that involved in the undelayed termination of this picture which is far more important to me than any pecuniary consideration. Until relieved of this burden I feel (and indeed know too well from bitter experience) that no attempt I might make, as to the portrait, could be successful. It is not with me now as in former days—when the original was painted—when I was young and in health, and with nothing extrinsic to overshadow my Art. For the last two years a succession of bodily complaints have griev-

* The unfinished portrait of Dr. C. in possession of his widow.

ously impeded the progress of the picture referred to, and the still feeble state of my health warns me that another suspension may be fatal to it forever. But once freed of this importunate, heavy load, I shall be, I trust, another man, and enabled to bring to this labor of love, fresh and unembarrassed, whatever powers I possess.

" I have made this frank statement, my dear Mrs. Channing, as what I owe both to you and myself; to your kind and generous nature, and to my honor and right feeling, for I know not what would distress me more, than that any misapprehended circumstance should lead you to doubt my inclination to fulfil my promise."

. . . .

CHAPTER XXVI.

DEATH OF ALLSTON. — HIS SUDDEN AND PAINLESS PASSING AWAY. —
ACCOUNT OF R. H. DANA, JR.

The death of Allston was almost an unfelt transition, so mercifully tempered was it to his delicate physical condition. Members of Mrs. Allston's family had dined and passed the evening with him. At seven o'clock of July 9, 1843, he had entered the house from his painting-room, where he had been hard at work on "Belshazzar." To reach the elevation of the soothsayer's face, on which he had been working, it had been necessary for him to ascend a ladder. The continual ascending and descending, to paint and see the effect of his work, would have been wearying to a strong man; to him it was extremely exhausting. He was evidently fatigued when he entered the house and greeted his guests, but after the refreshment of dinner he wore his usual animation, which imparted its wonted delightful and inspiring influence to all present. There was a refreshing interest in his manner that cannot be described. A kind of individualization, making each one feel that he was an object of special regard and attention; the gushing stream of kindliness from his heart reached, satisfied, and charmed everyone about him. This evidence of gentlemanly refinement singularly distinguished Allston. In separating for the night, even to those whom he was to see the next morning, he would make the most courteous acknowledgment for the pleasure he had derived from their society.

His last words to the retiring guests on that night of his departure were to his niece, Miss Charlotte Dana, whom he

regarded with the affection of a father. They were words coun-
selling intellectual, moral, and religious development unto perfection. And they were accompanied with his last benediction,
" God bless you, my child," and sealed with a kiss upon her
forehead.

Soon after he said to his wife, "I have a slight attack of indi-
gestion, I think I had better take a little soda." While she was
preparing it, he sat at the table in front of the fireplace, with
his head resting on his hand as if in thought, she turned to
speak to him, he did not answer; she, supposing him to have
fallen asleep, touched his hand; it fell limp. Thinking he had
fainted, she called aloud. Her sister and niece, who had just
retired, hastened to her assistance. They laid him upon the rug
in front of the fireplace, and chafed his body, hoping to revive
him. The doctor had been called. He came, felt his pulse, and
said, " He is gone." His wife's first thought was true, he had
fallen asleep.

Beautifully impressive are the words of the diary of R. H.
Dana, Jr., which we quote:

" I was awakened by the ringing of the door-bell on Sunday
morning at two o'clock. In answer to my inquiry, I was told
that I was needed at Cambridgeport immediately, that Mr.
Allston was dead. It went to my heart like a clap of thunder.
For the first time in my life I was confused upon an alarm, I
could hardly breathe. I was soon dressed and in the street.
The night air was chilly and the streets were as still as death.
The man had been to call Ned at Chestnut Street, and we
waited for him. In a moment we heard the fall of footsteps,
and Ned came up to us. We got into the chaise and rode out,
with hardly a word spoken. We reached the house. I saw a
light in the back room where he always sat, but none upstairs.
Where can he be? Where did he die? We opened the door.
Aunt Betsey met us in the entry and said a few words. He was

in the back room. I went to the door and just saw his body lying on the rug in front of the fire, and Aunt S. and Ned by his side. I could not for my life have gone up to the body. I went to the other end of the room and looked out of the window. I moved to the other window, but could not go up to it. Never did I force myself more than when I moved gradually and fearfully up to it. And there he lay. Excepting that his neckerchief had been removed he was dressed as usual, his gray and white curls lay about his forehead and shoulders, and his sublime countenance, with closed eyes, was turned upward. His candles were burning upon the table; by the side of them lay his spectacles; the remnant of his last cigar was upon the corner of the mantelpiece, where he always placed it; another, untouched, which he had taken out to use next, lay near it; a small plate, as usual, held the ashes of his cigar, and a few books, but none of them, however, open, lay upon the table and mantelpiece. Mrs. Allston had been taken upstairs.

"The day was now broken and there were the first twittering of birds and the sound of returning motion in the world. No rising sun was to awaken him from his rest, his spirit was in an eternal day to which no night cometh. The light being fully returned we could contemplate his sublime countenance. There was the highest grandeur of intellect, with the purity and peacefulness of one in the world, but not of the world.

"One could not but feel the absence of any signs of *force* in his intellect. It was rising, soaring, from one elevation to one higher, and especially into infinite space. There was no exercise of force against other intellects, no combat; no strife for mastery, which gives vigor and development to most minds, but which, compared with the growth of his intelligence, is like the shooting out of rays in horizontal lines compared with the rising upward, upward to the source of all light. Truth and beauty for the glory of God and the elevation of man were the great object for which his powers had been given him, and these he pursued without compulsion or conflict.

" At about eight o'clock I went over to announce the event to Uncle Edmund. He was in bed. I told it to him in a few words. He said nothing for some time, but lay with his eyes closed. At length he said, ' It is too horrible ! ' and after some time he repeated, ' It is too horrible ! ' I sat by his side and he said, ' I should like to have you come to see me to-morrow.' Upon this I left him.

" At about nine I went up to Cambridge to announce the death to father. He was visiting at Professor Channing's. I sent for the Professor, but he was at breakfast and did not come. I had to send again, and Cousin Harriette came, and this made a confusion, and father seemed to suspect that something was wrong, so we told him at once. ' Mr. Allston is dead! He died last night.' ' What does this mean? How? When? What is all this? What does this mean ? ' I said again, ' Pray be calm. He has gone peacefully and quietly; if you had been there you would not feel so.' Gracefully, like the clearing away of a mist or the rising of a curtain, his mental expression returned to his eye ; the cloud passed off, and the momentary aberration, for such it was, ceased. I then told him of all the consoling things, and among others mentioned that Aunt Martha was wonderfully calm, and seemed to have had a supernatural strength given her. This calmed father more than anything else had done. ' If Martha is only sustained, I have no fear ; I feared her nervous and frail nature.' Being assured on this point he became more composed. I then told him that my Aunts had feared the effect of this upon him, but that I had told them I knew that father had been predicting his dissolution, and I supposed he would not be surprised at any time to hear of his death. But far different was the effect. Father came toward me, and I went up to embrace him, but he clutched my hand convulsively and said not a word.

I led him to a chair. I sat down before him. He looked upon me, but his eye was that of one whose mind had been overthrown. It was not fancy in me, I could not be deceived in it. I placed my hands upon his shoulders as I would upon those of a child or an insane person, and told him to be calm. He heard me not, for his mind had no perception at the time. My blood returned to my heart, my limbs were cold, I could not speak, for I looked into his eye again and again and there was no change, and I thought I had crazed him. At length he said, in a broken, incoherent manner, 'How is this?' I said I had told them if it had been some embarrassment or trouble of worldly or pecuniary matters it would make him ill, but that so great a thing as this he could stand up against. This hit his feelings where I meant it should, and he said that was just the case with him, and added: 'Oh, I have had my mind too much fixed of late upon death, eternity, and the spiritual world, to be distressed by the fact of his death.' We then talked of the blessing—things attending his death. He had escaped that terrible vision—the nightmare, the incubus, the tormentor of his life—his unfinished picture."

The above unstudied and pathetic record prepares us for the singularly impressive character of the funeral. It was so timed as to meet the setting sun in its approach to the place of burial in Cambridge. Arrived at the churchyard, students of Harvard —Allston's Alma Mater—appeared bearing torches. Overshadowing clouds rendered their light needful. But soon the clouds opened, as if to let inhabitants of other spheres contemplate the scene. The moon and stars looked down with consecrating light as the service for the burial of the dead was voiced in solemn tones.

CHAPTER XXVII.

FIRST INSPECTION OF "BELSHAZZAR."—TECHNICAL ACCOUNT OF IT
    BY JOHN GREENOUGH.—ATTEMPTS AT RESTORATION. — TRAGIC
    INFLUENCE OF THE WORK ON ALLSTON'S LIFE.—ITS PRESENT
    POSITION.

Immediately upon the entombment of his body public interest turned to the unseen, yet famous, " Belshazzar." Mr. Dana,
with his son Richard, Mr. Edmund T. Dana, with his son Edmund, and Mr. John Greenough, on the 12th of July entered the
painting-room. The secret of many years' thought and labor
was opened, and the great work of Allston's life revealed. They
who first saw it were a committee appointed not by any special
authority so much as by a sense of fitness because of their sympathies and familiarity with the deceased. Interest was mingled
with sadness at the condition of the great picture. The King
had been finished, and Allston had expressed himself satisfied
with his success ; but now his entire figure is covered and blotted
out with a coat of dark brown paint. Upon seeing this the
elder Dana remarked, " That is his shroud." But we must not
attempt, by describing " Belshazzar " as it then appeared, to go
over ground so well covered by others. Among Mr. Dana's
" Notes," we find two descriptions of the picture, written after
Allston's death. The first is technical, given by Mr. John
Greenough, the second is extremely poetic, but without signature. We regret that we have no clue to its authorship. Both
are true to the subject and very interesting. Greenough's is as
follows :

" Belshazzar is here treated in strict accordance with the ac-

Belshazzar's Feast.

From the original study for the large unfinished picture in the Boston Museum of Art.

count in Daniel, chapter v. The scene is laid in the King's palace, where 'Belshazzar made a great feast to a thousand of his lords.' Belshazzar is seated upon his throne, in the foreground, on the left, near him, stands the Queen, supported by two Egyptian female slaves. The prophet Daniel, stands nearly in the centre of the foreground, his eyes fixed upon the King, and with his left hand pointing to the handwriting upon the wall, while he interprets the meaning of the mysterious words. The four figures on the right are the astrologers, Chaldeans, and soothsayers, who were 'unable to read the writing or interpret the meaning thereof.'

"The King has called for them and they have been brought into his presence. All have attempted, and all have failed to read the writing, or to show the interpretation thereof. Upon this the Queen, to whom word has come, has appeared in the hall and counselled the sending for Daniel, and he has been called. The King has addressed him and he has answered, setting before him the degradation, restoration, and piety of the King his father, and his own apostasy; and now, pointing toward the handwriting, he reads the words and shows the interpretation. All eyes but those of the Queen are turned from the supernatural writing to the Prophet, who is revealing the judgment.

"Receding a little from the immediate foreground is a group in shadow, their physiognomy and devout attitudes mark them to be Jews. They seem to be elevated by a consciousness of the truth of their religion, and deeply impressed with the triumphant display of the power of the true God. One of the females kneels in an attitude of reverence or prayer, while another reaches forward to touch the garment of the Prophet. Behind these, and forming a part of the same group, a youth of the Coptic race, in military habiliments, points to the vessels of gold and silver which were taken from the Jewish Temple by Nebuchadnezzar, the predecessor of Belshazzar, and were ordered by Belshazzar to be brought to his feast 'to serve wine to his lords and princes, their wives and concubines.'

"The middle distance is occupied by the banqueting-table, which, crowded with guests and laden with the holy vessels, is seen between the figures in the foreground. Large columns of porphyry, of barbaric order of architecture, support a gallery filled with spectators in attitudes of wonder and excitement. At the head of nine steps, under a large central light, is a colossal golden figure of Belas. The extreme distance shows an immense flight of steps with persons rushing up and down. As this picture is exhibited in an unfinished state, a few remarks in relation to its condition become necessary. It is known that Mr. Allston considered it virtually finished some fifteen or twenty years ago. He afterward, however, thought that by a change in the perspective the effect of the whole would be greatly improved. This change involved material alterations in nearly all the main figures of the picture then finished. After a consultation with Mr. Stuart the painter, he decided to undertake the labor, and, with this end in view, wrought upon the picture at intervals, carrying out his new design, but died before its completion.

"The picture now shows this later new design, in some parts perfected, in others commenced, while some portions remain precisely as they were before. A few outlines in chalk, made by Mr. Allston's hand over these latter portions, indicate that but trifling alterations were thought necessary to make them agree with the new design. It was found necessary to remove these outlines previous to varnishing the picture, but an accurate minute of them has been made.

"The alteration in the perspective required the size of the principal figures to be enlarged. This is particularly evident in the group of magicians, where new heads have been commenced on an enlarged scale, and the height of the figures is increased by half a head. A portion of one of the former heads is still to be seen under the chin of one of the new ones. The necks and shoulders remain the same as in the old design, though it is easy to trace the lines which were to have formed the shoulders to correspond with the last painted heads. The outline painted in oil-colors over the drapery of the principal figure of this group shows that having changed the height of this magician, Mr. Allston thought it necessary to paint the whole of the drapery anew, in order that every fold of the garment should be strictly true to the anatomy of the figure. The heads are unfinished, and probably are advanced very little beyond dead color. Near this group are to be seen the remains of two heads, which have the appearance of having at one time been finished, but afterward pumiced away to prepare a ground for raising the shoulders of the figure below. There are no means of judging whether Mr. Allston intended to dispense with these heads in his new composition, or whether they were to be repainted in different proportions.

" 'Belshazzar,' it will be seen by a glance, is now very far from perfect. It is, in fact, only the ghost of the figure which was once entirely finished, and afterward by his own hand pumiced down and covered with a solid coat of paint on which to paint a new figure on a larger scale. The left foot remains precisely as it was finished for the first figure. The right hand is evidently a new one, begun on a large scale to correspond with the intended proportions of the figure. It wants the glazing and finishing touches. As this figure was found, there was a perfect blank in the picture where the figure of Belshazzar was at one time seated on his throne entirely finished. The effect of the whole composition was marred not only by the want of one of the principal figures, but from the discord occasioned by this large spot of paint, which was entirely out of keeping with the rest of the picture.

" Those who were intrusted with the picture deliberated and debated a long time on the expediency of removing the covering from this important figure.   They feared that Mr. Allston, previously to painting it out, must have nearly obliterated it to form a proper ground for the new figure.   On the other hand, they thought it desirable to obtain even such a remnant of this important element of the design, and it was presumed that the coloring of the old figure, however much rubbed down, would restore in some measure the harmony of the picture.   They naturally felt a reluctance to tamper with anything in the work of so great an artist ; however, the consideration that they were about to remove a covering which could at any time be replaced by a common hand, and that its removal might work a most beneficial change, at length determined them.   The coat of paint has been by a peculiar process carefully taken off and the result has been as anticipated.   The figure was found to have been rubbed down to precisely the state in which it is now seen ; but the introduction of the color, even in its present state, at once threw light and brilliancy into other parts of the picture in a manner scarcely to be conceived except by those who saw it in its previous condition.

"In all other respects the picture is the same as it came from Mr. Allston's hand.   It is to be hoped that it may always remain so.   However much we may regret that he did not live to complete his work, it is very certain that no artist who has the ability to appreciate it would have the assurance to put his brush to it.   It is a consolation to reflect that to artists it is quite as valuable in its present condition, for in it are to be found specimens of Mr. Allston's methods in nearly every stage, from the beginning to the completion of a work, as they will be able to study in it the changes in the artist's manner since the first finishing of the picture as well as the last process.

"The figure of Daniel seems nearly perfect, with the exception of the right hand. This was at one time finished in accordance with the original design as seen in the colored sketch. It there hangs passive by his side; but Mr. Stuart, having suggested to Mr. Allston that by clenching the hand more animation would be given to the action, he began the alteration but proceeded no further than the dead color when he became satisfied of the superiority of his own conception, and mentioned to several of his friends that he intended to restore the hand as it was before. Since his death, one of these friends expressed a desire that the old hand might be restored by cleaning off the dead color, and the experiment was begun by uncovering a very small portion; it was found, however, that the old hand was so completely effaced before painting over it as to render the restoration hopeless. The new hand was not painted precisely over the old one, and the attempt was abandoned.

"In the upper part of the picture, on the right, are to be seen a number of lines laying down the perspective of the architecture. Some confusion here arises from the mixture of the outlines of the architecture with what are technically termed the working lines. They show that an alteration in this part was contemplated, and to a certain degree accomplished. The extreme corner which would have contained the writing is in a very unfinished state. The old painting has here again been rubbed down, and the picture loses much of its intended effect for the want of the supernatural light which was to have proceeded from this spot as a focus.

"It only remains to note the few chalk outlines which were necessarily removed before varnishing:

"1. A small outline around the toes of the left foot of the King, showing that it was to be lengthened a little.

"2. Another depressing the heel of the left foot of Daniel, a correction which probably became necessary from the change in the perspective.

"3. In the left upper corner of the picture there is a green curtain, which, hanging from the gallery, nearly covers one of the pillars. This curtain has been pumiced down, or cleaned nearly away with spirits. Over it the outlines of the whole of the pillar was laid down in chalk, as though Mr. Allston intended to represent it entire. These lines were drawn, not only over the curtain, but over a part of the 'golden candlestick.' It is a matter of conjecture whether this candlestick was to have been repainted in different proportion or form, or what was the nature of the change to be made. It could hardly have been his intention to dispense with it entirely, since in the account given in the Scriptures it serves to fix the locality of the handwriting, which is described as having been seen 'over against the golden candlestick.'"

Following is the other and anonymous account alluded to :

"You well know it has been the desire of my life to behold the 'great picture,' as Mr. Allston's 'Belshazzar' was called. It was a hope which I scarce believed would ever be realized, but it has been, and to-day, under circumstances of peculiar interest, I visited it, and felt a solemn awe stealing over my soul as I found myself standing before that mighty work. A hallowed presence seemed to pervade the room ; it was as if the spirit of Allston, in his calm majesty, stood near, and by silent thought conveyed the instruction, the deep and mighty meaning he there symbolized! Under hallowed influences, crowding fast on mind and heart, did I first behold this magnificent production. You wish to know my first impressions—under their immediate influence, therefore, I write you. The picture is unfinished ; the heart, the mind, the imagination of the artist grew with his work, and he could not be satisfied, in the advancing state of his mental and moral faculties, with that which did not fully develop and do justice to the feelings and passions he would delineate, and which with every year's life he more fully understood, as every Christian does, who, studying his own heart learns equally to read the hearts of others.

"There is an overwhelming power in every part of this glorious work. Belshazzar, who is the first figure on the left, and around whom is concentrated so much to interest the beholder, is formed, and was once entirely completed, but it is now the wreck of greatness ; and a fearful lesson, in his seemingly mutilated figure, of the crushing of the wicked. In the convulsed hand and foot one can almost see and touch the muscles quivering with horror, and from these more finished portions we can form some conception of the strength of emotion which the countenance was intended to express. It is a masterly production even as it is.

"Then the Queen—truly worthy her name. She looks the proud, imperious princess, a woman endowed with great power, and naturally accustomed to, and capable of, perfect self-control. There is an expression in her countenance as if she would rather die than betray her emotion ; but, nevertheless, the intense workings of her soul, which she vainly struggles to repress and conceal, are visible in every feature. The haughty eye quails before that awful and mysterious light which is shedding such supernatural brightness on every object, and her compressed lip and convulsed features evince but too plainly that she is under the influence of feelings too powerful to resist or subdue. Her hands also speak, as well as the countenance ; one might stand before her for hours, imagining the workings of her agitated soul.

"Daniel, the mighty and holy, 'the man of excellent spirit, in whom were found light and understanding and wisdom like the wisdom of the gods,' is the central figure, of most commanding power. Surrounded as he is by human passion in its stormiest aspects, his characteristic bearing as a prophet of the Most High, is made beautifully prominent. Majesty, truth, and a

heavenly repose are in him united, breathed in every lineament;
but that eye—in it is blended pity, severity, and calm self-possession, as he looks upon the guilty and terror-stricken monarch.
With the compassion of a man he would willingly have mercy
on the being he condemns, but in the stern necessity of his prophetic character he must reveal that which is shadowed forth in
his vision, the departing glory of Belshazzar, with all his honor
and brightness, as in violence and blood his kingdom is wrested
from him.

"Had Allston ever allowed himself to portray the Saviour,
and chosen as his subject 'Christ rebuking the people,' I think
the expression would not have been unlike that of Daniel. In
the whole attitude there seems to be this sentiment, I am the
prophet of Him who is God, and there is no other God beside
him. He who spake, and all things sprang into existence. He
whose honor, thou, O King, hast trampled in the dust, and whose
power thou hast scorned. *He* has sent me unto thee, and from
the message so mysteriously revealed there is no escape. Listen!
We seem to hear his lofty renunciation of Belshazzar's kingly
gifts and princely rewards, as he says, 'Let them be to thyself,
yet will I read the writing unto the king, and make known to
him the interpretation.' His left arm is uplifted, its power is
irresistible. Near the prophet are some fine female figures, apparently prostrate in reverence of him.

"The foreground is completed by a group of astrologers,
Chaldeans, and soothsayers, most majestic in form; but those
countenances! Of all the faces I ever saw on earth, or conceived
could dwell below, these are the most perfect embodiment of
every malignant passion which baffled skill and mortified pride
could call from the depths of a depraved human heart. Anger,
malice, bitterness, and hatred seem contending for mastery.
Their fierce glances, emanations of those inward fires which almost consume them, seem as if they would annihilate the de-

spised Hebrew captive, whose instantaneous comprehension and simple exposition of the mysterious and magical characters had

" ' Made Chaldea's wisdom dim ! '

" Directly above this group is the handwriting which has been the cause of their humiliation, its light is the light of the picture, and the intention of the artist was to have it of the intense brightness as in ' Uriel,' but the finishing touches can now never be given.

" A friend observed as a beautiful proof of the divinely imparted power of Daniel, that he could instantly discover the perfect form of those mystic characters, and as directly reveal them, and their interpretation, whereas the Chaldeans could not gaze into the depths of that glorious light with sufficient strength to read the symbols of their own language. ' Their eyes were holden, that they could not see ! ' But the moment the holy glance of the Almighty's prophet rested thereon, the mystery was solved, and this circumstance, added to the contempt with which they hitherto regarded Daniel, increased the mystification of their defeat.

" In the intervals between the figures which occupy the foreground is seen the banquet-table, gleaming with the rich treasures—once so sacredly consecrated to the Temple service in the holy city, now so ingloriously appropriated. All around, and in the gallery above, are seated the lords and princes who had gathered for the last time to join in the revels of the doomed monarch. In the background is seen the heathen idol who presides over this scene of revelry, so soon changed to agony and despair. A lamp, which is suspended above, pours upon the statue a strong, but still a distant, light. The effect is inimitable. The architecture is solemn and grand, but it is evidently a secondary consideration with the artist, whose great design was to delineate the Divine power, and the passions of the human heart under various influences; and most wonderfully has he succeeded.

"I feel that the memory or the fame of Allston can never die. I feel that the years to come will raise a proud monument to him in every heart that appreciates the noble art to which he devoted all the best powers of his intellectual, moral, and physical nature. Well may we say, 'The mind that was among us, in its works is embalmed.' With all the excellences of this splendid work many will find themselves unsatisfied in their anticipations—those who look at it hastily and without feeling, without knowledge of human nature, without appreciation of that wonderful art which can make the canvas seem to breathe. One who will read carefully the fifth chapter of Daniel, and then give himself thoughtfully to the study of 'Belshazzar's Feast' will find ample compensation in his own soul for the hours he spends there. The religious power of the picture will impress him at once, and the feeling will deepen continually. There is repose only on one brow, that of God's faithful servant.

"Sir Joshua Reynolds assures us that it took him three weeks to discover the beauty of the frescoes in the Vatican. To some observers the unfinished state in which 'Belshazzar's Feast' is presented to the world would be sufficient reason for their not beholding any beauty in it that they should desire it. But there are many circumstances that may one day be revealed to the world which would make it a thousandfold more interesting to behold it just as it is, and we view it as a precious relic, the dearer for lacking the finishing stroke of that masterly hand; and we, as a nation, are honored and happy in possessing this noble production of so lofty and pure a mind, and that on which the last trace of his pencil rested."

Allston's picture of "Belshazzar" is a symbol of artistic power; it is also a record of genius failing to fulfil its conceptions, not from lack of ability, but for want of mental stimulus and favoring circumstances. It was to be paid for by subscriptions of $1,000 each from ten gentlemen. A part of this amount was advanced when the order was given, thus imposing at the outset the obligation to finish it. That obligation was most unfortunate; it was a crushing weight upon Allston for over twenty years. It did, as it were, overreach and destroy its purpose; it introduced an incongruous and obstructive element into his motives and incitements to work. As a debt, it was an unfavorable and paralyzing influence. "I can paint under affliction," said he, "but to paint under debt!"

Had Allston been spared the feeling of obligation for the money advanced, his mind would have strengthened his hand with his former confidence, and "Belshazzar" would probably have been finished some twenty years before death arrested his brush wet with the color of the Soothsayer's face. Allston had demonstrated his ability to paint rapidly, and on his return to Boston from Europe, in 1818, "Belshazzar" was nearly completed.

Mr. J. H. Hayward, in a letter to Mr. Dana, wrote as follows: "A day or two previous to my departure for Europe he invited me to visit his picture of 'Belshazzar,' not only on my own account, but that I might give an account of it to Messrs. Leslie and Newton on my arrival in London. To the best of my recollection and belief, when I first saw it, it was finished, not in part, but *in toto.* I said to Mr. Allston, 'What more can you possibly add? Why, is not the picture done?' 'It is done,' he replied, 'and I am only glazing and retouching.' On taking leave I said, 'When shall I tell your friends in London that the picture will be open for exhibition?' 'You may tell them,' he replied, 'that it will certainly be out in the course of October.' This was, I think, on the 8th of September, 1821."

By encouraging approval or praise, an artist's friends may,

and often do, finish his pictures. "Belshazzar," so far as All-ston's work upon it was concerned, was finished in 1821. It was nearly done when he left London in 1818, but in bringing it to America he brought it away from all stimulating and reassuring influences. A sensitive imagination like Allston's is self-ques-tioning, self-critical, and self-doubting. When so important a work as "Belshazzar," one so charged with responsibility spring-ing from the consciousness of high expectation on the part of his friends concerning it, is left to the artist's sole judgment—when there is no one competent, whom he may call in to share the re-sponsibility of pronouncing it a success, he becomes a prey to doubts and fears, imagination quickens apprehension, and he is overcome by misgivings that he cannot control. The reaction of the mind upon itself in solitude is unhealthy, and most unfavora-ble to the execution of any work of genius. The stronger the imagination, the more important the fellowship with those of similar tastes and attainments.

A poet with nature and his books about him may need noth-ing more, but a painter must be among painters. The attrition of kindred minds is indispensable to great results in art. Imag-ination must have something human besides its own creations to strengthen it. The mind that feeds only upon itself has entered upon a process of mental starvation. Contact, even with inferior minds, may impart a modicum of strength, but isolation, for an artist, is always a condition of weakness and decline. Allston's transition from the society of artists in London, to that of his friends in Boston, was, in its relation to his art, for a while un-felt, and, it may be, unsuspected. The glow of his reception, the genial whole-heartedness of the welcome given him by his en-thusiastic admirers, buoyed his spirits, allowing no sense of loss. Fêted continually, encouraged with substantial and liberal patron-age on all sides, the central figure of interest in the society of in-tellectual men, whose appreciation manifested itself in words and deeds of refinement and generosity, there was no place for a sense of deficiency in artistic conditions.

This diversion of his mind continued to hold him up from a realization of his loss in leaving England. It may not have been till he opened his studio in Cambridgeport, and had passed through the exciting novelty of his situation there that he fully realized the want of artistic influences, which he had left in London. His mind was creative to a degree that could people his painting-room with visions of beauty. Thus gifted he might have whiled away the years unconscious of artistic loneliness or any sense of loss; but his dream-life, which could minister to him so constantly and pleasingly, was soon disturbed by pecuniary embarrassment, and we have the saddening picture of a man capable of the highest attainment in the sphere of the highest art, awakened and distressed by the cruel touch of want.

In his large, new painting-room, constructed to meet his requirements in painting large pictures, "Belshazzar" was unrolled, with its back to the eastern wall. Its 12 × 16 feet of surface was screened by a curtain so arranged as to be easily drawn aside. No eye but his was to see the picture during its progress. Leonard Jarvis, in his letter to Mr. Dana, extracts of which we have given elsewhere, says: " Whenever I visited your capital I made it a point to seek out my old friend (Allston). On one occasion I urged him to show me his ' Belshazzar.' He entreated me not to press my request, ' For,' said he, ' it gives me pain to refuse you, but if that picture were seen by any person, I should never finish it. I know,' continued he, ' that this is a weakness, but I cannot help it.' "

To the same purport is the following letter from Mr. Sargent:

"BOSTON, September 2, 1844.

" To R. H. DANA, ESQ.

DEAR SIR: In reply to your inquiries, in the note of 31st ult., this moment received, I can only say that I purchased an estate of the late John Prince, in Pearl and Milk Streets, January 22, 1828; there was a stable thereon about 25 × 45 feet. The stable is still standing. That stable was approached from Milk Street, over land now covered by stores; and there Mr. Allston wrought on the great picture. How long he had been the tenant of Mr. Prince, I know not; he was mine but a short time.

"His great simplicity of character struck me very forcibly. When he heard of my having purchased the estate, he came to see me, and appeared perplexed and pained by some prospective trouble, which for some time, I could not comprehend. 'I was wholly unprepared for this,' said he. 'I fear it will cause me a good deal of embarrassment.'

" 'Not at all, sir,' I replied. 'There is not the slightest occasion for it; you can remain perfectly at ease until you find better accommodations.'

" 'But my trouble, sir,' he rejoined, 'is as to the manner in which your men will enter the building.'

" 'My men will not have occasion to enter that building, Mr. Allston.'

" 'Yes, to take possession they will, you know, and I wish to ask if they cannot enter with their backs toward the picture?' I at once comprehended his difficulty, and assured him that the old English livery of seizin was unnecessary here, and that by our law a constructive delivery of possession was enough. He seemed highly delighted; but, after taking leave of me, and going part way down-stairs, he came back, with some anxiety on his countenance, to ask me if I was quite sure.

"Yours with regard,

"L. M. SARGENT."

It is painful to contemplate Allston's slavery to a morbid sensitiveness; to the unreasonable influence of a mistaken idea; to a conviction, upon the fifth unrolling of "Belshazzar," that he had no right to, and could not conscientiously, undertake any other work till that was done. The strength and control of his thought upon this subject is strikingly illustrated by the following incident, told by R. H. Dana, Jr.:

"When Lord Morpeth was in Boston, in the winter of 1841, he called on Allston, and in the course of his conversation alluded to 'Uriel in the Sun,' and the great delight his sister, the Duchess of Sutherland, took in having possession of it; and added, 'She requested me to say to Mr. Allston that, if she might be so bold, she would esteem it a favor if she could have another picture from his hand.' And then after examining various sketches, his Lordship added that if he might be allowed to dictate, he would suggest that it should be the 'Court of Titania.' To this Allston assented, and in taking leave said: 'Do me the honor of presenting my compliments to the Duchess of Sutherland, and say to her Grace, if you please, that my pictures are my children, and as she has treated one of them with so much kindness and courtesy, I shall be most happy to commit another to her care.'"

The writer, when a lad of sixteen, was privileged to hear Allston's description of this beautifully outlined sketch of the "Court of Titania," from "Midsummer-Night's Dream," with which he usually entertained visitors to his studio. It was very interesting, and the impression he received is among his indelible memories. Allston never showed this picture to one who had not seen it without describing and explaining its various points. While thus engaged he was himself the object of greatest interest. His expressive eye would kindle as his words, skilfully chosen and graphic, would flow in exposition from part to part. The canvas was not large, 4 × 6 feet. The compensation named and settled upon was £5,000, an amount at that time unprecedented for a picture by an American artist. Twenty-five thousand dollars for a work that he might have finished within a year! a competency which, it is obvious to con-

sider, would have disembarrassed him and enabled him to finish
"Belshazzar;" would have taken him out of daily stress for
money, and doubtless prolonged his life, by the assurance of a
peaceful independence. Certainly every consideration of prudence should have counselled his curtaining "Belshazzar" for a
time sufficient to execute so important and tempting a commission. But his conscience was imperious. He would accept the
order only on condition that the Duchess would wait till he had
finished his great picture. This was an indefinite postponement,
for "Belshazzar" was then more unfinished than it was when he
brought it to America, over twenty years before. "I would not,"
said he, "undertake to paint a picture for any crowned head in
Christendom till 'Belshazzar' is finished." This extravagance
of morbid sensibility was the outcome of a mind that had brooded
upon one subject till it had lost the power of estimating its true
relations to himself or to others—a mind that in solitude had
contemplated unimportant considerations till they were magni-
fied and distorted, till folly seemed wisdom, and reason impracticable. The Duchess of Sutherland's commission might have
been executed in a few months. Allston could have secured the
services of some young artist (there were several at the time in
Boston fully competent) who could have traced on a new canvas
the outlines of the picture, and, under his direction, laid it in, and
accomplished the greater portion of the manual labor requisite,
carrying it so far that Allston could easily have finished it in six
months. Moreover, according to custom in England, the Duchess would have advanced part of the compensation agreed upon,
an amount quite sufficient to pay his debts, and provide amply
for his expenses while at work on her picture. But to a mind so
hedged about by visionary considerations acting upon his moral
sensibility, no scheme, however simple and obvious, could enlist
the effort to carry it out.

The experiment of employing an assistant to work on "Bel-

Outline Sketch of Titania's Fairy Court.

From the original in the Boston Museum of Art.

shazzar " had been proposed, and he had received it favorably.
But that which commended itself to his judgment found no response in his energy or will. He seemed unable, at this period,
to diverge from the path and methods he had followed, though
they were carrying him farther and farther from his purpose.
The vigor of youth had passed, its ambitions and its sustaining
hopes were gone, when he undertook, single-handed, to complete
the difficult and laborious work of reconstructing his great picture on a new theory as to its perspective. This theory involved
a change in the point of sight. He had made it, as he thought,
too high for a picture which, from its size, would naturally be
placed above the eye of the spectator. But even a reconstruc-
tion so radical could have been accomplished with comparative
ease by starting *de novo ;* much perplexing confusion would have
been avoided by making on a new canvas the extensive altera-
ions involved. To alter the point of sight in a picture is to
change the relations of all its parts to each other, a work of
incalculable difficulty in so large a painting.

In estimating "Belshazzar " as a work of art, we cannot urge
too strongly a consideration of the unfinished and transition
state in which it was left by Allston, and is now seen. In the
accumulations of a studio there is usually much unfinished
work—outlines, sketches, dead colors, and studies—that the artist
would not show to anyone, and by which it would be unfair to
measure his capabilities as a painter. The accumulations of
many years were taken from Allston's studio, and are now placed,
with a discrimination that in many instances gives prominence
to his poorest work. We can find no justifying cause for an exposure so out of harmony with his known disposition to screen
his unfinished work from the public eye.

The propriety of exhibiting "Belshazzar " in its present condition was questioned, but the public interest in the picture
soon after Allston's death seemed to demand its exposition.

We think there should be appended to it a brief statement in explanation of its apparent incongruities and contradictions. When we consider how sensitive Allston was about showing this picture, how careful that it should not be seen, even when, with the exception of a little retouching and glazing, it was, as he said, finished, we feel that it is almost a breach of confidence to exhibit it, even under the best conditions of light and place. But to allow it to be seen where the position of the spectator distorts the perspective is, to say the least, a great injustice.

In the " Allston Room," so called, of the Boston Museum of Fine Arts, though shared by Stuart, Copley, and others, there are few pictures by Allston that the common observer would regard as the work of more than an ordinary artist, while there are several that do not rise even to that prominence. In a part of the building remote from the " Allston Room " there are a few outlines, very beautiful, though representing only the first stage of his work. But where is " Belshazzar," the picture upon which he had expended so much thought and labor—which had occupied him at intervals for more than half his working life—the picture about which so much has been said and more written than of any contemporaneous work of art—the most historic picture ever painted by an American? It is not in the " Allston Room," it is not in any of the galleries ; but high up in the hallway of the stairs leading to the galleries it hangs, where it cannot be judged intelligently and fairly.

The proper distance at which to view a picture is at least twice its length ; the proper place to stand in viewing it is at the point of station directly in front of the point of sight. It is impossible so to view " Belshazzar " where it now hangs. We cannot wonder that anyone whose opinion of Allston is formed from his pictures, as exhibited in the Boston Museum of Fine Arts, should express disappointment and a strong conviction that he is not entitled to the high rank given him by his contemporaries.

In arranging a gallery of paintings the demands of space and symmetry often prevent due and proper consideration of their requirements in reference to tone, light, and distance. The difficulty of assigning proper positions to a large number of pictures is well known to be very great. We are far from censuring as intentional the injustice to "Belshazzar," but certainly no artist could have so placed it without knowing that he was damaging the picture and the reputation of its author. The very object which led Allston to attempt the extremely difficult task of lowering the point of sight was to overcome the bad effect of a slight elevation above the eye of the spectator. It is obvious that no change contemplated by him could overcome the bad effect of its present elevation.

Why not put "Belshazzar" in the "Allston Room?" Why not let it hang on the wall opposite the large door of that room, thus occupying the place of honor, in which it could be seen at a good distance as you approach the entrance? The place is in every way suitable, and the difficulty of rearrangement involved by no means insurmountable. If grandeur of conception and forceful delineation of feeling, from its simplest to its subtlest manifestation; if ideality, imagination, fancy, and dramatic power are of value; if these enter into, and by their obvious presence measure greatness in pictorial representations, then "Belshazzar" is incomparably the greatest picture on the walls of the Museum of Art, and yet it is in a position unworthy of the poorest, and, as we think, needlessly so. In the interest of art, in the interest of the memory of a great man, who left his impress on foreign schools, and did more for art in America than any other painter of his time, "Belshazzar" should be so placed as to be seen to advantage. To retain it in its present position is, by disregarding the requirements of the picture, a great injustice to the memory of its author. Better roll it up once more, and forever.

CHAPTER XXVIII.

The late Richard H. Dana, Jr., whose father, it will be remembered, was Allston's brother-in-law, left interesting memoranda of recollections of Allston:

"When Mr. Allston was at Petworth he was one day looking at a portrait of Vandyke's, when Lord Egremont coming up, asked his opinion of it.

" 'Very fine,' said he, 'and had I not known it to be Vandyke's I should have supposed it to be one of Sir Joshua's.'

" 'Do you mean to compliment Vandyke or Sir Joshua?' said his Lordship.

" 'Vandyke,' answered Mr. Allston.

" 'Then you think him inferior to Sir Joshua?' said Lord Egremont.

" 'Yes, I do,' said Mr. Allston.

" 'So do I,' said his Lordship, 'though I hardly dare to say so.'

"This anecdote Mr. Allston related when nearly sixty years of age, and added that he had never seen reason for changing his opinion. 'Sir Joshua,' said he, 'wanted Vandyke's correctness. He did not draw so well, but he had more genius.'

"Allston took great pleasure in reading Talfourd's 'Life and Letters of Lamb.' He had been intimate with Lamb when in

London, and was much attached to him. He told several anecdotes of him, which, I believe, are not told by Talfourd. Among
them were the following :

"Lamb was present when a naval officer was giving an account of an action which he had been in, and to illustrate the
carelessness and disregard of life at such times said that a sailor
had both his legs shot off, and as his shipmates were carrying
him below, another shot came and took off both his arms ; they,
thinking he was pretty much used up, though life was still in
him, threw him out of a port.

" 'Shame, d——d shame,' stuttered out Lamb, ' he m-m-might
have l-lived to have been an a-a-ornament to society ! '

"Mr. Allston was on a visit to Coleridge, at Bath or Bristol,
when Coleridge received a letter from Lamb, in which he said
that he was to dine that evening with the Worshipful Company
of Fishmongers, and as he expected to have a glorious time he
had spoken for a couple of watchmen and a window-shutter to
take him home."

"Once, in company with Lamb and Coleridge, with a few
others, Coleridge spoke very highly of a ' Dr. Bell.' ' Pooh ! '
said Lamb, very gravely, ' that is only because you are so fond
of Mrs. Bell.'

"After Coleridge and Lamb had left, Allston asked a gentleman present if it was true that Coleridge was much attached
to Mrs. Bell, for he had never heard him speak of her.

" 'Oh,' said the gentleman, ' that's only Lamb's nonsense.
The poor woman has been in a madhouse these forty years.'

"Allston became intimately acquainted with Coleridge, and
they were continually together during a residence of several
months in Rome. When Coleridge was at Highgate he was
often there for days together. He had the highest admiration,
nay, reverence, for Coleridge's powers of mind, and he loved him
as a man and a friend ; and, what was still more, he looked up

to him as a sincere and humble Christian. He often spoke of Coleridge as having been of the greatest advantage to his mind in every way—in his art, in poetry, and in his opinions and habits of thought generally—and also to his religious character.

" Nothing ever pained Allston more than to hear anyone (as some men inclined to do from difference of political, but more especially of religious, opinions) speak slightingly of Coleridge, or sneeringly of him as a man, a husband, a friend, and a Christian.

" Allston once told me an anecdote, which he never told to more than one or two besides, and then with a wish that it might be kept secret.

" Many of Coleridge's enemies made a handle of his separation from his wife to injure his character, and Mr. Allston was often asked in America what he knew of the matter. He always answered that it was an amicable separation; that Coleridge always spoke very respectfully of his wife, and had behaved very honorably to her in the matter. However, he told my father and myself an anecdote which plainly showed the cause of the separation, but he enjoined upon us never to repeat it during the lifetime of Coleridge or himself; ' For,' said he, ' nothing ever could give Coleridge greater pain then to be defended at the expense of his wife, and therefore I have never told this anecdote before, and should not feel right in telling it generally, even after Coleridge's death; but as it goes to show one probable reason for his conduct, I cannot but wish to have it preserved.'

" Mrs. Gillman told Mr. Allston that the younger sister of Mrs. Coleridge, when upon her deathbed, said that Coleridge would never be able to live with her sister, for she had the most horrible temper that she had ever known or heard of; that she was both irascible and implacable, and that when they were girls at a boarding-school they were glad when the vacations were over, and they were to go back to school, for her terrible temper made the house so uncomfortable to them. This she told Mrs. Gillman upon her deathbed, when speaking of her family and of Mr. Coleridge. She lived with them some time after their marriage, and said that no one could behave better than Mr. Coleridge to her sister. Mrs. Gillman told this in serious and secret conversation with Mr. Allston.

"When Mr. Allston and Coleridge were travelling in Italy they stopped at a miserable inn, where Mr. Allston, for want of something better to do, took up an execrable book and was reading it when Coleridge came in. He showed it to him and said that he had been much amused with the exceeding badness of the style; but Coleridge advised him to put it down, saying:

"'You may think that it amuses you, but you had better be doing nothing. You cannot touch pitch without being defiled.'

"Coleridge knew human nature, but he was an indifferent discriminator of persons. Mr. Allston tells an anecdote which was related to him by a literary friend, whose name I have forgotten, illustrating this. He was travelling with Coleridge in Scotland when they fell in with a party of fashionables from London admiring a waterfall. 'Magnificent,' said one of the cockneys.

"Coleridge was struck with the appropriateness of the epithet, and without suspecting, as any man with a pair of eyes might have done, that it was the result of chance, turned to him and commenced talking about the waterfall and giving many reasons why 'magnificent' was the proper epithet, and not sublime, or beautiful, or any other. His friend thought that Coleridge was wasting time and sense, and the event proved it; for the cockney turned and lisped out, with a perfectly unmoved expression:

"'Very true, sir; not only magnificent, but sublime and beautiful.'

"'Come away, Coleridge,' said his friend, taking his arm.

"Allston spent the greater part of a day in walking through Caen wood with Coleridge, and talking upon future punishment. Coleridge expressed his belief in it very distinctly and strongly;

and Allston has often spoken of the emphasis and effect with which he brought in the words, 'As a tree falleth, so shall it lie.'

"Allston was sitting with Mrs. Gillman and Coleridge in the garden at Highgate, when Coleridge read to them something which he had written, in which was the following passage: 'A Scotchman is a superficial German and a dull Frenchman.' Mrs. Gillman remonstrated with him, and asked him how he could be willing, by a single sentence, to get the ill-will and hurt the feelings of a whole nation. After a little conversation between Coleridge and Allston, Mrs. Gillman said that she thought he had better strike it out, and added, 'And I will give you my reasons.'

"'No, madam; don't, for God's sake,' said Coleridge, 'for if you do you will spoil the whole. A woman judges by her instinct, and not by reason. I'll strike it out, but I've more respect for your first impression than I should probably have for your argument.'

"Coleridge told Allston that he was once travelling in a stage-coach with Southey, when they had for their fellow-passenger a watchmaker who was a self-taught man and was very much given to reading poetry. Hearing Southey call Coleridge by his surname he asked whether he was the Mr. Coleridge who had recently published a volume of poems, and finding he was the same, praised them very much, especially a dialogue, which he pronounced capital.

"'I don't remember any dialogue among them,' said Coleridge.

"'Oh, yes,' said the man; 'it was between Strophe (pronounced in one syllable) and Anti Strophe. It was capital, but, to tell the truth, I think Strophe had it, all hollow!'

"Coleridge was engaged for some time in writing for the *Courier*, and when he left it, the editor, Mr. Stewart, a clear-headed Scotchman, who had known a good deal of the world from having conducted for many years that leading political journal, said to him, 'Well, Mr. Coleridge, you say you must leave me. I am sorry you are going. Before I knew you, sir, I did not believe there was a man of principle in the world.'

"When Allston was in Italy there was an English artist there who had lived abroad more than in England, and affected to hate his own country, and was a man of rather bad character. Allston painted a picture which was much admired for its clouds. This artist asked him how he produced his effect, and Mr. Allston told him freely how he managed his colors.

"The English artist then began a picture and endeavored to paint clouds in the same manner. Allston went into his studio, and finding that he had been partly misunderstood, took the brush into his own hands and painted for him until he had made him master of the mode. Coleridge said to Allston, 'You are doing yourself no good, and him a favor for which he will not thank you.' Allston doubted the man's ingratitude, and said that at all events he was not sorry he had done him a kindness. Coleridge, to try the man, went to his studio and praised the picture, especially the clouds. The man made no explanation. Coleridge then went further and said, 'You've got Allston's clouds, or Allston's method of painting clouds.' 'Oh,' said the man, 'we knew all that before.'

"Allston told artists all that he knew. Other artists discover a mode and keep it to themselves. Allston opened his knowledge to all.

"My father said he never could forget the delightful expression with which Allston came from seeing Haydon's picture of 'Christ's Entry into Jerusalem.' His eye beamed, his whole face lighted up, and he looked as though he had received pure delight. My father, who had seen it, said, 'But is not there this and that defect?'

"'Oh, yes,' said Allston; 'but the picture has genius and

life in it. It has glorious parts, and one need not see its defects.' Nor did he ever speak of its defects.

"He always cited with approbation a story of an Italian artist who praised a statue, and when his pupils pointed out defects, glaring defects in one place and another, admitted them all, and said there were worse defects than those; 'You have not mentioned all, nor can you, but it's a glorious statue.'

"A picture painted by him called 'Alpine Scenery,' and owned by Mr. Isaac P. Davis, was retouched by a picture-finisher and restored in Boston. Allston saw it and said, 'It is not my picture now.' The foreground was altered and the tone taken out of it.

"He once told me he could paint the portraits of all his class in college, and he believed, of all who were in college with him, from recollection. If the names were given to him, he could call up the face to each name.

"This anecdote I had from Dr. Channing. Mr. Allston had engaged to paint a picture for Mr. J. Phillips for $1,000. Mr. Phillips advanced $500. When the picture was done it was worth much more, at least $1,500, even at the rate of sales in America. Mr. Phillips was told of this, and he (or his agent) wrote Mr. Allston a line enclosing the $500, and telling him they were aware that the picture was worth more than the sum agreed, and asking him if he was willing they should send him $500 more. To this Allston replied that he could not now agree for more than he had first contracted with Mr. Phillips to paint the picture for, or something to that effect. But at the same time he told a friend that if Mr. Phillips had sent him the $500 without asking him to ask it for the picture and change his bargain, he would have accepted it, and been very glad of it. He knew the picture was worth the whole, and he would have received it if sent, but could not ask more for his picture than he had agreed upon.

"Chester Harding told Alexander the artist that at one time Allston was very much distressed for money, and driven to great straits, and that Harding, being then very intimate with Allston, and confident of his friendship, suggested to him that he could easily relieve himself by painting two or three pictures off hand; that they would sell well, and though they might not do justice to his powers in all respects yet they would without doubt be clever and would pass muster very well, and be far better than any other of our artists could do. But he said he received as severe a rebuke from Allston as though he had suggested a forgery or peculation.

"A friend lent him Carlyle's sketch of the character of Mirabeau, extracted from his 'French Revolution' into the *Westminster Review*. Soon afterward someone asked him what he thought of it. 'I do not see any original ideas in it, but I see a great deal of original English. He takes a common thought and belabors it with his Babylonish jargon until it appears like something original. The man has made a god of his own intellect, and worships it with perpetual summersets.'

"Father says that Allston was invited to dine with Stuart Newton, who had just come from London, and that he went anticipating great pleasure from hearing of the English artists, and of all that was doing in the art in London. But he came back quite dejected. On being asked about it, he said, 'I have not heard a single man praised.'

"The last time Mrs. Dana spent an evening at Allston's this incident occurred, showing his great kindness and simplicity. She had mislaid her bag, and when we were ready to go she mentioned that she could not find it. Some search was made, but to no purpose, and it was given up for the time. We observed that Mr. Allston rose from his seat, lighted a lamp, and went out of the room; but as he often did this, we thought nothing particularly of it. A minute or two after this, as we passed

through the entry to go away, we gave another look into the parlor, thinking the bag might possibly be there, and, on opening
the door, there we saw Mr. Allston, infirm and suffering from
pain as he was, stooping down and looking under the sofa and
tables to search for this bag. So secret did he mean to be in his
kindness, that he actually blushed when we entreated him not to
put himself to so much trouble for it. But for our looking into
the room we should never have known that he had searched for
the bag, had he been unsuccessful. When, after his death, we
remembered this incident of so short a time before, it was very
affecting.

"The fall after his death, one day, a plain man, a house-car-
penter in Cambridgeport, by the name of Litchfield, called at my
office on business, and after he had got through the business he
spoke of Mr. Allston, and expressed extreme interest in the great
picture. Then he went on as follows: 'I always set a great
deal by that man. He was a real gentleman, that man was. A
good many sets up for it, but there are precious few. Now,
Mr. Allston was what I call a real gentleman. I knew him
very well. I lived next house to him ten years, and whenever
I met him he always had something pleasant to say.' He then
told me an anecdote of Allston which, he said, 'clinched' him in
his opinion. When the painting-room was building, this Litchfield was employed in some way to make an estimate, out of the
usual mode, for which he thought he ought to have been paid by
the agent. The agent would not pay him, and he abided by the
decision, yet he mentioned it to Mr. Allston, knowing that he
was not responsible for any of the expenses, but hoping that he
would mention it to the agent. Mr. Allston said at once, 'Mr.
Litchfield, you ought to be paid. Don't say that I said so, for
it is not my business, and I should not like to hurt the feelings
of the agent, but you ought to be paid.' Litchfield knew that
Allston did not own the building, and that he had no money to

spare, and thought no more of it. Some six or eight years after this, one evening Mr. Allston sent for him to come into his room. 'He was always polite,' said Litchfield, 'and he handed me a chair. He then brought to my mind the matter of the estimate, and said that he had always intended that I should be paid for it; that he had never forgotten it, although he had not had it in his power to pay. He then took out a ten-dollar bill and asked me if that would satisfy me. I told him, 'Mr. Allston, I can't take so much. This is more than I ask for the work.' He tried to make me take it, saying that I had been out of the money for several years. At last he told me to take the bill and satisfy myself out of it. I took it and brought him back the change, deducting no more than the lowest price I could fix upon my labor. Now, he was not bound to pay me. He never made the bargain, and he told me not to tell any one, lest it should hurt the agent's feelings. I never have, until since his death.' He then expatiated upon Mr. Allston again, upon his polite manners and kindness to all people, and repeated, 'Yes, sir; that man was a real gentleman; I set great store by that man.'

Following are some of Allston's sayings and comments, also recorded by Mr. Dana:

"Hazlitt began by being an artist. I once saw a work of his; it was a copy from Titian, and very well done. But he would not have gone far beyond copying, for he was entirely destitute of imagination. He once remarked to me that the English could have no great historical painters because the English face was a poor one for a model. He seemed to have no idea that there could be any faces but portraits, and no idea of the art beyond its mimetic character. In the article which he furnished for the 'Encyclopedie Métropolitaine' he argues against the ideal in the art—against the liberty of the artist in making use of the ideal; and supports himself by appealing to Raphael. Now this was the very point in which Raphael failed —in which he was inferior to Michael Angelo."

" Lawrence had the bravura touch of the pencil—slap-dash— which always takes with novices. I was once at Mr. Anger- stein's gallery with Walker and a young artist of genius who was much taken by a portrait of Angerstein by Lawrence. In the next room was a portrait by Vandyke, and a masterpiece. We were expressing our admiration of it when our young friend said:

" ' Yes, but I confess I like Sir Thomas better.'

" ' Do you, sir ? ' said Walker. 'Indeed! Well, sir, you won't think so long.' And he was right.

" There is something technically called ' handling,' which in- variably surprises and delights the novice, but which is easily gotten and soon palls. A great picture has a simplicity about it, and is so true to reality that it seldom dazzles and surprises."

" The finest head I ever painted, and for effect the best thing I ever did, or ever expect to do, was the agony of Judas, which I painted in Bristol, England. I showed it to a few friends who said that its effect upon them was as dreadful as it was upon me ; but I destroyed it in a few days, and for reasons which per- haps I could not make others understand as I felt them. It was not merely the distress I felt at looking on it, for I might have disposed of it and never seen it again, but I could not endure the thought of deriving an intellectual gratification or profes- sional reputation and pleasure from what I believed to be so dreadful a reality."

" While I was in Florence I saw in a dream a female whom I may call perfectly beautiful. In form, feature, expression, and dress she was more perfect than anything that my highest imagination had ever conceived. Nothing in ancient or modern art is an approach to it, and if I could have painted her with half her effect I should have painted the most beautiful object in the art. For several days afterward I was in a state of quiet, ethereal exaltation; I felt in whatever I was about that something peculiar had occurred to me, and could hardly realize that I was to act and be treated like other people. The vision, or perhaps the consciousness of something having occurred to me haunted me for months. It was a long time before I became fully awake on that subject."

"I saw Madame de Staël at the illumination of St. Peter's. She had a beautiful hand and arm, and displayed them to great advantage by waving a wreath which she held in her hand, but a face like a figure-head—coarse features and a vulgar mouth."

"Goethe must be a great man to carry so many great minds with him; but he certainly knows nothing of my art. He does not enter into the philosophy of it. He knows neither its height nor its depth. His notions are jejune and those of a mechanic; and even in the mechanical part he is for the most part false. He begins a paragraph as though he was going to lead his reader to some great truth, and when he has got him down to the middle of the well, he leaves him."

"Too much stress cannot be laid upon the conformity of art to nature, but it should be remembered that nature is only the artist's starting-point."

"Rembrandt was the Dryden of the art."

"I have been more affected by music than I have ever been by either painting or poetry."

"Père la Chaise, at Paris, which you hear so much talked about, is the most finical baby-house that you can imagine.

Mount Auburn is much more beautiful by nature, and less spoiled by bad taste in art."

"I never could feel that Canova had genius. The artists were doubting his genius twenty years ago in Italy, and now few artists call him a man of genius, though he has great value with the public."

"Titian was poetical in color, and perhaps it is the only way in which he was poetical. Yet no one can be truer in objects of the senses than Titian. Tintoretto, however, sometimes made higher poetic flights in color than his master, though he did not seem to know it."

"Raphael was in painting what I take Mozart to have been in music. He was the painter of the affections. He had not the genius of Angelo, yet he will always have the sympathies of mankind with him. The creatures of Michael Angelo are often superhuman, the results of a glorious imagination ; but the creatures of Raphael, beautiful as they are, have always a father and a mother."

"I never met with a French artist who had a sense of the sublime. One of them defined the sublime to me as the *Très bien*. I never saw a French painting that reached my higher nature. I have seen many such from the Italian, German, Dutch, Spanish, and English, but never from the French."

"Coleridge told me that he could introduce me to the acquaintance of nearly all the authors in London, but he would not do it, for he would be sorry to have me know them. He told me seriously that he did not know so entirely worthless and despicable a set of men as the authors by profession in London, and warned me solemnly to avoid any intercourse with them."

"I know the faults of my country, and there are few Americans who feel them more than I do, or have less confidence in our form of government, but I cannot endure to hear my country abused by a foreigner. It makes my blood boil. If I were a fighting man I could challenge him for it in an instant. I will agree with him in his reasoning upon general principles of politics, but he must not be personal."

Here are some lines that Mr. Dana preserved, written by Allston on an old pair of bellows :

> " Where'er I roam, whatever fires I see,
>   My heart, untravelled, still returns to thee,
>   My own dear bellows!
>   For gentle puff or energetic blast
>   At crackling wood or sputtering coal thou hast
>   Nowhere thy fellows!"

CHAPTER XXIX.

LETTERS ON ALLSTON TO R. H. DANA, SR., FROM WORDSWORTH; WILLIAM CULLEN BRYANT; C. R. LESLIE, R.A.; W. F. COLLARD; WILLIAM COLLINS, R.A.; PROFESSOR HENRY REED; COLONEL WILLIAM DRAYTON; W. Y. DEARBORN; CHARLES FRAZER, AND JOSHUA H. HAYWARD.

We give in this chapter evidences from distinguished men of the profound impression Allston made upon them. These evidences form a peculiar tribute; they are spontaneous attestations of kindred souls to the purity and grace of his character. Twenty-five years had passed since he took leave of his friends in England and sailed for America. He never saw them again, he seldom wrote, his correspondence with them ceased long before his death. And yet after a quarter of a century of separation he was still in their memories and in their hearts. This is not a common testimony. There are not many who thus command the tears of friendship to bridge a chasm of so many years—to cross an ocean of time, and waters, with loving tributes. But our purpose is to let the letters of friends speak his praise. Those which follow were addressed, except where otherwise specified, to R. H. Dana, Sr.

From Longfellow.

"CAMBRIDGE, March 13, 1847.

"MY DEAR SIR : I enclose you a few tributary lines, which I found in an out-of-the-way place, namely, Southey's 'Vision of Judgment,' and which peradventure you may have forgotten.

"Faithfully yours,

"HENRY W. LONGFELLOW."

". . . he who, returning
Rich in praise to his native shores, hath left a remembrance
Long to be honour'd and loved on the banks of Thames and of Tiber:
So may America, prizing in time the worth she possesses,
Give to that hand free scope, and boast hereafter of Allston."

From Wordsworth.

" I had heard much of Mr. Allston from Mr. Coleridge, and I should have thought it a high privilege to cultivate his friendship had opportunity allowed. Mr. Coleridge had lived on terms of intimacy with him at Rome; they returned from Italy about the same time, and it was in London, there only, that I had the pleasure of seeing Mr. Allston at his own lodgings. He was well known, both through Coleridge and his own genius, to one of my most intimate friends, Sir George Beaumont, who always passed the spring season in London. Coleridge and he took great delight in referring to Mr. Allston's observations upon art and the works of the great masters they had seen together in Rome, and the admiration was no doubt mutual from the commencement of their acquaintance.

" By such reports of his conversation and corresponding accounts of his noble qualities of heart and temper, I was led to admire, and with truth I may say to love, Mr. Allston, before I had seen him or any of his works. But opportunities did not favor me. His short stay in London occasioned me much regret, less on account of being cut off from his society (though to that I was anything but indifferent) than that I felt strongly that his works would surely be duly appreciated in England.

" His own country had a strong claim upon his talents, as it had upon his affections; nevertheless carefully as he had observed the works of the old masters, and deeply as he had studied them, and vivid as were his impressions of their excellence, I could not but entertain some fear, that when by residence in America he was removed from the sight of them, his genius, great as it was, might suffer, and his works fall more or less into mannerism. For my part there was such high promise in the few works of his pencil which I had the opportunity of seeing, that they stood high in my estimation, much above any artist of his day. They indicated a decided power of higher conceptions, and his skill in dealing with the material of art struck me as far beyond that of any other painter of his time. It was truly as Coleridge used to say, ' coloring, and not color.'

"Since Mr. Allston went back home I have had short letters from him frequently, introducing his American acquaintances ; and friendly messages have often passed between us, which I am certain were mutually acceptable. Your account of his last moments affected me deeply. I thank you sincerely for it. Much do I regret that it is not in my power to dwell more upon particulars, but after such a lapse of time I could not venture to attempt it, and I beg of you to take in good part the scanty tribute to the memory of a great man whom I highly honored.

" Sincerely yours,

" WILLIAM WORDSWORTH.

" RYDAL MOUNT, AMBLESIDE, October, 1843."

From William Cullen Bryant.

" NEW YORK, August 4, 1843.

"MY DEAR SIR : I would have answered your letter earlier if I had known what to say. All the circumstances which made the death of Allston a happy one, seem to increase the weight of his loss to his friends. Even the general sorrow with which he is mourned, and the honors paid to his memory, but remind them how great is that loss. I suppose that the only method of consolation is to fix the mind upon what death has been to him, rather than what it is to those whom he has left.

"For my part, I think of him as one who, without the usual approach of pain and decay, was taken by the gentlest transition into that better world, the light of which was always about him, and to which he seemed to belong rather than this. Do you remember the pilgrims in Bunyan's narrative, who, in passing over the dark river to the glorious land beyond, seemed scarcely to dip their feet in the waters?

"Weir, who has just put the last hand to his picture of the 'Embarkation of the Pilgrims,' on which he has earnestly been engaged for years, is a man of great simplicity of character and depth of feeling. 'It was encouragement to me during my long labors,' said he to me, last week, 'that when they should be finished, Allston would see what I had done. I thought of it almost every day while I was at work.' Such was the confidence with which the artists looked up to his true and friendly judgment, and so sure were they that what they had done well would give him pleasure.

"I hope you will admit that it is something to the credit of the country and the age that it can discern the worth of such a man as Allston, and can grieve that so bright an example both in life and out had been taken from our midst.

"Yours faithfully,

"WILLIAM CULLEN BRYANT."

From C. R. Leslie, R.A.

"As from what you have told me of our lamented Allston it was evident to many of his friends that his life was near its close, it is a great happiness to me to know that he was spared the sufferings of a sick-bed. I had a letter from him in October last, telling me of the long illness which had confined him to his chamber for the greater part of the preceding winter, and this with my previous knowledge of the delicacy of his constitution had somewhat prepared me to expect the sad intelligence of the last month. He was one of a very few excellent persons I have known in the course of my life, whose rare endowments have rendered it next to impossible that I should ' ever look upon his like again.'

.   .   .   .

"My obligations to Allston are very great, and now, that he is gone, they seem greater than ever. I was so fortunate as to become acquainted with him at the most critical period of my life, when, above all things, I wanted a safe guide to help me to distinguish truth from falsehood, not only in art but in matters of far higher moment. That I derived less benefit than I might have done from my intercourse with so rare a man as Allston, was my own fault. Indeed, I was far from estimating his full value, for I could not know, when I was but on the threshold of the world, how unlikely it was that I should ever meet again with equal purity of mind combined with equal purity of taste."

From Collard to Leslie.

"My Dear Sir: Your letter confirming the melancholy event of our friend Allston's death, and of which I had previously seen an account, with deep regret, in the public papers, has been forwarded to me. So many of the friends of my youth have passed away from me by distance and death that I begin to feel like one of another epoch who has outlived his proper age, and who wanders about among a race whose sympathies belong not to him but to a new generation. After Allston left England we exchanged a few letters, and I was constantly expecting that he would give me detailed accounts of the progress of his labors; but this he delayed to do, and our correspondence ceased. Every opportunity I have had since of inquiring after him among any of his countrymen whom I happened to meet I made use of; but, strange to say, to this hour I am ignorant of the nature or success of his efforts after he left this country.

"The gentle disposition, the love of quietly indulging in his own imagination, and the simple retiring habits of our excellent friend prevented his mingling much in the stirring scenes of life, so that his greatest enjoyments were found in his own studies and in the society of a few friends. I now see him, with a cigar in his hand, sitting in an easy-chair, and luxuriating in some interesting subject of conversation, or projecting designs which it would give me the greatest pleasure to find he had carried into successful execution.

"I have often regretted the interruption of our correspondence, and now regret it more than ever, for I always had a latent feeling that we should meet again and live over some of the pleasant hours of our youth. That hope, however, like most of those we fondly form, is now past, leaving its place unhappily supplied with unavailing sorrow.

"Believe me faithfully yours,

"W. F. COLLARD."

From William Collins, R.A.

"LONDON, September 6, 1843.

"MY DEAR SIR: I am exceedingly obliged for your kind and interesting letter, for although I had heard of the sudden death of our dear friend, I had been informed of few particulars, and the intelligence of his peaceful departure and the happy state of his mind, evinced in his conversation with your daughter so short a time before he 'fell asleep,' is to me, as it must be to all who loved him as I did, most gratifying.

"I shall have a melancholy satisfaction in telling you all I can recollect of the happy and uninterrupted intercourse I enjoyed during the few years I was honored by the confiding friendship of one of the best of men. My acquaintance with Mr. Allston began in 1814; I was introduced to him by my friend

Leslie, and from this moment, until he left England for America I saw more of him than almost any other friend I had. Every time I was in his company my admiration of his character and my high estimation of his mind and acquirements, as well as of his great genius as a painter, increased, and the affectionate kindness he showed toward my mother and brother upon his frequent visits to our abode, so completely cemented the bond of union that I always considered him as one of the family. Alas! that family, with the exception of your correspondent, are now no more seen. It is a source of great comfort to me to know that although we were for so many years separated by the Atlantic, he yet sometimes spoke of me, and especially that so short a time before his death he had me in his mind.

" Very shortly before the sad news arrived in England I had fully intended to write to my friend to thank him for the beautiful and interesting story of ' Monaldi,' which he had so recently sent me, making the inscription in his own handwriting an excuse for sending him a long letter. We had both been wretched correspondents. His name, however, was always before me, for in my high estimation of his character I had, by proxy, fifteen years ago, ventured to connect him with my family as godfather to my second son, who has been christened Charles Allston, and it is perhaps not unworthy of remark that he, having been left entirely to his own choice as regards a profession, has determined to follow that of painting, and is now carrying on his studies at the Royal Academy. I desire no better thing for him than that he may follow the example of his namesake, both as a painter and as a man."

From Professor Henry Reed.

"PHILADELPHIA, July 23, 1843.

" MY DEAR SIR: You will not, I hope, regard it as an intrusion or an impertience if I venture to write you a few lines to express the sincere sorrow with which I heard of the death of your eminent relative, Mr. Allston. Having long been in the habit of regarding him as in the front rank of his high vocation, I had it greatly at heart, when on a visit to Boston last summer, to gain the privilege of personal converse with him. The introduction by a friend, and the cordial courtesy with which Mr. Allston welcomed those who sought his society, removed from my mind all apprehensions of trespassing upon him, and enabled me to spend some four or five hours in his company at his house. This brief space of time has left a deep impression. I need not say how much there was of that instinctive politeness, which, for what he had reason to suppose would be the gratification of his visitor, gave a direction to the conversation in his recollections of Wordsworth, Coleridge, and Lamb. That these were full of interest to me you can well believe, but I do not know how to describe to you the feelings I found myself possessed of when I parted with him. The deepest of these feelings, as I come to reflect on them, was the sense of admiration and reverence for the gentleness and purity of his genius, characteristics that had been unconsciously and unaffectedly manifesting themselves, in various indescribable ways, in all that he said of his fellow-men, of his fellow-poets, and fellow-artists.

"I have treasured from that evening's interview my best belief of the placid magnanimity of a great and good man. Doubtless the height of his conceptions in art was owing, not to the native power of his genius alone, but to that moral culture which saved them from being depressed by the unworthy passions, the littleness and meanness which sometimes embitter and disfigure the artist's life. He appeared to be endowed with a power, the very virtue of purity, of not suffering such things to touch him, and not only this, but to have no sight for them in minds less happily constituted. Earth loses more than we can estimate when such a spirit is called away."

From Colonel Wm. Drayton.

"PHILADELPHIA, October, 1843.

"I sincerely sympathize with you in the death of Mr. Allston, to be deplored as a public and private loss. His brilliant talents reflected honor upon his country, and what constitutes a rare union with so bright an order of intellect, he possessed a sweetness of temper, a mildness of manner, and fascinating power of conversation which delighted all who had been in the habit of social intercourse with him, and must have bound to him by the most endearing ties the favored few who were in the enjoyment of his intimacy and friendship.

"I am, with great respect, your obedient servant,

"WM. DRAYTON."

From W. Y. Dearborn.

"HAWTHORN COTTAGE, ROXBURY, September 28, 1844.

"Most happy am I to learn that I was favorably remembered by Mr. Allston, for he was a gentleman whom it was necessary to have known to be duly capable of appreciating his character, as a man and an artist. From 1819 down to about the year 1829 I had the pleasure of seeing him often; but subsequent to that period a tempest passed over me and most unfortunately I was not in a condition to continue that most agreeable intimacy of acquaintance which had so long and happily subsisted, and was so precious in my estimation. The delightful years passed in his society rise up in my memory like verdant and sunny glades in the great desert of life, and although for many years I saw him not, still I constantly watched his progress with intense solicitude and the deepest interest, and felt how much I lost, while I rejoiced in that richly merited renown which was rapidly extending.

"Mr. Allston was one of the most remarkable men I ever

knew. With a mind of the very first order, a brilliant imagination, a genius so universal and comprehensive in its scope, and talents of such diversified excellence, that he was as distinguished for intellectual attainments in science and letters as for his refined taste and extensive knowledge in the exalted arts of painting, sculpture, and architecture.

" In conversation he was one of the most interesting, instructive, and eloquent men I ever had the good fortune to meet. As a gentleman, it is rare indeed that in the whole course of our lives we find an individual in whom all the high qualities of mind, heart, and manners are so harmoniously and admirably combined as they were in him. There was a rectitude of principle, a refinement of sentiment, a lifting of spirit, and a moral grandeur of character, united in him, which commanded the honor and esteem of all who knew him. I hope the period is not distant when a whole people will be emulous to do honor to the memory of a man who did so much to elevate the glory of their country.

" Your most obedient servant,

" W. Y. DEARBORN."

From Charles Fraser.

"We know Allston's qualities and honor his memory. I hope that his fame may ever be such as his genius and attainments justly entitle him to. His was a life of thought, feeling, sentiment, rather than action. All his views were philosophical. He considered art but the reflex of nature in her moral and intellectual workings, and valued its productions only as they exemplified and embodied her mysterious and inscrutable impulses. Hence character—character, was his constant aim. If he labored on a picture, it was not to attract notice to the work, but to make it more expressive of his design. If he employed art (and who could do it more successfully?) it was only to make it forgotten in its triumphs.

"His mind was so sensitively alive to external influences, and his heart so susceptible of kind and gentle impressions, his philanthropy so comprehensive, and his friendships so discriminating—his whole manner so bland and benignant that to do justice to these traits and to give each its proper shade one must be a congenial spirit. Few, if any, of the artists of the present age unite so much practical excellence with such profound science as he did. I never left his society without feeling improved. There was a moral elevation in his character and conversation in perfect keeping with his eminence as an artist."

From Joshua H. Hayward.

"His conversations were of such a character that to recall them would be like recalling the impressions made by some beautiful scenery in Nature where the grand outline and general effect remain, but the detail is lost. I cannot remember a single saying of his, and yet all his words, could they have been taken down, as they were uttered, would have been worth recording. The fact is, he never aimed at wit, sarcasm, or smartness; nor did he, like the late Mr. Stuart, ever deal in those epigrammatic remarks that were remembered rather from the bitterness of their sting than from their justice or truth. His conversations were humorous, didactic, or of a serious cast.

"He delighted, as you well know, in anecdote, and was as fond of listening to as of telling stories. When one was told he always seemed to have its companion ready, and was so remarkable in this last respect that I have no doubt he not infrequently drew upon his inventive faculty on the spur of the moment. I never heard him speak harshly of any human being. He has sometimes complained of ingratitude in some, who, receiving only favors from him had attempted to injure him, but this he did in sorrow rather than anger.

"He was remarkably free from suspicion. I recollect saying to him, when about to open ' Jeremiah ' for exhibition : ' What is to prevent your being imposed upon by the doorkeeper as to the receipts?' 'Nothing,' he replied, 'unless I should be lucky enough to find an honest man.' He evidently had studied at all the schools, but was an imitator of none. His style was his own, and his inspiration from a higher source. If he had less vigor than the old masters, he had far more sweetness and delicacy ; he scorned the tricks and traps of art, and chose to win by addressing himself to the heart rather than the eye. He was, if I may say so, the Dante of painters ; his impersonations breathed more of heaven than earth. Perhaps he resembled Correggio more than any other of the ancients in his general manner. And yet, had he been called upon to paint the same subjects, he would have given us Madonnas equally beautiful, but far less sensual.

"His talent, too, was more varied than that of most of the old masters. Portrait, landscape, cabinet, and humorous subjects seemed equally under his control with history ; and he had only to choose on which to exercise his talent to produce a masterpiece of the kind. He was remarkably fond of conversing upon art—its principles, objects, and means to be used to attain it. And these conversations were of such a nature as to produce as strong an impression of his knowledge and power as was experienced when viewing the greatest works of his hand.

"He was invariably kind to young artists. He loved to instruct them. No one, I believe, ever asked his advice without receiving it, and in such a way as to produce a lasting and grateful impression. He could criticise without offending, for amidst faults he would find some beauties. He seemed always to wish to impart knowledge, rather than to make a display of it. When opportunity presented he would take the crayon and correct the drawing of a picture, and not long since, happening to ask his advice as to the best color for the background of a portrait I was then painting, he took the palette and painted the whole background himself, merely saying as he finished, ' There, I would give it some such color as that.' It is needless to add that the background remains just as he left it.

" As an artist I consider Allston one of the greatest of this or any age. He possessed in an eminent degree a feeling for the true and beautiful, and the art so to embody them as to produce a corresponding feeling in others."

From an Unknown American Artist (Extract).

" FREYWALDEN, AUSTRIAN SILESIA, September 23, 1844.

.   .   .   .

" Were I in Italy I might obtain some details for you from the brothers Riepenhausen, who occupy a prominent position in the German school, both as painters and as writers on art. I am not personally acquainted with them, but know that Allston was well known to them, and that they still possess a work of his hand.

" If Mr. Leslie would consult Mr. Severn, who knew Allston when in London, and who was afterward intimate with his German friends in Italy, he could scarce fail to get valuable information on the subject that interests you. I am the more certain of this as I had a long conversation about Allston at Mr. Severn's house in London a year since, and he spoke of Allston's influence on the German school as a thing well known to him. Many persons conversant with art have been surprised that Allston's labors should have been so imperfectly known, so partially appreciated. Allston was an Idealist, and as the Ideal is a criticism of the Actual, he shared the fate of those who, in whatever branch of culture, rise where the mass cannot follow. From the landscape to the embodying of the highest religion, Allston's

The Sibyl—Outline in Chalk.

From the original in the Boston Museum of Art.

pictures were lofty, noble poetry. He owed the sympathy he won rather to the sweetness of his language than to his thought, rather to his vehicle than his substance. I believe that his influence would have been much greater could his works have stood before the body of the people in the interior. I know how necessary is a certain familiarity with the language of art to a full appreciation of the artist, but the wants of the country-folk in this respect are more than balanced by their freedom from the cant, the false taste, and the frivolity of self-sufficient society. In England we have seen portrait-painting constantly lead to the highest honors in the gift of Government. After portraiture come the illustration of the literature in vogue and the various ornamental branches of painting.

"High art leads straight to debt and jail. We are told that the Barry Haydonites were men of bad temper and exorbitant pretensions, and this they say was the cause of their ruin. What pride of English painter ever approached that of Michael Angelo, who, at a harsh word from the Pope, turned his back on the man, and that, too, in the palmy days of popedom? In America we have seen Copley, Stuart, and Trumbull absorb a large portion of the public attention and large sums of money. Thus far these facts are a command to quit the paths of high art and to ornament and amuse society.

"There is a battle, then—there is a battle between what is and what might be, between poetry and fact, between the passions and the tastes of the day and the eternal beauty of nature. Napoleon's feeling toward what he called the '*Ideologic*,' Johnson's feeling toward Milton, this is the feeling with which practical social life listens to the voice of genius. The conclusion is not very original. The battle is not merely in art, God knows. It is everywhere. Allston is the head, the chief, the Adam of American Idealists. He is the first of that noble Spartan band, sure to fall because the hosts of the Persian are overwhelming, but sure to carry with them to the ground, wherever they fall, not only the sense, but the proof of having acted the noblest part that God grants to man, that of sacrificing body to mind, expediency to right, fact to truth, now to hereafter.

" Let no man think the influence of these efforts is as small as the attention he gives to them. If the gifted minds of a country like ours are to join the current, echo the cry of the street, and hammer out their gold to bedizen the every-day life of the many, what will be the consequence ? The course will be downward, and when the gifted travel in that direction they travel fast.

" I hope that in your biography of Allston you will lay due stress on one feature of his artistical character. He never wrought but upon subjects capable of wholly absorbing his mind, and he never let his work go from him until that mind was reflected back from the canvas. To give an idea of his views of the objects of art, would be to name all his subjects ; to impress one with his sense of what was due to technical execution would be to show labors and studies through which I am not able to follow him. To appreciate the force of his genius one must have seen how deaf was his ear to the promise of gain, and of newspaper renown, through poverty and illness ; to feel what a heart he had, one must have seen him in all these struggles, generous, loving, forgetful of self, living in the life of others."

CHAPTER XXX.

LETTERS FROM HORATIO GREENOUGH EULOGIZING ALLSTON'S CHAR-
ACTER AND COMMENTING ON HIS WORKS.—A LETTER FROM W.
W. STORY, SUPPLEMENTED BY A TRIBUTE TO ALLSTON IN
VERSE.

Both the personal and the artistic sides of Allston are eloquently testified to in the two following letters from Horatio
Greenough to R. H. Dana, Sr. :

"PARIS, September 21, 1843.

"MY DEAR SIR: Your letter of the 13th ult. has just now
reached me, and has been a great relief to me. The thought of
having been so near Allston at the time of his death, yet not
with him, distressed me. I longed for a voice from one of you,
to hear what you have now told me. What would I not have
borne to have the memory which your daughter will ever retain
of having listened to the last breathings of his blessed spirit!
. . . But I knew all that I was enjoying when Allston lived.
I can truly say that I heard him as an angel, and that when far
from him he exercised over me a power no other man ever did.

"In my eagerness to do something, I wrote to Mr. Quincy
and to Mr. Gray to beg that they would use their influence to prevent tampering with the unfinished work which Allston had left.
I tried to make them feel that works like his are always finished,
because the first lines that declared his intention were a whole,
and never finished, because the last agony of elaboration was
but an approximation to his thought. I wished them to under-

stand that instead of endeavoring to help him, our task is but to receive gratefully and cherish as it is all that came from him.

"I can fully realize the anxiety with which you shrink from undertaking his biography. As a man you can record him—I know you will do it—worthily! As an artist you cannot record him! You will see that the news of his decease will elicit from England, from Italy, and Germany, tributes to his genius. Neither can these record Allston the artist. It is to the men who will be born of him that I look for a fit monument of his career, and hence my sense of the duty of collecting and preserving his unfinished works, because they are full of invaluable instruction to kindred minds.

"In whatever walk of culture a genius now labors he is a scourge. To the superficial, the heartless, to the time-serving, to the false, he must be a scourge! In the early ages of art a genius threw open new sources of light and stood in the blaze of his own creation a demi-god; but now the false prophets throw their rods on the ground and they become serpents; the rod of the genius, like that of Moses, devours them. In this sense it is that even the artist whose mission seems so peaceful bears a two-edged sword.

"America has always acted toward her artists like a hen who hatched ducklings; she cannot understand why they run to the water instead of thriving on the dunghill, which only asks to be scratched in order to feed them; she will learn better, but not yet.

"I will write to you what I have treasured of remembrance of Allston; I cannot do it now—I cannot bring myself to think calmly enough, but when I am in my own home I will write. I think that all should be recorded, but only a reserved biography as yet given. I know that it was impossible in America for Allston's career to be other than it was. I blame no one, but I think that we should withhold our testimony until the nation awakes to a sense of the worth of her noble child. Until she begs to hear of this man, who, doing more for thought and truth and love than all these of the ignorant present, entered not into the account of her treasures. Mr. Dana, you will remember how much of esteem and affection was lavished upon Allston by the higher minds of America, and you will perhaps feel surprised that I speak thus. If you could but see the career of a high artist here in Germany, or even in poor Italy, you would understand why I grieve.

"Wherever I have been I have found some one or two persons who owed to Allston the birth of their souls, and with these I have always found that what I had imbibed from him was a chain of sympathy, a bond of affection even. To look back to those hours when he was with us, to recall his words, his looks, to cherish the memory of his virtues, these must henceforth take the place of his presence. Is it not thus that our Father weans us from earth, and prepares us also to lie down by our departed friends?

"Very truly and affectionately yours,

"HORATIO GREENOUGH."

"FLORENCE, June 11, 1844.

"DEAR SIR: The few words which I shall say will be very general in their character, and I feel the more reconciled to this forced silence of mine from the reflection that Allston as a man will be fully recorded, while his work must ever be his monument as a poet. We have seen that a living Lawrence or David exerts an influence upon contemporary art which the example of a dead Raphael cannot counterbalance. The crowd of aspirants naturally seeks to reflect the qualities of the favorite of the age. This but shows that painting shares the fate of all human pursuits. What a deluge of would-be misanthropy has been poured forth by the imitators of Byron. But if this be true of the mass, the reverse is the case of the man of genius. Raphael first absorbed the masters who had preceded him, and then became their counterpart. Michael Angelo carried on a double war with the meagre imitation of the early Florentine sculptors and the measured and scientific grace of the antique. Carravaggio's fierce chiaroscuro was born of the emasculate gradations of Guido, and in one way Canova turned to the Greeks, satiated by the extravagance of Bernini's school. In some of these instances there would seem to have been as much of malice aforethought in the choice of style, as of sincere bias of the heart and of taste; but this we may venture to affirm, that we have not seen two men of strong decided genius work the same vein of thought in painting.

"Allston began the study of art in Rome at a time when a revolution in taste had just been effected throughout the Continent. The works of Winkelmann and Visconti were but symptoms of the reaction which pervaded the cultivated classes, a reaction whose first wave swept away the puny relics of Bernini, and whose second placed Canova on the pedestal of Phidias, and David on the throne of painting. To do justice to Allston, one should be familiar with the history of art at that epoch. He should see the color with which David achieved his fame to appreciate Allston's worship of the Venetians. He should know how extensively Roman history occupied public attention as a subject of art to feel Allston's unwavering adherence to the neglected poetry of the Bible. He should be aware how fully Michael Angelo had fallen into disrepute, how the simpler and earlier masters were laughed to scorn, in order to do justice to the mind of the American painter, who, without once failing to pay his tribute of admiration to the cleverness and executive vigor of the reigning artists, kept his eye and his heart unenthralled, daily absorbing from all that had gone before its most varied and precious results.

"Like all artists who have received a literary education, Allston began his studies by theory, by books, and amateur efforts. Like all artists who so begin he was forced to unlearn what he had thus acquired. 'When I first went abroad I groped for five years in the dark,' these were his words to me. They show his sense of what was wanting in his earlier means of instruction. In Rome Allston mastered painting as a language, proved his idea of the scope and object of his art, planned his processes and marked out his career. The Germans, who have raised so noble a school upon a philosophic study of the early painters, and who are said to owe to Allston their first clear idea of the means as well as the end of a modern school of art, they, and they alone, can do justice to that portion of his career.

"No artist ever felt the beautiful more keenly than Allston; none ever gave it more exactly its due place in his heart. It was with him always a means, never an end. Moral beauty was his idol, if so it can be called; religious truth his main inspiration. Through all his higher efforts there breathes the same spirit, and a voice comes from thence that fills the mind with awe. Whether in 'Jeremiah,' in 'Miriam,' in 'Saul,' or in 'Belshazzar,' we have the same dreadful words, 'I will repay.'

"Allston's style was extremely varied, as were the subjects he treated. His was no formal manner, operating with the regularity, fecundity, and swiftness of a machine. Who would assign to the same hand the landscapes at Boston and the 'Desert,' purchased by Mr. Labouchere? When I reflect upon the character of his works and the immense labor bestowed upon them, I am surprised that this age, so prone to regard art as a handmaid of luxury, should have employed him as it did. When I remember the astonishing rapidity of his execution, the ease with which his hand and eye mirrored the beauty before him, when I remember that his will alone stood between his poverty and the most prolific outpouring of production, with all the renown and emolument that accompany it, then I form a clear idea of the character of his genius.

"His was truly a great and a noble example. Was such ever thrown away? Surely never. More even than in his works do I believe that he will live in the awakened minds of American art, and who shall say where the republic will carry the achievements of painting with him for her first-born poet-painter?

.   .   .   .

"Very truly yours,
"Horatio Greenough."

Upon the occasion of the Allston Celebration in Boston, November 1, 1880, the following letter from the sculptor, W. W. Story, was received by the committee in charge, together with the lines given below:

"Venice, October, 1880.

".   .   . I am very glad to hear that there is to be a celebration in honor of Allston, and very happy to send my little contribution, which I only wish were far more worthy of the occasion. We have been singularly neglectful, thus far, of his great claims as an artist, upon our admiration. It seems to me high time that something should be done in his honor, some permanent memorial raised to keep alive the memory of his genius and his person. He is one of our great men. Pure in his life as a child, modest in his character, and of a delicacy and refinement of imagination in his art that entitles him to take rank with the great masters. When I remember the place in which he worked, the difficulties which he had to encounter, the absence of all stimulus save that which he found within himself, his prosaic surroundings, the want of models and means for his art, and in every way the restrictions of his position, the works that he produced were almost marvellous; but genius makes its own place, and time breaks the difficulties of circumstance.

"My memories of him are delightful. I saw him but seldom, for I was too young, too shy, to dare to intrude upon him before death took him away. I, in common with all who knew him, was carried away by the charm of his presence, the gracious dignity of his manners, the breadth and variety of his conversation, and the simple modesty and refinement of his character. One long evening I remember to have spent with him, being taken to his house by Mr. Sumner. Then under the spell of his delightful conversation the hours passed like moments. He talked of art and filled my mind with delightful visions; gave living anecdotes and reminiscences of the great men of England whom he had known; discoursed of pictures and galleries, of Titian and Raffaelle, and all the great names of art, which were then only names, and I left him after midnight with my brain afire, feeling as if a wondrous world had been opened before me. That, and the few other conversations that I afterward had with him (conversations I call them, but I was only a rapt listener), gave a color to the whole of my after-life and filled me with ideas, hopes and feelings, and aspirations of turbulent delight. Little then did I dream of being an artist myself, and possibly I never should have been one had it not been for his inspiring influence. What a grand and splendid career it seemed as he painted it. No low jealousy deformed it in his mind; no mean motives turned it aside from its great end of beauty. It was a mountain range of high imagination, of exquisite fancy, of tender sentiment, where no low spirit could ascend; where only the highest and best-winged spirit could soar and wander.

"He filled my mind with his own enthusiasm and taught me the dignity of art, the sincere devotion it demanded. The earnest study, the consecration of the whole mind and heart it required. And he led me into its precincts as a high-priest leads the trembling neophyte to the altar. I can never be grateful enough to him for the high standard which he set before me, as before all who came into his presence. There was something singularly attractive in his face, something ideal. His complexion was pale, as of a student and thinker; his eyes large, of a tender, swimming blue, and deeply set under the brow, but with the whole orbit, above and beneath filled out, and, so to speak, pulpy, so that they seemed even larger than they were, and filled with a mild, pure light, that I can liken to nothing else than a lake in which the blue sky is tenderly reflected; soft, large, luminous, dreamy. His hair, which was abundant, soft in texture, and nearly white, flowed in long waves down his neck behind, but was shorter and more curly in front, and seemed almost like a halo around his head, in perfect harmony of color with his pale face and soft blue eyes. It may be somewhat of the reverence with which I looked at him, and my own young and enthusiastic admiration, but he still remains in my memory as the most ideal and poetic person I ever saw—one from whom one might expect such exquisite sentiments, such tender grace as he introduces on his canvas.

"I remember specially that he expatiated at length one day on the peculiar effect of blue in the eye, and told me that in his studies for the head of 'Jeremiah,' he drew one from a Jew, and found that the mere change of color from blue to brown so altered the expression that whereas the blue seemed to gaze abstractedly into vacancy, when changed to brown they seemed to be fixed intently on some object. He tried it over and over again with the same results.

"It has always been a matter of regret to me that Mr. R. H. Dana did not carry out the intention, which he undoubtedly had, of writing Allston's life. I still hope that he has left his notes of Allston's conversations and ideas of processes of art which may be used in the life which remains to be written. Perhaps no one would be so capable of doing this as he, for he knew him intimately, was a poet himself, and in every way fitted to do this work. No time should be lost to gather together what remains of personal reminiscences, and I beg to urge this upon his friends, the few who still remain.

"For myself I wish to recall the great admiration for the man and the artist. He was, as we all know, extremely fastidious in his work, always aiming at the highest, and never satisfying himself. But what he did was in its quality of a most rare and exquisite character, showing an extreme refinement of sentiment, a grace of fancy, a harmony of composition, and a beauty of color in his best works that have seldom been surpassed, and in some qualities never reached. The sketches, chiefly in outline, which were so well engraved by Cheney, are in themselves sufficient to establish his claim as an artist of remarkable power.

"The figures of the angels, outlined by himself from his picture of 'Jacob's Dream,' are in spirit, design, and sentiment worthy to be placed in the same rank as the best work of Raffaelle. The composition of 'Titania's Court' is exquisite in grace and harmony, and produced by the most delicate fancy; so, too, the fairies on the seashore have the same refined and elegant charm. The ship in a storm, though merely sketched in white chalk, has the power and mastery of a finished work by a great hand. I know nothing finer than the sweep of the waves and the large feeling for nature that is there shown. Yet these are mere sketches which probably no eye ever saw till after his death, and which he seems to have considered of little importance.

"In his paintings his color is perhaps their greatest attraction. They have the best characteristics of the Venetian school, and beyond this a refinement and fastidious beauty specially belonging to Allston. It would be difficult to find in any school anything more exquisite in tone and color than, for instance, the group in the middle distance in 'Belshazzar's Feast;' more dreamy and perfect in sentiment than 'Rosalie Listening to the Music,' with its twilight, too, so perfectly in accord with the theme of the picture; more masterly than 'Isaac the Jew,' and especially the hand in the subdued light with its sparkling ring; more inspired in character and expression than the 'Jeremiah;' more large and broad in style and delightful in composition than his Italian and Swiss landscapes.

"I am here only rudely hinting at his excellences. Some of these pictures, which I have never seen since the exhibition of his works, just after his death, remain in my memory as the most charming things I ever saw. What, by the hand of man, was ever more idyllic and full of the spirit of unconscious nature than that delicate, nude, shepherd boy, piping to himself in the wood, with the glancing light striking against the trunks of the trees that show through the slope behind him, as he listens in sweet privacy to the pastoral notes of his pipe? "What more full of tender sentiment than the twilight picture of 'Lorenzo and Jessica,' with the pure light still lingering faintly in the sky, as they sit in the soft shadow of the coming night, their heads silhouetted against the light, above the dark bank that rises against the sky? It is all mystery and poetry. What is more fresh and glad than 'Una in the Wood?' But let me stop, I do not know that I should like to see them again, so charming is my recollection of them. You ask for a sonnet and I send you these. I have not said half that I wish to say, even though I have thrice exceeded my limits.

> "A gentle nobleness, a quiet grace
> From some ideal sphere of beauty caught,
> Hallowed the art of Allston, swayed his thought,
> Breathed thro' his manners and illumined his face.
> Here in life's prose he seemed half out of place,
> An exile, who from higher realms had brought
> Graces refined and lofty dreams, where naught
> Of low or mean or common had a trace.

Well may he walk as brother in the line
Of the great masters; scarcely less than they
In harmonies of color, grand design,
Imagination, power of fancy's play,
And none with tenderer feeling, sense more fine,
Thro' pathless realms could find the poet's way.

" We laid him with small honor in the tomb,
But trivial record of his life remains,
Save what his hand with tender, patient pains
Upon his canvas wrought (the perfect bloom
Of his high nature), and the faint perfume
Of delicate, fine verse, and patient strains
Of lofty ring, and prose where romance reigns,
And high philosophies of art have room ;
These for themselves will speak and live ; but we—
We have our task to do—his life to write,
That nought be lost by treacherous memory
Of that clear spirit—and, in all men's sight,
To build his monument, that it may be
A beacon, an encouragement, a light.

" If to the warrior who hath writ his name
On Victory's fields a monument we raise—
If to the statesman, who through perilous bays
Of peace hath steered and struck no rock of blame
Shall not the artist equal honors claim
Who by his genius on the canvas stays
The fleeting hour—the historic deed delays—
And rescues beauty from Time's blight and shame?
Oh ! shall not beauty plead for him whose art
Makes her immortal ; from her wide domain
Brings gracious gifts to cheer and lift the heart—
Bids even the banished dead revive again,
And for our joy creates a world apart
Peopled with silent children of the brain ? "

CHAPTER XXXI.

In the year 1813 Allston had published in London a book of
poems entitled " The Sylphs of the Seasons, and Other Poems."
This volume was favorably received by his friends and the more
critical public, and after his death was republished, with his
other poems, in R. H. Dana, Jr.'s edition of his works, entitled
" Lectures on Art, and Poems," by Washington Allston.

An eminent art critic and lecturer of the time, Mr. Joseph
Henry Green, wrote to a friend in America, in reference to Allston's poetry :

" My acquaintance with Washington Allston was the result
of the good offices of our mutual friend and our revered teacher
S. T. Coleridge. How lasting the impression of that intercourse,
brief indeed, but unreserved, has been, may be gathered, in part
at least, from the fact of my having quoted more then one passage from Allston's poems in my lecture delivered this season
at our Royal Academy.

" Who, indeed, who had enjoyed the inestimable privilege of
converse with such a man, could ever forget the purity, the depth
and simplicity of his mind ? Indeed Allston had himself studied
his art with poetic feeling and philosophic thought, and I doubt
whether his productive genius or aspiration as an artist can be
fully appreciated without a knowledge of his poems. From his

sonnets on some of the masterpieces of the great Italian painters, among whom he will take his rank, it will be seen what his
admirable works have realized; that however great his technical
skill and knowledge, his high aim and excellence were the imagination working in the service of the moral being, and the rep-
resentation of the ennobled character of humanity."

We do not propose an extended citation of Allston's poems;
our purpose is to show, as we think we may, by a few selections,
that the spirit of the true poet was native to him; that it was
not the resultant of special culture, but rather an element in his
intellectual and moral constitution; that it manifested itself not
by an effort of art, but naturally, spontaneously, and even necessarily. He did not make poetry, it was in him, and he could not
withhold it. He was in every sense of the word a poet, whether
in painting or writing or conversation. His mind was replete
with visions, and his sensitive, emotional nature could summon
them at will.

In a recent conversation Oliver Wendell Holmes narrated to
the writer the following incident:

"Some fifty years ago a question of public interest in Cambridgeport brought together a large assemblage in one of the
churches of the place. I was standing in one of the galleries, and
looking over to the other I saw among the people assembled a
man who looked so 'like an angel of light' that I knew him to
be Allston, although I had never seen him before."

His appearance was indeed impressive. No one could see
him without feeling something of his character. To those who
have seen him, it is not surprising that the genial poet of
Boston needed no one to designate Allston. There was in
him a remarkable symmetry of endowment. As an artist he
seemed to possess every gift requisite to produce the best effects
in every department. As a poet he had the same fulness of
natural qualities. His poem "Rosalie" breathes the true spirit

of poesy. It forms a part of a dual inspiration—a picture on canvas and a picture in verse. That on canvas is a young woman, with a pensive expression, as if listening to music that fills her soul with an ecstasy of sadness, and captivates her with a sensation so profound as to simulate melancholy—the melancholy of entranced emotion. The picture in verse expresses what that on canvas was intended to represent. We quote the poem in full:

> "O! pour upon my soul again
>   That sad, unearthly strain,
> That seems from other worlds to plain;
> Thus falling, falling from afar,
> As if some melancholy star
> Had mingled with her light her sighs,
>   And dropped them from the skies!

> "No,—never came from aught below
>   This melody of woe,
> That makes my heart to overflow,
> As from a thousand gushing springs,
> Unknown before; that with it brings
> This nameless light—if light it be,—
>   That veils the world I see.

> " For all I see around me wears
>   The hue of other spheres;
> And something blent of smiles and tears
> Comes with the very air I breathe.
> O! nothing, sure, the stars beneath
> Can mould a sadness like to this,—
>   So like angelic bliss."

> So, at that dreamy hour of day
>   When the last lingering ray
> Stops on the highest cloud to play,—
> So thought the gentle Rosalie,
> As on her maiden reverie
> First fell the strain of him who stole
>   In music to her soul.

Coleridge was so impressed by the poem " America to Great Britain," that he published it in his " Sybilline Leaves," with the following note: " This poem, written by an American gentleman, a valued and dear friend, I communicate to the reader for its moral no less than its patriotic spirit."

AMERICA TO GREAT BRITAIN.

All hail! thou noble land,
   Our Fathers' native soil!
O! stretch thy mighty hand,
   Gigantic grown by toil,
O'er the vast Atlantic wave to our shore!
   For thou with magic might
   Can'st reach to where the light
   Of Phœbus travels bright
     The world o'er!

The Genius of our clime,
   From his pine-embattled steep,
Shall hail the guest sublime;
   While the Tritons of the deep
With their conchs the kindred league shall proclaim.
   Then let the world combine,—
   O'er the main our naval line
   Like the milky-way shall shine
     Bright in fame!

Though ages long have past
   Since our Fathers left their home,
Their pilot in the blast,
   O'er untravelled seas to roam,
Yet lives the blood of England in our veins!
   And shall we not proclaim
   That blood of honest fame
   Which no tyranny can tame
     By its chains?

While the language free and bold
   Which the Bard of Avon sung,
In which our Milton told
   How the vault of heaven rung

When Satan, blasted, fell with his host;
    While this, with reverence meet,
    Ten thousand echoes greet,
    From rock to rock repeat
        Round our coast;

While the manners, while the arts,
    That mould a nation's soul,
    Still cling around our hearts—
    Between let Ocean roll,
Our joint communion breaking with the Sun;
    Yet still from either beach
    The voice of blood shall reach,
    More audible than speech,
        "We are One."

Allston was versatile in methods, but beauty was ever a conspicuous component in his style. He once said, in a conversation with his niece, Miss Charlotte Dana, that if there was any one thing which he was sure he possessed, it was an intense sense of harmony. Moral and physical harmony were one in his mind; a sentiment pervading his moral and intellectual natures, so blending them that they were almost indistinguishable.

Another time he said to the same person that if he had three lives to live he should be every day learning something new in his art. "The big, ardent mind must be doing something, or it pines and dies. It must be filling up the awkward void; storing time with acts and making life substantial."

Allston was not deficient in strength or in the adventuring boldness of genius. Beauty did not check, if we may so express it, the effrontery of his imagination, or smooth the rugged strength of his thought. Symmetry was ever present, but never to weaken his work. His exquisite adjustment of all elements in the production of effects, his love of symmetry, with harmony, distinguished him to a remarkable degree. The gentle stood not alone, or as overbalancing the grand. As verifying this we select a few stanzas, from his personification of Winter, in the "Sylphs of the Seasons:"

> And last the Sylph of Winter spake,
> The while her piercing voice did shake
>   The castle-vaults below:
> "O! youth, if thou, with soul refined,
> Hast felt the triumph pure of mind,
> And learnt a secret joy to find
>   In deepest scenes of woe;

> "If e'er with fearful ear at eve
> Hast heard the wailing tempests grieve
>   Through chink of shattered wall,
> The while it conjured o'er thy brain
> Of wandering ghosts a mournful train,
> That low in fitful sobs complain
>   Of Death's untimely call;

> "Or feeling, as the storm increased,
> The love of terror nerve thy breast,
>   Didst venture to the coast,
> To see the mighty war-ship leap
> From wave to wave upon the deep,
> Like chamois goat from steep to steep,
>   Till low in valley lost;

> "Then, glancing to the angry sky,
> Behold the clouds with fury fly
>   The lurid moon athwart—
> Like armies huge in battle, throng,
> And pour in volleying ranks along,
> While piping winds in martial song
>   To rushing war exhort:

> "O! then to me thy heart be given,
> To me, ordained by Him in heaven
>   Thy nobler powers to wake.
> And, O! if thou with poet's soul,
> High brooding o'er the frozen pole,
> Hast felt beneath my stern control
>   The desert region quake;

" Or from old Hecla's cloudy height,
  When o'er the dismal, half-year's night
    He pours his sulphurous breath,
Hast known my petrifying wind
Wild ocean's curling billows bind,
Like bending sheaves by harvest hind,
    Erect in icy death ;

" Or heard adown the mountain's steep
  The northern blast with furious sweep
    Some cliff dissevered dash,
And seen it spring with dreadful bound,
From rock to rock, to gulf profound,
While echoes fierce from caves resound
    The never-ending crash ;

.   .   .   .

" 'Twas I on each enchanting scene
  The charm bestowed, that banished spleen
    Thy bosom pure and light.
But still a *nobler* power I claim—
That power allied to poet's fame,
Which language vain has dared to name—
    The soul's creative might."

As an instance of easy flowing verse, in which thought is kept in motion, and the reader is entertained by frequent, unexpected and startling images, we cite " The Paint-King." It is said to have been written by Allston in burlesque of Scott's " Fire-King," and Lewis's " Cloud-King." This may account for the extravagance of its imagery without detracting from its merit as an example of truly poetic qualities.

The Paint-King.

Fair Ellen was long the delight of the young,
  No damsel could with her compare ;
Her charms were the theme of the heart and the tongue,
And bards without number in ecstasies sung
  The beauties of Ellen the Fair.

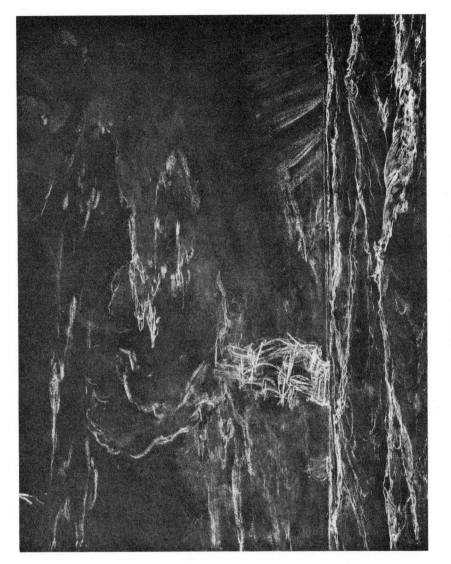

A Marine in Chalk.

From the original in the Boston Museum of Art.

Yet cold was the maid; and though legions advanced,
  All drilled by Ovidean art,
And languished and ogled, protested and danced,
Like shadows they came, and like shadows they glanced
  From the hard, polished ice of her heart.

Yet still did the heart of fair Ellen implore
  A something that could not be found;
Like a sailor she seemed on a desolate shore,
With nor house, nor a tree, nor a sound but the roar
  Of breakers high-dashing around.

From object to object still, still would she veer,
  Though nothing, alas! could she find;
Like the moon, without atmosphere, brilliant and clear,
Yet doomed, like the moon, with no being to cheer
  The bright barren waste of her mind.

But, rather than sit like a statue so still
  When the rain made her mansion a *pound*,
Up and down would she go, like the sails of a mill,
And pat every stair, like a woodpecker's bill,
  From the tiles of the roof to the ground.

One morn, as the maid from her casement inclined,
  Passed a youth, with a frame in his hand.
The casement she closed—not the eye of her mind;
For, do all she could, no, she could not be blind;
  Still before her she saw the youth stand.

"Ah, what can he do?" said the languishing maid;
  "Ah, what with that frame can he do?"
And she knelt to the Goddess of Secrets and prayed,
When the youth passed again, and again he displayed
  The frame and a picture to view.

"O beautiful picture!" the fair Ellen cried,
  "I must see thee again or I die."
Then under her white chin her bonnet she tied,
And after the youth and the picture she hied,
  When the youth, looking back, met her eye.

"Fair damsel," said he (and he chuckled the while),
　"This picture, I see, you admire;
Then take it, I pray you ; perhaps 'twill beguile
Some moments of sorrow (nay, pardon my smile),
　Or at least keep you home by the fire."

Then Ellen the gift with delight and surprise
　From the cunning young stripling received.
But she knew not the poison that entered her eyes,
When sparkling with rapture they gazed on the prize—
　Thus, alas ! are fair maidens deceived!

'Twas a youth o'er the form of a statue inclined,
　And the sculptor he seemed of the stone ;
Yet he languished as though for its beauty he pined,
And gazed as the eyes of the statue so blind
　Reflected the beams of his own.

'Twas the tale of the sculptor Pygmalion of old ;
　Fair Ellen remembered and sighed :
"Ah, couldst thou but lift from that marble so cold,
Thine eyes too imploring, thy arms should enfold
　And press me this day as thy bride,"

She said ; when, behold, from the canvas arose
　The youth, and he stepped from the frame ;
With a furious transport his arms did inclose
The love-plighted Ellen, and, clasping, he froze
　The blood of the maid with his flame !

She turned, and beheld on each shoulder a wing.
　"O Heaven!" cried she, " who art thou?"
From the roof to the ground did his fierce answer ring,
As, frowning, he thundered, " I am the Paint-King!
　And mine, lovely maid, thou art now ! "

Then high from the ground did the grim monster lift
　The loud-screaming maid like a blast;
And he sped through the air like a meteor swift,
While the clouds, wandering by him, did fearfully drift
　To the right and the left as he passed.

Now suddenly sloping his hurricane flight,
  With an eddying whirl he descends;
The air all below him becomes black as night,
And the ground where he treads, as if moved with affright,
  Like the surge of the Caspian bends.

"I am here!" said the fiend, and he thundering knocked
  At the gates of a mountainous cave;
The gates open flew, as by magic unlocked,
While the peaks of the mount, reeling to and fro, rocked
  Like an island of ice on the wave.

"O mercy!" cried Ellen, and swooned in his arms;
  But the Paint-King he scoffed at her pain.
"Prithee, love," said the monster, "what mean these alarms?"
She hears not, she sees not, the terrible charms
  That wake her to horror again.

She opens her lids, but no longer her eyes
  Behold the fair youth she would woo;
Now appears the Paint-King in his natural guise;
His face, like a palette of villainous dyes,
  Black and white, red and yellow, and blue.

On the skull of a Titan, that Heaven defied,
  Sat the fiend, like the grim Giant Gog,
While aloft to his mouth a huge pipe he applied,
Twice as big as the Eddystone Lighthouse, descried
  As it looms through an easterly fog.

And anon, as he puffed the vast volumes, were seen,
  In horrid festoons on the wall,
Legs and arms, heads and bodies, emerging between,
Like the drawing-room grim of the Scotch Sawney Beane,
  By the devil dressed out for a ball.

"Ah me!" cried the damsel, and fell at his feet.
  "Must I hang on these walls to be dried?"
"O no!" said the fiend, while he sprung from his seat;
"A far nobler fortune thy person shall meet;
  Into paint will I grind thee, my bride!"

Then, seizing the maid by her dark auburn hair,
  An oil-jug he plunged her within.
Seven days, seven nights, with the shrieks of despair,
Did Ellen in torment convulse the dun air,
  All covered with oil to the chin.

On the morn of the eighth on a huge sable stone,
  Then Ellen, all reeking, he laid;
With a rock for his muller he crushed every bone,
But, though ground to a jelly, still, still did she groan;
  For life had forsook not the maid.

Now, reaching his palette, with masterly care
  Each tint on its surface he spread;
The blue of her eyes, and the brown of her hair,
And the pearl and the white of her forehead so fair,
  And her lips' and her cheeks' rosy-red.

Then, stamping his foot, did the monster exclaim,
  "Now I brave, cruel Fairy, thy scorn!"
When lo! from a chasm wide-yawning there came
A light, tiny chariot of rose-colored flame,
  By a team of ten glow-worms upborne.

Enthroned in the midst on an emerald bright,
  Fair Geraldine sat without peer;
Her robe was a gleam of the first blush of light,
And her mantle the fleece of a noon-cloud white,
  And a beam of the moon was her spear.

In an accent that stole on the still, charmed air
  Like the first gentle language of Eve,
Thus spake from her chariot the Fairy so fair:
"I come at thy call—but, O Paint-King, beware
  Beware if again you deceive

"'Tis true," said the monster, "thou queen of my heart,
  Thy portrait I oft have essayed;
Yet ne'er to the canvas could I with my art
The least of thy wonderful beauties impart;
  And my failure with scorn you repaid.

"Now I swear by the light of the Comet-King's tail,"
　And he towered with pride as he spoke,
"If again with these magical colors I fail,
The crater of Etna shall hence be my jail,
　And my food shall be sulphur and smoke.

"But if I succeed, then, O fair Geraldine!
　Thy promise with justice I claim,
And thou, queen of Fairies, shalt ever be mine,
The bride of my bed; and thy portrait divine
　Shall fill all the earth with my fame."

He spake; when, behold, the fair Geraldine's form
　On the canvas enchantingly glowed;
His touches—they flew like the leaves in a storm—
And the pure, pearly white and the carnation warm,
　Contending, in harmony flowed.

And now did the portrait a twin-sister seem
　To the figure of Geraldine fair:
With the same sweet expression did faithfully teem
Each muscle, each feature; in short, not a gleam
　Was lost of her beautiful hair.

'Twas the Fairy herself! but, alas, her blue eyes
　Still a pupil did ruefully lack;
And who shall describe the terrific surprise
That seized the Paint-King when, behold, he descries
　Not a speck on his palette of black!

"I am lost!" said the Fiend, and he shook like a leaf;
　When, casting his eyes to the ground,
He saw the lost pupils of Ellen, with grief,
In the jaws of a mouse, and the sly little thief
　Whisk away from his sight with a bound.

"I am lost!" said the Fiend, and he fell like a stone.
　Then rising, the Fairy in ire
With a touch of her finger she loosened her zone,
(While the limbs on the wall gave a terrible groan,)
　And she swelled to a column of fire.

Her spear, now a thunderbolt, flashed in the air,
  And sulphur the vault filled around ;
She smote the grim monster, and now by the hair,
High-lifting, she hurled him in speechless despair
  Down the depths of the chasm profound.

Then over the picture thrice waving her spear,
  " Come forth ! " said the good Geraldine ;
When, behold, from the canvas descending, appear
Fair Ellen, in person more lovely than e'er,
  With grace more than ever divine !

The singleness of theme and the condensation required in
sonnets have made them a favorite form of poetic composition.
Allston's style was epigrammatic, yet flowing and perspicuous.
In poetry he seemed strongest when most circumscribed—the
smaller the compass for its expression, the richer his thought.
He was extremely fond of finish. He tells us that he once spent
four hours in writing twenty lines of prose, after he had the idea
perfectly in his mind.

"How poetically philosophical," says Dana, the poet, "is
Allston's sonnet on the 'Group of Angels' by Raphael; and how
perfectly true it is when applied to his own works in the art."

ON THE GROUP OF THE THREE ANGELS BEFORE THE TENT OF ABRAHAM,
BY RAPHAEL.

O ! now I feel as though another sense,
From Heaven descending, had informed my soul ;
I feel the pleasurable, full control
Of Grace, harmonious, boundless and intense.
In thee, celestial Group, embodied lives
The subtile mystery, that speaking gives
Itself resolved ; the essences combined
Of Motion ceaseless, Unity complete.
Borne like a leaf by some soft eddying wind
Mine eyes, impelled as by enchantment sweet,

From part to part with circling motion rove,
Yet seem unconscious of the power to move;
From line to line through endless changes run,
O'er countless shapes, yet seem to gaze on One.

" Though," continues Mr. Dana, " painting presents to the eye a moment of time, yet to the mind it is not limited in its suggestive power, but may carry our thoughts back into a long past, and at the same time forward into the future. Allston, I find, on recurring to his sonnet on the ' Falling Group' of Michael Angelo, has finely expressed this : "

ON A "FALLING GROUP," BY MICHAEL ANGELO.

How vast, how dread, o'erwhelming, is the thought
Of space interminable ! to the soul
A circling weight that crushes into naught
Her mighty faculties ! a wondrous whole,
Without or parts, beginning, or an end.
How fearful, then, on desperate wings to send
The fancy e'en amid the waste profound !
Yet, born as if all daring to astound,
Thy giant hand, O, Angelo ! hath hurled
E'en human forms, with all their mortal weight,
Down the dread void—fall endless as their fate !
Already now they seem from world to world
For ages thrown ; yet doomed, another past,
Another still to reach, nor e'er to reach the last !

" The remaining sonnets," adds Mr. Dana, " partake more or less of the same character; and it should be remembered that, with the exception of Wordsworth and Coleridge, who were but just then reopening upon us the depths of our being in a new form, poetry had not recovered its Metaphysic Idea, which had lain so long unseen."

Allston with poetic inspiration attributes to Rembrandt the highest characteristics of genius.

In Rembrandt; Occasioned by his Picture of Jacob's Dream.

As in that twilight, superstitious age
When all beyond the narrow grasp of mind
Seemed fraught with meanings of supernal kind,
When e'en the learned, philosophic sage,
Wont with the stars through boundless space to range,
Listened with reverence to the changeling's tale;—
E'en so, thou strangest of all beings strange:
E'en so thy visionary scenes I hail;
That, like the rambling of an idiot's speech,
No image giving of a thing on earth,
Nor thought significant in reason's reach,
Yet in their random shadowings give birth
To thoughts and things from other worlds that come,
And fill the soul, and strike the reason dumb.

In his lines on Michael Angelo he lays, as it were, at the feet of the great Tuscan, the tribute, we might almost say, of his idolatry. It is a brief expression of his exalted admiration. To Allston, Michael Angelo was alone, peerless, unapproachable—poet, painter, sculptor, architect; he styles him, "the mighty sovereign of the ideal, than whom no one ever trod so near, yet so securely, the dizzy brink of the impossible."

On Michael Angelo.

'Tis not to honor thee by verse of mine
I bear a record of thy wondrous power;
Thou stand'st alone, and needest not to shine
With borrowed lustre; for the light is thine
Which no man giveth; and, though comets lower
Portentous round thy sphere, thou still art bright;
Though many a satellite about thee fall,
Leaving their stations merged in trackless night,
Yet take not they from that supernal light
Which lives within thee, sole, and free of all.

The death of Coleridge touched Allston deeply, and would have overwhelmed him with sorrow but for that philosophy which his friend had assisted him in cultivating.

ON COLERIDGE.

And thou art gone, most loved, most honored friend!
No, never more thy gentle voice shall blend
With air of earth its pure ideal tones,
Binding in one, as with harmonious zones,
The heart and intellect. And I no more
Shall with thee gaze on that unfathomed deep,
The Human Soul,—as when, pushed off the shore,
Thy mystic bark would through the darkness sweep,
Itself the while so bright! For oft we seemed
As on some starless sea,—all dark above,
All dark below,—yet, onward as we drove,
To plough up light that ever round us streamed.
But he who mourns is not as one bereft
Of all he loved; thy living truths are left.

Coleridge's regard for Allston was not only that of a friend, it was like the tenderest affection of an elder brother. Next to Wordsworth, as he said, he loved and honored him more than anyone else.

The fragment on Rubens is a remarkable epitome. Its eight lines hold a volume of descriptive criticism and merited praise. It is certainly a wonderful condensation, teeming with thought poetically expressed. The writer remembers a conversation with Allston in which he said: "In my opinion Rubens has injured more artists than he has benefited." The voluptuous floridity of his style was constantly imitated by those who could not reach the height of his great qualities whereby a satisfying equipose was sustained.

ON RUBENS.

Thus o'er his art indignant Rubens reared
His mighty head, nor critic armies feared.

His lawless style, from vain pretension free,
Impetuous rolling like a troubled sea,
High o'er the rocks of Reason's ridgy verge
Impending hangs ; but, ere the foaming surge
Breaks o'er the bound, the under-ebb of taste
Back from the shore impels the watery waste.

Painting, sculpture, architecture, music, and poetry are manifestations of the same natural endowment or genius. They are influenced according to certain natural aptitudes and capabilities of eye or ear or hand. But though the arts have a common origin, and are branches from one root, few men of genius succeed in more than one branch. Allston may be numbered among that few. So balanced were natural qualities of genius in him that it is difficult to say whether he would have been less successful as a sculptor or poet than he was as a painter. His first attempt at modelling in clay was the head of St. Peter, of which West said, "There is no man in England who can equal it." As already related, he supposed it to be an antique, till informed that it was Allston's work. Of Allston's poetry Coleridge, Wordsworth, and Southey have spoken in terms entitling him to high rank. His prose, too, abounds in poetry. His "Lectures on Art" are poetic treatises, analytical and philosophical. In one of them he has drawn a comparison between Ostade and Raphael, which for descriptive force and beauty is, we think, unsurpassed. The exposition of genius in opposite manifestations is so effective and interesting that we reproduce it here :

"In order, however, more distinctly to exhibit their common ground of invention, we will briefly examine a picture by Ostade, and then compare it with one by Raphael, than whom no two artists could well be imagined having less in common. The interior of a Dutch cottage forms the scene of Ostade's work, presenting something between a kitchen and a stable. Its princi-

pal object is the carcass of a hog, newly washed and hung up
to dry, subordinate to which is a woman nursing an infant; the
accessories—various garments, pots, kettles, and other culinary
utensils. The bare enumeration of these coarse materials would
naturally predispose the mind of one unacquainted with the
Dutch school to expect anything but pleasure; indifference, not
to say disgust, would seem to be the only possible impression
from a picture composed of such ingredients. And such, indeed, would be their effect under the hand of any but a real artist. Let us look into the picture and follow Ostade's *mind* as it
leaves its impress on the several objects. Observe how he spreads
his principal light, from the suspended carcass to the surrounding objects, moulding it, so to speak, into agreeable shapes, here
by extending it to a bit of drapery, there to an earthen pot;
then connecting it, by the flash from a brass kettle, with his
second light, the woman and child; and again turning the eye
into the dark recesses through a labyrinth of broken chairs, old
baskets, roosting fowls, and bits of straw, till a glimpse of sunshine from a half-open window gleams on the eye, as it were,
like an echo, and sending it back to the principal object, which
now seems to act on the mind as the luminous source of all these
diverging lights. But the magical whole is not yet completed;
the mystery of color has been called in to the aid of light, and so
subtly blends that we can hardly separate them, at least until their
united effect has first been felt, and after we have begun the process of cold analysis. Yet even then we cannot long proceed before we find the charm returning. As we pass from the blaze of
light on the carcass, where all the tints of the prism seem to be
faintly subdued, we are met on its borders by the dark harslet,
glowing like rubies; then we repose awhile on the white cap and
kerchief of the nursing mother; then we are roused again by the
flickering strife of the antagonist colors on a blue jacket and red
petticoat; then the strife is softened by the low yellow of a straw-

bottomed chair; and thus with alternating excitement and repose do we travel through the picture till the scientific explorer
loses the analyst in the unresisting passiveness of a poetic
dream. Now all this will no doubt appear to many, if not absurd, at least exaggerated; but not so to those who have ever felt
the sorcery of color. They, we are sure, will be the last to question the character of the feeling because of the ingredients which
work the spell, and, if true to themselves, they must call it poetry. Nor will they consider it any disparagement to the all-
accomplished Raphael to say of Ostade that he also was an
artist.

"We turn now to a work of the great Italian—the 'Death
of Ananias.' The scene is laid in a plain apartment, which is
wholly devoid of ornament, as became the hall of audience of
the primitive Christians. The apostles (then eleven in number)
have assembled to transact the temporal business of the Church,
and are standing together on a slightly elevated platform, about
which in various attitudes, some standing, others kneeling, is
gathered a promiscuous assemblage of their new converts, male
and female. This quiet assembly (for we still feel its quietness,
in the midst of the awful judgment) is suddenly roused by the
sudden fall of one of their brethren; some of them turn and see
him struggling in the agonies of death. A moment before he was
in the vigor of life, as his muscular limbs still bear evidence; but
he had uttered a falsehood, and, an instant after, his frame is
convulsed from head to foot. Nor do we doubt for a moment as
to the awful cause: it is almost expressed in voice by those nearest to him, and, though varied by their different temperaments—
by terror, astonishment, and submissive faith—this voice has yet
but one meaning, 'Ananias has lied to the Holy Ghost.' The
terrible words, as if audible to the mind, now direct us to him
who pronounced his doom, and the singly raised finger of the
apostle marks him the judge; yet not of himself—for neither

his attitude, air, nor expression has anything in unison with the impetuous Peter — he is now the simple, passive, yet awful instrument of the Almighty; while another on the right, with equal calmness though with more severity, by his elevated arm, as beckoning to judgment, anticipates the fate of the entering Sapphira. Yet all is not done; lest a question remain, the apostle on the left confirms the judgment. No one can mistake what passes within him; like one transfixed in adoration, his uplifted eyes seem to ray out his soul, as if in recognition of the divine tribunal. But the overpowering thought of Omnipotence is now tempered by the human sympathy of his companion, whose open hands, connecting the past with the present, seem almost to articulate, 'Alas, my brother!' By this exquisite turn we are next brought to John, the gentle almoner of the Church, who is dealing out their portions to the needy brethren. And here, as most remote from the judged Ananias, whose suffering seems not yet to have reached it, we find a spot of repose—not to pass by, but to linger upon, till we feel its quiet influence diffusing itself over the whole mind; nay, till, connecting it with the beloved disciple, we find it leading us back through the exciting scene, modifying even our deepest emotions with a kindred tranquillity.

"This is Invention; we have not moved a step through the picture but at the will of the artist. He invented the chain which we have followed, link by link, through every emotion, assimilating many into one; and this is the secret by which he prepared us, without exciting horror, to contemplate the struggle of mortal agony. This, too, is Art, and the highest Art, when thus the awful power, without losing its character, is tempered, as it were, to our mysterious desires. In the work of Ostade we see the same inventive power, no less effective, though acting through the medium of the humblest materials.

"We have now exhibited two pictures, and by two painters

who may be said to stand at opposite poles, and yet, widely
apart as are their apparent stations, they are, nevertheless, tenants of the same ground, namely, actual nature ; the only difference being that one is the sovereign of the purely physical, the
other of the moral and intellectual, while their common medium
is the catholic ground of the imagination.

"We do not fear either sceptical demur or direct contradic-
tion when we assert that the imagination is as much the medium of the homely Ostade as of the refined Raphael. For
what is that which has just wrapped us as in a spell, when we
entered his humble cottage, which, as we wandered through it,
invested the coarsest object with a strange charm ? Was it the
truth of these objects that we there acknowledged ? In part, certainly, but not simply the truth that belongs to their originals ;
it was the truth of his own individual mind superadded to that
of nature, nay, clothed upon besides by his imagination, imbuing
it with all the poetic hues which float in the opposite regions of
night and day, and which only a poet can mingle and make visible in one pervading atmosphere. To all this our own minds,
our own imaginations, respond, and we pronounce it true to
both. We have no other rule, and well may the artists of every
age and country thank the great Lawgiver that there *is no other*.
The despised *feeling* which the schools have scouted is yet the
mother of that science of which they vainly boast."

Allston had a keen relish for novels, and his comments upon
them were extremely interesting. The writer recalls an evening
when, to a few friends, he discoursed upon Bulwer's "Eugene
Aram," which he had just read. The easy flow of language, em-
phasized by his expressive countenance and manner, made it a
memorable occasion to his privileged listeners. Allston's great
zest for novels was a kind of voucher for his capability in that
branch of art. This is verified by his beautiful story "Monaldi,"
published in 1841, a tale packed with imagination and fancy.

We may open " Monaldi " at random and we shall meet a degree of thought taxing our own. To cite an instance which in its exacting quality may be matched on nearly every page, we give the following :

" ' Nay,' said Monaldi, ' Raffaelle is one whom criticism can affect but little either way. He speaks to the heart, a part of us that never mistakes a meaning, and they who have one to understand should ask nothing in liking him but the pleasure of sympathy.'

" ' And yet there are many technical beauties,' said the Advocate, ' which an unpractised eye needs to have pointed out.'

" ' Yes, and faults too,' answered Monaldi ; ' but his execution makes only a small part of that by which he affects us. But had he even the color of Titian, or the magic chiaro-oscuro of Correggio, they would scarcely add to that sentient spirit with which our own communes. I have certainly seen more beautiful faces ; we sometimes meet them in nature, faces to look at, and with pleasure, but not to think of like this. Besides, Raffaelle does more than make us think of him ; he makes us forget his deficiencies, or rather, supply them.'

" ' I think I understand you, when the heart is touched, but a hint is enough,' said Rosalia.

" ' Ay,' said the Advocate, smiling, ' 'tis with pictures as with life, only bribe that invisible finisher and we are sure to reach perfection. However, since there is no other human way to perfection of any kind, I do not see that it is unwise to allow the allusion, which certainly elevates us while it lasts, for we cannot have a sense of the perfect, though imaginary, while we admit ignoble thoughts.'

" ' This is a great admission for you, sir,' said Rosalia. ' 'Tis the best apology for romance I have heard.' "

This citation may fitly introduce an extract from a review of

"Monaldi," written upon its publication, for the *North American Review*, by President Felton, of Harvard :

"We have often before pondered Allston's pages to admire the grace and delicacy of his English poetical style. The book is equally remarkable for its rich and harmonious prose. The nice selection of epithets, the faultless arrangement of the members of the sentences, and the rhythmical cadence to which thought and expression seem to move united, combine to make it one of the most finished works of American literature. We fall here and there upon a most delicately wrought picture of some natural scene which betrays the artist's eye and hand ; then a deep moral reflection, speaking a varied experience and observation of life, meets our attention and awakens a train of solemn thought ; then a maxim of art, worthy to be laid up among the treasures of memory is modestly put forth, but bears under its simple expression the wisdom of studious and thoughtful years. Such in our judgment is the character of this little volume by our great artist ; it is a work of high genius, of rare beauty, and of a moral purity and religious elevation which distinguishes it from most literary works of the age."

As Allston's Aphorisms are published in the volume entitled "Lectures on Art and Poems," we cite but few of them, and these only as giving further evidence of his philosophic and epigrammatic power :

"If an artist love his art for its own sake he will delight in excellence wherever he meets it, as well in the work of another as in his own. This is the test of a true love."

"Nor is this genuine love compatible with a craving for distinction ; where the latter predominates it is sure to betray itself before contemporary excellence either by silence or (as a bribe to the conscience) by a modicum of praise."

"The enthusiasm of a mind so influenced is confined to itself."

" Distinction is the consequence, never the object, of a great mind."

" The love of gain never made a painter ; but it has marred many."

" The most common disguise of Envy is in the praise of what is subordinate."

" Selfishness in art, as in other things, is sensibility kept at home."

" The most intangible, and therefore the worst, kind of lie is a half-truth. This is the peculiar device of a *conscientious* detractor."

" In the same degree that we overrate ourselves, we shall underrate others ; for injustice allowed at home is not likely to be corrected abroad. Never, therefore, expect justice from a vain man : if he has the negative magnanimity not to disparage you, it is the most you can expect."

" The phrenologists are right in placing the organ of self-love in the back of the head, it being there where a vain man carries his intellectual light ; the consequence of which is that every man he approaches is obscured by his own shadow."

" Some men make their ignorance the measure of excellence ; these are, of course, very fastidious critics ; for, knowing little, they can find but little to like."

" The painter who seeks popularity in art closes the door upon his own genius."

" Make no man your idol, for the best man must have faults ; and his faults will insensibly become yours, in addition to your own. This is as true in art as in morals."

" Originality in art is the individualizing the Universal ; in other words, the impregnating some general truth with the individual mind."

" The painter who is content with the praise of the world in respect to what does not satisfy himself, is not an artist, but an artisan ; for though his reward be only praise, his pay is that of a mechanic, for his time,—and not for his art."

" All excellence of every kind is but variety of truth. If we wish, then, for something beyond the true, we wish for that which is false. According to this test, how little truth is there in art ! Little indeed ! but how much is that little to him who feels it ! "

" What *light* is in the natural world, such is *fame* in the intellectual ; both requiring an *atmosphere* in order to become perceptible. Hence the fame of Michael Angelo is, to some minds, a nonenity ; even as the sun itself would be invisible *in vacuo*."

" A man may be pretty sure that he has not attained *excellence*, when it is not all in all to him. Nay, I may add, that if he looks beyond it, he has not reached it. This is not the less true for being good *Irish*."

CHAPTER XXXII.

Allston was a man who represented, and may be regarded as
the last great exemplar of the art of the sixteenth century.
He manifested in his work the spirit and power of the great
Italian masters. He copied none, but mingled indications of
Titian and Veronese in color, Michael Angelo in form, and Raphael in graceful delineation of the affections. He engrafted
upon his own style great qualities from the best examples
of the past, but never so as to obscure his individuality. Precedents stimulated and assisted in the development of himself.
His style was not that of any master, Roman or Venetian, German, Spanish, or French; it was his own, invigorated and inspired by the good in all.

They who have followed him in these pages will not think
the above statement demands more for him than he deserves.
We have endeavored to be true to our purpose to let the tributes of his friends suffice for his praise, and if, in this closing
chapter, or elsewhere, we seem to have departed from that purpose, we may appeal to those tributes to show that we have not
overstepped the truth.

Nature in her prodigality from age to age endows certain
men with transcendent gifts, by which they stand out conspicuously upon the background of their times. The tendency of

human thought in reference to specially endowed characters is to apotheosize; this tendency is a token of the highest in man, it is evidence of divinity within us thus to seek it in others. We bury the bodies of the departed, and we sepulchre in forgetfulness the evil they have done; the good remains and becomes more and more vivid with the lapse of time; a few years encircle with a halo of divinity characters by no means faultless. The common tendency to forget faults and magnify the virtues of men is so strong that it has deified founders of religions, teachers of philosophy, and princes. It is a tendency as old as the race and as young as the present generation. Our own brief history illustrates this. Washington has become immaculate, and Lincoln is rapidly approaching political canonization.

We claim only special gifts for Allston, or rather gifts special in degree. He was a man in whom truth and conscience were uncompromising. Honor, the outflowing of these, was as pure as a ray from the moon. We cannot suspect him of insincerity in his confession of moral defects; when he says, " I know I have faults enough and to spare," we take him at his word; but we think we have prepared the way justly to claim for Allston, without fear of being misunderstood, certain qualities and capabilities that entitle him to consideration as a genius, using the word in its highest and most inclusive sense.

He is a benefactor who ministers to a love of the beautiful through painting, sculpture, architecture, poetry, or music. Along the track of the world's history great men, like mountain-peaks, rise and reflect upon the masses below their higher, purer light; of these is he who transfixes on canvas thoughts, emotions, beauties—visions caught from that loftier communion with nature whereunto natural powers have lifted him.

Emotions have by their visible effects a potentiality in ethical development; by contemplation and by experience of them morality is evolved. The highest art is that which makes visible to the eye the emotions in their various incitements and consequences—which touches and makes apparent the affections and sensations embraced between the poles of love and hate. Such attainment presupposes mastery of artistic methods by extraordinary intellectual ability and mechanical aptitude. The man in whom the greatest intelligence and constructive power are associated with a strong moral sense, whether painter, sculptor, architect, poet, or musician, is in the fullest sense of the word, a genius. Such a man was Washington Allston.

Reputations are regulated by exact law, they are never accidental as to their true relations, though accidental causes may temporarily enhance or obscure them. At the age of thirty Allston's fame—we use the word interchangeably with reputation—was second to none, if, indeed, it was not greater than that of any artist of his years. In his very infancy greatness was predicted for him. The bent and quality of his mind were, from childhood to the culmination of his powers in mid-life, continually manifested, and men recognized in him the characteristics of the true artist. From the construction of little mud-houses and miniature trees, from the ship drawn in chalk on the bottom of a wooden chair in Mrs. Calcott's school, to the nearly completed "Belshazzar's Feast" in 1821, his ascent had been continuous and conspicuous beyond that of any of his American contemporaries. He never once faltered in his determination to pursue, and his devotion to, art. His associations were formed according to his artistic predilections. While at school in Newport his chief recreation was found in the shop of the quadrant-maker and portrait-painter, Mr. King. While in Cambridge he cultivated the acquaintance of the great miniature-painter, Malbone. His collegiate education gave that basis of discipline, that intellectual balance-wheel, if we may so express it, which is especially necessary, indeed indispensable, to the continuous progress of a mind in which imagination, as it was in his case, is so powerful as to need bridling and regulating. Many a great genius has fallen short of his promise simply from want of a thorough literary education.

Coincident with Allston's final return to America, and comparative isolation, he developed a morbid sensitiveness which was at once the cause and consequence of the succession of embarrassments that wore upon his spirits and destroyed his health. We are glad, however, to say, in vindication of his countrymen, that his embarrassments were not from lack of patronage, private or public, individual or governmental, but rather, and solely, from want of the stimulation of artistic environment. His extreme conscientiousness in reference to his obligations to finish "Belshazzar" was the constant source of his pecuniary troubles.

The splendid gifts wherewith nature had endowed him were met by a succession of untoward circumstances. While engaged on his first large picture, "The Dead Man Revived," he was stricken by a sickness from which, though he lived some thirty years after, he never wholly recovered.

His marriage with Miss Channing was full of promise for his future. A companionship so congenial and helpful as that which she brought him was of incalculable importance. In a thousand ways, by intelligent advice, criticism or approval, she could constantly aid him in his work. By sympathy she could lessen difficulties, soothe the pain of disappointment, and mitigate the many trials in the struggle of life. By wifely interest, affection, and care she could make his home an elysium, recreative and strengthening, during his intervals of rest. The quiet, unparaded influences of true wifehood upon an artist of a refined and sympathetic nature is inestimable ; no force external to him has such potency of stimulation and encouragement.

After his severe illness in Bristol, just as he had commenced housekeeping in London, Mrs. Allston was, by a brief sickness, taken from him, and he was alone, bereft of a loving and devoted wife, an incitement to work, and source of inspiration which nothing could supply. This most distressing calamity, involving so great loss, was soon followed by an event even more disastrous to his prospect of future distinction. His pictures were attracting great attention and rendering him conspicuous as a candidate for academic honors. Mr. West, President of the Royal Academy, was aged and infirm; no man in England was so competent and so eligible to succeed him as was Allston. His fame was rapidly increasing in London, when the presidential chair was about to become vacant. At this juncture various causes conspired to draw him to America. These causes seconding his patriotism were reinforced by tidings that through the mismanagement and dishonesty of his agent in South Carolina his patrimony was exhausted. This, though not the ostensible reason, was, we think, the superinducing influence that took him from his friends, and from his brilliant prospects in England.

Still another misfortune had its inception in his great picture "Belshazzar's Feast." Had he remained in London this would probably in a few months have been finished, but in taking it to America he took it to a process of retrogression, which left it, some twenty-five years after, hopelessly unfinished.

Another, for it may well be thought a most unfortunate event in its bearing upon Allston's fame was the throwing into the sea of Coleridge's notes on Rome. The result of seven months' writing upon the Eternal City and its art, while in intimate daily intercourse with the young American artist, in uttering whose praises he never seemed to tire, doubtless contained many a tribute to his genius as glowing as that which called forth the envious inquiry of Northcote, "Who is this Mr. Allston?"

Nor did this succession of unfortunate events cease with his death.   Nothing could be more detrimental to his fame than the present arrangement of his pictures in the Boston Museum of Art.   Most unfortunate, too, is the seclusion of his best works ; " Jacob's Dream " and " Uriel in the Sun " are in country-houses in England, where they are seldom seen.   His large picture, " The Angel Releasing St. Peter," is in effect hidden from view in the chapel of the Hospital for the Insane in Worcester, Mass.   This picture alone, could it be conspicuously exhibited, would attest Allston's ability, and introduce him to the present generation as worthy the high appreciation of his contemporaries.   It is hard to be reconciled to such a combination of misfortunes, it touches our sense of justice, and we feel that it is almost an outrage upon Allston's memory to expose so unfavorably his works where they are seen, and to seclude effectually some of his best.

R. H. Dana, Jr., records that about three weeks before Allston's death he told his wife that he would be obliged to stop for a while his work on his great picture, and finish a small one and sell it.   They were embarrassed for money, and he was troubled with little debts.   She prayed him not to do this, but he said he feared he must ; she said to him, " Why don't you finish the large picture and get the money for that ? "   " Martha, don't you think of me as all the rest of the world does," was his only reply, and she could say no more.

There is a deep pathos in this anecdote.   A man whose entire influence and work had ministered directly to the exaltation of human character ; a man of the highest genius allied to a feminine sensitiveness unfitting him to cope with his fellows in the struggle for subsistence ; a man in whom ideality and intellect pushed imagination into realms of the unseen that he might materialize visions of beauty to entertain, purify, and uplift his fellow-men, the gentlest and purest of beings burdened with poverty !   We cannot fix the obligation to assist such a man,

Uriel in the Sun.

From the original in the possession of the Duke of Sutherland.

but the simple fact of his want is an indictment against a state of things under which such a fact is possible. " I am growing old and losing my physical powers. I am ready to go, I only ask time and strength to finish ' Belshazzar.' " These words were addressed to his sister-in-law a few weeks before his departure; it was evidently toward evening with him.

Viewed in its extended influences upon his life we may regard "Belshazzar" as his greatest misfortune. If this picture had never been commenced he could, and doubtless would, have overcome the other obstacles in the way of his happiness, his health, and the wider acknowledgment of his powers. Begun in the zenith of his career, this picture soon became a great burden, and as such increased until he yielded to the pressure and left it upon the earth with his tired body. So burdened, what wonder that clouds of indifference have gathered about his fame, and men knowing nothing of him but what they learn from the scanty and abortive display of his pictures in Boston should doubt his ability and question his title to eminence. The greater wonder is that, so oppressed, he attained to the measure of acknowledgment accorded him by his distinguished contemporaries.

His associates have passed away ; they who were boys in his later life are old men now, but with those who knew him the sweet influences of his character linger in memory, refining and elevating. To them it is a saddening thought that so soon none who knew him will remain to tell of an individuality and presence so charged with inspiration for others. This consideration has influenced our efforts. But great characters are immortal in the reflex of their lives upon their fellow-men. Though but little known to the present generation, Allston yet lives, and in the better thought and discrimination that will wait upon a higher development of taste and æsthetic culture his fame is safe, and the acknowledgment of his powers assured. This conviction is the inevitable result of investigation into his character and genius.

With a feeling of sadness, as if parting from an inspiring and healthful influence ; with a feeling almost of self-reproach that though executing our task in all faithfulness, we have yet fallen short of justice to our subject, we take our leave of Allston. In our converse with his genius, in our study of his character as an artist and a man, we have gained much to strengthen, much to suggest high endeavor and encourage the development of what is best in character. Thus our own experience gives us heart to hope that beneficent influences may accompany this biography.

INDEX